POWER AND SOCIETY

An Introduction to the Social Sciences

---

by **THOMAS R. DYE**

FLORIDA STATE UNIVERSITY

With the assistance of
SUSAN A. MacMANUS
University of Houston

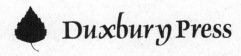 **Duxbury Press**

NORTH SCITUATE • MASSACHUSETTS

Duxbury Press
A DIVISION OF WADSWORTH PUBLISHING COMPANY, INC.

Power and Society: An Introduction to the Social Sciences was edited and prepared for composition by Julia Stair. Interior design was provided by Dorothy Booth and the cover was designed by Oliver Kline.

L.C. Cat. Card No.: 75-11275
ISBN 0-87872-064-2

PRINTED IN THE UNITED STATES OF AMERICA

3 4 5 6 7 8 9 10 — 79 78 77

In memory of
James C. "Jeff" Dye

Contents

v

PART THREE: THE USES OF POWER

Preface

Power and Society: An Introduction To The Social Sciences is designed as a basic text for an introductory, interdisciplinary social science course. It is written specifically for freshman-sophomore students at community and junior colleges, four-year colleges and universities which offer a basic studies program.

Power and Society introduces students to central concepts in

Anthropology	Psychology
Sociology	History
Economics	Political Science

But, more importantly, it does so by focusing these disciplinary perspectives on a central integrative theme—the nature and uses of power in society. In this way, students are made aware of the *interdependence* of the social sciences. Compartmentalization is avoided and students are shown how each social science discipline contributes to an understanding of power.

Power and Society also introduces students to some of the central challenges facing American society:

Ideological Conflict	Crime and violence
Race relations	Population and pollution
Poverty and powerlessness	Urban crisis

Each of these national challenges is approached from an interdisciplinary viewpoint, with power as the integrating concept.

Power has been defined as the capacity to modify the conduct of individuals through the real or threatened use of rewards and punishments. Doubtlessly there are other central concepts or ideas in the social sciences which might be employed to develop an integrated framework for an introduction to social science. But certainly *power* is a universal phenomenon which is reflected in virtually all forms of human interaction. Power is intimately related to many other key concepts and ideas in the social sciences—personality, behavior, aggression, role, class, mobility, wealth, income distribution, markets, culture, ideology, change, evolution, authority, oligarcy, elites, etc. Power is also a universal instrument in approaching the various crises which afflict man and society—racism, poverty, violence, crime, pollution, urban decay.

Several special features are designed to assist the student in understanding the meaning of the concepts presented. The first is the identification of specific *masters of social thought* and the clear, concise presentation of their central contributions to social science. Specific attention is given to the contributions of

Sigmund Freud   Charles Beard
B. F. Skinner   C. Vann Woodward
Rollo May   John Locke
David Riesman   Thomas Hobbes
Adam Smith   Martin Luther King, Jr.
John M. Keynes   Ruth Benedict
John K. Galbraith   Karl Marx
Konrad Lorenz   Edmund Burke
Louis Wirth   Herbert Marcuse

The second special feature is the presentation of *timely, relevant case studies* at the end of each chapter to illustrate important concepts:

The Aztec Empire
The Military-Industrial Complex
The Power Elite
The Authoritarian Personality
Watergate and the Resignation of Richard Nixon
Reconstruction and Black History
Marxism-Leninism in the Soviet Union
The Busing Controversy
Welfare Reform and the Work Ethnic
The Ghetto Riots
Federal Urban Policy

Finally, each of the social sciences is described, the scientific method is explained, and problems in the application of the scientific method in the social sciences are explored.

I am especially indebted to Professor Susan A. MacManus of the University of Houston who made many significant contributions to this volume. Professor MacManus's four years of teaching experience at Valencia Community College, Orlando, Florida, proved very valuable in making this book a better instructional tool. Specifically, she prepared the Performance Objectives, Key Terms and Concepts, Testing Yourself, and Discussion Questions for each chapter, as well as an Instructor's Manual.

I am grateful for the many constructive comments and criticisms made at various stages of this work by Merlin G. Cox, University of Florida; Leonard J. Mills, Northern Virginia Community College; Matthew H. Epstein, Michigan State University; Richard D. Humphrey, City Colleges of Chicago (The Loop College); Donald L. Uppendahl, Portland Community College; Ruth Gruenberg, Montgomery Community College; R. Bruce Donlan, Brevard Community College; Charlton D. Keen, Jr., Chipola Junior College; Steven W. Valavanis, Brevard Community College; William Scalapino, College of Marin (California).

Thomas R. Dye

PART ONE

The Nature of Power

CHAPTER 1

Power, Society, and Social Science

PERFORMANCE OBJECTIVES

The student should be able to:

1. Define power and identify the characteristics or properties of power.

2. Discuss how one studies power in an interdisciplinary fashion.

3. Identify each of the social science disciplines: anthropology, sociology, economics, psychology, political science, and history.

4. Discuss Bertrand Russell's views on power and identify what he saw as the "chief motive producing the changes which social science has to study."

5. Differentiate between behavioral psychologists, social psychologists, and Freudian psychologists.

6. Define ideology. Identify the purpose of ideologies in society. Differentiate between the ideologies of: classical liberalism; modern liberalism; modern conservatism; fascism; Marxism; Leninism; socialism; and "New Left" radicalism.

7. List the social problems which the book will discuss and discuss how each involves the concept of power.

8. Identify the two definitions of a science. Discuss the goals of science.

9. Define: significant relationship, hypotheses, validity, random, universe, probabilities, and inference.

10. Identify the "weakness" of a statistical relationship.

11. Differentiate between normative (prescriptive) and explanatory (descriptive) techniques.

12. Define theory. Contrast a theory with a low level of generality with a theory with a high level of generality.

3

13.   Define the scientific method. Identify: what types of phenomena it deals with; its assumptions regarding human behavior; and its basic "attitude."

14.   List the obstacles to the development of a truly scientific social science.

15.   Define:

Elites
Masses
Stratification system
"Power elite"
Personality

Authority
Legitimate
Poverty
Powerlessness

THE NATURE OF POWER

Ordinary men and women are driven by forces in society which they neither understand nor control. These forces are embodied in governmental authorities, economic organizations, social values and ideologies, accepted ways of life, and learned patterns of behavior. However diverse the nature of these forces, they have in common the ability to modify the conduct of individuals, to control their behavior, to shape their lives.

Power is the capacity to modify the conduct of individuals through the real or threatened use of rewards and punishments. Power is exercised over individuals or groups by offering them some things they value or by threatening to deprive them of these things. These values are the "power base," and they may include: physical safety, health, and well-being; wealth and material possessions; jobs and means to a livelihood; knowledge and skills; social recognition, status, and prestige; love, affection, and acceptance by others; a satisfactory self-image and self-respect. To exercise power, then, control must be exercised over the things which are valued in society.

Power can rest on various power bases. The exercise of power assumes many different forms—the giving or withholding of many different values. Yet power bases are usually interdependent—individuals who control certain base values are likely to control other base values as well. Wealth, economic power, prestige, recognition, political influence, education, respect, and so on, all tend to "go together" in society.

Power is never equally distributed. "There is no power where power is equal." For power to be exercised, the "power holder" must control some base values. By *control* we mean that the power holder is in a position to offer these values as rewards to others, or to threaten to deprive others of these values.

Power is a relationship between individuals, groups, and institutions in society. Power is not really a "thing" which an individual possesses. Instead power is a relationship in which some individuals or groups have control over certain base values.

"*All right folks, we'll be landing in a few minutes. You first-class passengers gather on my left. You huddled masses and wretched refuse gather on my right.*"

Drawing by O'Brian; © 1973 The New Yorker Magazine, Inc.

The elite are the few who have power; the masses are the many who do not. The elites are the few who control what is valued in society and use that control to shape the lives of all of us. The masses are the many whose lives are shaped by institutions, events, and leaders over which they have little control. Political scientist Harold Lasswell writes, "The division of society into elites and masses is universal," and even in a democracy "a few exercise a relatively great weight of power, and the many exercise comparatively little."[1]

Power is exercised in interpersonal relations. Psychologist Rollo May writes that "power means the ability to affect, to influence, and to change other persons." He argues that power is essential to the individual's "sense of significance"—his conviction that he counts for something in the world, that he has an effect on others, and that he can get recognition of his existence from others. Power is essential to the development of personality. An infant who is denied the experience of influencing others or of winning the attention of others to his existence withdraws to a corner of his bed, does not talk or develop in any way, and withers away physiologically and psychologically. So power is essential to being. Political scientist Robert Dahl also defines power in terms of individual interaction: "A has power over B to the extent that he can get B to do something he would not otherwise do." He argues that every exercise of power depends upon interpersonal relations between the power holder and the responder. Since there are many different aspects of power in interpersonal situations, Dahl thinks it unlikely that there will ever be two cases in which power is exercised in precisely the same fashion.

Power is exercised in large institutions—governmental, corporate, educational, military, religious, professional, occupational. Power which stems from positions in the social structure of society is stable and far-reaching. Sociologist C. Wright Mills observes: "No one can be truly powerful unless he has access to the command of major institutions, for it is over these institutional means of power that the truly powerful are, in the first instance, powerful."[2] Not all power, it is true, is anchored in or exercised through institutions. But institutional positions in society provide a continuous and important base of power. As Mills explains:

> If we took the one hundred most powerful men in America, the one hundred wealthiest, and the one hundred most celebrated away from the institutional positions they now occupy, away from their resources of men and women and money, away from the media of mass communication that are now focused upon them—then they would be powerless and poor and uncelebrated. For power is not of a man. Wealth does not center in the person of the wealthy, to have power, requires access to major institutions, for the institutional positions men occupy determine in large part their chances to have and to hold these experiences.[3]

POWER AND THE SOCIAL SCIENCES

Social science is the study of human behavior. Actually, there are several social sciences, each specializing in a particular aspect of human behavior and each using different concepts, methods, and data in its studies. Anthropology, sociology, psychology, economics, history, and political science have developed into separate "disciplines," but each shares an interest in human behavior.

Power is *not* the central concern of the social sciences, yet all of the social sciences deal with power in one form or another. Each of the social sciences contributes to an understanding of the forces which modify the conduct of individuals, control their behavior, and shape their lives. So in order to fully understand power in society, we must approach this topic in an *interdisciplinary* fashion—using ideas, methods, data and findings from all of the social sciences.

Anthropology. Anthropology is the study of man and his ways of life. Anthropology is the most comprehensive social science. *Culture* is all of the common patterns and ways of living that characterize a society. The anthropologist tries to describe and explain a great many things: child-rearing and education; family arrangements; language and communication; technology; ways of making a livelihood; the distribution of work; religious beliefs and virtues; social life; leadership patterns; and power structures.

Power is part of the culture or the way of life of a people. Power is exercised in all societies, because all societies have systems of sanctions designed to control the behavior of their members. Perhaps the most enduring structure of power in society is the family: power is exercised within the family when patterns of dominance and submission are established between male and female and parents and children. Societies also develop structures of power outside of the family to maintain peace and order among their members; to organize individuals to accomplish large-scale tasks; to defend themselves against attack; and even to wage war and exploit other peoples.

In our study of power and culture we will examine how cultural patterns determine power relationships. We will examine patterns of authority in traditional and modern families and the changing power role of women in society. We will examine the origins and development of power relationships outside of the family—in the band (Polar Eskimos), in the tribe (Crow Indians), and in the emerging state (the Aztec Empire).

Sociology.   Sociology is the study of relationships among men and groups. Sociologists describe the structure of formal and informal groups, their functions and purposes, and how they change over time. They study social institutions (families, schools, churches, etc.), social processes (conflict, competition, assimilation, change, etc.), and social problems (crime, race relations, poverty, etc.). They also study social classes.

All societies have some system of classifying and ranking their members—a system of "stratification." In modern industrial societies, social status is associated with the different roles in which an individual plays in the economic system. Individuals are ranked according to how they make their living and the control they exercise over the living of others. Stratification into social classes is determined largely on the basis of occupation and control of economic resources.

Power derives from social status, prestige, and respect as well as control of economic resources. Thus, the stratification system involves, among other things, the unequal distribution of power.

In our study of power in society, we will describe the stratification system in America, explore popular beliefs about "getting ahead," and examine the actual extent of social mobility. We will discuss the differential lifestyles of upper, middle, and lower classes in America, and the extent of class conflict. We will examine the ideas of Karl Marx about the struggle for power among social classes. We will describe the differential in political power among social classes in America. Finally, we will explore the ideas of sociologist C. Wright Mills about a top "power elite" in America which occupies powerful positions in the governmental, corporate, and military bureaucracies of the nation.

Economics. Economics is the study of the production, distribution, and consumption of goods and services. The fact that there are not enough goods and services to satisfy everyone's demands implies the necessity of choice. Economists study how individuals, firms, and nations make choices about goods and services.

Economic power is the power to decide what will be produced, how much it will cost, how many people will be employed, what their wages will be, what the price of goods and services will be, what profits will be made, how these profits will be distributed, and how fast the economy will grow. Control over these decisions is a major source of power in society.

In our study of economic power, we will examine America's vast wealth—how it is measured, where it comes from, and where it goes. We will examine the relationship between wealth and the quality of life, which are not always equivalent things. In a capitalist society, the market mechanism is heavily relied upon to determine who gets what—what is to be produced, how much it will cost, and who will be able to buy it. We want to explore both the strengths and weaknesses of the market system, including the ideas of economic philosophers Adam Smith and John M. Keynes. Our study of economic power must consider the role of government in the economy, which has increased over the years. But we are also interested in the concentration of private wealth and corporate power in America. Finally, we will inquire into the power relationships among government, corporations, and the defense establishment—"the military-industrial complex."

Psychology. Psychology is the study of the behavior of men and animals. This simple definition, however, fails to convey the richness and diversity of psychological inquiry. *Behavioral psychologists* study the learning process—the way in which men and animals learn to respond to stimuli. They frequently study in laboratory, experimental situations, with the hope that the knowledge gained can be useful in understanding more complex human behavior outside of the laboratory. *Social psychologists* study interpersonal behavior—the way in which social interactions shape an individual's beliefs, perceptions, motivations, attitudes, and behavior. They generally study the whole person in his total environment. *Freudian psychologists* study the impact of unconscious feelings and emotions, and early childhood experiences, on the behavior of adults. Finally, there are many psychologists who combine theories and methods in different ways to better understand behavior.

Personality is all of the enduring, organized ways of behavior that characterize an individual. Psychologists differ over how personality characteristics are determined—whether they are learned habits acquired through the process of reinforcement and conditioning (behavioral psychology), or products of the individual's interaction with the significant people and groups in his life (social psychology), or the results of unconscious drives and long-repressed emotions stemming from early childhood experiences (Freudian psychology), or some combination of all these.

The study of personality is essential in understanding how individuals react toward power and authority. Power is a personal experience. Everyone is subject to one form of power or another during all the waking hours of his life. And everyone has exercised some power, if only in microscopic degree, at some time. Individuals react toward these experiences with power in different and characteristic ways. Some individuals seek power for personal fulfillment. Philosopher Bertrand Russell writes, "of the infinite desires of man, the chief are the desires for power and glory."[4] Other individuals are submissive to authority, while still others are habitually rebellious. It is said that "power corrupts, and absolute power corrupts absolutely." But there is ample psychological evidence the powerlessness also corrupts. The feelings that one cannot influence anyone else, that he counts for little, that nobody pays attention to him, and that he has no control over his own life all contribute to the loss of personal identity.

In our study of power and personality, we will examine various theories of personality determination—behavioral psychology, social psychology, and Freudian psychology—in an effort to understand the forces shaping the individual's reaction to power. We will explore the power implications of B. F. Skinner's ideas of behavioral conditioning for the control of human behavior. We will examine social psychologist David Riesman's notion of the "other-directed" man, and the effect of individual powerlessness in mass society. Finally, we will study the "authoritarian personality"—the individual who is habitually dominant and aggressive towards others over whom he exercises power, yet submissive and weak towards others who have power over him—the individual who is extremely prejudiced, rigid, intolerant, cynical, and power-oriented.

Political Science.   Political science is the study of government and politics. Governments possess a particular form of power: the legitimate use of physical force (authority). By "legitimate" we mean that people generally consent to the government's use of this power. Of course, other individuals and organizations in society—muggers, street gangs, the Mafia, or violent revolutionaries—use force. But only government can legitimately threaten people with the loss of freedom and well-being to modify their behavior. Moreover, governments exercise power over all individuals, institutions, and individuals in society—corporations, families, schools, etc. Obviously the power of government in modern society is very great, extending to nearly every aspect of modern life—"from the womb to the tomb."

Political scientists, from Aristotle to the present, have been concerned with the dangers of unlimited and unchecked governmental power. We will examine the American experience with limited, constitutional government; the philosophical legacy of English political thought; and the meaning of democracy in modern society. We will observe how the U.S. Constitution divides power, first between states and the national government, and second among the legislative, executive, and judicial branches of government. We will examine the growth of power in Washington and the struggle for power among the different branches. We will also explore competition between political parties and interest groups and popular participation in decision-making through elections. We will discuss whether or not governmental elites are really responsive to the wishes of the people. Finally, in our study of "Watergate and the Resignation of Richard Nixon," we will look at what happens when political elites in America fail to abide by "the rules of the game."

History.   History is the recording, narrating, and interpreting of man's experience. The historian recreates the past by collecting recorded facts, organizing them into a narrative, and interpreting their meaning. History is also concerned with change over time. History provides a perspective on the present by informing us of the way men lived in the past. It helps us to understand how society developed into what it is today.

Power relationships develop and change over time. An understanding of power in society requires an understanding of historical development of power relationships. The foundations of power vary from age to age. As new power bases are developed, power shifts to those new groups and individuals who acquire control over them.

Our interest in power in society requires us to examine the changing sources of power over time in American history and the characteristics of men and groups who have acquired power. We will examine the men of power in the early days of the Republic and how they shaped the Constitution and the government which it established. We will discuss Charles Beard's interpretation of the Constitution as a document designed to protect the economic interests of these early power-holders. We will discuss historian Frederick Jackson Turner's ideas about how western expansion and settlement created new bases of power and new power-holders. We will explore the struggle for power between Northern commercial and industrial interests and Southern planters and slaveowners for control of western land, and the Civil War which resulted from that struggle. We will also explore the development of an industrial elite in America after the Civil War, the impact on that elite of the Depression, and resulting growth of "New Deal" liberal reform. Finally, we will examine how history occasionally overlooks the experiences of powerless minorities and later reinterprets their contributions to society, in our brief examination of "Reconstruction and black history."

BERTRAND RUSSELL: Power Is to the Social Sciences What Energy Is to Physics

Bertrand Russell (1872 - 1970), the English philosopher and mathematician, is regarded as one of the twentieth century's greatest thinkers for his contributions to mathematics and symbolic logic. But Russell possessed a great breadth of interest, ranging from history, economics, and political science to education, morals, and social problems. He received the Nobel prize in literature "in recognition of his many-sided and significant authorship, in which he has constantly figured as a defender of humanity and freedom of thought." He summarized his views about the importance of power in society in a book significantly entitled *Power: A New Social Analysis.*

The fundamental concept in the social sciences is power, in the same sense in which energy is the fundamental concept in physics. . . .

The orthodox economists, as well as Marx, who in this respect agreed with them, were mistaken in supposing that economic self-interest could be taken as the fundamental motive in the social sciences. The desire for commodities, when separated from power and glory, is finite, and can be fully satisfied by a moderate competence. The really expensive desires are not dictated by a love of material comfort. Such commodities as a legislature rendered subservient by corruption, or a private picture gallery of Old Masters selected by experts, are sought for the sake of power or glory, not as affording comfortable places in which to sit. When a moderate degree of comfort is assured, both individuals and communities will pursue power rather than wealth: they may seek wealth as a means to power, or they may forgo an increase of wealth in order to secure an increase of power, but in the former case as in the latter their fundamental motive is not economic. . . .

Like energy, power has many forms, such as wealth, armaments, civil authority, influence on opinion. No one of these can be regarded as subordinate to any other, and there is no one form from which the others are derivative. The attempt to treat one form of power, say wealth, in isolation can only be partially successful, just as the study of one form of energy will be defective at certain points, unless other forms are taken into account. Wealth may result from military power or from influence over opinion, just as either of these may result from wealth. The laws of social dynamics are laws which can only be stated in terms of power, not in terms of this or that form of power. In former times, military power was isolated, with the consequence that victory or defeat appeared to depend upon the accidental qualities of commanders. In our day, it is common to treat economic power as the source from which all other kinds are derived: this, I shall contend, is just as great an error as that of the purely military historians whom it has caused to seem out of date. Again, there are those who regard propaganda as the fundamental form of power . . . It has about the same measure of truth and falsehood as the military view or the economic view. Propaganda, if it can create an almost unanimous opinion, can generate an irresistible power; but those who have military or economic control can, if they choose, use it for the purpose of propaganda. To revert to the analogy of physics: power, like energy, must be regarded as continually passing

Bertrand Russell

Although Bertrand Russell is most recently remembered for his campaign against nuclear arms, he also made significant contributions in a wide variety of fields and received the Nobel prize for literature. *Wide World Photo*

from any one of its forms into any other, and it should be the business of social science to seek the laws of such transformations. The attempt to isolate any one form of power, more especially, in our day, the economic form, has been, and still is, a source of errors of great practical importance . . .

Those whose love of power is not strong are unlikely to have much influence on the course of events. The men who cause social changes are, as a rule, men who strongly desire to do so. Love of power, therefore, is a characteristic of the men who are causally important. We should, of course, be mistaken if we regarded it as the sole human motive, but this mistake would not lead us so much astray as might be expected in the search for causal laws in social science, since love of power is the chief motive producing the changes which social science has to study.[5]

Bertrand Russell

SOCIAL SCIENCES AND SOCIAL PROBLEMS

Social problems—the major challenges confronting society, including ideological conflict, racism, poverty, crime, violence, pollution, and urban decay—do not confine themselves to one or another of the disciplines of social science. They spill over the boundaries of anthropology, economics, sociology, political science, psychology, and history—they are *interdisciplinary* in character. Each of these problems has its historical antecedents, its social and psychological roots, its cultural manifestations, its economic consequences, and its impact on government and public policy.

Ideological Conflict. Ideas have power. Indeed, whole societies are shaped by systems of ideas which we call "ideologies." The study of ideologies—liberalism, conservatism, socialism, communism, fascism, radicalism—is *not* a separate social science. Rather, the study of ideology spans all of the social sciences, and it is closely related to philosophy. Ideologies are integrated systems of ideas which rationalize a way of life, establish standards of "rightness" and "wrongness," and provide emotional impulses to action. Ideologies usually include economic, political, social, psychological, and cultural ideas, as well as interpretations of history.

Ideologies rationalize and justify power in society. By providing a justification for the exercise of power, the ideology itself becomes a base of power in society. Ideology "legitimizes" power, making the exercise of power acceptable to the masses and thereby adding to the power of the elite. But ideologies also affect the behavior of the elites, because once an ideology is deeply rooted in society, power-holders themselves are bound by it.

In our study of power, we want to learn first about the ideology of classical liberalism—an ideology which attacked the established power of a hereditary, feudal system and asserted the dignity and worth and freedom of the individual. Classical liberalism and capitalism justify the power of private enterprise and the market system. While "classical" liberalism limits the powers of government, "modern" liberalism accepts governmental power as a positive force in freeing men from poverty, ignorance, discrimination, and ill health. It justifies the exercise of governmental power over private enterprise and the establishment of the welfare state. In contrast, modern conservatism doubts the ability of the governmental planners to solve society's problems; conservatism urges greater reliance on family, church, and individual initiative and effort.

We will then look at ideologies which have influenced other societies. Fascism is a power-oriented ideology which asserts the supremacy of the nation or race over the interests of individuals, groups, and other social institutions. Marxism attacks the market system, free enterprise, and individualism; it justifies revolutionary power in overthrowing liberal, capitalist systems and the establishment of a "dictatorship of the proletariat." Socialism calls for the evolutionary democratic replacement of the private enterprise system with government ownership of industry. We also want to examine the ideology of the "New Left" in America and the meaning of "campus radicalism." In our study of "Marxism-Leninism in the Soviet Union," we will see how an ideology justified the exercise of unlimited political and economic power by a totalitarian communist party. Finally, we will construct a framework for comparing all of these ideologies.

Racial Equality.   In our discussion of racial problems in American society, we will briefly describe the history of the civil rights movement and the response of the national government in the Civil Rights Acts. We will examine the power of protest activities and the strategies available to powerless minorities to affect social change. Of course, other minorities in America—Chicanos, Indians, and Puerto Ricans, for example—face similar problems of powerlessness. But we will try to understand these problems by studying America's black urban ghettos and the development of black militancy and the black power movement. We will also describe the growth of black political power in America. Finally, we will explore one of the more explosive racial issues: "the busing controversy."

Poverty and Powerlessness.   The American economy has produced the highest standard of living in the world, and yet a significant number of Americans live in poverty. We will observe that poverty can be defined as economic hardship or as economic inequality, and that each definition implies a different governmental approach to this problem. Poverty can also be defined as powerlessness—a social-psychological condition of hopelessness, indifference, lack of motivation, distrust, and cynicism. We will discuss whether or not there is a culture of poverty—a way of life of the poor which is passed on to future generations—and what its implications are for government policy. We will describe government efforts to cope with poverty, including the "war on poverty" and the current welfare programs. Finally, we will discuss the problems involved in "welfare reform and the work ethic."

Crime and Violence.   Social power must be balanced against individual freedom. A democratic society must exercise police powers to protect its citizens, yet must not unduly restrict individual liberty. We will explore the problem of crime in society, the constitutional rights of defendants, the role of the courts, the wisdom of capital punishment, and the difficult tasks of the police. We will also describe briefly the history of violence in American society. We will summarize social-psychological explanations of violence; violence as a form of political activity; and violence as an aspect of lower-class culture. Finally, we will try to describe and explain urban violence and "the ghetto riots" of the 1960s.

The Quality of Life.   There are a variety of social problems which affect the quality of life in America. We will look first at the worldwide population problem and its implications. We will contrast the global picture with the situation in the United States, especially in the light of the 1973 Supreme Court ruling on abortion. We will then turn to the problem of environmental pollution and the causes and effects of the "energy crisis."

We will explore the growth of urban and suburban populations in America. We will also explore the social patterns of urban life—the characteristic forms of social interaction and organization which typically emerge in a large metropolis—and the socioeconomic conflicts between cities and suburbs. We will examine the fragmented governmental structure of the large metropolis and the failure of "metro" government schemes. Finally, we will examine the dilemmas of creating an effective "federal urban policy."

THE SOCIAL SCIENCES AND THE SCIENTIFIC METHOD

Broadly speaking, a *science* is any organized body of knowledge. In this general sense, all of the social sciences can be considered sciences. But if we were to narrow our definition of a science to only those disciplines which employ the *scientific method*, then some questions arise about whether the social sciences are really scientific. In other words, if science is defined as a *method of study*, rather than a *body of knowledge*, then not all studies in the social sciences are truly scientific.

The scientific method is a method of explanation which develops and tests theories about how real-world, observable phenomena are related.

The goal of science is explanation. Science seeks to answer the question "Why." Of course science must begin by observing and classifying things. Just as biology begins with the careful observation, description, and classification of thousands upon thousands of different forms of life, the social sciences also must begin with the careful observation, description, and classification of various forms of human behavior. But the goal is explanation, not description. Just as biology seeks to develop theories of evolution and genetics to explain the various forms of life upon earth, the social sciences seek to develop theories to explain why human beings behave as they do.

To answer the question of "why," *science searches for relationships.* All scientific hypotheses assert some relationship between phenomena. Social sciences seek to find relationships which explain men's behavior. The first question is whether two or more events or behaviors are related in any way—that is, do they occur together consistently? The second question is whether either event or behavior is the *cause* of the other. Social scientists first try to learn whether human events have occurred together merely by chance or accident, or whether they occur together so consistently that their relationship cannot be a mere coincidence. A relationship which is not likely to have occurred by chance is said to be *significant*. After observing a significant relationship, social scientists next ask whether the phenomena occurred together because one is the cause of the other, or whether both are being caused by some third phenomena.

Science seeks to develop statements ("hypotheses") about how events or behaviors might be related, and then to determine the validity of these statements by careful, systematic, and logical tests. Scientific tests are really exercises in logic. For example, if we want to find out something about the relationship between race and party voters, we might collect and record data from a national sample of black and white voters chosen at random. ("Random" means that the sample was chosen in such a fashion that every voter had an equal chance of getting into the sample, and therefore the sample should (if it is large enough) be an accurate reflection of the *universe* of voters. If our data showed that all blacks voted Democratic and all whites Republican, it would be obvious that there was a perfect relationship between race and voting. If both blacks and whites had voted Republican and Democratic in the same proportions, then it would be obvious that there was *no* relationship. But in the social sciences we rarely have such obvious, clear-cut results. Generally our data will show a mixed pattern: in the 1972 presidential elections, for example, 85 percent of blacks voted Democratic and 58 percent of whites voted Republican. In other words, social sciences must deal in statistical *probabilities*. If there was *no* relationship between race and voting, then blacks and whites would vote Democratic and Republican in roughly the *same* proportions. But it turns out that in 1972 blacks voted Democratic in far heavier proportions (85 percent) than whites (42 percent). This difference is not likely to have occurred by chance—it is "significant." So we can make the *inference* that blackness is related to Democratic voting.

However, the existence of a statistically significant relationship does not prove cause and effect. We must employ additional logic to find out which phenomenon caused the other or whether both were caused by a third phenomenon. We can eliminate the possibility that voting Democratic causes one to become black as illogical: being black comes first in life and voting Democratic comes later. That leaves us with two possibilities: blackness may cause Democratic voting, or blackness and Democratic voting may both be caused by some third condition. For example, the real causal relationship may be between low incomes and Democratic voting: low income groups, which would include most blacks, tend to identify with the Democratic party. This new hypothesis can be tested by looking at the voting behavior of other low income groups to see if they voted Democratic in the same proportions as blacks. (It turns out that blacks vote more heavily Democratic than white low income groups, so the low income explanation can be rejected. Race must therefore be independently related to voting behavior.) There are many other possible alternatives to our explanation of the relationship between race and voting behavior. Perhaps blackness does not cause Democratic voting, but both are related to urban residence; or lower educational levels; or lower social status.

Every time we test and reject an alternative explanation for the relationship which we have observed, we increase our confidence that the relationship between race and voting behavior is a causal one. Of course, since someone can always think of a new alternative explanation, it is impossible to establish for certain that a causal relationship exists. Some social scientists react to the difficulties of proving "cause" by refusing to say that the relationships they find are anything more than *correlations,* or simply statistical relationships. The decision whether or not to call a relationship "causal" is a difficult one. Statistical techniques cannot guarantee that a relationship is causal. Social scientists must rely, finally, on the "feel" which comes from their familiarity with the details of the phenomena they are studying.

The scientific method deals only with observable—"empirical"—phenomena. In other words, the scientific method deals with *facts;* it deals with what *is,* rather than what *should be.* It cannot test the validity of values, or norms, or feelings, except insofar as it can test for their existence in a society, or group, or individual. For example, the scientific method can be employed to determine whether voting behavior *is* related to race, but it cannot determine whether voting behavior *should be* related to race. The latter question is a *normative* one (dealing with "oughts" and "shoulds"), rather than an empirical one (dealing with "is's"). The scientific method is *descriptive* and *explanatory,* but not *prescriptive.* The social sciences can explain many aspects of human behavior but cannot tell men how they ought to behave. For guidance in values and norms—for prescriptions about how men should live—we must turn to ethics, or religion, or philosophy.

Science strives to develop a systematic body of theory. Science is more than crude empiricism—the listing of facts without any statement of relationships among them. Of course, especially in the early stages of the science, research may consist largely of collecting data without the help of any theoretical statements about how the data may be related. But the ultimate goal of science is the development of verifiable statements about relationships among phenomena. It is the task of social scientists to find patterns and regularities in human behavior, just as it is the task of physicists and chemists to find patterns and regularities in the behavior of matter and energy. Their use of the scientific method, then, assumes that human behavior is not random, but rather that it is regular and predictable.

Theories are developed at different *levels of generality*. Theories with low levels of generality explain only a small or narrow range of behaviors. For example, the statement that blacks tend to vote Democratic is a fairly low-level generality about political behavior. Theories with higher levels of generality explain a greater or wider range of behavior. For example, the statement that differences among men cause political conflict has a higher level of generality. Strictly speaking, a *theory* is a set of interrelated concepts at a fairly high level of generality. Some social scientists concentrate on theory building rather than empirical research; they try to develop sweeping social theories to explain all, or a large part of, human behavior. Still other social theorists provide merely insights, hunches, or vague notions that serve to suggest possible explanations of human behavior, thus developing new hypotheses for empirical research.

Perhaps more than anything else, *the scientific method is an attitude of doubt or skepticism*. It is an insistence upon careful collection of data and systematic testing of ideas, a commitment to keep bias out of one's work, to collect and record all relevant facts, and to interpret them rationally regardless of one's own feelings. For the social scientist, it is the determination to test explanations of human behavior by careful observations of real-world experiences. It is a recognition that any explanation is tentative and may be modified or disproved by careful investigation. Even the scientific theories that constitute the core knowledge in any discipline are not regarded as absolutes by the true social scientist; rather they are regarded as probabilities or generalizations developed from what is known so far.

WHY THE SOCIAL SCIENCES AREN'T ALWAYS "SCIENTIFIC"

Not all of the knowledge in social science is derived scientifically. A great deal of knowledge about human behavior comes to us through insight, intuition, random observation, folklore, and common sense rather than by careful scientific investigation. The scientific method was devised in the physical and biological sciences. There are many difficulties in applying this method to study individuals, groups, economies, classes, governments, nations, or whole societies. Let us examine some of the obstacles to the development of truly *scientific* social sciences.

First of all, social science deals with very subjective topics and must rely on interpretation of results. The social scientist is part of what he is investigating—he belongs to a family, class, political party, interest group, profession, nation; he earns money and consumes goods like everybody else. He finds it much harder to suppress his personal bias than does the investigator in the physical sciences, when the topic is a very emotional one. It is easier to conduct an unbiased study of migratory birds than of migrant workers.

It is difficult to conduct "value free" research. Even the selection of a topic reveals the values of the researcher—he studies what he thinks is important in society and what he thinks is important is affected by his personal values. If it were only in the selection of the topic that the researcher's values were reflected, there would be no great problem in social science research. But the researcher's values are also frequently reflected in his perceptions of the data itself, in his statement of the hypotheses, in his design of the test for his hypotheses, and in his interpretation of the findings. "Value intrusion" can occur in many stages of the research process, which is why social scientists studying the same problems and using the same methods frequently end up with contradictory results. Perhaps it is impossible to separate facts and values in social science research. As sociologist Louis Wirth explains:

> The distinctive character of social science discourse is to be sought in the fact that every assertion, no matter how objective it may be, has ramifications extending beyond the limits of science itself. Since every assertion of a "fact" about the social world touches the interests of some individual or group, one cannot even call attention to the existence of certain "facts" without quoting the objections of those whose very raison d'etre in society rests upon a divergent interpretation of the "factual" situation.[6]

Another problem in the scientific study of human behavior centers on public attitudes toward social science. Few laymen would consider arguing with atomic physicists or biochemists about their respective fields, but most people believe they know something about social problems. Many people seemingly know exactly what should be done about juvenile delinquency, unwed mothers, expanding welfare roles, Vietnam, and race relations. Very often their information is limited and their view of the problem is a simplistic one. When a social scientist suggests that a problem is very complex, that it has many causes, and that information on the problem is incomplete, the layman believes that the social scientist is simply obscuring matters that to him seem obvious.

Social science sometimes develops explanations of human behavior which contradict established ideas. Of course, the physical and biological sciences have long faced this same problem: Galileo faced the opposition of the established church when he suggested that the earth revolved around the sun, and the theory of evolution continues to be a public issue. But social science generates even more intense feelings when it deals with poverty, crime, sexual behavior, race relations, and other heated topics.

Another set of problems in social science centers on the limitations and design of social research. It is not really possible to conduct some forms of controlled experiments on human beings. For example, we cannot subject people to poverty and deprivation just to see if it makes them violent. Instead, social researchers must find situations which have been produced naturally in order to conduct their research. They must, therefore, find situations of poverty and deprivation in order to make the necessary observations about causes of violence. In a laboratory we can control all or most of the factors that go into the experimental situation. But in real-world observations, we cannot control factors present, and it is difficult to pinpoint precisely what it is that causes the behavior we are studying. Moreover, even where some experimentation is permitted, human beings frequently modify their behavior simply because they know they are being observed in a social science experiment. It is difficult to know whether the behavior observed is a product of the stimulus being introduced, or merely a product of the experimental situation itself.

Perhaps the most serious reservation about social science research is that human behavior is shaped by so many different forces that it resists scientific explanation. A complete understanding of such a complex system as human society is beyond our current capabilities. At present human behavior can be as well understood through art, literature, music, intuition, and experience as through scientific research.

NOTES

1. Harold Lasswell and Abraham Kaplan, *Power and Society* (New Haven: Yale University Press, 1950), p. 219.

2. C. Wright Mills, *The Power Elite* (New York: Oxford University Press, 1956), p. 9.

3. Ibid., p. 10.

4. Bertrand Russell, *Power: A New Social Analysis* (New York: W. W. Norton, 1938), p. 11.

5. Ibid.

6. Louis Wirth, Preface to Karl Mannheim, *Ideology and Utopia: An Introduction to the Sociology of Knowledge* (New York: Harcourt Brace Jovanovich, 1936).

TESTING YOUR PERFORMANCE

Note to the Student. The following questions are to test how well you achieved the Performance Objectives identified for you at the beginning of this chapter. The correct answers are supplied, accompanied by corresponding pages for you to review if you have answered incorrectly. The questions are coordinated numerically with the Performance Objectives at the beginning of the chapter. This exercise will assist you in determining the type of questions you have the most difficulty in answering (discussion, identification, explanation, definition, etc.) and will prepare you for test questions likely to be asked by your instructor.

1. (a) The capacity to modify the conduct of individuals through the real or threatened use of rewards and punishments defines _____.
    (b) The existence of several value bases; unequal distribution; a relationship between individuals, groups and institutions in society; a property of the elite rather than the masses; exercised in interpersonal relations; and exercised in large institutions, are all _____.
2. One who studies power in society by using ideas, methods, data, and findings from all of the social sciences would be using an _____ approach.
3. Identify the social science discipline which:
    (a) Studies the history and the development of man and his cultures ___

    _____.
    (b) Studies the relationships between men and groups _____.
    (c) Studies the production and distribution of scarce goods and services

    _____.
    (d) Studies the behavior of men and animals _____.
    (e) Studies government and politics _____.
    (f) Records, narrates, and interprets man's experiences _____.
4. (a) "The fundamental concept in the social sciences is power, in the same sense in which energy is the fundamental concept in physics. . . . When a moderate degree of comfort is assured, both individuals and communities will pursue power rather than wealth . . . Love of power is the chief motive producing the changes which social science has to study." These statements would be used to discuss _____

    _____.
5. Identify the type of psychologist who studies:
    (a) The learning process—the way in which men and animals respond to stimuli. _____.
    (b) Interpersonal behavior—the way in which social interactions shape an individual's beliefs, perceptions, motivations, attitudes, and behavior.

    _____.
    (c) The impact of unconscious feelings and emotions, and early childhood experiences on the behavior of adults. _____.
6. (a) An integrated system of ideas which rationalizes a way of life, establishes standards of "rightness" and "wrongness," and provides emotional impulses to action, defines _____.

(b) The rationalization and justification of power in society, the provision of a power base, and the adding to the power base of the elite by "legitimizing" power-making, all identify _____ .

Identify the ideology which:

(c) Justifies the power of private enterprise, the market system, and limits the power of government. _____

(d) Justifies the exercise of governmental power over private enterprise, and the establishment of the welfare state. _____

_____

(e) Doubts the ability of the governmental planners to solve society's problems and urges greater reliance on family, church, and individual initiative and effort. _____

(f) Asserts the supremacy of the nation or race over the interests of individuals, groups, and other social institutions. _____

(g) Attacks the market system, free enterprise, and individualism, and justifies revolutionary power in overthrowing liberal, capitalist systems. _____

_____

(h) Justifies the exercise of unlimited political and economic power by a totalitarian, communist party. _____

(i) Calls for the evolutionary democratic replacement of the private enterprise system with government ownership of industry. _____

7. (a) Racism, poverty, crime, violence, pollution, and urban decay (the quality of life) all involve the concept of power and are _____

_____ .

(b) Power exercised through protest activity; powerlessness in the black urban ghettos; the black power and black militancy movements; black political power; poverty defined as powerlessness; violent power; police power; social power; and power in the big cities and suburbs resulting in different conditions of life all would be used in a discussion of _____

_____ .

8. (a) A "method of study" and a "body of knowledge" are two definitions of _____ .

(b) Explanation, search for significant relationships, development of hypotheses about how events or behaviors might be related, determination of the validity of hypotheses by careful, systematic, and logical tests would be used in a discussion of the _____ .

9. Identify the term defined by the following statements:

(a) A relationship which is not likely to have occurred by chance. _____

_____

(b) Scientific statements about how events or behaviors might be related. _____

(c) The truth of hypotheses. _____

(d) A sample chosen in such a fashion so that every voter had an equal chance of getting into the sample. _____

(e) The total number of voters from which a random sample is taken.

_____

(f) The lack of clear-cut results means that social sciences must deal in statistical _____ .

(g) A deduction from the data provided by a significant relationship.

_____

10. The impossibility of establishing for certain that a causal relationship exists identifies the _____

_____ .

11. (a) A technique which attempts to determine what "ought" to be or what "should" be is _____ .

(b) A technique which attempts to deal with empirically verifiable observations ("is's") is _____ .

12. (a) A set of interrelated concepts at a fairly high level of generality is a

_____ .

(b) Theories which explain only a small or narrow range of behaviors as opposed to theories which explain a greater or wider range of behavior represent theories with different _____ .

13. A method of explanation which develops and tests theories about how real-world, observable phenomena are related, assumes that human behavior is regular and predictable, and is characterized by a basic attitude of "doubt or skepticism" is the _____ .

14. Dealing with "subjective" topics, reliance on "interpretation" of results, difficulty in suppressing personal bias or conducting "value free" research, skeptical public attitudes about the research, the difficulty of conducting some forms of controlled experiments on human beings, and the complexity of human behavior are all _____

_____ .

15. Identify the term defined by the following statements:
   (a) The few who control what is valued in society (have power). _____

_____

   (b) The many whose lives are shaped by institutions, events, and leaders over which they have little control. _____

   (c) A system which enables societies to classify and rank their members.

_____

   (d) The persons who occupy powerful positions in the government, corporate, and military bureaucracies of the nation (identified by C. Wright Mills).

   (e) All of the enduring, organized ways of behavior that characterize an individual. _____

   (f) The legitimate use of physical force. _____

   (g) General acceptance by people that government can use physical force to control behavior. _____

   (h) Economic hardship, economic inequality, and powerlessness. _____

_____

   (i) A social-psychological condition of hopelessness, indifference, lack of motivation, distrust, and cynicism. _____

Correct Responses

1. (a) Power (p. 4); (b) Characteristics of power (pp. 4 - 6).

2. Interdisciplinary (p. 4).

3. (a) Anthropology (pp. 6 - 7); (b) Sociology (p. 7); (c) Economics (p. 8); (d) Psychology (p. 8); (e) Political Science (p. 9); (f) History (p. 10).

4.   Bertrand Russell's views on power (pp. 11 - 12).

5.   (a) Behavioral psychologist (p. 8); (b) Social psychologist (p. 8); (c) Freudian psychologist (p. 8).

6.   (a) Ideology (p. 13); (b) Purposes of ideology in society (p. 13); (c) Classical liberalism (p. 13); (d) Modern liberalism (p. 13); (e) Modern conservatism (p. 13); (f) Fascism (p. 13); (g) Marxism (p. 13); (h) Leninism (p. 14); and (i) Socialism (p. 14).

7.   (a) Social problems (pp. 14 - 15); (b) How social problems involve the concept of power (pp. 14 - 15).

8.   (a) Science (p. 15); (b) Goals of science (pp. 15 - 16).

9.   (a) Significant relationship (p. 16); (b) Hypotheses (p. 16); (c) Validity (p. 16); (d) Random sample (p. 16); (e) Universe (p. 16); (f) Probabilities (p. 16); (g) Inference (p. 16).

10.   Weakness of a statistical relationship (pp. 16 - 17).

11.   (a) Normative (prescriptive) technique (p. 17); (b) Explanatory (descriptive) technique (p. 17).

12.   (a) Theory (p. 18); (b) Levels of generality (p. 18).

13.   Scientific method (pp. 15 - 18).

14.   Obstacles to a truly "scientific" social science (pp. 15 - 18).

15.   (a) Elites (p. 5); (b) Masses (p. 5); (c) Stratification system (p. 7); (d) "Power elite" (p. 6); (e) Personality (p. 8); (f) Authority (p. 9); (g) Legitimate (p. 9); (h) Poverty (p. 14); (i) Powerlessness (p. 14).

DISCUSSION QUESTIONS

1.   You are assigned the task of describing the concept of "power" to a group of students:
   (a) How would you define "power"?
   (b) What characteristics of "power" would you discuss?

2.   Discuss how you would study the forms of power from the perspective of a (an):
   (a) anthropologist
   (b) sociologist
   (c) psychologist
   (d) economist
   (e) historian
   (f) political scientist

3.   Identify the purpose of ideologies in society. Describe how ideology itself can become a base of power in society. Discuss the approach to governmental power of four of the following ideologies:*
   (a) classical liberalism
   (b) modern liberalism
   (c) modern conservatism

   (d) fascism
   (e) Marxism
   (f) Leninism
   (g) Socialiam

4. Choose two of the following social problems and briefly explain how it involves power:*
   (a) Racial equality
   (b) Poverty
   (c) Crime and violence
   (d) The quality of life

5. You are about to begin a research project and you wish to be "scientific" rather than normative (prescriptive).
   (a) What method would you choose?
   (b) How does the method work?
   (c) What are the goals of the method?
   (d) Can the method prove cause and effect? Why or why not?

6. Discuss the reasons offered for why the social sciences are not always "scientific."

7. Discuss *The Authoritarian Personality:*
   (a) Its goal
   (b) Methodological tools employed (F-scale)
   (c) Characteristics of the authoritarian personality
   (d) Sources of authoritarianism
   What are the weaknesses and criticisms of it?

* Instructor may offer "extra credit" for students capable of discussing all of the items.

SUGGESTED READINGS

BERNARD BERELSON (ed.), *The Behavioral Sciences Today* (New York: Basic Books, 1963).

FRANK J. BRUNO, *The Story of Psychology* (New York: Holt, Rinehart, Winston, 1972).

HENRY STEELE COMMAGER, *The Study of History* (Columbus, Ohio: Merrill, 1966).

SEYMOUR MARTIN LIPSET, *Politics and the Social Sciences* (New York: Oxford University Press, 1969).

RICHARD S. MARTIN and REUBEN G. MILLER, *Prologue To Economic Understanding* (Columbus, Ohio: Merrill, 1966).

PERTTI J. PELTO, *The Nature of Anthropology* (Columbus, Ohio: Merrill, 1966).

CAROLINE B. ROSE, *The Study of Sociology* (Columbus, Ohio: Merrill, 1966).

FRANK J. SORAUF, *Perspectives on Political Science* (Columbus, Ohio: Merrill, 1966).

PART TWO

Power and Social Science

CHAPTER 2

Power and Culture

PERFORMANCE OBJECTIVES

The student should be able to:

1. Contrast informal sanctions with formal sanctions.

2. List the four broad purposes for which power is exercised in society.

3. Explain how the family or kinship group creates power relationships in society. Explain how warfare affects power relationships in society.

4. Define culture. Identify the social science discipline which most closely studies culture.

5. Differentiate between ideal cultural patterns and real behavioral patterns.

6. Define symbol. Discuss the roles symbolism plays in culture.

7. Define the various cultural categories: technology, economics, social organization, religion, and symbolic culture.

8. Define the approach known as functionalism. Contrast biological needs with social and psychological needs.

9. Discuss how Ruth Benedict in her book *Patterns of Culture* viewed each culture and how she viewed "abnormality" and "normality." Define configurationism.

10. Identify which group is the most important of all social groups. Discuss the reasons *why* it is so important.

11. List the six common characteristics of families in all societies.

12. Define the following variations in family arrangements: institutional (monogamy, polygyny, or polygamy); selection (parental, elders of the community, or individuals concerned); descent (patrilineal, matrilineal, or bilineal); residence (patrilocal, matrilocal, or neolocal); and domination (patriarchal, matriarchal, or diffused).

13. Contrast the family and authority in agricultural societies with the family and authority in industrialized societies.

28

14. Discuss the factors that have contributed to male dominance in society.

15. Discuss the legal, social, and medical changes and developments that have enabled women to acquire greater power over their own lives.

16. Discuss the three stages of development of power relationships in society (family; band, clan, or tribe; and state) and the types of societies and societal characteristics which exemplify each stage. Match the three case studies presented in the chapter (polar Eskimos; Crow Indians; and the Aztec empire) with the appropriate stage of development.

17. Outline the basic contributions anthropological studies can make to the understanding of the growth development of power relationships in society.

THE ORIGINS OF POWER

Power is exercised in all societies. Every society has a system of sanctions, whether formal or informal, designed to control behavior of its members. Informal sanctions may include expressions of disapproval, ridicule, or fear of supernatural punishments. Formal sanctions involve recognized ways of censoring behavior—for example, ostracism or exile from the group, loss of freedom, physical punishment, mutilation or death, or retribution visited upon the offender by a member of the family or group that has been wronged.

Power in society is exercised for four broad purposes:

1. To maintain peace within the society.
2. To organize and direct community enterprises.
3. To conduct warfare, both defensive and aggressive, against other societies.
4. To rule and exploit subject peoples.

Even in the most primitive societies, power relationships emerge for the purposes of maintaining order, organizing economic enterprise, conducting offensive and defensive warfare, and ruling subject peoples.

At the base of power relationships in society is the family or kinship group. Power is exercised, first of all, within the family, when work is divided between male and female and parents and children, and when patterns of dominance and submission are established between male and female and parents and children. In the simplest societies, power relationships are found partially or wholly *within* family and kinship groups. True political (power) organizations begin with the development of power relationships *between* family and kinship groups. As long as kinship units are relatively self-sufficient economically and require no aid in defending themselves against hostile outsiders, political organization has little opportunity to develop. But the habitual association of

This Carl Schuachardt illustration of agricultural work in a prehistoric village shows how labor is divided between male and female in the simplest of human societies. *The Bettmann Archive*

human beings in communities or local groups generally leads to the introduction of some form of (power) organization. The basic power structures are voluntary alliances of families and clans who acknowledge the same leaders, habitually work together in economic enterprises, agree to certain ways of conduct for the maintenance of peace among themselves, and cooperate in the conduct of offensive and defensive warfare. Thus, power structures begin with the development of cooperation between families and kinship groups.

Warfare frequently leads to another purpose for power structures—ruling and exploiting peoples who have been conquered in war. Frequently primitive societies which have been successful in war learn that they can do more than simply kill or drive off enemy groups. Well-organized and militarily successful tribes learn to subjugate other peoples for purposes of political and economic exploitation, retaining them as subjects. The power structure of the conquering tribe takes on another function—that of maintaining control over and exploiting conquered peoples.

CULTURE: WAYS OF LIFE

The ways of life which are common to a society make up its *culture*. The culture of any society represents the generalizations about the behavior of many

South African women carry grass to be used in building fires. This is one example of a culturally-originated sex-related role. *Courtesy of the Boston Public Library*

members of that society; culture does not describe the personal habits of any one individual. Common ways of behaving in different societies vary enormously. For example, some societies view dogmeat as a delicacy, while others find the idea of dogmeat nauseating. Some peoples paint their entire bodies with intricate designs, while others paint only the faces of the females. In some cultures a man is required to support, educate, and discipline his children, while in others these functions belong to the children's uncle.

The concept of culture is basic to what *anthropology* is all about. One could say that anthropology is the study of culture. Anthropologist Clyde Kluckhohn has defined culture as all of the "historically created designs for living, explicit and implicit, rational, irrational, and nonrational which may exist at any given time as potential guides for the behavior of man."[1] In contrast to psychologists, who are interested primarily in describing and explaining individual behavior, anthropologists tend to make generalizations about behavior in a whole society. Of course, generalizations about behavior in a whole society do not describe the personal habits of any one individual. Some of them apply only to a portion of that society's membership. In other words, there may be variations in ways of life among different groups within one society, variations frequently referred to as *subcultures*.

Actually the term *culture* encompasses two major types of behavioral patterns: the ideal and the real. Ideal cultural patterns are what the people of a society would do or say if they conformed completely to the standards of their culture. Real behavioral patterns, on the other hand, are derived from observations of how people actually behave. For example, the anthropologist Morris Opler reports that when an Apache husband discovers that his wife has been unfaithful he is supposed to mutilate or kill her and then find and kill her lover. However, affronted husbands do not always take such extreme steps. In one account, the husband simply "didn't care. He married right away to a Comanche."[2] Thus, the ideal patterns of a culture represent the "musts" and "shoulds," but these patterns may differ to a greater or lesser extent from actual behavior patterns.

Most anthropologists believe that various aspects of culture are interrelated—the religious rituals, the work habits, the beliefs and ideologies, the marriage relationships, and so forth, form a whole system whose parts are related to one another and affect one another. Anthropologists frequently attempt to analyze each aspect of culture in terms of its relationship to other aspects and to the functioning of the total system. Thus, for example, religious rituals will be associated with agricultural activities in a society which relies upon farming for its food; but religious activities will center about hunting in a society which hunts for its food. Anthropologists frequently search for underlying themes that give unity to a culture. Only recently has anthropology departed from this "holistic" approach. Some anthropologists now believe that many cultures, perhaps even a majority, are not dominated by a single unifying idea, but instead encompass a number of general themes, which may not be interrelated at all. Nevertheless, most anthropologists still hold that culture is systematically related, its parts influencing one another.

Culture is learned. Culture is transferred from one generation to another, but it is *not* genetically transmitted. It is passed down through the generations because people are brought up differently. Individuals learn from other people how to speak, think, and act in certain ways.

Symbolism plays a key role in culture, for it is the ability to create and use symbols—including words, pictures, and writing—that distinquishes human beings from other animals. A symbol is anything that has meaning bestowed upon it by those who use it. Words are symbols, and language is symbolic communication. But other objects or artifacts can also be symbols: A cross can be a symbol of Christianity; the color red may stand for danger or it may be the symbol of revolution. Mathematics is symbolic. It is the creation and use of symbols that enable men to transmit their learned ways of behaving to each new generation. The child is not limited to knowledge acquired through his own experiences and observations; he can learn about the ways of behaving in society through symbolic communication, receiving, in a relatively short time, the result of centuries of experience and observation. Man therefore can learn more rapidly than animals, and he can employ symbols to solve increasingly complex problems. Because of symbolic communication, man can transmit a body of learned ways of life accumulated by many men over many generations.

It is possible to divide culture into several categories. Anthropologists commonly use the following divisions:

1. Technology: the ways in which men create and use tools and other material artifacts.
2. Economics: the patterns of behaving relative to the production and distribution and consumption of goods and services.
3. Social organization: characteristic relations among individuals within a society including the division of labor and the social and political organization; and the relationships between a society and other societies.
4. Religion: ways of life relative to man's concern for the unknown.
5. Symbolic culture: systems of symbols used to acquire, order, and transfer knowledge, including language, art, music, literature, etc.

THE FUNCTIONS OF CULTURE

Culture assists people in adapting to the conditions in which they live. Even ways of life which at first glance appear to be quaint or curious may play an important role in helping individuals or society cope with problems. Many anthropologists approach the study of culture by asking what function a particular institution or practice performs for a society: How does it serve individual or societal needs? Does it work? How does it work? Why does it work? This approach is known as *functionalism*.[3]

Functionalism assumes that there are certain minimum biological needs which must be satisfied if individuals and society are to survive, as well as social and psychological needs. The biological needs are fairly well defined: food, shelter, bodily comfort, reproduction, health maintenance, physical movement, and defense. Despite great variety in the way these needs are met in different cultures, we can still ask how a culture goes about fulfilling them and how well it does so. Social and psychological needs are less well defined, but they probably include affection, communication, education in the ways of the culture, material satisfaction, leadership, social control, security, and a sense of unity and belongingness. Functionalists tend to examine every custom, material object (artifact), idea, belief, and institution in terms of the task or function it performs.

To understand a culture functionally, we have to find out how a particular item relates to biological, social, or psychological needs, and how it relates to other aspects of the culture. For example, a hunting culture may lead to the worship of animals, but agriculture leads to new deities, perhaps the sun, or rain, etc. Magic gives man courage to face the unknown; myth preserves social traditions; religion fosters individual security and social solidarity; and so forth.

Technology, with its tools, weapons, and artifacts, underlies nearly all of these human activities. Variations in ways of life reflect different attempts by human beings to adjust or adapt to their environment.

Technology can be viewed as a cultural screen that man sets up between himself and his environment. While most animals simply utilize the environment for food and shelter, changing it very little in the process, man alters or transforms the environment. As a result, man, who probably originated as a tropical animal like the ape, can live almost anywhere on the earth's surface. Of course, peoples differ widely in the degree to which they exploit environmental resources. A society without means of transportation is restricted to a single area and depends on that area's resources. The technologies of "primitive" societies are not necessarily simple; the products of Eskimo technology, for example, are often ingenious and complex and require great skill in their manufacture. Societies with more advanced technologies exploit their environment more fully. Indeed, the technological advance of Western societies threatens to exhaust environmental resources.

RUTH BENEDICT *and* Patterns of Culture

The concept of culture assists man in understanding himself by allowing him to see himself in relation to other men in other societies and other cultures. Not only does culture explain many of the regularized behaviors of people—for example, eating, sleeping, dress, or sex habits—but perhaps more importantly it helps us to gain a wider perspective on our own behavior. Through the study of diverse cultures we realize that there are many different ways of living—many different ways in which men can satisfy their social and psychological needs as well as their biological requirements; that our own culture is not "the only possible way to live." Awareness of culture provides us with some perspective on the conscious and unconscious values and assumptions of our own culture. The realization that there are other ways of life besides our own may make us more tolerant, even appreciative, of alien cultures. Thus, we not only learn more of the variety of human experience but become more sensitive to values and lifestyles of others.

Perhaps this perception of the diversity of human existence was the really important contribution of cultural anthropologist Ruth Benedict in her widely read

Ruth Benedict

Cultural anthropologist Ruth Benedict introduced the concept that each culture has unique patterns which are manifested in its social organization, religious beliefs and artistic expressions. *Wide World Photo*

Patterns of Culture. Professor Benedict (1887 - 1947), as professor of anthropology at Columbia University, popularized the notion that different cultures can be organized around characteristic purposes or themes. "A culture, like an individual, is a more or less consistent pattern of thought and action. Within each culture there come into being characteristic purposes not necessarily shared by other types of societies."[4] According to Benedict, each culture has its own patterns of thought, action, and expression dominated by a certain theme which is expressed in social relations, art, and religion.

For example, Benedict identified the characteristic theme of life among Zuñi

Ruth Benedict

Pueblo Indians as moderation, sobriety, and cooperation. There was little competition, contention, or violence among tribal members. In contrast, the Kwakiutls of the northwestern United States engaged in fierce and violent competition for prestige and self-glorification. Kwakiutls were distrustful of one another, emotionally volatile, and paranoid. Members of the Dobu tribe of New Guinea, too, were suspicious, aggressive, and paranoid:

> Life in Dobu fosters extreme forms of animosity and malignancy which most societies have minimized by their institutions. Dobuan institutions, on the other hand, exalt them to the highest degree. The Dobuan lives out without repression man's worst nightmares of the ill-will of the universe, and according to his view of life virtue consists in selecting a victim upon whom he can vent the malignancy he attributes alike to human society and to the powers of nature. All existence appears to him as a cut-throat struggle in which deadly antagonists are pitted against one another in a contest for each one of the goods of life. Suspicion and cruelty are his trusted weapons in the strife and he gives no mercy, as he asks for none.[5]

Yet Benedict was convinced that *abnormality* and *normality* were relative terms. What is "normal" in Dobuan society would be regarded as "abnormal" in Zuñi society, and vice versa. She believed that there is hardly a form of abnormal behavior in any society which would not be regarded as normal in some other society. Hence, Benedict helped social scientists realize the great variability in the patterns of human existence. Men can live in competitive as well as cooperative societies, in peaceful as well as aggressive societies, in trusting as well as suspicious societies.

Today many anthropologists have reservations about Benedict's idea that the culture of a society reflects a single dominant theme. This idea is now known as *configurationism,* and it includes the notion that societies, like individuals, have characteristic personalities. But it is doubtful that societies can really be as well integrated as individuals. There are probably a multiplicity of themes in any society, and some societies may be poorly integrated indeed. Moreover, Benedict may have underestimated the fact that, regardless of the importance of culture in shaping individual behavior, even within a single culture wide variations of individual behavior exist.

AUTHORITY IN THE FAMILY

The family is the principal agent of socialization into society. It is the most intimate and most important of all social groups. Of course, the family can assume different shapes in different cultures, and it can perform a variety of functions and meet a variety of needs. But in *all* societies the family relationship centers on sexual and child-rearing functions. A cross-culture comparison reveals that in all societies the family possesses these common characteristics:[6]

Ruth Benedict

1. Sexual mating.
2. Child-bearing and child-rearing.
3. A system of names and a method of determining kinship.
4. A common habitation.
5. Socialization and education of the young.
6. A system of roles and expectations based on family membership.

These common characteristics indicate why the family is so important in human societies. It replenishes the population and rears each new generation. It is within the family that the individual personality is formed. The family transmits and carries forward the culture of the society. It establishes the primary system of roles with differential rights, duties, and behaviors. And it is within the family that the child first encounters *authority*.

Family arrangements vary. First of all, the marriage relationship may take on such institutional forms as monogamy, polygyny, and polyandry. *Monogamy* is the union of one husband and one wife; *polygyny*, the union of one husband and two or more wives; *polyandry*, the union of one wife and two or more husbands. Throughout the world, monogamy is the most widespread marriage form, probably because the sex ratio (number of males per 100 females) is near 100 in all societies, meaning there is about an equal number of men and women.

Second, marriage mates may be selected by parents, or by the elders of the community, or by the individuals concerned.

Third, the reckoning of descent may be through the male line (patrilineal), through the female (matrilineal), or through both (bilineal).

Fourth, the newlyweds may reside with the family of the husband (patrilocal residence), or with the family of the wife (matrilocal), or in a new residence together (neolocal).

Fifth, the family may be dominated by the husband-father (patriarchal) or the wife-mother (matriarchal), or the dominance pattern may be diffused, so that both parents (and in some instances even the children) have considerable authority (democratic or equalitarian).

In all societies the child's first experience with authority is within the family. Indeed, the entire culture first appears to the child as something his father or mother wants him to do. Differences in the type of authority exercised, and whether or not the authority is exercised primarily by the mother or father, can shape the character and personality of the growing individual.

In most agricultural societies the family is *patriarchal;* the male is the dominant authority and kinship is determined through the male line. The family is an economic institution as well as a sexual and child-rearing one. Land is owned by families, many artifacts are produced within the family, and the family cares for its old as well as its young. Male family heads exercise power in the wider community; the village or tribe may be governed by the patriarchs. Male authority frequently means the subjection of both women and children. This family arrangement is buttressed by traditional moral values and religious teachings that emphasize discipline, self-sacrifice, and the sanctity of the family unit.

Women face a lifetime of child-bearing, child-rearing, and work in the house. Families of 10 or 15 children are not uncommon. The property rights of a woman are vested in her husband. Women are taught to serve and obey their husbands. Women are not considered to be as mentally competent as men. The economic enterprise of the family is owned and managed by the husband. Tasks are divided, with men raising crops, tending animals, and performing heavy work; and women making clothes, preparing food, tending the sick, and performing endless household services.

Industrialization alters the economic functions of the family and brings about changes in the traditional patterns of authority. In industrialized societies the household is no longer an important unit of production, even though it retains an economic role as a consumer unit. Work is to be found outside of the home, and industrial technology enables women to find gainful employment as well as men. This means an increase in opportunities for women outside of the family unit and the possibility of economic independence. The number of women in the labor force increases; today in the United States nearly 40 percent of adult women are employed outside of the home.

The patriarchal authority structure of the family in an agricultural economy is altered by the new opportunities for women in an advanced industrial nation. Not only do women acquire employment alternatives, but their opportunities for education also expand. This independence permits them to modify many of the more oppressive features of patriarchy. Women in an advanced industrialized society have fewer children (and closer together) and generally end their child-bearing by age 30. Divorce becomes a realistic alternative for an unhappy marriage, and the trend in divorce rates in industrialized societies is upward.

At the same time, governments in industrialized societies assume many of the traditional functions of the family, further increasing opportunities for women. The government steps into the field of formal education—not just in instruction in reading, writing, and arithmetic, but in support of home economics, driver training, health care, and perhaps even sex education, all areas once the province of the family. Government welfare programs provide assistance to mothers of dependent children where a family breadwinner is absent or unable to provide for the children. The government undertakes to care for the aged, the sick, and others incapable of supporting themselves, thus relieving families of still another traditional function.

The authority of the male also may be threatened by unemployment. The failure of the male to find gainful and respectable employment in an industrialized society can seriously undermine his self-esteem, status, and role as the family breadwinner. The problem is compounded if the female can find employment while the male cannot, or if the female can obtain public assistance and the male is an obstacle to her receiving it. The result can be the emergence of the female-dominated family.

Despite these characteristics of industrial society, however, the family remains as the fundamental social unit. The family is not disappearing; marriage and family life are as popular as ever. But the father-dominated authority structure, with its traditional duties and rigid sex roles, is changing. The family is becoming an institution in which both husband and wife seek individual happiness, rather than the perpetuation of the species and economic efficiency. A majority of women still choose to seek fulfillment in marriage and child-raising rather than in outside employment. The important point is that now this is a *choice* and not a cultural requirement.

POWER AND SEX

Sex roles involve power relationships. The recent reconsideration of woman's role in American society, including the publicity given to the women's liberation movement, has brought about a new realization that sexual roles in our culture specify differential treatment, status, and power. The traditional American family was patriarchal, and many cultural practices continue to reflect male dominance. Men still hold most of the major positions in industry, finance, universities, the military, politics, and government. Authority in most families still rests with the male. Only one-third of the work force in America is female, and the average wage of these women is only half the average income of men. Women who work must generally continue to bear the major burden of domestic service and child care in their homes. Women have many special protections in the law, but often these protections limit opportunities for advancement and even encourage women to remain dependent upon men. Sex roles assign domestic service and child care to women, and human achievement, interest, and ambition beyond these to men.

Male dominance stems from a combination of biological factors and cultural practices. Often arguments over women's liberation center around the issue of how much of male dominance can be attributed to *biology* and how much to *culture*. Many advocates of women's liberation deny that biological differences necessitate *any* distinctions between male and female in domestic service or child-care responsibilities, or authority in the family, or economic roles in society, or political or legal rights. They contend that existing sex differences are culturally imposed upon women from earliest childhood. The very first item in personality formation is the assignment of sex roles (you are a boy, you are a girl)

Even though nearly 40% of adult American women are employed outside the home, child rearing and household management are still primarily female responsibilities. *Eugene Richards Photo*

and the encouragement of "masculine" and "feminine" traits. Aggression, curiosity, intelligence, initiative, and force are encouraged in the boy; passivity, refinement, shyness, and virtue are encouraged in the girl. Girls are supposed to think in terms of domestic and child-care roles, while boys are urged to think of careers in industry, the professions, etc. Deeply ingrained symbols, attitudes, and practices are culturally designated as "masculine" or "feminine" behaviors. ("Is it a boy or a girl?" "What a big boy!" "Isn't she pretty.") There are masculine and feminine subjects in school: science, technology, and business are male; teaching, nursing, and secretarial are female. Boys are portrayed in roles in which they master their environment; girls, in roles in which they admire the accomplishments of men. It is this *cultural* conditioning which leads a woman to accept a family- and child-centered life and an inferior economic and political role in society—not her *physiology*.

Many writers have complained bitterly about the social-psychological barriers to a woman's full human development. There is a double standard of sexual guilt in which women are subject to greater shame for any sexual liaison, whatever the circumstances. The family and society inculcate greater sexual inhibitions in women, frequently leading to an inability to enjoy sex fully and achieve orgasm. Yet, while denied sexual freedom herself, the female is usually obliged to seek advancement through the approval of males. She may try to overcome her powerlessness by using her own sexuality, perhaps at the cost of her dignity and self-respect. The prevailing male attitude is to value women for their sexual traits rather than their qualities as human beings. Women are frequently portrayed as "sex objects" in advertising, magazines, and literature. They are supposed to entertain, please, gratify, and flatter men with their sexuality; it is seldom the other way around. There is even evidence of self-rejection among women similar to that encountered among minority groups: Female children are far more likely to wish they had been born boys than male children are to wish they had been born girls.[7] The "cult of virginity" continues as a traditional sign that the new husband's "property" is received "unused." The power aspects of sex roles are also ingrained in male psychology. Young men are deemed feminine (inferior) if they are not sufficiently aggressive, physical, or violent.

Marriage laws also imply superiority-inferiority relationships for male and female. Marriage involves the female's loss of name, her obligation to adopt her husband's place of living, and the exchange of sexual relationships for financial support. Divorce is most states is granted to a male for his wife's failure to grant sexual consortion, but it is not granted to him for his wife's failure to provide financial support. On the other hand, divorce is granted a woman for her husband's failure to support her financially, but it is not granted to her for his failure to engage in sexual relationship. Women are seldom required to pay alimony or child support upon divorce, while men are.

In contrast to these arguments about *culturally* imposed sex roles, other observers have contended that *physiological* differences between men and women account for differential sex roles. The woman's role in reproduction and care of the young is biologically determined. To the extent that she seeks to protect her young, she also seeks family arrangements which will provide maximum security and support for them. Men acquire dominant positions in industry, finance, government, etc., largely because women are preoccupied with family and child-care tasks. Men are physically stronger than women, and their role as economic providers is rooted in this biological difference. Whether there are any biologically determined mental or emotional differences between men and women is a disputed point, but the possibility of such differences exists. Thus, differential sex roles may be partly physical in origin.

Sexual attraction between men and women has certainly been a great force in human affairs since the beginning of time. Attempts to eliminate sex differences —"unisex" in dress, behavior, and manner—may run counter to the biological urges of a great many people, not to mention their preferences. While most Americans today agree that women should have equal opportunities in education and employment, and receive equal pay for equal work, it is quite another matter to try to eliminate all of the distinctions between men and women.

"I had a dress once."

Drawing by B. Tobey;
© 1971 The New Yorker
Magazine, Inc.

Women in America have made great progress in acquiring equal rights over the years. The earliest active "feminist" organizations grew out of the pre-Civil War antislavery movement. The first generation of feminists, including Lucretia Mott, Elizabeth Cody Stanton, Lucy Stone, and Susan B. Anthony, learned to organize, to hold public meetings, and to conduct petition campaigns as *abolitionists*. After the Civil War, the feminist movement concentrated on winning civil rights and the franchise for women. The suffragettes employed mass demonstrations, parades, picketing, and occasional disruptions and civil disobedience—tactics not dissimilar to those of the civil rights movement of the 1960s. The more moderate wing of the American suffrage movement became the League of Women Voters; in addition to women's vote, they sought protection of women in industry, child welfare laws, honest election practices, and the elimination of laws discriminating against the rights of women.

The culmination of the early feminist movement was the passage in 1920 of the Nineteenth Amendment to the Constitution:

> The right of citizens of the United States to vote shall not be denied or abridged by the United States or by any State on account of sex.

The movement was also successful in changing many state laws which abridged the property rights of the married woman and otherwise treated her as the "chattel" (property) of her husband. But active feminist politics declined after the goal of women's voting rights had been achieved.

Renewed interest and progress in women's rights came with the civil rights

The efforts of early feminists, like these 1912 Cleveland suffragettes, were rewarded eight years later by passage of the Nineteenth Amendment to the Constitution, giving women the right to vote. *The Bettmann Archive*

movement of the 1960s. The Civil Rights Act of 1964 prevents discrimination on the basis of *sex*, as well as race, in employment, salary, promotion, and other conditions of work. In addition, Congress had passed and sent to the states for their ratification an Equal Rights Amendment to the Constitution which states:

> Equality of rights under the law shall not be denied or abridged by the United States or by any State on account of sex.

The purpose of this amendment is to eliminate sex as a factor in determining the legal rights of men and women, and to ensure "the fundamental dignity and individuality of each human being."[8] Debate over ratification in the states has suggested that this amendment may eliminate some legal protections for women —financial support by husbands, alimony and child support, an interest in the husband's property, etc.

Women are also acquiring greater power over their own lives by means of a series of social and medical developments. First of all, the changing of sexual mores and the lifting of prohibitions against women's pleasure in sexuality have brought about changes in women's attitudes in sex. Women no longer accept sexual relations as an exclusively male domain. Increased physiological un-

A group of demonstrators observing Women's Rights Day in 1972 protest the lack of women brokers on the floor of the American Stock Exchange in New York City. *Wide World Photo*

derstanding and improved sexual technique have contributed to the reassertion of feminine sexuality. Advances in birth control techniques, including "the pill," have freed women's sexuality from the reproductive function. Legal abortions in the early months of pregnancy are now a recognized, constitutional right. Women can now determine for themselves whether and when they will undertake childbirth and child-rearing.

STAGES OF DEVELOPMENT
OF POWER RELATIONSHIPS

As a general guide to the study of development of power relationships in society, we can identify the following stages:

1. Societies in which there is no separate power organization outside of the family or kinship group. These are societies in which the local group has no continuous or well-defined system of leaders over or above those who

head the individual families that make it up. Nor do these societies have any clear-cut division of labor or economic organization outside of the family; and there is no structured method of resolving differences and maintaining peace among members of the group. These societies do not engage in organized offensive or defensive warfare. They tend to be small and widely dispersed, to have economies that yield only a bare subsistence, and to lack any form of organized defense. Power relationships are present, but they are closely tied to family and kinship.

2. Societies in which families are organized in larger bands, tribes, or confederacies and which have reorganized sets of power arrangements extending beyond family ties. In these societies population tends to be somewhat more concentrated; the economy yields a richer subsistence but no real surplus; and warfare, although frequent and often of great importance, is usually a matter of raiding between neighboring societies. When wars are decisive, they result in the killing or driving off of enemy tribes, rather than their conquest for exploitation.

3. Societies which are organized as permanent states and which have a more or less well-defined territory and a recognized organization to make and enforce rules of conduct. In these societies populations are large and highly concentrated; the economy produces a surplus; and there are recognized rules of conduct for the members of the society with positive and negative sanctions. These societies have a more or less organized military establishment for offensive and defensive wars; in war, conquered people are not usually destroyed but instead held as tributaries or incorporated as inferior classes into the state. In the vast majority of these societies power is centered in a small, hereditary elite.

These stages of development in power relationships in societies certainly do not exhaust the variety of current and past power arrangements. They represent only broad divisions, each of which can be subdivided. (For example, states can be classified in Aristotelian fashion as monarchy, aristocracy, or democracy— rule by the one, the few, or the many.) Sharp lines cannot be drawn among these three stages; each stage shades into the next, and there are many transitional forms.

POWER AMONG THE POLAR ESKIMOS

Societies lacking formal power organizations are found today only in the very marginal areas of the world. Societies with no formal power structures outside the family and kinship groups exist only in the most difficult environments, where physical hardship and a lack of adequate food resources keep the human

The primary family is the main social organization among Eskimos and other peoples living where harsh environments preclude large permanent groupings. *Wide World Photo*

population small and thinly scattered. Among the polar Eskimos of northern Greenland, for example, a harsh environment and a limited food supply, together with a crude technology, force families to wander great distances to maintain themselves. Inadequate food resources make it physically impossible for these Eskimos to maintain, except temporarily, any groupings larger than one or two families. As a result, there is little in the way of power organization outside of the family. No leadership system develops, and social control is vested in the family.

Anthropologists who have observed Eskimo culture note that it has just two social units: the primary family, a small but autonomous kinship group; and the winter village, an unstable association of primary families who are not necessarily linked by kinship ties. The winter village is only partially a power grouping; its member families do not stay together long enough or undertake the common enterprises necessary for the development of a stable leadership system. Ordinarily the families in a winter village, though temporarily united by common residence, act independently of each other. Their technology, whether in food-gathering or house-building, requires no high degree of cooperative labor. In times of stress, when a storm or lack of game reduces food stores to the danger point, a *shaman*, respected for his supernatural powers, may call the families together to participate in a ceremony intended to restore the food supply. But the shaman's authority is limited to such occasions; at other times he has no right to direct or command.

A strong and aggressive hunter may gain the esteem and respect of his fellows, but there are few occasions when he may capitalize on this prestige to assume a position of leadership. In short, the winter village has little need for leadership outside of the family. Not even warfare exists to organize its primary families for offensive or defensive action. Leadership resides only within the primary family, where it is shared by husband and wife, each in his or her sphere of activity. The family maintains itself largely through its own efforts. It is linked to other families through intermarriage, remote kinship, or ties of mutual affection and regard. Conflicts are often resolved by song sessions in which the disputants lampoon each other in songs before their fellows. More aggressive behavior is inhibited by fear of retaliation by kinsmen of the victims. Protracted disputes may be resolved among some Eskimos by one party's moving to another winter village, although an overbearing and abusive individual may be speared while on a hunt.

Among these Eskimos, then, there is no structure of power outside the family group. Families rarely work together as a unified force. Leadership outside of the family is evidenced only rarely, when some particularly able member of the community takes charge in a crisis. Ecological circumstances prohibit large permanent groupings of people, and the technology of the society is so simple that it utilizes individual and not group effort. Variations on this fundamental family kinship type of power system are also found among other primitive peoples living in harsh environments.

POWER AMONG THE CROW INDIANS

Perhaps the simplest form of power arrangement outside of the family is a band or clan or tribe. Although its members may be linked by kinship, such a group is generally made up of many kinship units, not all of which need to be related by marriage. Bands form the next stage of development in power relationships above that of the family or kinship groups. The band or clan or tribe consists of numbers of individuals and families who (1) live and travel together; (2) regularly engage in one or more large community enterprises—for example, an organized hunt; (3) regulate conflict and maintain order among themselves; and (4) organize to protect themselves from their enemies and wage war against them. Within the band there is as a rule an acknowledged leader— a chief—together with other respected individuals who assist in implementing authority. This authority may be backed by force, but more often it rests upon the ability of the leadership to persuade and influence its followers. The leaders generally owe their status to their personal achievements as hunters or warriors. Members of the band or tribe share a common language and culture.

Antropological research on the American Crow Indians in the early nineteenth century provides an example of development of power relationships at the tribal level. The Crows were more or less continually hostile to their neighbors. Any non-Crow was automatically an enemy. Warfare, however, was largely a matter of small-scale raiding, either to steal horses or to avenge the death of a tribesman. Horse-stealing parties tried to take as many horses as they could without disturbing the enemy camp; they fought only when necessary to defend themselves. When revenge was the object of a war party, however, they tried to surprise the enemy and to kill as many as possible without losing any of their own men. A war leader, whether he set out to capture horses or to get revenge, was not considered successful unless he brought his own party home intact.

Success in warfare was very important. Crow men achieved reputation and prestige through the slow accumulation of war honors. War honors were clearly defined; they were awarded for (1) leading a successful war party, (2) capturing an enemy's weapon in actual combat, (3) being first to strike an enemy in the course of a fight, and (4) driving off a horse tethered in an enemy encampment. A man who performed all of these deeds became, in Crow terms, a "good and valiant man," and his status increased as the number of his earned war honors increased. A Crow who had not yet attained the minimum four honors was regarded as not yet a man, but only an untried youth.

The warriors formed a kind of military aristocracy that made up the band council. One of their number, usually an older man with many war honors, was recognized as chief. He decided when the band was to move or settle down in its yearly wanderings in search of food and when war parties were to be sent out. He directed the annual buffalo hunt, a cooperative endeavor in which the whole band united to secure a store of winter food.

But the chief's authority was by no means absolute; he was "neither a ruler nor a judge." In effect, the chief was a leader rather than a ruler; it was his function to persuade and influence rather than to command. This point is illustrated by the procedure employed among the Crows to settle internal disputes. When quarrels and violence occurred between members of the same clan, these were resolved by the older kin, acting as clan heads. But when a feud threatened between clans, the chief, his council, and influential warriors belonging to neutral clans exerted their powers to prevent further hostilities and restore peace. Their efforts were often successful, because the Crows, continually at war with their neighbors, fully realized the values of band solidarity.

On some occasions, mainly the annual buffalo hunts, the chief and other council warriors could resort to force rather than persuasion to maintain order. In such instances the senior warriors "severely whipped anyone who prematurely attacked the herd, broke his weapons, and confiscated the game he had illegally killed."[9] The need for a winter's supply of food, and the fact that this need could not be adequately served without the closest coordination of effort, clearly justified, in Crow eyes, the chief's authority over his tribesmen. However, apart from such special occasions as the community buffalo hunt, members of the band were allowed to act pretty much as they pleased, subject only to the discipline of public opinion. The threat of ridicule and the obligations imposed by kinship were normally sufficient deterrents to antisocial behavior.

Band or tribal organizations similar to that of the Crow are widespread among nonliterate peoples. As environment and technology permit higher concentrations of population, bands form into larger tribes. Then emerge even larger political units with recognized power structures.

POWER AND CULTURE: A CASE STUDY
The Making of the Aztec Empire

The most fully developed system of power relationships is the *state*—the last of our major categories. Power in the state is employed to maintain order among peoples and to carry on large-scale community enterprises, just as in the band or tribe. But power in the state is also closely linked to defense, aggression, and the exploitation of conquered peoples. Frequently states emerge in response to attacks by others. Where there is a fairly high density of population, frequent and continuing contact between bands, and some commonality of language and culture, there is the potential for "national" unity in the form of a state. But a state may not emerge if there is no compelling motivation for large-scale cooperation. This motivation is very often provided initially by the need for defense against outside invasion. States differ from bands or tribes to the extent that there is a centralized authority with recognized power, backed by force, to carry out its decrees. This legitimate use of force distinguishes the state as a form of power structure from the band or tribe, in which power depends largely on persuasion or the personal achievements of individuals. Power in the state is a more impersonal kind of authority.

The Making of the Aztec Empire

The Aztec empire that was conquered by the Spaniards under Cortez in 1521 is an excellent example of a primitive state. Anthropologists have been able to trace its beginnings to an earlier tribal order confined to the valley of Mexico. The rich agricultural economy developed by the Aztecs produced far in excess of their immediate needs. With the exchangeable surplus there soon evolved a complex specialization of labor and an extensive trade that brought the Aztecs in frequent and profitable contact with neighboring groups.

Early in the fifteenth century the Aztecs embarked on a series of military conquests that led ultimately to their economic and political control over most of central and southern Mexico. But the conquered cities and states were not destroyed. On the contrary, the commercially minded Aztecs permitted them to retain local autonomy, demanding only political allegiance and a yearly tribute in goods and services to the Aztec emperor. It was this economic empire, politically a loose aggregate of city-states controlled from the Aztec capital city of Tenochtitlán, that Cortez took over in 1521.

At the time of the conquest, the Aztec aristocracy was divided into 20 *calpulli*, small groups composed of nuclear families organized in ranked lineages. Each *calpulli* owned a tract of arable land, a council house, and a temple. The land was allotted in small farms to each family within the *calpulli*, to hold as long as the family continued its cultivation. Families could cultivate their own land, retaining the proceeds for their own support, or rent it to others, but it could not be sold or otherwise alienated from the *calpulli*. Should the family line die out or a family fail to cultivate its land for two successive years, the land reverted to the *calpulli* for reallotment. Some lands within the territory of a *calpulli* belonged to the chief, and some were cultivated by subordinates. Others were set aside for the support of religious establishments and for the payment of tributes to the central government. These were cultivated communally.

Calpulli were governed by a council of family heads. It was under the leadership of a chief (the *calpullec*), who was in charge of land distribution and who kept a record of landholdings. Together with the council, the chief adjudicated property disputes and other conflicts between *calpulli* members, administered the public stores, and carried on various other administrative and judicial duties. The chief was selected by the council, but the successor to the position was customarily chosen from among the sons or other near relatives of the chief. The chief was exempt from the need to cultivate his own lands; all full-time *calpulli* officers were supported from the *calpulli's* land reserve. Each *calpulli* had two other elected officers besides the chief. A warlord led warriors in battle, instructed young men in the arts of war, and acted as the police chief. A speaker or delegate represented the *calpulli* in the state council.

The state council consisted of the 20 speakers, who met at frequent intervals to administer affairs of state, declare war, make peace, and judge disputes between *calpulli*. In addition, there was a great council, which included the 20

The Making of the Aztec Empire

This Salvador Tarazona mural shows the ancient Aztecs taking part in an annual Festival of Flowers. The powerful Aztec chiefs would sacrifice a 16-year-old girl to the gods and then select a newborn girl to die in the same manner 16 years later. *Wide World Photo*

chiefs, the speakers, the warlords, the ranking priests, and a number of other state officials. This council judged exceptional legal cases submitted to it by the state council and, at the death of the king, selected a successor. The king was always chosen from a single royal family and was usually a younger son or nephew of the deceased king. The king was the supreme military commander and collector and distributor of tribute from conquered peoples.

The early Aztec power structure, although more complicated than that of primitive tribes, still retained a measure of democratic procedure. The core of the Aztec empire was ruled by its citizens, the members of the *calpulli*. While the positions of chief and king were in part hereditary (they were customarily chosen from particular families), the choice of a leader also depended upon reputation and ability. Although the king had great power as a military leader in a state more or less continuously at war, this power was modified by the councils.

But as the Aztecs grew in wealth from their numerous conquests and ever widening control of trade, the power structure gradually underwent a change. Most important, there developed a class division in Aztec society along socioeconomic lines. An upper class appeared, composed of honorary lords known as *tecutin*. These were men, *calpulli* members, who were given titles for outstanding services to the state as warriors, merchants, public officials, or

The Making of the Aztec Empire

priests. They were universally esteemed, had many privileges including certain exemptions from taxation, were preferred for high governmental and military positions, and were given large estates and shares of tribute by the king, to be held as private property during their lifetime. These rewards clearly made the *tecutin* economically independent of their *calpulli* and, moreover, allied them with the king, from whom their honors came and who could also withdraw them.

A middle class also emerged, made up of *calpulli* members who were not *tecutin*. These formed the bulk of the population of the capital city; they were self-supporting through their membership in the *calpulli* and had a voice in the government through their representatives in the state and great councils. Often they rented their *calpulli* lands, and some acquired great wealth.

Finally, a lower class was divided into propertyless freemen and serfs attached to the lands of the nobility as slaves. The former were men exiled from the *calpulli* for various crimes and so without any way of making a living except by hiring themselves out as agricultural laborers or as porters in the caravans of the merchants. Slaves were similarly dependent for a living on their labor. Neither had a voice in the government. Though initially small, the lower class grew as conquests increased.

As class lines become more sharply drawn, Aztec government moved inevitably in the direction of an absolute, hereditary monarchy. *Tecutin* clearly supported this tendency to their advantage and increasingly, by various devices, managed to pass on their titles and private property to their heirs. Slowly a hereditary nobility arose. At the time of the conquest, the Aztec empire was essentially in the hands of an emergent feudal order, with political power centered more and more in the king and his *tecutin* rather than in the elected representatives of the *calpulli*.

POWER AND SOCIETY—
SOME ANTHROPOLOGICAL OBSERVATIONS

Let us summarize the contributions that anthropological studies can make to our understanding of the growth of power relationships in societies. First, it is clear that the physical environment plays an important role in the development of power systems. Where the physical environment is harsh and the human population must of necessity be spread thinly, power relationships are restricted to the family and kinship groupings. Larger political groupings are essentially impossible. Elites emerge only after there is some concentration of population, where food resources permit groupings of people larger than one or two families.

Second, power relationships are linked to economic patterns of culture. In subsistence economies, power relationships are limited to the band or tribe level. Only in surplus-producing economies do we find states or statelike power systems. Developed power systems are associated with patterns of settled life, a certain degree of technological advance, and economic surplus.

Third, patterns of warfare are linked to the development of power relationships. Warfare is rare or lacking among people such as Eskimos who have no real power system outside of the family. Where power relationships emerge at the band or tribe level, as in the culture of the Crows, warfare appears to be continuous, in the form of periodic raiding for small economic gains or the achievement of personal glory and status; victory assumes the form of killing or driving off enemy groups. Only at the state level is warfare well organized and pursued for the purpose of conquest and economic exploitation. This does not mean necessarily that statelike power systems *cause* war, but rather that some common factor underlies both the rise of state power systems and organized warfare. Warfare and conquest are not essential to the maintenance of the state; in fact, in the modern world warfare between major states may slowly give way to other forms of competition, if only because of the increasing threat of total destruction.

Fourth, anthropological research makes it clear that power relationships may exist in simple forms in primitive societies (no society is void of a power structure). Power structures become more complex and hierarchical, and more impersonal and based on physical force, as societies move from the subsistence level with simple technology to a surplus-producing level with advanced technology and large cooperative enterprises. The simpler power systems are frequently headed by chiefs and councils selected for their age, wisdom, or demonstrated capacity as hunters or warriors. These leaders tend to rule more by example and persuasion than by formal decree or force. As more complex state systems emerge, leaders are endowed with the exclusive right to coerce. Characteristically, political and economic power in the state is concentrated in a small hereditary elite. Modern representative government, in the form of European and American democracies, is relatively rare in the history of human societies.

NOTES

1. Clyde Kluckhohn and William Kelly, "The Concept of Culture," in Ralph Linton (ed.), *The Science of Man in the World Crisis* (New York: Columbia University Press, 1945), p. 97.

2. Morris E. Opler, *An Apache Life Way* (Chicago: University of Chicago Press, 1941), pp. 409 - 410.

3. This approach was developed by Bronislaw Malinowski, *A Scientific Theory of Culture and Other Essays* (Chapel Hill: University of North Carolina Press, 1944).

4. Ruth Benedict, *Patterns of Culture* (Boston: Houghton Mifflin, 1934), p. 46.

5. Ibid., p. 172.

6. William H. Stephens, *The Family in Cross-Cultural Perspective* (New York: Holt, Rinehart & Winston, 1963).

7. Goodwin Watson, "Psychological Aspects of Sex Roles," in *Social Psychology, Issues and Insights* (Philadelphia: Lippincott, 1966), p. 477. See also Philip Goldberg, "Are Women Prejudiced Against Women?" *Transaction*, April 1968.

8. *Congressional Quarterly*, March 25, 1972, p. 693.

9. Robert H. Lowie, *The Crow Indians* (New York: Rinehart, 1935), p. 5.

TESTING YOUR PERFORMANCE

Note to the Student. The following questions are to test how well you achieved the Performance Objectives identified for you at the beginning of this chapter. The correct answers are supplied, accompanied by corresponding pages for you to review if you have answered incorrectly. The questions are coordinated numerically with the Performance Objectives at the beginning of the chapter. This exercise will assist you in determining the type of questions you have the most difficulty in answering (discussion, identification, explanation, definition, etc.) and will prepare you for test questions likely to be asked by your instructor.

1. (a) The sanctions used by society to control behavior of its members which include expressions of disapproval, ridicule, or fear of supernatural punishments are ___*Internal Sanctions*___ .

(b) Recognized ways of censoring behavior such as ostracism, loss of freedom, physical punishment, mutilation, or death are ___ *Formal* ___ sanctions.

2. To maintain peace within the society, to organize and direct community enterprises, to conduct warfare against other societies, and to rule and exploit subject peoples are ___*powers in society*___ .

3. (a) A division of work between male and female and parent and children, the establishment of patterns of dominance and submission, and the development of power relationships between groups can be used to explain ___

(b) Success in subjugating other peoples for purposes of political and economic exploitation, and the retaining of the "conquered" as subjects, can be used to explain ___ .

4. (a) The term which describes the common patterns of behavior and ways of life that characterize different societies is ___*Culture*___ .

(b) The social science discipline which most closely studies culture is ___*Anthropology*___ .

5.   (a) Patterns which define what the people of a society would do or say if they conformed completely to the standards of their culture are *Ideal Culture Patterns*

(b) Patterns derived from observations about how people actually behave are *Real Behavioral Patterns* .

6.   Anything that has meaning bestowed upon it by those who use it is known as a *Symbol* .

7.   Identify the cultural categories associated with the following:

(a) The ways in which men create and use tools and other material artifacts. *Technology*

(b) The patterns of behaving relative to the production and distribution and consumption of goods and services. *Economics*

(c) Characteristic relations among individuals within a society, and the relationships between a society and other societies. *Political Science*

(d) Ways of life relative to a man's concern for the unknown. *Religion*

(e) Systems of symbols used to acquire order and transfer knowledge. *Education*

8.   (a) The approach to the study of culture which asks how a particular item relates to biological, social, or psychological needs, and how it relates to other aspects of the culture, is *Functionalism*

(b) The needs which are fairly well defined, as for food, shelter, bodily comfort, reproduction, health maintenance, physical movements, and defense, are *Biological Needs* needs.

(c) Less well-defined needs, as for affection, communication, education in the ways of the culture, material satisfaction, leadership, social control, security, and a sense of unity and belongingness, are *Social + physological* needs.

9.   (a) The belief that each culture has its own characteristic patterns of thought, action, and expression; that this pattern is dominated by a certain theme which is expressed in social relations, art, and religion; and that "abnormality" and "normality" are relative terms, represent _____

(b) The idea that the culture of a society reflects a single dominant theme and that societies, like individuals, have characteristic personalities is known as _____ .

10.   (a) The group which is the most important of all social groups is the *Family* .

(b) The replenishment of the population and the rearing of each new generation, the formation of the individual personality, the transmission and carrying forward of the society's culture, the establishment of the primary system of roles with differential rights, duties, and behaviors, and the first encounter with authority are all *The importance of the family*

11.   Sexual mating, child-bearing and child-rearing, a system of names and a method of determining kinship, a common habitation, socialization and education of the young, and a system of roles and expectations based on family membership are *Characterist of the family* .

12.   Identify the *institutional* variations in family arrangements described by the following:
   (a) The union of one husband and one wife. _____
   (b) The union of one wife and two or more husbands. _____
   (c) The union of more than two spouses. _____
Identify the *descent* variations in family arrangements:
   (d) Descent through the male line. _____
   (e) Descent through the female. _____
   (f) Descent through both the male and female line. _____
Identify the *residence* variations of family arrangements:
   (g) Residence with the family of the husband. _____
   (h) Residence with the family of the wife. _____
   (i) Establishment of a new residence together. _____
Identify the *domination* variation of family arrangements:
   (j) Domination by the husband-father. _____
   (k) Domination by the wife-mother. _____
   (l) Diffused domination so that both parents (and even children) have considerable authority. _____

13.   (a) The type of society likely to be characterized by a democratic or equalitarian dominance; bilineal descent, a family with an economic role but not an important unit of production, government assumption of many of the traditional family functions, and an increase in the opportunities for women outside the family unit is an ____*Industrial*____ society.
   (b) The type of society likely to be characterized by patriarchal dominance; patrilineal descent; a family which is an economic institution as well as a sexual and child-rearing one; governance by patriarchs; subjection of both women and children; traditional moral values and religious teachings that emphasize discipline, self-sacrifice, and the sanctity of the family unit is an ____ ____*Agriculture*____ society.

14.   A combination of biological factors (sex identification, reproduction, and care of the young) and cultural factors (a set of symbols, attitudes, and practices to designate "masculine" and "feminine" behaviors, marriage laws, sexual double standards) have both contributed to *Man in society* ____ _____ .

15.   The Nineteenth Amendment to the Constitution, the Civil Rights Act of 1964, the changing of sexual mores and the lifting of prohibitions against woman's pleasure in sexuality, increased physiological understanding and improved sexual technique, and advances in birth control techniques can be used to discuss ____*Women Power*____ _____ .

16.   Identify the power group associated with the following stages of development of power relationships in society:
   (a) Societies in which local groups have no well-defined system of leaders, no clear-cut division of labor or economic organization, no structural method to resolve differences and maintain peace among group members, and no organized offensive or defensive welfare, and which are small and widely dispersed, are dominated by ____*Family kinship*____ .
   (b) Larger, more concentrated societies, which employ reorganized sets of power arrangements extending beyond family ties, which have richer

economies, and which use warfare in the raiding of neighboring societies, are dominated by ___*Clan tribes Bands*___ .

(c) Societies with more or less well-defined territories, recognized organizations to make and enforce rules of conduct, large highly concentrated populations, economic surpluses, and military establishments for offensive and defensive wars are societies dominated by *States, Nations* .

Identify the cultures associated with the following stages of development:

(d) Family or kinship type of society. ___*Polar Eskomos*___

(e) Band, clan, tribe, or confederacy type of society. *Crow Indians*

_____ (f) Permanent state. *Aztec Indians (Empire)*

17. Studies of the physical environment, the economic patterns of culture, the patterns of warfare, the existence of power relationships in primitive and complex societies alike are all _____

_____ .

Correct Responses

1. (a) Informal sanctions (p. 29); (b) Formal sanctions (p. 29).

2. The broad purposes of power in society (p. 29).

3. (a) Creation of societal power relationships through family or kinship groups (p. 29); (b) The effect of warfare on societal power relationships (p. 30).

4. (a) Culture (p. 30); (b) Anthropology (p. 31).

5. (a) Ideal cultural patterns (pp. 31 - 32); (b) Real behavioral patterns (p. 32).

6. Symbol (p. 32).

7. (a) Technology (p. 33); (b) Economics (p. 33); (c) Social organizations (p. 33); (d) Religion (p. 33); (e) Symbolic culture (p. 33).

8. (a) Functionalism (p. 33); (b) Biological needs (p. 33); (c) Social and psychological needs (p. 33).

9. (a) Ruth Benedict's views of culture (pp. 34 - 36); (b) Configurationism (p. 36).

10. (a) Family (p. 36); (b) Reasons for the importance of the family as a social group (pp. 36 - 37).

11. Common characteristics of families (p. 37).

12. (a) Monogamy (p. 37); (b) Polygyny (p. 37); (c) Polyandry (p. 37); (d) Patrilineally (p. 32); (e) Matrilineally (p. 32); (f) Bilineally (p. 37); (g) Patrilocal (p. 37); (h) Matrilocal (p. 37); (i) Neolocal (p. 37); (j) Patriarchal (p. 37); (k) Matriarchal (p. 37); (l) Democratic or equalitarian (p. 37).

13. (a) Industrialized society (p. 38); (b) Agricultural society (pp. 37 - 38).

14. Male dominance in society (pp. 39 - 41).

15. Legal, social, and medical changes enabling women to acquire greater power (pp. 42 - 44).

16. (a) Family or kinship group (pp. 44 - 45); (b) Bands, tribes, or confederacies;

(p. 45); (c) Permanent states (p. 45); (d) Polar Eskimos (pp. 45 - 47); (e) Crow Indians (pp. 47 - 49); (f) Aztec empire (pp. 49 - 52).

17.   Basic contributions of anthropological studies to the understanding of the growth of power relations in society (pp. 52 - 53).

KEY TERMS

informal sanctions

formal sanctions

culture

subcultures

ideal cultural patterns

real behavioral patterns

symbolism

functionalism

biological needs

social and psychological needs

configurationism

monogamy

polygyny

polygamy

sex ratio

patrilineal descent

matrilineal descent

bilineal descent

patrilocal residence

matrilocal residence

neolocal residence

patriarchal family

matriarchal family

democratic or equalitarian family

monarchy

aristocracy

democracy

family

band, clan, or tribe

state

calpulli

calpullec

hereditary

DISCUSSION QUESTIONS

1.   Discuss the four broad purposes for which power exists in society.

2.   Compare and contrast the approaches of studying culture:
    (a) Functionalism
    (b) Configurationism

3.   We know that the family is the principal agent of socialization into society. Discuss the different variations in family arrangements by:
    (a) Institutional form
    (b) Selection of mate
    (c) Descent
    (d) Residence
    (e) Domination

4. Contrast an agricultural society and an industrialized society. Include in your answer discussion of:
    (a) The functions of the family
    (b) Employment and work arrangements
    (c) The role of women
    (d) The exercise of power and authority

5. Discuss the biological and cultural factors which have been used to justify male dominance of society within each of the following areas:
    (a) Domestic service or child-care responsibilities
    (b) Authority in the family
    (c) Economic role in the society
    (d) Political and legal rights
What evidences are there that society may be becoming more equal sexually?

6. Contrast the *family and kinship group* with *bands, tribes, or confederacies* and with *permanent states* (the three stages in the development of power relationships) on the basis of:
    (a) System of leadership
    (b) Economic system
    (c) Governmental (rule-making) system
    (d) Type of warfare
    (e) Size and density of population

SUGGESTED READINGS

RALPH L. BEALS and HARRY HOIJER, *An Introduction to Anthropology* (New York: Macmillan, 1971).

RUTH BENEDICT, *Patterns of Culture* (Boston: Houghton Mifflin, 1934).

RUTH BUNZEL and MARGARET MEAD, *The Golden Age of American Anthropology* (New York: Braziller, 1960).

CLYDE KLUCKHOHN, *Mirror for Man* (New York: Fawcett, 1960).

RALPH LINTON, *The Tree of Culture* (New York: Vintage Books, 1959).

MARGARET MEAD, *Coming of Age in Samoa* (New York: Mentor Books, 1949).

WILLIAM H. STEPHENS, *The Family in Cross-Cultural Perspective* (New York: Holt, Rinehart & Winston, 1963).

CHAPTER 3

Power and Social Class

PERFORMANCE OBJECTIVES

The student should be able to:

1. Define stratification of society. Distinguish between classification and ranking. Identify the most important bases of stratification in a modern industrial society. Discuss the characteristics associated with the stratification system.

2. Define power. Define social class.

3. Differentiate between the subjective method, the reputational method, and the objective method of identifying and measuring social stratification.

4. Describe the American ideal. Identify the authors whose writings exemplify the American ideal.

5. Discuss how Americans self-evaluate (rank) themselves into social classes. Identify the class which a majority of Americans see themselves falling into. Identify the direction of the trend in subjective class evaluation.

6. Compare and contrast the subjective (self) evaluation of class with the objective ideas of social scientists about class.

7. Compare knowledge and consensus about occupational-prestige rankings in socialist and capitalist, developed and underdeveloped nations.

8. Identify the principal objective criteria of social class.

9. Define status inconsistency. Identify the possible sources of status inconsistency.

10. List the purposes of ideology in a stratification system.

11. List the major points of the American ideology of equality of opportunity.

12.   Contrast Americans' acceptance of general statements about equality of opportunity with their acceptance of specific statements about opportunity. Give some examples of this contrast. Discuss the different levels of support for both specific and general statements about equality of opportunity in America by social class.

13.   Define subcultures. Identify the various aspects of class subcultures as described by many sociologists.

14.   Compare and contrast the ways of life of the upper class, the middle class, the working class, and the lower class.

15.   Contrast social mobility in a caste society with social mobility in American society.

16.   Explain how social mobility is usually measured.

17.   Identify the most important factor contributing to an excess of upward mobility over downward mobility in America.

18.   Discuss the important reservations about opportunity and mobility in America.

19.   Distinguish between vertical occupational movement and horizontal (adjacent) occupational movement.

20.   Differentiate between class consciousness and class awareness. Identify which of these two terms is more prevalent in America.

21.   Explain the similarities between black consciousness and class consciousness. Explain the difference between the two.

22.   List the factors which appear to help stabilize the existing class system in America and reduce class conflict.

23.   Outline the major characteristics of power as presented by Karl Marx in *The Communist Manifesto*. Identify the determinant of man's interests, beliefs, and actions. Identify what Marx saw as the important prerequisite to successful proletarian revolution. Define the classless society.

24.   List the reasons why neither capitalist societies nor communist societies conformed to Marx's analysis.

25.   Describe the relations between social class and political power. Identify the social, economic, and occupational characteristics of government officeholders. Identify the people who have the best opportunities for getting into politics and explain the reasons why Identify the factors in addition to high social status that affect political election to office.

26.   Compare the elitist view of society and the pluralist view of society as they relate to political power being largely in the hands of individuals from the upper class.

27.   Identify the power elite as defined by C. Wright Mills in *The Power Elite*. Identify the factors contributing to the emergence of the power elite.

28.   Contrast the institutional explanation of how the power elite holds

power with the individual-qualities explanation of how the power elite holds power. List the factors contributing to the unity of the top elite.

29.   Define what C. Wright Mills meant by higher immorality.

POWER PYRAMIDS AND PECKING ORDERS

All known societies have some system of ranking their members along a superiority-inferiority scale. While some societies claim to grant "equality" to their members, in no society have men in fact been considered equal. The "stratification" of society involves the *classification* of individuals and the *ranking* of classifications on a superiority-inferiority scale. This system of classification and ranking is itself a source of prestige, wealth, income, authority, and power.

Individuals can be classified on a wide variety of characteristics—physical strength, fighting prowess, family lineage, ethnic or racial category, age, sex, religion, birth order, and so on. But *the most important bases of stratification in a modern industrial society are the different roles which individuals play in the economic system*. Individuals are ranked according to how they make their living and how much control they exercise over the livelihood of others. The ranking of individuals by their occupation and their control of economic resources occurs not only in the United States but in most other modern nations as well; both communist and noncommunist nations have stratification systems based on these same factors.[1]

The evaluation of individuals along a superiority-inferiority scale means, of course, a differential distribution of prestige. Thus the elite strata will receive the *deference* of individuals who are ranked below them. Deference may take many forms: acquiescence in the material advantages or objective privileges of the elite (the use of titles and symbols of rank, distinctive clothing, housing, and automobiles), accordance of influence and respect, acceptance of leadership in decision-making, and so on. The stratification system also involves different styles of life: foods eaten, magazines and books read, place of residence, favorite kind of sports, schools attended, pronunciation and accent, recreational activities, and so forth. In addition, of course, the stratification system is associated with the uneven distribution of *wealth* and *income*: In every society persons ranked higher enjoy better housing, clothing, food, automobiles, and other material goods and services than persons ranked lower in the scale.

Finally, the stratification system involves the unequal distribution of *power*—the ability to control the acts of others. Sociologists agree that power and stratification are closely related, but they disagree on the specific value of this relationship. Some theorize that power is a product of economic well-being

"Charisse, are we too sophisticated to order some Girl Scout cookies?"
Drawing by Weber;　©1974 The New Yorker Magazine, Inc.

or prestige or status. Others believe that power *determines* the distribution of wealth, prestige, and status.[2]

It is the stratification system that creates social classes. The term *social class* simply refers to all individuals who occupy a broadly similar category and ranking in the stratification system. Members of a social class may or may not interact, or even realize that they have much in common. Since all societies have stratification systems, all societies have social classes.

STRATIFICATION IN AMERICAN SOCIETY

There are several methods of identifying and measuring social stratification: (1) the subjective method, in which individuals are asked how they see themselves in the class system; (2) the reputational method, in which individuals are asked to rank positions in the class system; and (3) the objective method, in which social scientists observe characteristics that discriminate between patterns of life associated by them with social class.

The American ideal, set forth in the writings of John Locke and Thomas Jefferson, is that position should be based upon personal qualities and achievements. The individual in a free society should have the opportunity to achieve the social ranking that he can earn by ability, effort, and moral worth. He is supposed to rise or fall according to his merits. The American ideal does not deny the existence of a superiority-inferiority scale for evaluating men in society; nor does it call for absolute equality or "leveling," with all men given equal income, wealth, position, and prestige regardless of their individual deserving. But it does call for equality of opportunity; that is, all should have an equal *opportunity* to achieve high position in accordance with their individual merits and endeavors. In the American ideal "anyone who has it in him can get ahead," and therefore in general those who are at the top are worthy of being there because of their talents and efforts.

In view of this ideal it is not surprising that most Americans think of themselves as middle class. Nearly nine out of ten will describe themselves as middle class when they are forced to choose between this term and either upper or lower class. It is apparent that to characterize oneself as upper class is regarded as "snobbish"; and to view oneself as lower class is to admit that one is a loser in the great game of life. Even people who admit to being poor consider it an insult to be called lower class.[3]

TABLE 3-1. Subjective Class Identifications of Americans

1945		1968	
Upper class	3%	Upper class	2.2%
Middle class	43%	Upper-middle class	16.6%
Working class	51%	Middle class	44.0%
Lower class	1%	Working class	34.3%
Deny idea of class	1%	Lower class	2.3%
		Deny idea of class	1.0%

Source: Derived from Robert W. Hodge and Donald J. Treiman, "Class Identification in the United States," *American Journal of Sociology,* 73 (March 1968), 535–547.

But the fact that most Americans label themselves as middle class does not mean American society is one big middle class society. In fact, when *working class* is added to the list of choices, and individuals are asked to subjectively evaluate their own class membership, a different picture emerges. Table 3-1 shows the distribution of responses over time when people are asked to rank themselves on more precise scales. In 1945 over half of a national sample ranked themselves as "working class," compared to 43 percent who ranked themselves as "middle class" and 4 percent who ranked themselves as "lower class" or "upper class." Obviously the inclusion of "working class" reveals that Americans by no means see themselves all as members of a single class. However, note that class identification changes over time. By 1968 only one-third of a national sample placed themselves in the "working class." Many more

Americans viewed themselves as members of the "middle class," and a substantial portion ranked themselves as "upper-middle." The inclusion of the "upper-middle" option makes precise comparison difficult, but it seems reasonable to conclude that there is an *upward trend* in subjective class evaluation. This may be due to higher levels of educational attainment and the increase in consumer goods which were once available only to the well-to-do.[4]

How well does subjective evaluation of class conform to the ideas of social scientists about the objective meaning of class? As we have already noted, social scientists view occupation and control of economic resources as the principal determinant of social class in America. Sociologist Richard Centers writes, "A man's way of getting his livelihood dominates much of his waking life, and it is out of the forces acting upon him in this economic sphere that class consciousness has been seen to emerge."[5] In an interesting test of this idea, sociologists Hodge and Treiman sought the correlation between individuals' subjective identification of their own class with their actual income, occupation, and education and their ownership of real estate, savings bonds, and corporate stocks and bonds. It turned out that occupation, income, and education were all associated with class identification (occupation was more intimately connected with class identification than anything else), but these objective criteria of class were *not* as closely related to subjective evaluations as expected. The authors found it difficult to predict what class a person would put himself in on the basis of his occupation, income, or education. More importantly, they found that ownership of real estate, savings bonds, or corporate stocks and bonds had almost nothing to do with subjective class identification. Persons who did not own these resources were just as likely to rank themselves as middle or upper-middle class as those who did. Hodge and Treiman also report that the social class of an individual's friends and neighbors affected his self-identification. One whose friends were in the upper occupation and income categories tended to rank himself as middle class while one whose friends and neighbors were blue-collar workers tended to rank himself working class. In short, there is some relationship between subjective and objective measures of social class, but subjective evaluation of one's own social class can be affected by factors other than objective circumstances.

Social scientists have spent a great deal of time studying the prestige ranking of occupations as another aspect of the stratification system of modern society. Individuals are asked in national surveys to make a superiority-inferiority ranking of specific occupations. For example, "For each job mentioned, please pick out the statement that best gives *your own personal opinion* of the *general standing* that such a job has" offers respondents a choice of "excellent," "good," "somewhat below average," or "poor" as their answer. The resulting prestige scores for 90 separate occupations are shown in Table 3-2. It is interesting to note that these rankings remained stable for several decades. U.S.

TABLE 3-2. Prestige Ratings of Occupations

Occupation	Prestige Rank	Occupation	Prestige Rank
U.S. Supreme Court justice	1	Railroad engineer	39
Physician	2	Electrician	39
Nuclear physicist	3.5	County agricultural agent	39
Scientist	3.5	Owner-operator of a print-	
Government scientist	5.5	ing shop	41.5
State governor	5.5	Trained machinist	41.5
Cabinet member in the federal		Farm owner and operator	44
government	8	Undertaker	44
College professor	8	Welfare worker for a city	
U.S. representative in Con-		government	44
gress	8	Newspaper columnist	46
Chemist	11	Policeman	47
Lawyer	11	Reporter on a daily news-	
Diplomat in the U.S. foreign		paper	48
service	11	Radio announcer	49.5
Dentist	14	Bookkeeper	49.5
Architect	14	Tenant farmer—one who owns	
County judge	14	livestock and machinery and	
Psychologist	17.5	manages the farm	51.5
Minister	17.5	Insurange agent	51.5
Member of the board of		Carpenter	53
directors of a large corpora-		Manager of a small store in	
tion	17.5	a city	54.5
Mayor of a large city	17.5	Local official of a labor	
Priest	21.5	union	54.5
Head of a department in a		Mail carrier	57
state government	21.5	Railroad conductor	57
Civil engineer	21.5	Traveling salesman for a	
Airline pilot	21.5	wholesale concern	57
Banker	24.5	Plumber	59
Biologist	24.5	Automobile repairman	60
Sociologist	26	Playground director	62.5
Instructor in public schools	27.5	Barber	62.5
Captain in the regular army	27.5	Machine operator in a	
Accountant for a large		factory	62.5
business	29.5	Owner-operator of a lunch	
Public school teacher	29.5	stand	62.5
Owner of a factory that em-		Corporal in the regular army	65.5
ploys about 100 people	31.5	Garage mechanic	65.5
Building contractor	31.5	Truck driver	67
Artist who paints pictures		Fisherman who owns his own	
that are exhibited in gal-		boat	68
leries	34.5	Clerk in a store	70
Musician in a symphony		Milk route man	70
orchestra	34.5	Streetcar motorman	70
Author of novels	34.5	Lumberjack	72.5
Economist	34.5	Restaurant cook	72.5
Official of an interna-		Singer in a nightclub	74
tional labor union	37	Filling station attendant	75

TABLE 3-2. (Cont.)

Occupation	Prestige Rank	Occupation	Prestige Rank
Dockworker	77.5	Clothes presser in a	
Railroad section hand	77.5	laundry	85
Night watchman	77.5	Soda fountain clerk	86
Coal miner	77.5	Sharecropper—one who owns	
Restaurant waiter	80.5	no livestock or equipment	
Taxi driver	80.5	and does not manage farm	87
Farm hand	83	Garbage collector	88
Janitor	83	Street Sweeper	89
Bartender	83	Shoe shiner	90

Source: Robert W. Hodge, Paul M. Siegel, and Peter H. Rossi, "Occupational Prestige in the United States," *American Journal of Sociology,* 69 (November 1964), 286–302. By permission of the University of Chicago Press.

TABLE 3-3. The Distribution of Income, Occupation, and Education in the United States

Family income	Percent
Less than $4,000	15.2
$ 4,000– 7,000	16.9
7,000–10,000	20.6
10,000–15,000	26.6
15,000–25,000	16.0
Over $25,000	4.6

Median family income = $9,590

Education	Percent of Persons 25 Years Old and Older
Less than 5 years	5.5
Less than 1 year high school	28.3
Four years high school or more	52.3
Four years college or more	10.7

Median years completed = 12.1

Occupation	Percent of Employed Males	Females
Professional	13.5	14.8
Managerial and administrative	10.6	3.5
Sales	6.8	6.9
Clerical	7.2	32.9
Craftsmen	19.7	1.7
Operatives	18.2	13.2
Laborers	6.1	0.9
Farmers and farm managers	2.7	0.2
Farm labor	1.6	0.5
Service	7.7	18.8
Not reported	5.9	6.8

Source: *1970 Census of Population,* General Social and Economic Characteristics, United States Summary, PC(1)-C1.

Supreme Court justice and physician were ranked number 1 and number 2 respectively from the end of World War II at least through 1964. Sharecropper, garbage collector, street sweeper, and shoe shiner occupied the last four rankings respectively over these years. Furthermore, *knowledge* about occupational prestige and relatively strong *consensus* on relative ratings of occupations are widespread throughout the American population. Even more noteworthy is the fact that occupational-prestige rankings are similar from nation to nation among modern societies, both socialist and capitalist, developed and underdeveloped.

The principal objective criteria of social class are income, occupation, and education. If social scientists are correct in the assumption that occupation and control of economic resources are the source of stratification in society, then these indices are the best available measures of class. Certainly income, jobs, and education are unequally distributed in American society, as they are in all other societies. Table 3-3 reveals the distribution of income, occupation, and education in the United States.

These three measures of social class are related; generally individuals with prestigious occupations have acquired good educations and enjoy high incomes. Table 3-4 shows that occupations ranked high in social prestige are well paid. Table 3-5 reveals that individuals who have acquired higher educations tend to enjoy higher annual incomes.

TABLE 3-4. Median Incomes—Different Occupations

Physicians and surgeons	$39,000
Dentists	23,400
Lawyers	22,100
Engineers	19,500
Managers and proprietors	
Salaried	15,600
Self-employed	14,600
Foremen	13,700
Teachers—grade and high school	12,300
Skilled craftsmen	11,500
Operatives	9,900
Service workers—sales clerks	
and so on	8,900
Secretaries	8,500
Unskilled workers—nonfarm	8,400
Unskilled workers—farm	4,300

Source: U.S. Bureau of the Census. Figures are for 1969.

However, the existence of several measures of class raises the possibility of *status inconsistency*. Status inconsistency occurs, for example, when a well-educated, prestigiously employed person receives a low income, or when a

TABLE 3-5. Education and Income

Years of School Completed	Mean Income, 1969
Elementary	
0–7	$ 3,981
8	5,467
High School	
1–3	6,769
4	8,148
College	
1–3	9,397
4	12,938

Source: *Statistical Abstract of the United States, 1972,* p. 114.

poorly educated person acquires great wealth. Status inconsistency may occur when individuals are in the process of rising or falling in the class system—for example, when well-educated individuals lose their jobs or when poorly educated persons "strike it rich." Status inconsistency may be a source of severe discomfort. Political scientists have even suggested that class inconsistency predisposes individuals and groups to accept extremist political views. Extremist political attitudes may develop when the economic security of a middle class group is threatened, or when the status strivings of ascending groups are blocked.

IDEOLOGY AND STRATIFICATION:
DREAMS ABOUT GETTING AHEAD

The ideology of a stratification system explains and justifies the distribution of power and rewards in society. The ideology helps to reduce tensions between classes by explaining and justifying differences in their well-being. At the same time the ideology helps to consolidate the power of the elite by giving legitimacy to their superior standing in society. Thus, ideology itself is a source of power (see Chapter 8).

In the American ideal, a man who works hard ought to get ahead, does get ahead, and in getting ahead proves that he has worked hard. The American ideology is one of equality of opportunity. Its major points are:

1. The belief in an open opportunity structure in the United States, with equality of chances for upward and downward mobility.
2. Personal responsibility for movement upward or downward in the class

Prospectors finding gold at Rockerville, Dakota, in 1889. Their success made them an example of status inconsistency. *The Bettmann Archive*

system, with movement based largely upon personal effort, ambition, hard work, skill, and education.

3.   Relative accessibility of education to everyone who has the ability.
4.   The impartial functioning of the political and legal systems.

Do Americans believe in this ideology? A majority of them endorse it when it is presented to them in very general statements. However, when general statements are translated into specific questions, there is much less agreement. Moreover, acceptance of both general and specific statements about opportunity in America varies widely from one social class to another. Wealthy white Americans believe more strongly in the American ideal of equality of opportunity than black Americans.

To test beliefs about the opportunity structure, sociologists asked a sample of Americans a series of questions relating to the American ideology. First was a general question about the existence of "plenty of opportunity" to get ahead:

Some people say there's not much opportunity in America today—that the average man doesn't have much chance to really get ahead. Others say there's plenty of opportunity and anyone who works hard can go as far as he wants. How do you feel?

Then came a more specific question about opportunities to get ahead:

Do you think that a boy whose father is poor and a boy whose father is rich have the same opportunity to make the same amount of money if they work equally hard, or do you think that the boy whose father is rich has a better chance of earning a lot more money?

A general question regarding equal access to education: "Do you feel that all young people of high ability have fairly equal opportunity to go to college, or do you feel that a large percentage of young people do not have the opportunity to go to college?" was followed by a more specific question: "Do you think that most young people in college come from families who can give them financial help, or do you think that young people whose parents are poor are just as likely to be in college as anyone else?" Finally, on power and influence in general terms: "Some people think that voting is a vital part of the governmental process in this country while others think it really doesn't make much difference who gets elected because the same people go on running things anyway. What do you think?" And a more specific question: "Some people say that, regardless of who gets elected, people who are rich get their way most of the time, while others say that people who are poor have just as much influence in government as people who are rich. What do you think?"

The responses to these questions clearly indicate that Americans believe in the ideology of opportunity only when it is stated in the most general and vague terms (see Table 3-6). There is far less belief in the existence of equal opportunity when the ideology is presented in concrete, specific situations. White Americans, who feel there is "plenty of opportunity" in general terms, divide over the question of whether or not a boy whose father is poor can achieve as much by working hard as a boy whose father is rich. Likewise the majority of whites think that "all young people of high ability" have a fairly equal opportunity to go to college, but at the same time they do not believe that young people of ability from poor families are as likely to be in college as anyone else. Most Americans will agree with the general proposition that voting influences government, but few are willing to assert that poor people have "just as much influence in government" as rich people. Moreover, support for both specific and general statements about equality of opportunity in America declines with social class; lower classes have less faith in equality of opportunity than upper classes. Finally, it is significant that black Americans are far less likely than white Americans to believe in the existence of equal opportunity.

CLASS AS A DETERMINANT OF "STYLE OF LIFE"

Life in each social class is different. Differences in ways of life mean differences in culture, or rather (since the style of life in each class is really a variant of one common culture in American society), a division of the culture

TABLE 3-6. Beliefs About Getting Ahead in America

	Percent in Agreement					
	Plenty of Opportunity (General)	Rich and Poor Have Equal Opportunity (Specific)	Equal Access to College (General)	Rich and Poor Equal in College (Specific)	Voting Influences Government (General)	Rich and Poor Have Equal Influence (Specific)
Lower income						
Black	56	11	22	11	76	3
White	90	47	57	38	88	30
Middle income						
Black	58	21	41	28	89	15
White	80	49	75	37	89	30
Upper income						
White	93	57	96	43	94	55
Total	78	42	64	38	88	35

Source: Derived from figures presented in Joan H. Rytina, William H. Form, and John Pease, "Income and Stratification Ideology: Beliefs About the American Opportunity Structure," *American Journal of Sociology,* 75 (January 1970), 703–716; from a sample of residents in Muskegon, Michigan.

into "subcultures." Class subcultures have been described by many sociologists. There are class differences in almost every aspect of life: health, hygiene, vocabulary, table manners, standards of right and wrong, recreation and entertainment, religion, sexual activity, family and child-rearing practices, political beliefs and attitudes, club memberships, dress, birth rates, attitudes toward education, toilet training, reading habits, and so on. It is impossible to provide a complete description of all of the class differences which have been reported by sociologists. Moreover, class lifestyles overlap, and there are no rigid boundaries in America between classes. Class subcultures should be thought of as a continuous scale with styles of life that blend; hence there are many "in between" positions. And finally, it should be remembered that any generalizations about broad classes in America do not necessarily describe the style of life of any particular individuals. So the following paragraphs are merely a general summary of these subcultures.

The Upper Class. The typical upper class individual is future-oriented and cosmopolitan: He expects a long life, he looks forward to this future and the future of his children and grandchildren, and he is concerned about what lies ahead for his community, the nation, and mankind. He is self-confident: He believes that within limits he can shape his own destiny and that of his community. He is willing to "invest" in the future—that is, to sacrifice some present satisfaction in the expectation of enjoying greater satisfaction in time to come. He is self-respecting; he places great value on independence, creativity, and "developing potentialities to the fullest." In rearing his children, he teaches them to be guided by abstract standards of social justice rather than by conformity to a given code ("Do things not because you're told to but because you take the other person into consideration"). Child-rearing is permissive, and the only coercive measures taken against the child are verbal and emotional. Instructions to the child are always rationalized. The upper class parent is not alarmed if his children remain in school or travel to the age of 30. Sex life in upper classes is innovative and expressive, with great variety in sexual practices. Women enjoy nearly equal status with men in family relationships. The goals of life include individuality, self-expression, and personal happiness. Wealth permits a wide variety of entertainment and recreation: theater, concerts, and art; yachting, tennis, skiing; travel abroad; etc.

The upper class individual takes a tolerant attitude toward unconventional behavior in sex, the arts, fashions, lifestyles, and so on. He deplores bigotry and abhors violence. He feels he has a responsibility to "serve" the community and to "do good." He is active in "public service" and contributes time, money, and effort to worthy causes. He has an attachment to the community, the nation, and the world, and he believes he can help shape their future. This "public-

Wealth in the upper class permits an extensive variety of expensive recreation.
United Press International Photo

regardingness" inclines him toward "liberal" politics; the upper classes provide
the leadership for the liberal wings of both Republican and Democratic parties.

The Middle Class.   The middle class individual is also future oriented; he
plans ahead for himself and his children. But he is not likely to be as
cosmopolitan as the upper class person, being more concerned with his immediate family than about "mankind" in the abstract. He is confident about his
ability to influence his own future and that of his children, but he does not really
expect to have an effect on community, state, or national events. He shows some
independence and creativity, but his taste for self-expression is modified by his
concern for "getting ahead."

The middle class individual is perhaps even more self-disciplined and willing
to sacrifice present gratification for future advantage than the upper class individual. In the lower middle class, investing time, energy, and effort in self-
improvement and getting ahead is a principal theme of life. Middle class people
strongly want their children to go to college and acquire the kind of formal

Recreation in the middle and working class is somewhat limited and often child centered. However, there is usually enough leisure time and available transportation for an outing to the beach. *Eugene Richards Photo*

training that will help them get ahead. Child-rearing in the middle class is only slightly less permissive than in the upper class; it is still based largely upon verbal and emotional punishment. This can be quite severe, however, and the middle class child may be more closely supervised and disciplined than either upper or lower class children. Authority is rationalized for the child, but values and standards of behavior are drawn from surrounding middle class society rather than from abstract concepts of social justice. In matters of sex, the middle class individual is outwardly conventional. The middle class adolescent experiences first intercourse at a later age than the lower class youth. However, in adult life, vis-à-vis lower class individuals, he enjoys greater variety in sexual activity, women have greater equality in the family, and the family has fewer children (though home activities are frequently child-centered). Recreation and entertainment include golf, swimming, movies, sports events, travel in the United States, with only a minimum of interest in theater, art, symphonies, or travel abroad.

As a rule a middle class individual deals with others according to established codes of conduct and behavior. He is likely to be middle-of-the-road or conservative in politics; he tends to vote Republican. He has regard for the rights of others, and he generally opposes bigotry and violence. However, he does not hold these attitudes as strongly as do members of the upper class, nor does he feel as much responsibility to the community as the upper class individual does. Though he joins voluntary organizations, many of which are formally committed to community service, he is less willing to give his time, money, and effort to public causes.

The Working Class.   The working class individual does not "invest" heavily in the future; he is much more oriented toward the present. He expects his children to make their own way in life. He has less confidence than the middle class person in his ability to shape the future, and a stronger sense of being at the mercy of fate and other uncontrollable forces. He attaches more importance to "luck" in getting ahead than to education, hard work, or self-sacrifice. He is self-respecting and self-confident, but these feelings extend over a narrower range of matters than they do in the middle class individual. The horizon of the working class is limited by job, family, immediate friends, and neighborhood. Self-improvement or getting ahead is not a major concern of life; there is more interest in having a "good time" with family and companions. The working class family has more children than do middle class or upper class families.

The working class individual works to maintain himself and his family; he does not look upon his job as a means of getting ahead and certainly not as a means of self-expression. In rearing his children he emphasizes the virtues of neatness, cleanliness, honesty, obedience, and respect for authority. He seldom rationalizes authority over his children ("Because I said so, that is why") and frequently uses physical punishment. He is not interested in stimulating his children to self-expression, but rather in controlling them—teaching them traditional family values. He would like his children to go to college, but if they do not do so he does not mind much. The working class youth experiences his first sexual intercourse at an earlier age, than do middle and upper class young people, but he is much more likely to categorize women as "good" or "bad" depending on their sexual activity. There is very little variety in the adult sexual behavior of the working class, and the female is relegated to a subordinate role in sexual and family affairs. Frequently a double standard allows promiscuity in the male whereas extramarital sex by the female can be the cause of family disruption.

In his relationships with others the working class individual is often intolerant and sometimes aggressive. Open bigotry is more likely to be encountered in the working class than in the middle or upper classes. Violence is less shocking to the working class than to middle class persons; indeed, sometimes it is regarded as a normal expression of a masculine style. To the working class, the upper class appears somewhat lacking in masculinity. The working class individual's deepest attachment is to his family. Most of his visiting is done with relatives rather than friends. He does not belong to many organizations other than his union and church. Whether Protestant or Catholic, his religious beliefs are fundamentalist in character; he believes in the literal meaning of the scriptures and respects the authority of the church. In his views toward others in the community he is very private-regarding; he believes he works hard for a living himself and feels others should do the same. He is not interested in public service or "do-goodism"; he looks down on people who accept welfare or charity, unless they are forced to do so by circumstances over which they have no control. When he votes, he generally votes Democratic, but he is often apathetic about politics. His opinions on public matters are more likely to be clichés or slogans than anything else. He is liberal on economic issues (job security, fair labor standards, government guarantees of full employment, etc.) but conservative on social issues (civil rights, welfare, youth, etc.). His position in politics is motivated not by political ideology but by ethnic and party loyalties or the appeal of personalities or the hope for occasional favors. For recreation he turns to bowling, stock-car racing, circuses, fairs, carnivals, drive-in restaurants, and drive-in movies.

The Lower Class. The lower class person lives from day to day, with little interest in the future. He has no confidence in his ability to influence what happens to him. Things happen *to* him; he does not *make* them happen. He does not discipline himself to sacrifice for the future because he has no sense of future. He looks for immediate gratification, and his behavior is governed largely by impulse. When he works at all, it is often from payday to payday, and he frequently drifts from one unskilled job to another, taking scant interest in the work. His self-confidence is low, and occasionally he even suffers from feelings of self-contempt. In his relations with others he is suspicious, hostile, and aggressive. He feels little attachment to community, neighbors, and friends and resents all authority (for example, that of policemen, social workers, teachers, landlords, and employers). The lower class individual is a nonparticipant—he belongs to no voluntary organizations, he seldom attends church, he has no political interests, and he seldom votes.

The lower class family is frequently female-headed. Lower class women not only have more children than middle or upper class women but have them earlier in life. A woman may have a succession of mates who contribute intermittently to the support of the family but take almost no part in rearing children. In child-rearing, the mother (or the grandmother) is impulsive; children may be alternately loved, disciplined, neglected, and abused, and often they do not know what to expect next. The mother may receive welfare aid or work at a low-paying service job, but in either case children are generally un-

Lower class housing conditions are often overcrowded, and children have less parental supervision and variety of recreation. Youngsters in this neighborhood enjoy playing in an open fire hydrant on a hot day. *Eugene Richards Photo*

supervised once they have passed babyhood. Physical punishment is frequent. When the child enters school, he is already behind other children in verbal abilities and abstract reasoning. For the male offspring of a lower class matriarchal family, the future is often depressing, with defeat and frustration repeating themselves throughout his life. He may drop out of school in the eighth or ninth grade because of lack of success. Without parental supervision, and having little to do, he may get in trouble with the police. The police record will further hurt his chances of getting a job. With limited job skills, little self-discipline, and low aspiration levels, the lower class male is not likely to find a steady job which will pay enough to support a family. Yet he yearns for the material standard of living of higher classes—a car, a television set, and other conveniences. He may tie up much of his income in installment debts; because of his low credit rating he will be forced to pay excessive interest rates, and sooner or later his creditors will garnish his salary. If he marries, he and his family will have overcrowded substandard housing. As pressures mount, he may decide to leave his family, either because his inability to support a wife and children is humiliating, or because he is psychologically unprepared for a stable family relationship, or because only in this way will his wife and children be eligible for welfare payments.

Frequently, to compensate for defeat and frustration the lower class male will resort to risk-taking, conquest, and fighting to assert his masculinity. Lower class life is violent. The incidence of mental illness is greater in the lower class than in any others. While the lower class youth may have engaged in sexual activities from a very early age, these are stereotyped in a male dominant-female subordinate fashion. Entertainment may be limited to drinking and gambling. Many aspects of lower class culture are unattractive to women. Sociologist Herbert Gans writes:

> The woman tries to develop a stable routine in the midst of poverty and deprivation; the action-seeking man upsets it. In order to have any male relationships, however, the woman must participate to some extent in his episodic lifestyle. On rare occasions, she may even pursue it herself. Even then, however, she will try to encourage her children to seek a routine way of life. Thus the woman is much closer to working class culture, at least in her aspirations, although she is not often successful in achieving them.[6]

SOCIAL MOBILITY: GETTING AHEAD IN LIFE

The American ideal is not a classless society but a society in which the individual is free to move ahead on the basis of his merit, talent, and hard work. In a *caste* society individuals have no opportunity to move from one class to another. But in American society social mobility is valued highly, and there are no formal or legal barriers to moving up the social ladder. America is pictured as a land of opportunity where individuals with talent and effort can better themselves. Let us explore the accuracy of this picture.

There is, indeed, a great deal of social mobility in America. In every major occupation category the fathers of more than half of the individuals followed other occupations. This is a far cry from the pure caste system in which the occupations of the fathers are visited upon the sons for generation after generation. Social mobility is usually measured by comparing the current occupation of individuals with either their own previous occupations or the occupations of their fathers. The results of a typical study of social mobility are shown in Table 3-7. This table suggests that few sons have occupations with the same prestige value as those of their fathers. Furthermore, upward mobility exceeds downward mobility, reflecting the fact that economic growth is promoting upward mobility for successive generations of Americans. Finally, education is a vital factor in occupational advancement. The greatest upward mobility is experienced by individuals with college preparation.

However, there are some important reservations about this generally rosy picture of opportunity and mobility. First of all, most social mobility occurs within a narrow range of occupations. Vertical occupational movement largely occurs step by step—from unskilled to skilled labor, from clerk to manager, from

TABLE 3-7. Social Mobility: Occupational Mobility of Sons
in Relation to Fathers by Educational Level

	Upward	Stable	Downward
Total	54%	11%	35%
College	69	17	14
High school	49	6	45
Some high school	52	12	36
Grade school	48	11	41

Source: Derived from Chicago Labor Mobility Sample figures reported by Otis Dudley
Duncan and Robert W. Hodge, "Education and Occupational Mobility," *American Journal
of Sociology,* 68 (May 1963), 629–644.

business proprietor to professional, and so forth. The vast majority of persons in high-prestige occupations had fathers who were in roughly *adjacent* occupations. There are few jumps from occupations very low in income and prestige to those very high, or vice versa. In terms of intergenerational movement from manual to nonmanual occupations, the United States shows approximately the same proportions of upward mobility as western European nations.[7]

Moreover, the stratification system is much more rigid at the bottom and the top than in the middle. Studies of top business, financial, and governmental elites reveal that the ranks of labor, craftsmen, lower white-collar employees, and farmers are seldom represented. Over two-thirds of the richest men in America gain their wealth through inheritance. At the bottom of the social ladder, mobility is curtailed by educational failure. As we have already noted, educational achievement is a major factor in determining occupational mobility. In general, children from lower classes have less opportunity to stay in school, receive less encouragement to go to college, and have little motivation for educational and occupational success. The lesser value placed upon educational achievement in the lower classes is undoubtedly an obstacle to mobility. An optimistic note: There is probably more opportunity for upward social mobility in America today than ever before; in recent decades the proportion of people from lower class backgrounds who rise to fairly high positions in the system has noticeably increased.

Social mobility has its costs as well as its benefits. An open society which encourages relatively high levels of aspiration and rewards energy, merit, and ambition creates tensions in its members. Young men who would be happier as auto mechanics or TV repairmen or plumbers are pushed through college to become frustrated clerks and salesmen. Moreover, there is some evidence that upwardly mobile individuals are often discontented. Among the consequences of upward mobility, sociologists have observed overconformity, lower levels of family cohesion, anxiety, tension, and difficulty in adjustment. Among downwardly mobile individuals, sociologists have observed political conservatism, aggressiveness, authoritarianism, lower levels of family cohesion, and extreme anxiety. While most people are unaffected by moderate amounts of either upward or downward mobility, these problems may afflict individuals who have experienced a great deal of mobility. The upwardly mobile, status-seeking man is often isolated and lonely. His loneliness may be a product of his excessive devotion to getting ahead, or getting ahead may be a way that he uses to compensate for a lack of recognition and love denied him at an early age. Devotion to getting ahead also tends to take its toll in early life; the status-seeking man may neglect his family, or change wives as he moves from one level to another. And upward mobility may involve changes in location, friendships, and other adjustments in life.

SOCIAL CLASSES: CONFLICT AND CONCILIATION

An awareness of class membership is not the same as class consciousness. Class consciousness is the belief that all members of one's social class have similar economic and political interests which are adverse to the interests of other classes and ought to be promoted through common action. As we have already seen, Americans are aware of class membership, but members of the same class do not always share political interests, or feel that collective class action is necessary, or see themselves as locked in a struggle against opposing classes. Few Americans believe in the militant ideology of class struggle. Americans do not have a strong sense of class consciousness.

Nonetheless, there is some evidence of an awareness of class interest in voting behavior. While Democratic and Republican candidates draw their support from all social classes in America, social class bases of the Democratic and Republican parties are slightly different (see Chapter 6). Professional and managerial groups and other white-collar employees give greater support to the Republican party than skilled, semiskilled, and unskilled workers. Likewise, people with some college education tend to vote Republican more than those with a high school or grade school education do. Of course not all of the upper class vote goes to the Republican party, and not all of the lower class vote goes to the Democratic party. In fact the differences in voter support are not very great. But there is some indication that class has an impact on voting behavior.

In recent years, the *black consciousness* which has developed in America is similar in many ways to class consciousness. A prominent theme in militant black politics has been the necessity to foster black pride and dignity, bring about an awareness of oppression, reject the idea of coalition with whites, promote black solidarity, and engage in collective political action to advance black interests. But black consciousness is based on race and not upon class membership. Only insofar as the new black consciousness draws attention to the general problems of lower classes in America will it be contributing to the growth of class consciousness.

Why is there no militant class consciousness in America? This is a difficult question to answer precisely, but we can summarize some of the factors which appear to help stabilize the existing class system in America and reduce class conflict:

1. The high level of real income of Americans of all social classes and the relatively wide distribution of a very comfortable standard of living.
2. A great deal of upward mobility in the American system which diverts lower class attention away from collective class action toward individual efforts at "getting ahead."
3. The existence of a large middle-income, middle-prestige class.
4. Widespread belief in the legitimacy of the class structure and the resulting acceptance of it.
5. Many cross-cutting allegiances of individuals to churches, communities, races, unions, professional associations, voluntary organizations, and so forth, which interfere with class solidarity.

The American system has produced a high level of material comfort for the great majority of the population. The real possibilities in acquiring greater income and prestige have reinforced efforts to strive within the system rather than to challenge it. Even individuals who realize that their own social mobility is limited can transfer their hope and ambition to their children. A large middle class, diverse in occupation and ambiguous in political orientation, helps to blur potential lines of class identification and conflict. It stands as a symbol and an embodiment of the reality of opportunity. A widely accepted set of ideologies, beliefs, and attitudes supports the existing system. Finally, cleavages centering around religious affiliations, ethnic backgrounds, and racial categories, as well as other types of diversity (region, skill level, occupational group) have all worked against the development of a unified class movement.

KARL MARX *and the* Class Struggle

Conflict between social classes is a central feature of communist ideology. In the opening of his famous *Communist Manifesto*, Karl Marx wrote:

Karl Marx

The history of all hitherto existing society is the history of class struggles. Freeman and slave, patrician and plebeian, lord and serf, guild-master and journeyman, in a word, oppressor and oppressed, stood in constant opposition to one another, carried on uninterrupted, now hidden, now open fight, a fight that each time ended, either in a revolutionary re-constitution of society at large, or in the common ruin of the contending classes. . . . Our epoch, the epoch of the bourgeoisie, possesses, however, this distinctive feature: it has simplified the class antagonisms. Society as a whole is more and more splitting up into two great hostile camps, into two great classes directly facing each other: Bourgeoisie and Proletariat.

Karl Marx was born in Prussia in 1818. His parents were Jews who converted to Christianity when Marx was a child. He studied history, law, and philosophy at Bonn, Berlin, and Jena and received his doctor of philosophy degree in 1841. Soon after, he entered revolutionary socialist politics as a journalist and

Karl Marx was author of *Das Kapital* and the *Communist Manifesto*. While his predictions of worldwide proletarian revolution and a subsequent withering away of the states have proved untrue, he was still an original thinker who heightened awareness of social classes, their inter-relationships, and alternatives to capitalist society. *Wide World Photo*

Karl Marx

pamphleteer; he was expelled from Prussia and engaged in conspiratorial activities in France and Belgium from 1843 to 1849. *The Communist Manifesto*, written with Friedrich Engels, appeared in 1848 as a revolutionary pamphlet. In 1849 Marx fled to London where he spent the remainder of his life writing occasional pamphlets on socialism, advising socialist leaders, and setting forth his views in a lengthy work, *Das Kapital.* He lived largely on the money given him by Friedrich Engels, who was the son of a wealthy textile manufacturer.

According to Marx, social classes develop on the basis of the different positions which individuals fulfill in the prevailing "mode of production"—that is, the economy. In an agricultural economy, the principal classes are landowner and serf or tenant, or slave; in a handicraft economy, guildmaster and apprentice; and in an industrial economy, the capitalist owner of the factory and the non-property-owning worker. Marx believed that a man's position in the economy determined his interests, beliefs, and actions. The bourgeoisie who own the factories have an interest in maximizing profit and seek to keep for themselves the surplus of profit which has been created by the worker. The worker is exploited because he produces more than he receives in wages; this "surplus value" is stolen from him by the capitalist. In the long run, bourgeois society is doomed to destruction because gradually the workers will realize they are being exploited, will become aware of their historic role and act collectively to improve their situation, and ultimately will take over the ownership of the instruments of production in violent revolution. In Marx's opinion it was inevitable that development of capitalism would lead eventually to the proletarian revolution. He believed that as the capitalist became richer the workers would become poorer:

> Accumulation of wealth at one pole is, therefore, at the same time accumulation of misery, agony of toil, slavery, ignorance, brutality, mental degradation, at the opposite pole.[8]

Class consciousness was viewed by Marx as an important prerequisite to successful proletarian revolution. Class consciousness would increase as the proletariat grew in numbers, as factories concentrated them in greater masses, as workers communicated among themselves and achieved solidarity in unions and political organizations, and as conflict between workers and owners intensified. The bourgeoisie would not relinquish their control over the means of production without a fight, and therefore violent revolution was necessary and inevitable. Marx said little about the details of revolution; this aspect of communist ideology was developed later by Lenin (see Chapter 8). But after the successful proletarian revolution, Marx envisioned a society without social classes. This *classless society* would be a "dictatorship of the proletariat" with all other social class eliminated. The state would control the means of production, and everyone

Karl Marx

would be in the same relationship to the state as everyone else. Only when all were employees of the state would true equality exist. Class distinctions and class antagonisms would then be abolished. Social relations would be based upon the rule: "From each according to his ability; to each according to his needs." The state, which functions in bourgeois society to help the bourgeoisie oppress the masses, would gradually wither away in a communist society. As soon as there was no longer any social class to be held in subjection, the special repressive force, the state, would no longer be necessary.

The truth of the matter is, of course, that in the end neither capitalist societies nor communist societies conformed to Marx's analysis. First, men in capitalist societies do not define their interests strictly on the basis of their class membership. Allegiances to church, ethnic group, racial category, voluntary organizations, union and occupational groups, and so forth, prevent the emergence of the militant class consciousness. Second, and perhaps more important, the workers in America did not become poorer over time but improved their standard of living. It turned out that capitalism provided workers with considerable material comfort. Third, American society provided a great deal of social mobility enabling many individuals in the working class to move into the middle class. This growth of the middle class was unforeseen by Marx. Moreover, social mobility encouraged people in the working class to work within the system to improve their life and the life of their children, rather than to organize to destroy the system. Finally, with regard to communist societies, even though the bourgeois class was eliminated at great cost in human lives, new social groups emerged which were just as oppressive as the former bourgeoisie, if not more so. Now Communist party officials, government bureaucrats, and military officers monopolized power, prestige, and wealth. The state did not wither away but became all-encompassing and all-powerful.

SOCIAL CLASS AND POLITICAL POWER

Government leadership is recruited mainly from the upper social classes. Government officials, particularly at the national level (cabinet officers, presidential advisers, congressmen, Supreme Court judges, etc.), are recruited primarily from the well-educated, prestigiously employed, successful, and affluent upper and upper-middle classes. Political scientist Donald Matthews studied the occupations of the fathers of congressmen in order to obtain a reasonably accurate indicator of the class origins of congressmen. With few exceptions, congressmen are the sons of professional men, business owners and managers, or successful farmers and landowners.[9] Only a small minority are the sons of wage earners or salaried workers. The occupational characteristics of

Karl Marx

congressmen themselves also show that they are generally of higher social standing than their constituents; professional and business occupations dominate the halls of Congress. One reason is, of course, that candidates for Congress are more likely to be successful if their occupations are socially "respectable" and provide opportunities for extensive public contacts. The lawyer, insurance agent, farm implement dealer, and real estate dealer establish in their business the wide circle of friends necessary for political success. Another more subtle reason is that candidates and elected congressmen must come from occupational groups with flexible work responsibilities. The lawyer, landowner, or business owner can adjust his work to the campaign and then the legislative schedule, whereas the office manager cannot.

The overrepresentation of lawyers as an occupational group in Congress and other public office is particularly marked, since lawyers constitute no more than two-tenths of 1 percent of the labor force.[10] Lawyers have always played a prominent role in the American political system. Twenty-five of the 52 signers of the Declaration of Independence and 31 of the 55 members of the Continental Congress were lawyers. The legal profession has also provided 70 percent of the presidents, vice-presidents, and cabinet officers of the United States and approximately half of all United States senators and members of the House of Representatives. Lawyers are in a reasonably high-prestige occupation, but so are physicians, businessmen, and scientists. Why then do lawyers, rather than members of these other high-prestige groups, dominate the halls of Congress?

It is sometimes argued that the lawyer brings a special kind of skill to Congress. Since his occupation is the representation of clients, he makes no great change in occupation when he moves from representing clients in private practice to representing constituents in Congress. Also, he is trained to deal with public policy as it is reflected in the statute books, so he may be reasonably familiar with public policy before entering Congress. But professional skills alone cannot explain the dominance of lawyers in public office. One answer is evident in the fact that of all those in high-prestige occupations only lawyers can really afford to neglect their careers for political activities. For the physician, the corporate businessman, and the scientist such slighting of their vocation is very costly. But political activity can be a positive advantage to the occupational advancement of a lawyer; free public advertising and opportunities to make contacts with potential clients are two important benefits. Another answer lies in the fact that lawyers naturally have a monopoly on public offices in the law and the court system, and the office of judge or prosecuting attorney often provides a stepping stone to higher public office, including Congress.

To sum up, information on the occupational background of congressmen indicates that more than high social status is necessary for election to Congress. It is also helpful to have experience in interpersonal relations and public contacts, easy access to politics, and a great deal of free time to devote to political activity.[11]

Congressmen are among the most educated occupational groups in the United States. They are much better educated than most members of the populations they represent. Of course, their education reflects their occupational background and their middle and upper class origins.

Power in the *executive branch*, which most analysts now see as more important than Congress in policy formulation, is also exercised by individuals from upper and upper-middle class backgrounds. Cabinet secretaries, undersecretaries, and top civil servants tend to come from eastern Ivy League schools; most are lawyers or businessmen at the time of their appointment; many accept lower salaries out of a sense of obligation to perform "public service."[12] The same class origins are found among judges in federal courts, particularly the Supreme Court.[13]

We know that political power is largely in the hands of individuals from upper social classes, but what does this really mean for the great majority of Americans? We might *infer* that people drawn from upper social classes share values and interests which are different from those of the majority of people. We might also *infer* that these elites will use their power to implement upper social class values, and that, consequently, public policy will reflect upper class values more than mass values. These inferences would be consistent with the "elitist" view of society.

On the other hand, several factors may modify the impact of upper social classes in politics. *First*, there may be considerable conflict among members of upper social classes about the basic directions of public policy. That is, despite similarity in social backgrounds, individuals may *not* share a consensus about public affairs, and competition rather than consensus may characterize their relationships.

Second, elites may be very "public-regarding" in their exercise of power; they may take the welfare of the masses into account as an aspect of their own sense of well-being. Indeed, there is a great deal of evidence that America's upper classes are liberal and reformist, and that do-goodism is a widespread impulse. Many public leaders from very wealthy families of the highest social status (e.g., Franklin D. Roosevelt, Adlai Stevenson, John F. Kennedy) have championed the interests of the poor and the downtrodden. Thus, upper class values do not foster political exploitation but public service.

Third, upper class leaders, whatever their values, can be held accountable for their exercise of power by the majority in elections. Our system of parties and elections forces public officials to compete for mass support in order to acquire public office and the political power that goes with it. This competition requires them to modify their public statements and actions to fit popular preferences. Hence, in a democracy the fact that the upper social classes tend to hold public office does not necessarily mean that the masses are oppressed or exploited or powerless. This interpretation of the relationship between social class and political power reflects the pluralist view of society (see Chapter 6).

POWER AND CLASS: A CASE STUDY

The Power Elite

The most popular and controversial analysis of power in America is *The Power Elite,* by sociologist C. Wright Mills.[14] Since its appearance in 1956 most writers have been unable to discuss national power without reference to this important study.

According to Mills, power in America is concentrated at the top of America's corporate, governmental, and military organizations, which closely interlock to form a single structure of power—a "power elite." Power rests in these three domains: "the corporation chieftains, the political directorate, and the warlords." Occasionally there is tension among them, but they share a broad consensus about the general direction of public policy and main course of society. Other institutions—the family, churches, schools, etc.—are subordinate to the three major institutions of power:

> Families and churches and schools adapt to modern life; governments and armies and corporations shape it; and, as they do, they turn these lesser institutions into means for their ends.

The emergence of the power elite is a product of technology, bureaucratization, and centralization. The economy—once a scatter of many small competing units—is now dominated by a few hundred giant corporate and financial institutions. The political system—once a decentralized structure of states and communities with a small central government—has become a giant centralized bureaucracy in Washington which has assumed power over nearly every aspect of American life. The military—once a slim establishment depending largely on citizen-soldiers to meet specific crises—has become the largest and most expensive function of government and a sprawling bureaucratic domain.

> The history of modern society may readily be understood as the story of the enlargement and the centralization of the means of power—in economic, in political, and in military institutions. The rise of industrial society has involved these developments in the means of economic production. The rise of the nation-state has involved similar developments in the means of violence and in those of political administration.[15]

As each of these sectors of society enlarged and centralized, they increasingly came together to coordinate decision-making.

> At the pinnacle of each of the three enlarged and centralized domains, there have arisen those higher circles which make up the economic, the political, and the

The advancement of technology has contributed to the emergence of the power elite. Here automobile designer and manufacturer, Henry Ford (left), and inventor, Thomas Edison (center), two of America's best known successes in the field of technology, socialize in the early 1920's with a man of comparable stature in politics — President Warren Harding. From Stefan Lorant's *The Glorious Burden*.

military elites. At the top of the economy, among the corporate rich, there are the chief executives; at the top of the political order, the members of the political directorate; at the top of the military establishment, the elite of soldier-statesmen clustered in and around the Joint Chiefs of Staff and the upper echelon. As each of these domains has coincided with the others, as decisions tend to become total in their consequences, the leading men in each of the three domains of power—the warlords, the corporation chieftains, the political directorate—tend to come together, to form the power elite of America.[16]

The power elite holds power because of its position at the top of the institutional structures of society. These men are powerful *not* because of any individual qualities—wealth, prestige, skill, or cunning—but because of the institutional positions they occupy. As society has concentrated more and more power in a few giant institutions, the men in command of these institutions have acquired enormous power over all of us.

If we took the one hundred most powerful men in America, the one hundred wealthiest, and the one hundred most celebrated away from the institutional

The Power Elite

positions they now occupy, away from their resources of men and women and money, away from the media of mass communication that are now focused upon them—then they would be powerless and poor and uncelebrated. For power is not of a man. Wealth does not center in the person of the wealthy. Celebrity is not inherent in any personality. To be celebrated, to be wealthy, to have power requires access to major institutions, for the institutional positions men occupy determine in large part their chances to have and to hold these valued experiences.[17]

Mills is aware that his description of power in America conflicts with the "pluralist" interpretation. But he believes that notions of balancing and compromising interests, competition between parties and groups, "countervailing centers of power," and so forth, apply to middle levels of power in America and not to the top power elite. Political journalists and scholars write about middle levels because this is all they know about or understand; these levels provide the noisy content of most "political" news and gossip. The major directions of national and international policy are determined by men beyond the "clang and clash of American politics." Political campaigns actually distract attention from the really important national and international decisions.

The unity of the top elite rests on several factors. First of all, these people are recruited from the same upper social classes; they have similar education, wealth, and upbringing. Moreover, they continue to associate with each other and reinforce their common feelings. They belong to the same clubs, attend the same parties, meet at the same resorts, and serve on the same civic, cultural, and philanthropic committees. Each member of the elite incorporates into his own viewpoint the viewpoints, expectations, and values of those "who count." Factions exist and individual ambitions clash, but their community of interest is far greater than any divisions that exist. Perhaps what accounts for their consensus more than anything else is their experience in command positions in giant institutions. "As the requirements of the top places in each of the major hierarchies become similar, the types of men occupying these roles at the top— by selection and by training in the jobs—become similar."

Mills finds American democracy severely deficient, and his work is frequently cited by radical critics of American society. According to Mills, the power elite is guilty of "a higher immorality," which is not necessarily personal corruption or even mistaken policies and deeds, but rather the more insensitivity of institutional bureaucracy. More importantly, it is the failure of the power elite to be responsive and responsible to "Knowledgeable publics." Mills implies that true democracy is possible only where men in power are truly responsible to "men of Knowledge." He is not very specific about who the "men of Knowledge" are, but the reader is left with the impression that he means intellectuals like himself.

The Power Elite

NOTES

1.   Alex Inkeles and Peter Rossi, "National Comparisons of Occupational Prestige," *American Journal of Sociology*, 61 (January 1956), 320 - 339; R. Murray Thomas, "Reinspecting a Structural Position on Occupational Prestige," *American Journal of Sociology*, 67 (March 1962), 561 - 565.

2.   Gerhard Lenski, *Power and Privilege* (New York: McGraw-Hill, 1966); Jack Roach, Llewellyn Gross, and Orville R. Gursslin, *Social Stratification in the United States* (Englewood Cliffs, N.J.: Prentice-Hall, 1969).

3.   Richard Centers, *The Psychology of Social Classes* (Princeton, N.J.: Princeton University Press, 1949).

4.   Robert W. Hodge and Donald J. Treiman, "Class Identification in the United States," *American Journal of Sociology*, 73 (March 1968), 535 - 547.

5.   Op. cit., p. 218.

6.   Herbert Gans, *The Urban Villagers* (New York: Free Press, 1962), p. 246. See also Edward C. Banfield, *The Unheavenly City* (Boston: Little, Brown, 1968), Chap. 3.

7.   W. J. Goode, Reinhard Bendix, and Seymour Martin Lipset, *Class Status and Power: Social Stratification in Comparative Perspective*, 2nd ed. (New York: Free Press, 1966), pp. 585 - 589.

8.   Karl Marx, *Capital* (New York: Modern Library, 1936), p. 709.

9.   See Donald Matthews, *Social Background of Political Decision-Makers* (Garden City, N.Y.: Doubleday, 1954).

10.   Heinz Eulau and John D. Sprague, *Lawyers in Politics* (Indianapolis, Ind.: Bobbs-Merrill, 1964).

11.   See Joseph A. Schlesinger, *Ambition and Politics* (Chicago: Rand McNally, 1968).

12.   David T. Stanley, Dean E. Mann, and Jameson W. Doig, *Men Who Govern* (Washington: Brookings, 1966).

13.   John Schmidhouser, "The Justices of the Supreme Court: A Collective Portrait," *Midwest Journal of Political Science*, 3 (1959), 1 - 10.

14.   C. Wright Mills, *The Power Elite* (New York: Oxford University Press, 1956).

15.   C. Wright Mills, "The Structure of Power in American Society," in Irving L. Horowitz (ed.), *Power, Politics and People: The Collected Writings of C. Wright Mills* (New York: Oxford University Press, 1963), p. 24.

16.   Mills, *The Power Elite*, pp. 8 - 9.

17.   Ibid., p. 10.

TESTING YOUR PERFORMANCE

Note to the Student. The following questions are to test how well you achieved the Performance Objectives identified for you at the beginning of this chapter. The correct answers are supplied, accompanied by corresponding pages for you to review if you have answered incorrectly. The questions are coordinated numerically with the Performance Objectives at the beginning of the chapter. This exercise will assist you in determining the type of questions you have the most difficulty in answering (discussion, identification, explanation, definition, etc.) and will prepare you for test questions likely to be asked by your instructor.

1.   Identify the terms defined by the following statements:
     (a)   The classification of individuals and the ranking of classifications on a superiority-inferiority scale is _____ .
     (b)   A wide variety of characteristics such as physical strength, fighting prowess, family lineage, ethnic or racial category, age, sex, religion, and birth order are used for _____ of the members of a society.
     (c)   Individuals' occupations and their control of economic resources are used for _____ of the members of a society.
     (d)   The most important bases of stratification in a modern industrial society are _____
_____ .
     (e)   Differential distribution of prestige, differential lifestyles, uneven distribution of wealth and income, and unequal distribution of power can be used to discuss _____
_____ .

2.   (a)   The term used to define the ability to control the acts of others is _____ .
     (b)   All the individuals who occupy a broadly similar category and ranking in the stratification system make up a _____
_____ .

3.   Identify the method used to identify and measure social stratification:
     (a)   Where individuals are asked how they see themselves in the class system. _____
     (b)   Where individuals are asked to rank positions in the class system. _____
     (c)   Where social scientists observe characteristics which discriminate between patterns of life they associate with social class. _____
_____

4.   (a)   The idea that positions should be based upon personal qualities and achievements and that all individuals have an equal opportunity to achieve high position based upon their individual merits and efforts is a description of _____ .
     (b)   The authors whose writings exemplify the American ideal are
_____ .

5.   (a)   The fact that nine out of ten Americans describe themselves as middle class when forced to choose between the middle, upper, and lower classes

(because to characterize oneself as upper class is regarded as snobbish, and to view oneself as lower class is to admit to being a loser) would be mentioned in a discussion of _____

_____ .

(b) The direction of the trend in subjective class evaluation among Americans is _____ .

6. An individual's subjective identification of his own class was *not* found to be closely correlated to his actual income, occupation, and education, or his ownership of real estate, savings bonds, and corporate stocks and bonds, which are all _____

_____ .

7. On what subject are knowledge and consensus *similar* in both socialist and capitalist, developed and underdeveloped nations? _____

_____ .

8. The principal objective criteria of social class are _____

_____ .

9. (a) The term used to define the condition when a well-educated, prestigiously employed individual receives a low income, or when a poorly educated individual acquires great wealth, is _____

_____ .

(b) Situations in which individuals are rising or falling in the class system, well-educated individuals are losing their jobs, or poorly educated persons are "striking it rich," all indicate _____

10. To explain and justify the distribution of power and rewards in society, to reduce tensions between classes by explaining and justifying differences in their well-being, to consolidate the power of the elite by giving legitimacy to their superior standing in society, and to act as a source of power are all _____

_____ .

11. The belief in an open opportunity structure in the United States with equality of chances for upward and downward mobility; personal responsibility for movement upward or downward in the class system, with movement based largely upon personal effort, ambition, hard work, skill, and education; relative accessibility of education to everyone who has the ability; and the impartial functioning of the political and legal systems are the major points of the American ideology of _____ .

12. Americans accept general statements about equality of opportunity but disagree when these are translated into specific statements about equal education, family background characteristics, and so forth. The class *less likely* to believe in both specific and general statements about equality in America is the _____ .

13. (a) The term used to define differences in the style of life in each class is _____ .

(b) Such things as health, hygiene, vocabulary, standards of right and wrong, recreation and entertainment, religion, sexual activity, family and child-rearing practices, political beliefs and attitudes, birth rates, and reading habits are all _____ .

14. Identify the class described by the following:

(a)   Future-oriented and cosmopolitan; self-confident; invests in the future; self-respecting; permissive in child-rearing; innovative in sex life; public-regarding; liberal. _____

(b)   Concerned with immediate family; desirous of "getting ahead"; willing to sacrifice for the future; invests time, energy, and effort in self-improvement; less permissive in child-rearing; conventional in sex attitudes; conservative. _____

(c)   More oriented toward the present; believes in "luck"; interested in having a "good time" with family and companions; has more children; strictly rules children; female is relegated to a subordinate sex role; very fundamentalist in religious beliefs; private-regarding; liberal on economic issues but conservative on social issues. _____

(d)   Looks for immediate gratification; behavior largely governed by impulse; takes little interest in work; resents all authority; is a nonparticipant; family is frequently female-headed; has more children earlier in life; physical punishment frequent; in trouble with the police; higher incidence of mental illness. _____

15.   (a)   The type of society in which individuals have no opportunity to move from one class to another (social mobility) is _____ .

(b)   A society in which social mobility is valued highly and there are no formal or legal barriers to moving up the social ladder is _____ .

16.   To compare the current occupation of individuals with either their own previous occupations or the occupations of their father is _____ .

17.   The most important factor contributing to an excess of upward mobility over downward mobility in America is _____ .

18.   The occurrence of most social mobility within a very narrow range of occupations, the greater rigidity at the bottom and the top of the stratification system than in the middle, and the presence of discontentment and frustration among upwardly mobile people, all can be used to discuss _____ .

19.   (a)   The type of occupational movement which largely occurs step by step (from unskilled to skilled labor, from clerk to manager, etc.) is _____ .

(b)   The type of occupational movement which occurs when one moves to a different job paying relatively the same and similar to his old job or his father's job is _____ .

20.   (a)   The term used to define the belief that all members of one's social class have similar economic and political interests which are adverse to the interests of other classes and which ought to be promoted through common action is _____ .

(b)   The term used to define the belief that all members of one's social class have similar economic characteristics but do not necessarily share political interests or feel that collective class action is necessary is _____ .

21.   (a)   The ways in which black consciousness developed which stressed awareness of "place," similar political ideas, and promotion of collective political actions indicate _____

(b)   The fact that black consciousness is based on race, not on class membership, indicates _____
_____ .

22.   The high level of real income of Americans of all social classes and the relatively wide distribution of a comfortable standard of living; a great deal of upward mobility which diverts lower class attention away from collective action toward individual efforts at "getting ahead"; the existence of a large middle-income, middle-prestige class; widespread belief in the legitimacy of the class structure and the resulting acceptance of it; and many cross-cutting allegiances of individuals to organizations which interfere with class solidarity—all are _____
_____ .

23. (a)   Karl Marx identified the basic source of power in society as _____
_____ .

(b)   Marx identified the determinant of a man's interests, beliefs, and actions as his _____ .

(c)   Marx identified an important prerequisite to a successful proletarian revolution as _____ .

(d)   What type of society would a dictatorship of the proletariat, with all other social classes eliminated, be? _____

24.   The existence of cross-cutting allegiances which prevent the emergence of the militant class consciousness, the improvement of the standard of living of capitalist workers, the existence of adequate social mobility, the consequential growth of the middle class, and the emergence of equally oppressing new social classes in communist societies are all reasons for _____
_____ .

25. (a)   Being primarily from the well-educated, prestigiously employed, successful, and affluent upper and upper-middle classes characterizes those who hold what type of power? _____

(b)   People who have the best opportunities for getting into politics are _____ .

(c)   The social respectability, opportunities for extensive public contracts to deal out, a wide circle of friends, and flexible work responsibilities all explain why certain professions _____
_____ .

26. (a)   The view of society which infers that people drawn from upper social classes share values and interests different from those of the majority of people and that these persons will use their power to implement upper social class values is _____ .

(b)   The view of society which sees the impact of upper social classes being modified in politics by conflict and competition among the members of upper social classes over the basic direction of public policy, a public-regarding attitude, and a democratic system of elections is _____

27. (a)   The corporate chieftains, the political directorate, and the warlords closely interlock to form a single structure of power which C. Wright Mills identifies as the _____ .

(b)   The factors contributing to the emergence of the power elite are _____

28. (a)   The explanation that the power elite holds power because of their positions at the top of important structures of society is the _____ _____ explanation.

(b)   The explanation that the power elite holds power because of wealth, prestige, skill, or cunning is the _____ _____ explanation.

(c)   Recruitment from the same upper social classes, continued association with each other and the reinforcement of common feelings, and similar experiences in command positions in giant institutions are all factors contributing to the _____ .

29.   The term used to by C. Wright Mills to define the moral insensitivity of institutional bureaucracy and its failure to be responsive and responsible to "Knowledgeable publics" is _____ .

Correct Responses

1.   (a) Stratification (p. 62); (b) Classification (p. 62); (c) Ranking (p. 62); (d) Roles individuals play in the economic system (p. 62); (e) Characteristics of the stratification system (pp. 62 - 63).

2.   (a) Power (p. 62); (b) Social class (p. 63).

3.   (a) Subjective method (p. 63); (b) Reputational method (p. 63); (c) Objective method (p. 63).

4.   (a) The American ideal (pp. 63 - 64); (b) John Locke and Thomas Jefferson (p. 63).

5.   (a) Self-evaluation of Americans into social classes (p. 64); (b) Upward (p. 65).

6.   Objective ideas of social scientists about class (p. 65).

7.   Occupational-prestige rankings (pp. 65 - 68).

8.   Income, occupation, and education (p. 68).

9.   (a) Status inconsistency (pp. 68 - 69); (b) Possible sources of status inconsistency (p. 69).

10.   Purposes of ideology in a stratification system (p. 69).

11.   Equality of opportunity (pp. 69 - 70).

12.   Lower class (p. 71).

13.   (a) Subcultures (p. 73); (b) Aspects of class subcultures (p. 73).

14.   (a) Upper class (pp. 73 - 74); (b) Middle class (pp. 74 - 76); (c) Working class (pp. 76 - 77); (d) Lower class (pp. 77 - 79).

15.   (a) Caste society (p. 79); (b) American society (p. 79).

16.   How to measure social mobility (p. 79).

17.   Education (p. 79).

18.   Important reservations about opportunity and mobility in America (pp. 79 - 80).

19.   (a) Vertical occupational movement (pp. 79 - 80); (b) Horizontal (adjacent) occupational movement (p. 80).

20. (a) Class consciousness (p. 81); (b) Class awareness (p. 80).

21. (a) Similarities between black consciousness and class consciousness (p. 81); (b) Differences between black consciousness and class consciousness (pp. 81 - 82).

22. Factors helping to stabilize the existing class system in America (p. 82).

23. (a) Ownership of the instruments of production (p. 84); (b) Position in the economy (p. 84); (c) Class consciousness (p. 84); (d) Classless society (p. 84).

24. Failure of capitalist and communist societies to conform to Marx's analysis (p. 85).

25. (a) Political power (pp. 85 - 86); (b) Lawyers, landowners, and businessmen (p. 86); (c) Dominate political officeholding (p. 86).

26. (a) Elitist view of society (p. 87); (b) Pluralist view of society (p. 87).

27. (a) Power elite (p. 88); (b) Technology, bureaucratization, and centralization (p. 88).

28. (a) Institutional explanation (p. 89); (b) Individual-qualities explanation (p. 89); (c) Unity of the power elite (p. 90).

29. Higher immorality (p. 90).

KEY TERMS

stratification

classification

ranking

deference

power

social class

subjective method

reputational method

objective method

leveling (absolute equality)

opportunity

the American ideal

working class

lower class

middle class

upper class

status inconsistency

the American ideology

subcultures

public-regarding

caste society

social mobility

vertical mobility

horizontal mobility

class consciousness

class awareness

black consciousness

The Communist Manifesto

Das Kapital

Karl Marx

classless society

elitist view of society

do-goodism

pluralist view of society

The Power Elite

C. Wright Mills

power elite

DISCUSSION QUESTIONS

1.   Suppose you are studying social class and you go out and ask someone to rank himself in a social class:
  (a) Which class would the average American choose? Why?
  (b) How would the respondent's *subjective evaluation* differ from the results you as a social scientist would obtain?
  (c) What are the *objective criteria* you as a social scientist use to identify social class?
  (d) What is meant by status inconsistency?

2.   Discuss what is meant by the American ideal.

3.   You are conducting a survey and are out interviewing people from all social classes (a random sample). You ask two questions in this order:

Question 1: "Some people think voting is a vital part of the governmental process in this country while others think it really doesn't make much difference who gets elected because the same people go on running things anyway. What do you think?"

Question 2: "Some people say that regardless of who gets elected, people who are rich get their way most of the time, while others say that people who are poor have just as much influence in government as people who are rich. What do you think?"

  (a) Which of the above statements will most Americans agree on? Why?
  (b) How does this response pattern represent American views on ideology?
  (c) What effect does one's social class and race have on his answers to the questions?

4.   Choose two of the social classes (upper, middle, working, lower) and contrast them according to:
  (a) Orientation toward the direction of life
  (b) Individual self-confidence
  (c) Attitude toward child-rearing
  (d) Sex life
  (e) Role of women
  (f) Life goals
  (g) Activities and interests
  (h) Participation in politics
  (i) Party identification

5.   Contrast *class consciousness* with *class awareness*. Discuss the factors which appear to stabilize the existing class system in America and to reduce class conflict.

6.   Suppose you are interested in getting into politics:
  (a) What social class membership would be most advantageous?
  (b) What occupational characteristics would be best for you to have in order to get elected? Why?

(c) In addition to your social class, what else might be helpful in your election?

(d) What educational level would you probably have in comparison with the general population?

(e) If you hold an elitist view of society, what would be your attitude toward influencing public opinion if elected? A pluralist view?

SUGGESTED READINGS

EDWARD C. BANFIELD, *The Unheavenly City* (Boston: Little, Brown, 1968).

W. J. GOODE, REINHARD BENDIX, and SEYMOUR MARTIN LIPSET, *Class Status and Power: Social Stratification in Comparative Perspective*, 2nd ed. (New York: Free Press, 1966).

SUZANNE KELLER, *Beyond the Ruling Class* (New York: Random House, 1963).

GERHARD LENSKI, *Power and Privilege* (New York: McGraw-Hill, 1966).

DONALD MATTHEWS, *Social Background of Political Decision-Makers* (Garden City, N.Y.: Doubleday, 1954).

C. WRIGHT MILLS, *The Power Elite* (New York: Oxford University Press, 1956).

JACK ROACH, LLEWELLYN GROSS, and ORVILLE R. GURSSLIN, *Social Stratification in the United States* (Englewood Cliffs, N.J.: Prentice-Hall, 1969).

CHAPTER 4

Power and the Economic Order

PERFORMANCE OBJECTIVES

The student should be able to:

1. List the decisions made by economic organizations.

2. Identify the system used to measure America's wealth. Define the gross national product (GNP). Define a transfer payment and explain why transfer payments are not part of the GNP. Identify the components of the GNP.

3. Identify the basic factors of production.

4. Explain why the national income is always less than the net national product.

5. Define personal income and disposable personal income.

6. Differentiate between *real* increases in the GNP and *dollar* increases in the GNP. Define constant dollars. Cite the annual growth rate of the real GNP.

7. List the reasons why the gross national product does not necessarily measure the quality of life in American society.

8. Identify the social indicators movement. List the problems or obstacles facing this movement.

9. Identify the components of the economic system.

10. Define a private enterprise system. Describe the operation of the market in a private enterprise system. Describe the role of prices, profits, willingness to pay, ability to pay, labor market, and competition in the private enterprise system.

11. List the factors which determine prices.

12. Define monopolistic and oligopolistic, monopsonistic, spillover effects, and mobile economy.

13. Define a mixed economic system. List the reasons why the government intervenes in the free market.

14. Outline the laissez-faire economics (classical economics) of Adam Smith in his *Wealth of Nations*. Compare laissez-faire economics with traditional democracy.

15. Outline the "Keynesian" mixed economies of John M. Keynes in *The General Theory of Employment, Interest and Money*. Contrast Keynesian economics with laissez-faire (classical) economics with regard to self-adaptability of the free enterprise system.

16. Differentiate between fiscal policy and monetary policy. Identify which of the policies Keynes relied upon more heavily to bring about economic recovery and list the reasons why.

17. Contrast inflation with depression. Explain the fiscal and monetary policies Keynes recommended to cure each of these conditions. Cite the act which specifically pledges the federal government to assume responsibility for the economy, created the Council of Economic Advisers, and requires the president to submit annual economic reports to Congress.

18. List the government programs and explain how they act as automatic stabilizers to counter the effects of economic cycles.

19. Define a "tight money" policy as imposed by the Federal Reserve Board.

20. List the practical difficulties in governmental use of fiscal and monetary policy. Cite the congressional act passed to help stabilize the economy and to allow the president to impose direct wage and price controls.

21. Outline the provisions of the Sherman Anti-Trust Act of 1890 and the Clayton Anti-Trust Act of 1914.

22. Distinguish between horizontal business combinations, vertical business combinations, and conglomerates.

23. List the independent regulatory commissions. Define "cease and desist" actions. Describe the legal powers of the independent regulatory commissions.

24. Outline the provisions of the National Labor Relations Act of 1935 (Wagner Act). Differentiate between collective bargaining and compulsory arbitration.

25. Outline the provisions of the Labor-Management Relations Act of 1947 (Taft-Hartley Act).

26. Define: closed shop, union shop, right-to-work laws, secondary boycott, jurisdictional strike, and featherbedding.

27. List the taxation provisions commonly known as tax loopholes. Explain the effect of taxation on the distribution of income.

28. List the factors contributing to the increasing concentration of corporate power.

29.   Describe the emergence of a "management technostructure." Define "corporate conscience."

30.   Define the military-industrial complex. Contrast the views of the radicals toward the military-industrial complex with the views of the author.

31.   Describe the relationship between government and business and the military-industrial complex and the "technostructure" as seen by John K. Galbraith in *The New Industrial State*.

POWER AND ECONOMIC ORGANIZATION

A great deal of power in America is centered in large economic organizations —corporations, banks, utilities, investment firms, and government agencies charged with the responsibility of overseeing the economy. Not all power, it is true, is anchored in or exercised through these institutions; power is also embodied in class, cultural, political, and ideological institutions and processes, as discussed elsewhere in this volume. But control of economic resources provides a continuous and important base of power in any society. Economic organizations decide what will be produced, how it will be produced, how much will be produced and how much it will cost, how many people will be employed, who will be employed and what their wages will be, how the goods and services which are produced will be distributed, what technology will be developed, what profits will be made and how they will be distributed, how much money will be available for loans and what interest rates will be charged, how fast the earnings will grow, and so forth.

The decisions of steel companies to raise prices, of defense industries to develop new weapons, of banks to raise or lower interest rates on home mortgages, of electrical companies to market new home products, of the president to freeze wages and prices, of the Federal Reserve Board to tighten credit and to reduce the supply of money—all affect our lives directly. The economic decisions, made by both governments and private corporations, require choices by individuals, corporations, and governments. Control over these choices is obviously a major source of power in society.

MEASURING AMERICA'S WEALTH:
NATIONAL INCOME ACCOUNTING

The United States can produce over $1 trillion worth of goods and services in a single year for its 200 million people. This is over $5,000 worth of output per person. To understand America's vast wealth, we must learn how to measure it. We need to know where the wealth comes from and where it goes. The system of *national income accounts* provides these measures.

Let us begin with the gross national product. *The gross national product (GNP) is the nation's total production of goods and services for a single year valued in terms of market prices.* It is the sum of all the goods and services that people have been willing to pay for, from wheat production to bake sales, from machine tools to maid service, from aircraft manufacturing to bus service, from automobiles to chewing gum, from wages and salaries to interest on bank deposits. The gross national product is not a moral or an ethical concept; producing and selling cigarettes is part of the GNP, just as physician services and hospital care are. *The gross national product is also the total income received by all sellers of goods and services.* It really does not matter whether we view the GNP as the value of all goods and services produced, or the sum of all expenditures on these goods and services, for they are the same thing. To compute the GNP, economists sum up all the expenditures, plus government purchases. Care is taken to count only the final product sold to consumers, so that raw materials will not be counted twice—that is, both in original sale to a manufacturer and in the final price of the product. Business investment includes only new investment goods (buildings, machinery, and so on) and does not include financial transfers such as the purchase of stocks and bonds. Government purchases for goods and services include the money spent on goods (weapons, roads, buildings, parks, etc.) as well as the wages paid for the services of government employees. "Transfer payments" such as welfare payments, unemployment insurance, or social security payments are not part of the gross national product because they are not payments for currently produced goods or services. Thus, the gross national product becomes a measure of the nation's production of goods and services. It can be thought of as the total national pie for a given year and it is the most widely used measure of total national production.

National income accounting helps us to understand the circular flow which makes up both the income and expenditure sides of the gross national product. Figure 4-1 shows the circular flow of goods and services. Note that the GNP is composed of consumer outlays, plus business investment, plus government purchases of goods and services. On the income side, the gross national product is accounted for as shown in Table 4-1.

The "net national product" is the sum of all goods and services produced (GNP) less "depreciation" or the wearing out of producer goods which must be replaced to maintain the nation's productive capacities. The "national income" is the total of all income earned by the basic factors of production—land, labor, capital, and management. The national income is always less than the net national product because the factors of production do not actually receive the full value of their output; businesses must pay many indirect taxes to government which cut down on the income left to pay for the factors of production. "Personal income" is the total received by all individuals in the country—what people actually have to spend or to save to pay their taxes with. Personal income is what remains of national income after corporations have paid their income

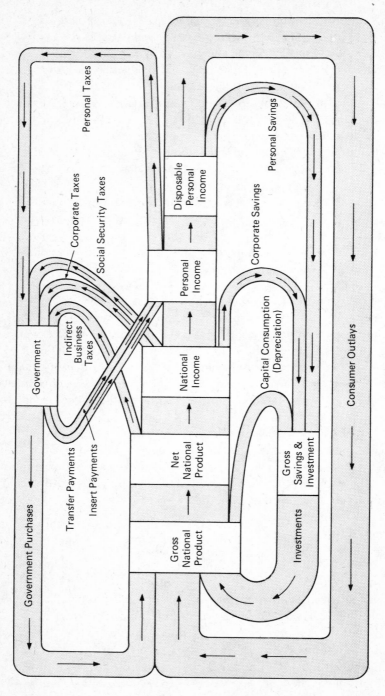

FIGURE 4-1.

TABLE 4-1. National Income Accounting and the GNP

	In Billions (1971)
Gross National Product	$1,294.9
Less Capital consumption	–110.8
(Depreciation of capital goods which must be replaced)	
Net National Product	1,184.1
Less Indirect business taxes	–119.5
(Sales, excise, property taxes which must be paid to government)	
National Income	1,065.6
Less Corporate profit taxes	–105.1
Social security taxes	– 91.2
Plus Government transfer payments	113.0
(social security, welfare)	
Government interest payments	38.3
Dividends	29.6
Buisness transfer payments	4.6
Personal Income	1,055.1
Less Personal taxes	–151.3
Disposable Personal Income	903.7
Personal Savings	74.7
Consumer Outlays	$ 829.0

taxes, made their social security contributions, and decided upon their corporate savings—how much they want to plow back into the business rather than pay out to stockholders. "Disposable personal income" is what people have left after they pay their taxes. Disposable personal income goes either to personal savings or to consumer outlays.

Since prices have increased over time (inflation), to get a meaningful measure of actual growth and output we must view the gross national product in *constant* dollars. Doubling the GNP by merely doubling prices is no real gain in production, so in order to separate "real" from merely "dollar" increases we must adjust for changes in the value of the dollar over the years. Economists account for changes in the value of a dollar by establishing the value of a dollar in a particular time base (for example, 1958) and then using "constant dollars" to measure the value of goods over time. Table 4-2 shows that the GNP has grown rapidly and vigorously both in "real" dollars *and* in "constant" dollars. Thus, America's economic growth is not merely a product of inflation. Gross national product in actual prices has risen from $40 billion to $1 trillion over this century. Even if inflation is taken into account, the growth is still phenomenal—from

TABLE 4-2.   Growth of the GNP in Real and Constant Dollars

Year or Yearly Average	Gross National Product (in billions of current dollars)	Gross National Product (in billions of 1958 dollars)
1899–1908	22	90
1909–1918	40	121
1919–1928	85	162
1929	104	218
1931	76	184
1933	56	153
1939	90	227
1945	214	393
1949	258	352
1955	398	438
1960	504	488
1965	685	618
1968	865	726
1972	1,152	790

Source: *Statistical Abstract of the United States, 1973,* p. 320; together with U.S. Bureau of the Census, *Historical Statistics of the United States* (Washington: Government Printing Office, 1960).

about $90 billion to $900 billion—a tenfold increase. Real GNP has grown between 3 and 3½ percent per year. An annual growth rate of 3½ percent enables the GNP to double every two decades.

THE GROSS NATIONAL PRODUCT AND THE QUALITY OF LIFE

While the gross national product is our best measure of economic well-being, it does not necessarily measure the quality of life in American society. First of all, it measures the size of the pie and not how the pie is cut up. Extremes of wealth and poverty can exist in the nation at any level of GNP. We will return to a discussion of the distribution of wealth, but for the moment it is important to realize that the GNP is not necessarily a measure of the extent of poverty.

The GNP says nothing about *what* goods and services get produced. The GNP includes military output—weapons, munitions, and the services of troops and other war activities—as well as expenditures for education, highways, food, and medical care. Not all of these expenditures contribute equally to improving the quality of life.

Some expenditures which are reflected in the GNP represent *costs* of life in a modern industrial society, rather than *benefits*. For example, we must build elaborate subways and mass highway transport systems in our cities to move

Smoke billowing from stacks in midtown Manhattan obscures the view of the Empire State building. The cost of this air pollution, in terms of damage to the environment, is one of many factors that is not reflected in the GNP. *United Press International Photo*

millions of people to and from work each day. The billions of dollars spent contribute to the annual GNP. But do they mean increased well-being for city dwellers? Or do they simply mean that money must be spent on a painful necessity of life in crowded cities?

Moreover, the GNP does not give any negative weight to the adverse side effects of economic development. For example, until recently producers could pollute the air and water freely, and the cost of their products did not reflect the costs of this pollution. Increasingly, efforts to control pollution will add to the cost of goods. But to the extent that the cost of goods does not include the damage done to the environment in the process of production, the GNP is misleading.

Nor does the GNP reflect the costs of goods and services that are not reflected in money transactions. The services of women who work in their own home and care for their own children are not included in the GNP; yet if women hire housekeepers and child-care personnel, their wages become part of the GNP.

The GNP places no value on leisure. Over the past 50 years, the average workweek has been cut from six long days (over 60 hours) to five short days (less than 40 hours) and vacations have greatly lengthened. In consequence, the quality of life has certainly improved. Yet the GNP does not reflect this increase in leisure. The fact that the GNP has continued to rise *despite* the growth in leisure is further evidence of the success of our system in producing goods and services.

Since national income accounting focuses largely on quantity of production rather than on the quality of life, social scientists have recently concerned themselves with producing measures of other social indicators. A special task force of distinguished social scientists prepared a document, *Toward a Social Report*, for the U.S. Department of Health, Education and Welfare suggesting the development of better social indicators of such things as (1) health and illness, (2) social mobility, (3) physical environment, (4) income and poverty, (5) public order and safety, (6) the learning of science and art, (7) participation and alienation. But the social indicators movement has a long way to go because there are no adequate national data, comparable to the GNP, to measure the quality of life in all these areas. Moreover, determining what is "quality" in life is frequently a controversial issue. The selection of the social condition to measure implies the judgment that this social condition has something to do with the quality of life, and even suggests that government ought to do something about it. The political implications of social reporting are obvious: Different interests will argue over what should be measured, what is important in life, and what shall be done about it.

THE MARKET SYSTEM, HARD-BOILED AND IMPERSONAL

The economic system consists of the institutions and processes by which a society produces and distributes scarce resources. There is not enough of everything for everyone to have all that he wants; if nature provided everything that everyone wanted without work, there would be no need for an economic system. But resources are "scarce," and some scheme must be created to decide who gets what. Scarcity and the problem of choice that it raises is a fundamental problem of economics.

The American economic system is largely "unplanned"; no government bureau tells all 80 million workers in the United States where to work, what to do, or how to do it. The private enterprise system largely organizes itself, with a minimum of central planning or direction. It would be difficult to consciously plan such a vast and complex cooperative arrangement. The American system relies chiefly on private individuals, in search of wages and profits, to get the job done. No government agency directs that shirts be produced: If people want shirts, there is profit to be made in producing them, and businessmen recognizing this potential profit will begin turning them out. No government agency directs how many shirts shall be produced: As shirt output increases, a point is

While open air markets grow considerably less common, they, like their larger and more complex counterparts, are still regulated by the basic economic laws of supply and demand. *Boston Globe Photo*

reached at which there are so many shirts that the price people are willing to pay falls below the cost of producing them; then businessmen begin curtailing their production of shirts. This same production-in-search-of-profits goes on for thousands of other products simultaneously. No government agency directs where workers shall work: Millions of workers go where they wish and search for the best jobs available. A private enterprise economy decides what is to be produced, how it is to be produced, and how it is to be distributed, all in a fashion which is for the most part automatic and impersonal. Everyone, by following his own self-interest, decides who gets what. The absence of planning and control does not mean chaos. Rather, it means a complex system of production and distribution that no single mind, and probably no government planning agency, could organize or control in all its infinite detail.

Under the private enterprise system, the *market* determines what is to be produced, how much it will cost, and who will be able to buy it. Consumers decide what shall be produced by expressing their preferences with regard to the amount of money they spend on various goods and services. When consumers are willing and able to pay for something, they will bid up the price of that item. The price is an indication of how much of the item consumers want produced. Businessmen are out to make profits. They gain profits when selling prices are higher than the costs of production. Businessmen move into industries in which consumers bid prices up and the businessmen can bring costs down. Where consumer demand bids prices up, businessmen can afford to pay higher wages, and consequently workers tend to move toward those industries with higher pay and better working conditions. So consumer demand shifts business and labor into industries in which prices are high. The businessman plays a key role in a free enterprise system because he channels production toward industries having the strongest consumer demand and organizes productive activity in the most efficient (lowest cost) way possible. Profits are the mainspring of the system. In seeking profits, businessmen perform a vital economic function. And prices play a key role in determining what profits will be, and prices are determined by consumer demand.

Who gets the goods that are produced? The price system allocates them to those who have both the *willingness to pay* and the *ability to pay*. The willingness to pay determines the desirability of producing a certain item. No government agency determines whether we "need" goods and services, but the market determines whether individuals are willing to pay for them. Consumers, however, must also have the ability to pay: They must earn incomes by working to produce goods and services that consumers want. The income received for their labor depends largely on their worth to the businesses they work for. They are worth more when they contribute more to production and profit. Where production and profits are low, wages will be low and individuals will be frequently unemployed. The "labor market" largely determines where people will work and how much they will be paid.

The market is hard-boiled and impersonal. If businessmen produce too much of a particular item—more than consumers are willing to buy at a particular price—the price will have to be lowered or production will have to be cut back. Competition among businessmen also checks prices, for a businessman who sets his price higher than that set by his competitors will lose sales. Thus consumer demand, product supply, and competition determine prices. In the absence of interfering factors, the price depends upon a relationship of supply and demand at any given time. If demand increases, prices tend to rise; if demand falls, prices tend to fall. If supply increases, prices tend to fall; if supply decreases, prices tend to rise.

Private enterprise economy, then, is really a continuous flow around a closed circle (see Figure 4-2). Businessmen pay wages, interest, and other income to the public. The public, as consumers, spends the income in payment to businesses for finished goods and services. This demand, in turn, leads businessmen to hire workers to produce more goods and services for consumers and at the same time to pay out money in wages. The continuous flow of labor and products is matched by a counterflow of money, and the whole thing is guided by the price system.

A *market* is any place or arrangement which enables people to exchange

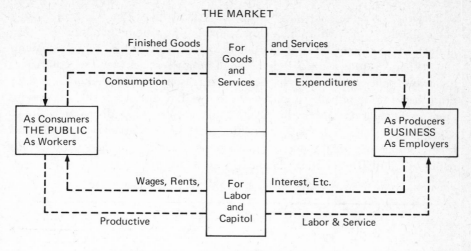

FIGURE 4–2.

money for goods or services or labor. The exchange rate is called the *price*. The market reconciles the interests of buyers and sellers, labor and business, in the process of getting people to agree on prices. The market undertakes this reconciliation automatically, without assistance from outside individuals or forces. The ideal conditions for a market operation are as follows: (1) A perfect competition exists, in which the market has so many buyers and sellers that no single trader has any control over the price of the good or service being exchanged, and the price is made by the market through the impersonal forces of supply and demand. (If one or a few sellers have control over supply, the market is said to be *monopolistic;* if one or a few buyers have control over demand, the market is said to be *monopsonistic.*) (2) The buyer of the good is able to exclude others from the satisfactions that it provides, and no one can enjoy the benefits of someone else's purchase. (When people benefit from the purchases of others, there are said to be *spillover* effects, as in the case, for example, of national defense, which cannot be sold on the open market.) (3) There is complete mobility of resources and labor so that they can move in response to changes in prices. (In a completely mobile economy, each individual (or business) is prepared to alter his pattern of spending and working in response to changes in prices of goods and labor.)

The free enterprise system just described is subject to major modifications by the activities of government. In fact, government is now so involved in the economy that we might call the American economic system a "mixed" rather than a "private enterprise" economy. Government intervenes in the free market for many reasons: (1) to assure competition among businessmen by breaking up monopolies and prohibiting unfair competitive practices; (2) to set minimum standards for wages and working conditions; (3) to regulate industries (like communications, broadcasting, and transportation) in which there is a strong public interest and in which unbridled competition may hurt more than it helps; (4) to protect the consumer from phony goods and services and false or misleading advertising; (5) to provide a wide range of public services (defense, education, highways, police protection) that cannot be reasonably provided on a private-profit basis; (6) to provide support and care (welfare, social security, unemployment compensation, Medicare, health care, etc.) to individuals who cannot supply these things for themselves through the free market system; (7) and finally, to ensure that the economic system functions properly and avoids depression, inflation, or unemployment.

ADAM SMITH
and Laissez-faire Economics

In the same year the Declaration of Independence was signed, Adam Smith, a Scottish professor of philosophy, published his *Wealth of Nations* and thereby secured recognition as the founder of free enterprise economics. Today the economic model set forth by Adam Smith is frequently referred to as "classical" economics or "laissez-faire" economics from the French phrase "allow to do as one pleases." Smith wrote *The Wealth of Nations* as an attack on the "mercantilism" of nations in his day—that is, the attempt of governments to intervene in the economy with special tariffs, regulations, subsidies, and exclusive charters to businesses, all designed to maximize the acquisition of gold and silver in government treasuries. Smith argued instead for free competition in the marketplace. He believed that a worldwide market, unfettered by government restrictions or subsidies, would result in lower prices and high standards of living for all. A free market would allow businesses and nations which could produce particular goods more cheaply and efficiently than anyone else, to do so. There would be greater specialization as each business and nation concentrated on what it did best. The outcome of the specialization and efficiency created by free competition would be a high standard of living for everyone. Thus, pursuit of private profit was actually in the public interest.

Every individual endeavors to employ his capital so that its produce may be of greater value. He generally neither intends to promote the public interest, nor knows how much he is promoting it. He intends only his . . . own gain. He is in this

Adam Smith

led by an invisible hand to promote an end which was no part of his intention. By pursuing his own interest he frequently promotes that of society more effectively than if he really intended to promote it.[1]

Laissez-faire economics is based on the idea that men are rational, that they will pursue their own economic self-interest, that they are mobile and able to shift their resources and labor as the market demands. There should be no artificial blocks to the most efficient use of men and materials. The market has a large number of competitors buying and selling products, services, and labor, and no one alone has control over supply or demand or price. Buyers buy from producers who make the best goods at the lowest price. Thus efficiency is rewarded and inefficiency driven out of the economy. Guided by demand and high prices, producers constantly shift to new lines of production. As competition increases supply and lowers prices, some producers again shift to more lucrative lines. The market continually corrects unproductive use of resources. The system is self-adjusting and self-regulating.

Smith objected to government interference in the natural operations of the marketplace. Government should do only two things: (1) create an environment for an orderly marketplace: maintain law and order, protect private property, enforce contracts, and provide a monetary system; and (2) supply those services that the marketplace cannot provide, such as defense, public works, and care of widows, orphans, and other helpless people.

Laissez-faire economics has much in common with traditional democracy. It is important to realize that Adam Smith was setting forth a model economic system which stressed individual rationality, freedom of choice, and limited government intervention, at the same time that democrats in America were developing a model political system emphasizing individual responsibility, freedom of expression, rational voter choice, and limitations on governmental power over individual liberty. *A free enterprise economic system paralleled a democratic political system.* In politics, every man was to be free to speak out, to form a political party, and to vote as he pleased—to pursue his political interests as he thought best. In economic life, every man was to be free to find work, start a business, and spend money as he pleased—to pursue his economic self-interest as he thought best. The ballot box in politics and the market in economics were the impartial arbiters of conflict in society. Government was to be restricted in both its power over individual liberty and its power over economic life.

Today many "classical" economists echo Adam Smith's ideas. Although it is now widely recognized that government must play an important role in stabilizing the economy (avoiding both inflation and depression), protecting consumers, regulating business and labor practices, and assisting individuals who cannot care for themselves, nonetheless, classical economists argue that economic planning by government is incompatible with personal freedom. They

Adam Smith

contend that bureaucratic intervention in the economy not only is inefficient and wasteful but gradually erodes individual freedom and initiative.

This fear is not unfounded; political scientist Roland Pennock warns of the political consequences of the government-controlled economy:

> The existing freedom to choose one's vocation, one's employer, and the way one would manage his savings or spend his income would give way in greater and lesser degree to regimentation in all these areas by governmental fiat. It might provide greater security or more equality, but it could hardly fail to reduce liberty.[2]

And conservative economist Friedrich Hayek writes:

> We have progressively abandoned the freedom in economic affairs without which personal and political freedom have never existed in the past. . . .
> What our planners demand is central direction of all economic activity according to a single plan, saying how the resources of the society should be "consciously directed" to serve particular ends in a definite way.[3]

Thus, the appeal of laissez-faire economics is based not only upon the efficiency of the marketplace in channeling labor and resources into their most productive uses, but also on the personal freedom in economic affairs which this system guarantees.

JOHN M. KEYNES
and the Mixed Economy

The Great Depression of the 1930s significantly altered American thinking about laissez-faire economics. It is difficult to realize today what a tremendous economic disaster befell the nation in those days. Following the stock market crash of October 1929 and in spite of President Herbert Hoover's assurances that prosperity lay "just around the corner," the American economy virtually collapsed. The gross national product was cut in half between 1929 and 1933. Businesses failed, factories shut down, new construction practically ceased, banks closed, and millions of savings were wiped out. One out of four American workers was unemployed, and one out of six was receiving welfare relief. Persons who had never known unemployment before lost their jobs, used up their savings or lost them when the banks folded, cashed in their life insurance, gave up their homes and farms because they could not continue the mortgage payments. Economic catastrophes struck far into the ranks of the middle classes.

John M. Keynes

John M. Keynes contradicted the popularly accepted doctrine of laissez-faire economics by asserting that government intervention in the economy is necessary to reverse adverse economic developments. This theory greatly influenced Franklin D. Roosevelt's policies in combating the Depression of the 1930's. *Wide World Photo*

Some business executives sold apples and pencils on the street to eke out a living. Homeless men and women stood in breadlines, slept on park benches, or took to the roads searching for work. Tramps abounded and panhandlers plied the streets. Mines were no longer worked; steel mills, foundries, and every variety of industrial plant put out only a fraction of the goods that they could produce; trains ran with no more than a handful of passengers; stores lacked customers, and many closed their doors; hospitals were empty, not because they were unneeded but because people could not afford them. Crops rotted in fields while people suffered hunger and malnutrition. Farmers lost their farms and either stayed on as sharecroppers or wandered the roads as migrant labor. Fear was widespread that violent revolution would soon sweep the country. Many

John M. Keynes

lost faith in the free enterprise system and urged the abandonment of the market economy. The "solutions" of fascism in Italy and Germany and communism in the Soviet Union were looked to as alternatives to a "doomed" capitalist system.

Laissez-faire economics recognized the possibilities of economic cycles. When consumer demand declines for any reason, businessmen are expected to cut back on production. Cutbacks involve laying off workers and postponing plans for capital investment in new plants or facilities. The resulting increase in unemployment means fewer dollars in the hands of consumers and thus a *further* cutback in consumer demands, leading to *further* cutbacks in production. But classical economics believed that the system would eventually adjust itself, reverse this downward cycle, and resume a forward movement. The turnabout would happen largely because of the effect of interest rates: When businessmen were postponing capital investment, savings would pile up, and the price of money (the interest rate) would decline; the interest rate would fall so low that businessmen would be encouraged to borrow money again, to invest in new plants and facilities, and thereby to stimulate employment. As employment rose, consumer demand would increase, and the economy would revive. In short, classical economics relied upon low interest rates as incentives to businessmen to reinvest in the economy. At the same time, the lower prices in a recession would presumably result in an increase in consumer demand. President Hoover, a believer in laissez-faire economics, waited three years for the economy to adjust itself according to the classical model. But the economy continued its downward spiral, and Hoover was overwhelmingly defeated in the 1932 presidential election by Franklin D. Roosevelt.

In 1936 John M. Keynes, a British economist, wrote a landmark book called *The General Theory of Employment, Interest and Money.* Keynes attacked the basic notion of classical economics that the free enterprise system was a self-adapting mechanism which tended to produce full employment and maximum use of resources. He believed that not all savings went into investment. When there was little prospect of profit, savings were likely to be hoarded and unused. This removal of money from the economy cycle brought depression. Moreover, he argued, low interest rates would not necessarily stir businessmen to reinvest; it was the expectation of profit, not the availability of money, that motivated businessmen to invest. Keynes believed that as confidence in the future is diminished, investment will decline, regardless of interest rates.

In Keynes's view, only *government* can reverse a downward economic cycle. Private businessmen cannot be expected to invest when consumer demand is low and there is no prospect of profit. And consumers cannot be expected to increase their purchases when their incomes are falling. So the responsibility rests on the government to take *countercyclical* action to increase aggregate income and aggregate consumption.

John M. Keynes

This man takes an original tack in trying to survive the 1930's Depression. *Wide World Photo*

Governments can act, first of all, by means of *fiscal policy:* decisions regarding government expenditures, taxes, and debt. In recessions, government can increase expenditures or lower taxes or both in order to raise total demand and private income. Government purchases add directly to total demand and stimulate production and employment. Government payments to individuals in the form of social security, unemployment compensation, or welfare make more money available to individuals for consumption. Reducing taxes also makes more money available to individuals for purchasing. Of course, increasing expenditures or lowering taxes or both means an *increase in government debt*, but only in this fashion can government pump money into the economy.

At the same time, government can act in a countercyclical way by means of *monetary policy:* decisions regarding the availability of money and credit and rates of interest. By expanding the money supply, through lowering interest rates and increasing the amount of money obtainable for circulation, government can encourage investment. However, monetary policy may not have a really direct or immediate impact on the economy if businessmen do not take

John M. Keynes

advantage of the availability of cheaper money. Thus, Keynes relied more heavily on fiscal policy than monetary policy to bring about economic recovery.

Keynes also argued that governments should pursue countercyclical, fiscal, and monetary policies to offset *inflation,* as well as depression. Inflation means the general rise in the price level of goods and services. Inflation occurs when total demand exceeds or nears the productive capacity of the economy. An excess of aggregate demand over aggregate supply forces up prices. Keynes believed that when inflation threatens, government should reduce its own expenditures, or increase taxes, or both. Reducing government purchases would reduce total demand and bring it back into equilibrium with supply. Raising taxes would reduce the money available for consumption and therefore also help bring demand back into equilibrium with supply. These fiscal policies (to be pursued during the inflationary times) would enable the government to reduce its debt (which was incurred during depressions). At the same time, governments would pursue monetary policies to fight inflation. Government could reduce the total amount of money in circulation and increase interest rates. These policies are fairly certain to reduce total demand. In fact, monetary policy is more effective in fighting inflation than it is in fighting recession.

Keynes was no revolutionary. On the contrary, he wished to preserve the private enterprise system by developing effective governmental measures to overcome disastrous economic cycles. In December 1933 he wrote an open letter to Roosevelt emphasizing the importance of saving the capitalist system:

> You have made yourself the trustee for those in every country who seek to mend the evils of our condition by reasoned experiment *within the framework of the existing social system.* If you fail, rational change will be gravely prejudiced throughout the world, leaving orthodoxy and revolution to fight it out.[4]

GOVERNMENT AND ECONOMIC STABILIZATION: CUSHIONING THE UPS AND DOWNS

Today the government of the United States is fully committed to preserving economic prosperity and using fiscal and monetary policies to try to offset the effects of inflation and recession. This much of Keynesian economics is contained in the Employment Act of 1946, which specifically pledges the federal government to assume responsibility for the economy:

> The Congress hereby declares that it is the continuing policy and responsibility of the Federal Government to use all practicable means . . . to coordinate and utilize all its plans, functions, and resources for the purposes of creating and maintaining, in a manner calculated to foster and promote free competitive enterprise and the general welfare, conditions under which there will be afforded useful employment,

John M. Keynes

for those able, willing, and seeking to work, and to promote maximum employment, production, and purchasing power.

To implement this commitment, the act created the Council of Economic Advisers to "develop and recommend to the President national economic policies." The CEA is composed of three economists, appointed by the president, and a staff of analysts to collect data on the economy and advise the president on what to do to offset cycles of inflation or recession. The act also requires the president to submit an annual economic report to Congress in which he assesses the state of the economy and recommends economic legislation.

Fiscal Policy. During recessions, when consumer demand must be increased, Congress can increase government spending or it can cut taxes and thereby put more money into the pockets of consumers. Conversely, during inflations, when strong consumer demands are pushing up prices, Congress may cut its own spending or it may raise taxes in order to restrict spending power of consumers. During recessions, Congress must increase its spending even if it does not have sufficient funds to pay the costs. Governments must run a deficit (debt) in order to pour money into the economy in periods of recession. During inflation, the government must cut its spending or raise taxes and create a surplus in its budget. That is, it is taking money out of the economy and reducing its debt in order to lower consumer demand and stabilize prices.

Automatic Stabilizers. Some government programs automatically act to counter the effects of economic cycles. For example, since income taxes increase in proportion to one's earnings, the income tax automatically restricts spending habits in times of prosperity by taking large bites of income. In times of adversity and low earnings, taxes drop automatically. Welfare programs also act automatically to counter economic cycles. In recessions, more people apply for welfare and unemployment payments, and these payments help to offset declines in income.

Monetary Policy. Since banks are the major source of money and credit for investors, businessmen, and manufacturers, government can control investment spending by making it easy or difficult to borrow money from banks. The Federal Reserve Board (FRB) was created in 1913 to regulate the nation's supply of money through its power to control the amount of money that commercial banks can lend. The FRB is headed by a seven-man board of governors, appointed by the president, for overlapping terms of 14 years. In periods of recession, the FRB can loosen controls on lending and encourage banks to loan more money to businessmen at lower interest rates. During inflation, the FRB can pursue "tight money" policies—policies making it more difficult for banks to lend money and thus reducing inflationary pressures.

In practice there have been many difficulties in government use of fiscal and monetary policy. (1) Economic prediction is not an exact science; honest economists will admit to a lot of uncertainty about just what policy should be adopted and when. Actions taken by the government may not impact the economy until six or nine months later, when conditions have changed from those which existed at the time the policy was adopted. There is a "lag" between government action and its effect. (2) The prospect for being blamed for a depression is very scary to presidents and congressmen. Inflation frequently goes unchecked because public officials are afraid that "tight money" or reduced spending or higher taxes might set off a recession. Besides, all of these counterinflationary actions are politically unpopular. Hence, deficit spending continues even when the nation is not confronting a recession. (3) Monetary policy often results in overreaction to short-run economic disturbances and contributes to long-run instability. Very tight money can check an inflation, but it may later cause a recession. Likewise, easy credit may check a temporary downswing but contribute to long-run inflation. Economist Milton Friedman has suggested that the money supply be stabilized through thick and thin with a constant rate of moderate expansion. This would allow minor economic fluctuations but avoid big swings. (4) Inflation and recession can occur at the same time if prices are pushed up by union demands for higher wages and the expectations of businessmen that inflation is a permanent way of life. Thus, even with high unemployment, prices can continue to climb. In such a situation, the government is forced into the difficult choice of fighting inflation at the cost of continued high unemployment or reducing unemployment at the cost of runaway inflation. (5) Fiscal and monetary policy must be effectively coordinated for optimum results. Unless they are, one may offset the other. But the president and Congress largely determine fiscal policy, while the independent Federal Reserve Board determines monetary policy. Occasionally, the FRB has disagreed with politicians about what policy should be applied at what time. The FRB is frequently more concerned with inflation than is the president or Congress (usually more concerned with unemployment).

In the Economic Stabilization Act of 1970, Congress recognized some of the practical problems in stabilizing the economy, particularly the problem of "cost-push" inflation during times of high unemployment (problem 4 above). The act authorized the president to impose wage and price controls as a means of halting inflation. These direct controls add another tool to the arsenal of government, together with fiscal and monetary policy, to counter inflation. Direct controls on wages and prices are supposed to hold the line against inflation while the government continues fiscal and monetary policies—deficit spending and easy credit—designed to maintain full employment. In 1971 President Richard Nixon used the powers given him in this act first to impose a moratorium on all wage and price increases and later to establish a Pay Board and a Price Board to regulate wages and prices and slow the rate of inflation. But wage and price controls proved ineffective in halting inflation in the early 1970s, and they were gradually phased out. Some economists think their failure was due to poor enforcement, while other economists do not believe such controls can ever halt serious inflation.

Recent inflation in America is not merely a product of our own government's deficit fiscal policies and expansionist monetary policies. Growing worldwide demand for food and increases in the worldwide price of oil imposed by a new cartel of oil-producing nations (the Organization of Petroleum Exporting Countries—OPEC) have contributed to *worldwide* inflation. Today the United States faces "double-digit" inflation—inflation rates exceeding 10 percent a year. It is small comfort to know that inflation in many other nations is even higher than in the United States. An annual decline in the value of the dollar (10 to 12 cents) is a serious threat to the stability of the economy. President Ford referred to this kind of inflation as "public enemy number one," convened a "summit conference" of the nation's leading economists to suggest means of dealing with it, and proposed a series of measures to Congress and the public designed to reduce demand and keep prices steady.

But it is difficult for any democratically elected government to curb inflation by deliberate "belt-tightening"—that is, by cutting down government spending, increasing taxes, and holding down the supply of money and credit. Although these policies are *economically* sound in an inflationary period, they are *politically* unpopular. Congressmen (and elected officials in other democratic nations) are reluctant to cut favorite spending programs, or confront their constituents with a tax increase, or allow unemployment to rise as a result of cutbacks in the supply of money and credit for business expansion and home buying. In short, good economics is not always good politics.

GOVERNMENT REGULATION OF BUSINESS

American public policy also attempts to maintain competition in the economy. The decline of business competition and the rise of monopolies accompanied America's industrial revolution in the late nineteenth century. As business became increasingly national in scope, only the strongest or the most unscrupulous of the competitors survived. Great producers tended to become the cheapest producers, and little companies tended to disappear. Industrial production rose rapidly while the number of industrial concerns steadily diminished. The result was the emergence of monopolies and near monopolies in each of the major industries of America.

Largely to appease farmer hostility toward eastern railroads—a hostility which was reflected in the Populist movement—Congress passed the *Sherman*

Anti-Trust Act of 1890. The Sherman Act is a vague statement condemning monopolies and restraint of trade, but despite its ambiguities it remains a cornerstone of national policy toward business. By neglecting to define "monopoly" or "restraint of trade," Congress left to the courts the problem of defining antitrust policy. The result was that the courts chose to adopt a "rule of reason" on antitrust policy, saying that only "unreasonable" monopolies or "unreasonable" restraints of trade were prohibited. The "rule of reason" allows the courts and the Justice Department great flexibility in antitrust policy. Yet flexibility brings with it uncertainty as to what particular courses of action will be held illegal.

The Clayton Anti-Trust Act of 1914 was an attempt to define antitrust policy in general, and monopoly and restraint of trade in particular. Various specific business activities that interfered with competition were prohibited, including price discrimination, exclusive agreements, and interlocking directorates for the purchase of stock in competing corporations. The Clayton Act also facilitated the bringing of suits by injured parties against businesses violating the Sherman and Clayton Acts. The Clayton Act was as important for American labor as it was for business because it specifically exempted labor unions from federal prosecutions under the antitrust laws. Finally, the Clayton Act struck at monopoly in its famous Section 7 prohibiting a corporation from acquiring the capital stock of another corporation "where the effect of such acquisition may be to substantially lessen competition." Potentially Section 7 could bring about the rearrangement of the business structure of America, but neither the Antitrust Division of the Justice Department nor the federal courts have attempted a literal enforcement of Section 7. The number of business mergers has increased dramatically in recent years.

On the whole, the Justice Department has been more likely to initiate antitrust action against business combinations which are *horizontal* in form (that is, those made up of separate businesses engaged in the production or sale of the same articles). Only recently have *vertical* combinations (that is, those composed of businesses engaged in various stages in the production process from raw materials to marketing finished products) touched off antitrust action. Not until 1961 did the Supreme Court order the I. E. duPont Company to divest itself of the General Motors stock it held. DuPont was convicted of using its control over GM to be sure that GM purchased only duPont products for its automobiles. A clear antitrust policy has not yet developed on *conglomerates* (that is, combinations of totally different businesses operating in different industries).

Another approach to business policy in America is the establishment of administrative commissions with rule-making, administrative, and judicial powers to regulate business practices. The first of the national regulatory commissions was the Interstate Commerce Commission, set up in 1887. The purpose of the

ICC was to regulate railroad practices, including rate-making. In 1914 Congress created the Federal Trade Commission, which was empowered to define and forbid unfair and dishonest methods of competition in interstate commerce. The activities of the Federal Trade Commission were extended by the Truth-in-Packaging Act of 1966 and the Truth-in-Lending Act of 1968, both of them specifically designed to protect the consumer against false or misleading advertising, packaging, or consumer credit terms.

Other regulatory commissions have been established in a variety of industries: the Civil Aeronautics Board, the Securities and Exchange Commission, the Federal Power Commission, the Federal Communications Commission, and the Atomic Energy Commission. Typically these commissions are constructed to be "independent" and "expert." Independence was to mean freedom from direct pressure of political party interests, and it was to be achieved (1) by the appointment of members for fixed overlapping terms longer than those of the president, and (2) by the requirement that the commissions be bipartisan in composition. Commission members are expected to have the experience and expertise necessary to deal with the complex field of business regulation. The commissions do not have the power to initiate criminal proceedings against businesses, but they may initiate civil action to compel businesses to "cease and desist" from engaging in prohibited activities. Often commissions have very vague mandates—"unfair methods of competition in commerce are hereby declared unlawful"—and the commissions must engage in rule-making for their respective industries. Typically, rules govern rates, discriminatory practices, adequacy of service, control of entry into the industry, unfair methods of competition, and so on.

The regulatory approach implies that competition alone is not sufficient to guarantee protection of the public interest. It implies that direct government regulation is better insurance against abuse of the public by business than reliance upon the indirect effects of competition. However, commissions often come under the influence of the industries they are trying to regulate. Regulated interests complain of bureaucratic red tape which prevents them from offering innovative or improved public service. Consumers charge that the commissions represent the interests of the industries rather than those of the general public. The cumbersome "cease and desist" system, dependent as it is upon protracted litigation for its enforcement, is weakened by long delays. The commission system, with its reliance upon detailed case-by-case regulation, appears ill adapted to modern problems.

Business is also governed by labor laws. The keystone of American labor policy is the *National Labor Relations Act of 1935*, sometimes called the Wagner Act. In this act, government guarantees labor's right to organize into unions and its right to bargain collectively through union representatives. Employers are forbidden to interfere with the rights of workers to organize and to bargain

While the position of unions in America improved greatly with the passage of the National Labor Relations Act of 1935, unions were still active even in the nineteenth century. This is a poster of the United Mine Workers emblem of 1890. *The Bettmann Archive*

collectively. The National Labor Relations Board is authorized to hold elections to determine which labor union the employees desire to represent them and to make decisions on alleged violations of the act by employers. It is important to note that, while the act requires collective bargaining, it does not require unions or employers to reach agreements. Unions are free to strike, and employers are free to fire strikers, and neither employers nor unions have to come to any agreement over wages, benefits, or conditions of work. Employers and unions are not compelled to submit their differences to any government agency for binding decisions. In other words, the act relies upon "collective bargaining" rather than "compulsory arbitration."

Employers' dissatisfaction with the increased strength of organized labor under the Wagner Act led to a dramatic shift in public policy in the *Labor-Management Relations Act of 1947* (the Taft-Hartley Act). While the Taft-Hartley Act reserves for labor all of the basic guarantees of the earlier Wagner Act, it places severe restrictions on the activities of unions. Technically, the Taft-Hartley Act was a series of amendments to the Wagner Act. The Taft-Hartley Act had to do with unfair labor practices of *unions* whereas the Wagner Act was concerned with unfair labor practices of *management*. Among other things, the act prohibits the "closed shop," in which a person cannot be hired unless he is already a member of a union, and permits a "union shop," in which a person is required to join a union after his employment only if a majority of workers vote

Telephone exchange equipment installers, members of the Communications Workers of America, picket the American Telephone and Telegraph office in New York City. The strike is labor's ultimate weapon in management-labor disputes. *Wide World Photo*

for union shop in an NLRB-supervised election. And Section 14B further restricts the union shop by giving states the power to outlaw union shops through "right-to-work" laws. The Taft-Hartley Act also outlaws the "secondary boycott," in which union members refuse to work with nonunion-made goods; the "jurisdictional strike," in which one union strikes to force an employer to recognize it rather than another union; and "featherbedding," in which a union tries to cause an employer to pay persons for services which are not performed or are unnecessary. Unions are forbidden to coerce an employee to join or not to join a union, or to cause an employer to discriminate against nonunion employees.

WEALTH, TAXES, AND LOOPHOLES

Personal wealth in America is distributed in an inverted pyramidal form. The top 20 percent (one-fifth) of income earners earn about 41 percent of all the income. The lowest 20 percent of income earners earn less than 6 percent of all the income. The top 5 percent of income earners earn about 15 percent of all of the nation's income. But this income concentration has been declining over time. In 1929 the top 5 percent of income earners received 30 percent of the total income, and the highest one-fifth of income earners received 54 percent of all in-

"I'm afraid a raise is quite out of the question, Hopkins, but perhaps one of our lawyers can suggest some tax loopholes for you."

Drawing by J. Mirachi; © 1974 The New Yorker Magazine, Inc.

come. Even since World War II, the decline in income concentration can be observed. The share of the total income received by the top 5 percent of income earners fell from 17.2 percent in 1947 to 14.7 percent in 1970 (see Table 10-2 in Chapter 10). The income received by the highest one-fifth of the population went from 43 percent in 1947 to 41 percent in 1970. Note, however, that this is only a very modest decline in income concentration over the last 25 years.

Although federal income taxes are "progressive" (large incomes are subject to higher tax rates than small ones), they do not succeed in leveling incomes in America. In 1972 an average family of four paid no income tax unless its income exceeded about $3,500. On the first $2,000 of income over this figure the family was taxed at 14 percent. The percentage rate increased rapidly as the family acquired more income. Income received over $44,000 was taxed at 50 percent, and the tax rate reached a maximum of 70 percent on income over $200,000. But *effective tax rate* (taxes paid as a percentage of total income) is not the same as *marginal tax rate* (the percentage of the last, highest dollar paid into taxes). For example, the family receiving $22,000 in income would be in the 32 percent marginal rate bracket, but its income tax bill would actually total only 18 percent of its income. The first $3,500 or so of income would be free of taxes, the next $1,000 would be taxed only 14 percent, the next $1,000 would be taxed 15 percent, and so on up the rate structure; only that portion of taxable income (after exemptions) over $20,000 would be taxable at the marginal rate of 32 percent.

Moreover, various forms of income are either tax exempt or taxed at lower rates, and a great many deductions are permitted for interest payments, depreciation, business and professional expenses, state and local taxes, etc. For example, capital gains (profits on assets bought and sold) are taxed at only half the rate of income, if the assets are held more than six months. This provision encourages investment in growing industries, but it also allows investors to receive income on which they pay less than the regular tax rates. Traditionally, interest on state and local government bonds has been exempt from federal income tax. Thus, not only are investors encouraged to assist state and local governments in community projects, but wealthy investors can receive tax-exempt income. While each of these tax provisions has special purposes (for example, the capital gains provision is supposed to encourage investment in growing industries, the tax-exempt status of state and local bonds is supposed to encourage investment in state and local governments, etc.), taken as a whole, they can act to reduce the effective tax rate on wealthy taxpayers. Hence, they are frequently referred to as "tax loopholes."[5]

Effective federal income tax rates are shown in Figure 4-3. The top line shows the steady rise of marginal tax rates under the law, but the bottom line shows the effective tax rate after exemptions, deductions, and provision for capital gains at different income levels. Plainly, taxation in America does not greatly change the distribution of income.

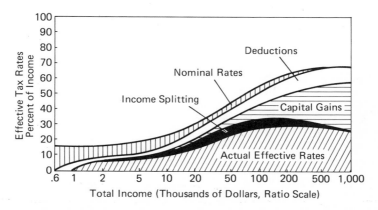

FIGURE 4–3.   Effective Federal Income Tax Rates (From C. Joseph Pechman, *Federal Tax Policy,* Washington, D.C.: Brookings Institution, 1968, p. 66.)

THE CONCENTRATION OF CORPORATE POWER

Control over the economic resources of the nation is becoming increasingly concentrated in the hands of a very few men, largely because of the consolidation of economic enterprise into a small number of giant corporations. The following statistics can only suggest the scale and concentration of modern corporate enterprise in America: The 500 largest corporations hold over two-thirds of the industrial assets in the nation. The 100 largest corporations hold half of the nation's industrial assets (see Table 4-3). The 50 largest corporations hold over one-third of all industrial assets; the five largest corporations possess over 12 percent of all of the assets of the nation. The combined revenues of three industrial corporations—General Motors, Standard Oil of New Jersey, and Ford Motor Company—exceed the total revenues of all of the American states combined. The revenues of General Motors alone are 50 times those of Nevada, eight times those of New York, and slightly less than one-fifth those of the federal government. The rate of corporate mergers in recent years suggests that this concentration is continuing to increase.

A. A. Berle, Jr., a corporation lawyer and corporate director who has written extensively on the modern corporation, commented on the concentration of corporate power:

> Since the United States carries on not quite half of the manufacturing production of the *entire world* today, these 500 corporations—each with its own little dominating pyramid within it—represents a concentration of power over economics which makes the medieval feudal system look like a Sunday School party. In sheer economic power, this has gone far beyond anything we have yet seen.[6]

According to Berle, corporate power is lodged in the hands of the directors of these corporations plus the holders of large "control blocks" of corporate stock:

> The control system in today's corporations, when it does not lie solely in the directors as in the American Telephone and Telegraph Company, lies in a combination of the directors of a so-called control block (of stock) plus the directors, themselves. For practical purposes, therefore, the control of power element in most large corporations rests in its group of directors, and it is autonomous—or autonomous if taken together with a control block. . . . This is a self-perpetuating oligarchy.[7]

TABLE 4-3. **Concentration in Manufacturing:**
Largest 100 Manufacturing Corporations

	1948	1955	1970
Percent of total assets held by all manufacturing corporations	40.3	44.3	48.2

TABLE 4-3. (Cont.)

Companies with Largest Total Assets

1. American Telephone & Telegraph
2. Standard Oil (New Jersey)
3. General Motors
4. Ford Motor
5. U.S. Steel
6. Texaco
7. Socony Mobil Oil
8. Gulf Oil
9. Sears, Roebuck
10. Standard Oil of California
11. General Telephone & Electronics
12. International Business Machines
13. Standard Oil (Indiana)
14. Consolidated Edison (N.Y.)
15. General Electric
16. Pacific Gas & Electric
17. Pennsylvania RR
18. Southern Pacific
19. E. I. duPont de Nemours
20. Chrysler
21. Bethlehem Steel
22. Tennessee Gas Transmission
23. New York Central RR
24. Shell Oil
25. Western Electric
26. Union Carbide
27. Santa Fe RR
28. Commonwealth Edison (Chicago)
29. Phillips Petroleum
30. Southern Calif. Edison
31. Southern Co.
32. Union Pacific RR
33. American Electric Power
34. Public Service Electric & Gas
35. International Telephone & Telegraph
36. International Harvester
37. Sinclair Oil
38. Aluminum Co. of America
39. Norfolk & Western Ry
40. Westinghouse Electric
41. Cities Service
42. Continental Oil
43. Monsanto
44. Columbia Gas & Electric
45. El Paso Natural Gas
46. Goodyear Tire & Rubber
47. Procter & Gamble
48. Eastman Kodak
49. Anaconda
50. Republic Steel

51. Dow Chemical
52. Consumers Power
53. Philadelphia Electric
54. Niagara Mohawk Power
55. General Public Utilities
56. Firestone Tire & Rubber
57. Allied Chemical
58. Radio Corp. of America
59. International Paper
60. Texas Eastern Transmission
61. Celanese
62. Detroit Edison
63. Armco Steel
64. Texas Utilities
65. Reynolds Metals
66. National Steel
67. Northern Pacific Ry
68. R. J. Reynolds Tobacco
69. Tidewater Oil
70. Great Northern Ry
71. American Natural Gas
72. American Can
73. Olin Mathieson Chemical
74. Atlantic Refining
75. Sun Oil
76. Inland Steel
77. Southern Ry
78. Middle South Utilities
79. Consolidated Natural Gas
80. Jones & Laughlin Steel
81. Kaiser Aluminum
82. Virginia Electric & Power
83. Union Oil of California
84. Kennecott Copper
85. W. R. Grace
86. Louisville & Nashville RR
87. Sperry Rand
88. Deere
89. Montgomery Ward
90. F. W. Woolworth
91. Chicago, Burl & Quincy RR
92. Continental Can
93. Caterpillar Tractor
94. Youngstown Sheet & Tube
95. Singer
96. Pacific Lighting
97. National Dairy Products
98. American Tobacco
99. U.S. Rubber
100. Great Atlantic & Pacific Tea

Source: *Statistical Abstract of the United States, 1971,* p. 467; listing of 100 largest corporations by size of assets from *Fortune,* March 1971.

Corporate power does not rest in the hands of masses of corporate employees or even in the hands of millions of middle and upper-middle class Americans who own corporate stock.

Corporate power is further concentrated by a system of interlocking directorates and by a corporate ownership system in which control blocks of stock are owned by financial institutions rather than by private individuals. Interlocking directorates, in which a director of one corporation also sits on the boards of other corporations, enable key corporate elites to wield influence over a large number of corporations. It is not uncommon for top elites to hold six, eight, or ten directorships. Let us illustrate the concept of interlocking directorates by examining the positions held by a few top corporate elite members. We shall also note the key positions that these top corporate elites hold outside the corporate system—in government, in the arts and sciences, and in charities, education, and civic affairs.

Richard King Mellon: chairman of the board of Mellon National Bank and Trust Company; president, Mellon and Sons; member of the board of directors of Aluminum Company of America, of General Motors Corporation, of Gulf Oil Corporation, of the Koppers Company, of the Pennsylvania Company, and of the Pennsylvania Railroad. *Fortune* magazine lists Mellon's personal wealth in excess of one-half billion dollars. He is a lieutenant general in the Reserves, a member of the board of trustees of the Carnegie Institute of Technology, of the Mellon Institute, and of the University of Pittsburgh.

David Rockefeller: chairman of the board of directors of the Chase Manhattan Bank; member of the board of directors of the B. F. Goodrich Company, of the Rockefeller Brothers, Inc., and of the Equitable Life Insurance Society; a trustee of the Rockefeller Institute for Medical Research, of the Council on Foreign Relations, of the Museum of Modern Art, of Rockefeller Center, and of the Board of Overseers of Harvard College.

Paul C. Cabot: partner, State Street Research and Management Company (investment firm); member of the board of directors of J. P. Morgan and Company, of the Continental Can Company, of the Ford Motor Company, of the National Dairy Products Corporation, of the B. F. Goodrich Company, and of the M. A. Hanna Company; former treasurer of Harvard University, and a trustee of the Eastern Gas and Fuel Association.

Crawford H. Greenewalt: chairman of the board of directors of E. I. du Pont de Nemours; member of the board of the Equitable Trust Company, of the Christiana Securities Company, and of the Morgan Guaranty Trust Company; a trustee of Massachusetts Institute of Technology, of Wilmington General Hospital, of the Philadelphia Academy of Natural Sciences, of the Philadelphia Orchestra Association, of the American

Museum of Natural History, of the Carnegie Institute of Technology, and of the Smithsonian Institution.

Arthur A. Houghton: president and chairman of the board of directors of Corning Glass Works; member of the board of directors of the Steuben Glass Company, of the Erie-Lackawanna Railroad Company, of the New York Life Insurance Company, and of the United States Steel Corporation; trustee of the Corning Museum of Glass, of the J. Pierpont Morgan Library, of the Philharmonic Symphony Society of New York, of the Fund for the Advancement of Education, of the Lincoln Center of Performing Arts, of the Cooper Union, of the Metropolitan Museum of Art, of the New York Public Library, of the Rockefeller Foundation, and of the Institute for Contemporary Art of Boston.

James R. Killian, Jr.:   member of the board of directors of the American Telephone and Telegraph Company, of the Cabot Corporation, of the Polaroid Corporation, and of General Motors Corporation; former Special Assistant to the President for Science and Technology; member of the Board of Visitors of the U.S. Naval Academy; a trustee of Mt. Holyoke College, of Mellon Institute, of the Alfred P. Sloan Foundation, and of the National Merit Scholarship Corporation; chairman and member of the board of the Institute for Defense Analysis.

James Stillman Rockefeller: chairman and director of First National City Bank of New York; member of the board of directors of the International Banking Corporation, of the National City Foundation, of the First New York Corporation, of the First National City Trust Company, of the Mercantile Bank of Canada, of the National City Realty Corporation, of Kimberly-Clark Corporation, of the Northern Pacific Railway Company, of the National Cash Register Company, of Pan American World Air Lines, of Monsanto Company.

A. A. Berle, Jr., has suggested that managers, rather than major stockholders, have come to exercise dominant influence in American corporations. Berle describes power in corporations:

> Management control is a phrase meaning merely that no large concentrated stockholding exists which maintains a close working relationship with the management or is capable of challenging it, so that the board of directors may regularly expect a majority, composed of small and scattered holdings, to follow their lead. Thus, they need not consult with anyone when making up their slate of directors, and may simply request their stock holders to sign and send in a ceremonial proxy. They select their own successors. . . . Nominal power still resides in the stockholders; actual power in the board of directors.[8]

In contrast to Berle's thesis, other scholars continue to assert the importance of having large stockholders operate through holding companies, "street names," and family trusts. It is generally conceded that a 5 percent ownership stake in a large corporation is sufficient in most cases to give corporate control. The Rockefellers, Fords, duPonts, Mellons, and others are still said to exercise prevailing influence over the large corporations.

Economist Gabriel Kolko summarizes the impact of the concentration of corporate power:

> The concentration of economic power in a very small elite is an indisputable fact. . . . A social theory assuming a democratized economic system—or even a trend in this direction—is quite obviously not in accord with social reality. Whether the men who control industry are socially responsive or trustees of the social welfare is quite another matter: it is one thing to speculate about their motivations, another to generalize about economic facts. And even if we assume that these men act benevolently toward their workers and the larger community, their actions still would not be the result of social control through a formal democratic structure and group participation, which are the essentials for democracy; they would be an arbitrary noblesse oblige by the economic elite. When discussing the existing corporate system, it would be more realistic to drop all references to democracy.[9]

THE MANAGEMENT TECHNOSTRUCTURE

Today the requirements of technology and planning have greatly increased the need in industry for specialized talent and skill in organization. Capital is something that a corporation can now supply to itself. Thus there is a shift in power in the American economy from capital to organized intelligence, and we can reasonably expect that this shift will be reflected in the deployment of power in society at large.

Individual capitalists are no longer essential to the accumulation of capital for investment. Approximately three-fifths of industrial capital now comes from retained earnings of corporations, rather than from the investments of individual capitalists. Another one-fifth of industrial capital is borrowed, chiefly from banks. Even though the remaining one-fifth of the capital funds of industry come from "outside" investments, the bulk of these funds are from large insurance companies, mutual funds, and pension trusts, rather than from individual investors. Thus, *the individual capitalist investor is no longer in a position of dominance in American capital formation.*

American capital is primarily administered and expended by managers of large corporations and financial institutions. Stockholders are supposed to have ultimate power over management, but individual stockholders seldom have any control over the activities of the corporations they own. Usually "management slates" for the board of directors are selected by management and automatically approved by stockholders. Banks and financial institutions and pension trust or mutual fund managers occasionally get together to replace a management-selected board of directors. But more often than not, banks and trust funds sell

"Happy days are here again.
The shares you hold
have split again.
We plan to raise the dividend.
Happy days are here again."

Drawing by H. Martin; ©
1973 The New Yorker
Magazine Inc.

their stock in corporations whose management they distrust, rather than use the voting power of their stock to replace management. Generally, banks and trust funds vote their stock for the management slate. The policy of nonaction by institutional investors means that the directors and managements of corporations whose stock they hold become increasingly self-appointed and unchallengeable; and this policy freezes absolute power in the corporate managements.

Of course, the profit motive is still important to the corporate managers, since profits are the basis of capital formation within the corporation. Increased capital at the disposal of corporate managers means increased power; losses mean a decrease in the capital available to the managers, a decrease in their power, and perhaps eventual extinction for the organization.

There is some evidence that management today has more concern for the interests of the public than did the individual industrial capitalists of a few decades ago. The management class is more sympathetic to the philosophy of the liberal establishment, to which it belongs; it is concerned with the public interest and expresses a devotion to the "corporate conscience." As Adolph Berle explains:

This is the existence of a set of ideas, widely held by the community and often by the organization itself and the men who direct it, that certain uses of power are "wrong," that is, contrary to the established interest and value system of the community. Indulgence of these ideas as a limitation on economic power, and regard for them by the managers of great corporations, is sometimes called—and ridiculed as—the "corporate conscience." The ridicule is pragmatically unjustified. The first sanction enforcing limitations imposed by the public consensus is a lively appreciation of that consensus by corporate managements. This is the reality of the "corporate conscience."[10]

Management fears loss of prestige and popular esteem. While the public has no direct economic control over management, and government control is more symbolic than real, the deprivation of prestige is one of the oldest methods by which any society enforces its values upon individuals and groups. Moreover, most of the values of the prevailing liberal consensus have been internalized by corporate managers themselves; that is, they have come to believe in a public-regarding philosophy.

POWER AND ECONOMICS: A CASE STUDY

The Military-Industrial Complex

In his farewell address to the nation in 1961, President Dwight D. Eisenhower warned of "an immense military establishment and a large arms industry." He observed:

> The total influence—economic, political, even spiritual—is felt in every city, every statehouse, every office of the federal government. We recognize the imperative need for this development. Yet we must not fail to comprehend its grave implications. Our toil, resources, and livelihood are all involved; so is the very structure of our society.
>
> In the councils of government, we must guard against the acquisition of unwarranted influence, whether sought or unsought, by the military industrial complex. The potential for the disastrous rise of misplaced power exists and will persist. We must never let the weight of this combination endanger our liberties or democratic processes. We should take nothing for granted. Only an alert and knowledgeable citizenry can compel the proper meshing of the huge industrial and military machinery of defense with our peaceful methods and goals, so that security and liberty may prosper together.

These words were prepared by political scientist Malcolm Moos, an Eisenhower adviser who was later to become president of the University of Minnesota. But they accurately reflect Eisenhower's personal feelings about the pressures which had been mounting during his administration from the military and from private defense contractors for increased military spending. The "military-industrial complex" refers to the armed forces, the Defense Department, military contractors, and congressmen who represent defense-oriented constituencies.

While radicals view the military-industrial complex as a conspiracy to promote war and imperialism, it is not really anything like that. Liberal economist John K. Galbraith portrays the military-industrial complex as a far more subtle interplay of forces in American society:

> It is an organization or a complex of organizations and not a conspiracy. . . . In the conspiratorial view, the military power is a coalition of generals and conniving industrialists. The goal is mutual enrichment; they arrange elaborately to feather each other's nests. The industrialists are the *deus ex machina;* their agents make their way around Washington arranging the payoff. . . .
>
> There is some enrichment and some graft. Insiders do well. . . . Nonetheless, the notion of a conspiracy to enrich the corrupt is gravely damaging to an understanding of military power. . . .
>
> The reality is far less dramatic and far more difficult of solution. The reality is a complex of organizations pursuing their sometimes diverse but generally common goals. The participants in these organizations are mostly honest men. . . . They live on their military pay or their salaries as engineers, scientists, or managers, or their pay and profit as executives, and would not dream of offering or accepting a bribe. . . .
>
> The men who comprise these organizations call each other on the phone, meet at committee hearings, serve together on teams of task forces, work in neighboring offices in Washington or San Diego. . . . The problem is not conspiracy or corruption, but unchecked rule. And being unchecked, this rule reflects not the national need but the bureaucratic need—not what is best for the United States, but what the Air Force, Army, Navy, General Dynamics, North American Rockwell, Grumman Aircraft, State Department representatives, intelligence officers, and Mendel Rivers and Richard Russell believe to be best.[11]

What are the facts about the military-industrial complex? Military spending runs about $90 billion per year—less than one-third of the federal government's budget and only about 7 *percent of the gross national product.* The 100 largest industrial corporations in the United States depend on military contracts for *less than 10 percent of their sales.* In other words, American industry does not depend upon war or the threat of war for any significant proportion of its income or sales.

Nonetheless, there are a few companies which rely heavily on defense contracts: Lockheed Aircraft, General Dynamics, McDonnell Douglas, Boeing Co., Martin-Marietta Co., Grumman Aircraft, Thiokol, and Newport News Shipbuilding. But in the world of corporate giants, these firms are considered only medium-sized. None appears in the list of the top 100 corporations in America.

The Military-Industrial Complex

While General Electric and American Telephone and Telegraph, among the real corporate giants, have large defense contracts, their military sales are only *a small proportion of total sales.* Yet there is enough military business to make it a real concern of certain companies, the people who work for them, the communities in which they are located, and the congressmen and other public officials who represent these communities.

A frequent criticism of the military-industrial complex is that defense-oriented industries have become dependent on military hardware orders. Any reduction in military spending would result in a severe economic setback for these industries, particularly the ones that rely almost totally upon defense contracts, so they apply great pressure to keep defense spending high. The military, always pleased to receive new weapons, joins with defense industries in recommending to the government that they be purchased. The military identifies and publicizes "gaps" in United States weapon strength relative to that of the Soviet Union—the missile gap, the bomber gap, the atomic submarine gap, the surface ship gap—frequently overestimating Soviet military capabilities to obtain new weapons. Finally, congressmen from constituencies with large defense industries and giant military bases can usually be counted on to join with the armed forces and defense industries in support of increased defense spending for new weapons. Of course, heavy military spending by the United States prompts the Soviet Union to try to keep pace, thus accelerating the arms race.

But American business is definitely not interested in war or international instability. The defense industry is considered an unstable enterprise—a feast or famine business for industrial companies. The price-earnings ratios for military-oriented companies are substantially lower than for civilian-oriented companies. More importantly, corporate America seeks planned stable growth, secure investments, and guaranteed returns. These conditions are disrupted by war. The stock market, reflecting the aspirations of businessmen, goes *up* when peace is announced, not *down.*

A more rational critique of the relationship between government and business centers is based on the gradual blurring of the distinction between private and public activity in the economy. In his popular book *The New Industrial State,* John K. Galbraith argues effectively that the military-industrial complex is part of a general merger of corporate and governmental enterprise into a giant "technostructure." Corporate planning and governmental planning are replacing market competition in America. Corporations avoid vigorous price competition, and the government also endeavors to fix overall prices. Both corporations and governments seek stable relations with large labor unions. Solid prosperous growth is the keynote of the planned economy, without undue, disruptive, old-style competition. Wars, depressions, or overheated inflations are to be avoided in the interest of stable growth. Big government, big industry, and big labor

The Military-Industrial Complex

organizations share in this consensus, within which the big quietly grow bigger and more powerful. Government protects this secure world of corporate giants unless they abuse the accepted standards of behavior or openly try to aggrandize their positions.

According to Galbraith:

> The industrial system, in fact, is inextricably associated with the state. In notable respects the mature corporation is an arm of the state. And the state, in important matters, is an instrument of the industrial system. This runs strongly counter to the accepted doctrine. That assumes and affirms a clear line between government and private business enterprise. The position of this line—what is given to the state and what is accorded to private enterprise—tells whether the society is socialist or non-socialist. Nothing is so important. Any union between public and private organization is held, by liberal and conservative alike, to be deviant sin. To the liberal it means that public power has been captured for private advantage and profit. To the conservative it means that high private prerogative has been lost to the state. In fact, the line between public and private authority in the industrial system is indistinct and in large measure imaginary, and the abhorrent association of public and private organizations is normal. When this is perceived, the central trends in American economic and political life become clear.[12]

Galbraith is concerned with the dangers in a merger of governmental and corporate power. He believes that the industrial system has proved its ability to serve man's material desires but that it threatens his liberty. He expresses his fear of this "new industrial state" in his concluding section:

> Our wants will be managed in accordance with the needs of the industrial system; the policies of the state will be subject to similar influence; education will be adapted to industrial need; the disciplines required by the industrial system will be the conventional morality of the community. All other goals will be made to seem precious, unimportant or antisocial. We will be bound to the ends of the industrial system. The state will add its moral, and perhaps some of its legal, power to their enforcement. What will eventuate, on the whole, will be the benign servitude of the household retainer who is taught to love her mistress and see her interests as her own, and not the compelled servitude of the field hand. But it will not be freedom.[13]

NOTES

1. Adam Smith, *The Wealth of Nations* (New York: Modern Library), p. 423.

2. J. Roland Pennock, *Liberal Democracy: Its Merits and Prospects* (New York: Holt, 1950), p. 333.

The Military-Industrial Complex

3.   Friedrich Hayek, *The Road to Serfdom* (Chicago: Phoenix Books, 1957), p. 35.

4.   Richard Hofstadter, *American Political Tradition* (New York: Knopf, 1948), p. 332.

5.   C. Joseph Pechman, *Federal Tax Policy* (Washington: Brookings, 1968); Tax Foundation, *Tax Burdens and Benefit of Government Expenditures by Income Class* (New York: Tax Foundation, 1966).

6.   A. A. Berle, Jr., *Economic Power and the Free Society* (New York: Fund for the Republic, 1958), p. 14.

7.   Ibid., p. 10.

8.   A. A. Berle, Jr., *Power Without Property* (New York: Harcourt, Brace & World, 1959), p. 73. See also Ferdinand Lundberg, *The Rich and the Super Rich* (New York: Lyle Stuart, 1968).

9.   Gabriel Kolko, *Wealth and Power in America* (New York: Praeger, 1962), pp. 68 - 69.

10.   Berle, *Power Without Property*, pp. 90 - 91.

11.   John Kenneth Galbraith, *How to Control the Military* (New York: Signet Books, 1969), pp. 23 - 31.

12.   John Kenneth Galbraith, *The New Industrial State* (New York: Signet Books, 1968), pp. 304 - 305.

13.   Ibid., p. 316.

TESTING YOUR PERFORMANCE

Note to the Student. The following questions are to test how well you achieved the Performance Objectives identified for you at the beginning of this chapter. The correct answers are supplied, accompanied by corresponding pages for you to review if you have answered incorrectly. The questions are coordinated numerically with the Performance Objectives at the beginning of the chapter. This exercise will assist you in determining the type of questions you have the most difficulty in answering (discussion, identification, explanation, definition, etc.) and will prepare you for test questions likely to be asked by your instructor.

1.   What to produce, how to produce it, who gets the product, how much it will cost, how many people will be employed, who will be employed, and what their wages will be are all _____

_____ .

2.   (a) The system used to measure America's wealth is _____

_____ .

(b) The term used to define the nation's total production of goods and services for a single year valued in terms of market prices is _____

_____ .

(c) Payments such as welfare payments, unemployment insurance, or social security payments which are not part of the GNP because they are not payments for currently produced goods or services are _____ .

(d) Consumer outlays, business investment, government purchases of goods and services are all _____ .

3. The basic factors of production are _____ .

4. National income is always less than the net national product because the _____ .

5. (a) The term used to define the total income received by all individuals in the country which individuals have to spend or to save to pay their taxes with is _____ .

(b) The term used to define the income people have left after they pay their taxes and which goes either to personal savings or to consumer outlays is _____ .

6. (a) The type of increase in the GNP which is calculated by adjusting for changes in the value of the dollar over the years is _____ .

(b) The type of increase in the GNP measured by the yearly increase in dollars without accounting for inflation or recession is _____ .

(c) Dollars used to measure the value of goods over time by establishing their value in a particular time base are _____ .

(d) The annual growth rate of the GNP is _____ .

7. Failures to measure the extent of poverty, to identify what goods and services get produced, to identify expenditures that represent costs of life in a modern industrial society, to give any negative weight to the adverse side effects of economic development, to reflect the cost of goods and services that do not pass through money transactions, and to place a value on leisure are all reasons why the GNP does not necessarily measure the _____ .

8. (a) The movement begun by a task force of social scientists who suggested better measures of health and illness, social mobility, physical environment, income and poverty, public order and safety, the learning of science and art, and participation and alienation in a report entitled *Toward a Social Report* was the _____ .

(b) Lack of adequate national data, comparable to the GNP, to measure the quality of life, and trying to determine what is "quality" in life are both _____ .

9. The institutions and the processes by which a society produces and distributes scarce resources are components of the _____ .

10. (a) The type of economic system which largely organizes itself, with a minimum of central planning or direction is a _____ .

(b) In a private enterprise system the determinant of what is to be produced, how much it will cost, and who will be able to buy it is the _____ .

(c) The key role in determining what profits will be, which are themselves determined by consumer demand, is played by _____ .

(d) The mainsprings of the private enterprise system which are sought by businessmen are _____ .

(e) The determinant of the desirability of producing a certain item is the public's _____ .

(f) The earning of incomes by working to produce goods and services that customers want determines people's _____ .

(g) The large determinant of where people will work and how much they will be paid is the _____ .

(h) The best check on prices in a private enterprise system is _____ .

11.   The factors which determine prices are _____ .

12.   (a) If one or a few sellers have control over supply, the market is said to be _____ .

(b) If one or a few buyers have control over demand, the market is said to be _____ .

(c) When people benefit from the purchases of others, there are _____ .

(d) In what type of economy is each individual and business prepared to alter his pattern of spending and working in response to changes in the prices of goods and labor? _____

13.   (a) The type of economic system, as in America, which is created when the government modifies and becomes involved in the economy is a _____ .

(b) To assure competition among businessmen by breaking up monopolies and prohibiting unfair competitive practices; to set minimum standards for wages and working conditions; to regulate industries where there is a strong public interest and where unbridled competition may hurt more than it helps; to protect the consumer from phony goods and services and false or misleading advertising; to provide a wide range of public services that cannot be reasonably provided on a private-profit basis; to provide support and care to individuals who cannot provide these things for themselves through the free market system; and to ensure that the economic system functions properly and avoids depression, inflation, and unemployment are all _____ .

14.   (a) The type of economics developed by Adam Smith in his *Wealth of Nations,* which calls for free competition in the market place and no government restrictions or subsidies and which supposedly produces lower prices and higher standards of living for all as well as greater specialization and efficiency, is _____ .

(b) The emphasis in a political system on individual responsibility, freedom of expression, rational voter choice, and limitations on governmental power over individual liberty and the emphasis in an economic system on individual rationality, freedom of choice, and limited government intervention are demonstrative of the comparability of _____ .

15.   (a) The type of economics expressed in *The General Theory of Employment, Interest and Money,* which identifies the role of the government as essen-

tial in reversing downward economic cycles and inflation through exercising fiscal and monetary policy, is _____ .

(b) The classical economics' reliance upon low interest rates as incentives to businessmen to reinvest in the economy and lower prices to increase consumer demands, and the Keynesian economics' insistence that low interest rates would *not* necessarily stir businessmen to reinvest, basically represent conflicting ideas regarding _____
_____ .

16.   (a) The type of governmental policy involving decisions regarding governmental expenditures, taxes, and debt is _____
_____ .

(b) The type of governmental policy involving decisions regarding the availability of money and credit and rates of interest is _____
_____ .

(c) The fact that monetary policy may not have a really direct or immediate impact on the economy if businessmen do not take advantage of the availability of cheaper money is an explanation for Keynes's greater reliance on what type of governmental policy? _____

17.   (a) The term for the condition that occurs when total demand exceeds or nears the productive capacity of the economy, accompanied by a general rise in the price levels of goods and services, is _____ .

(b) The term for the condition that occurs when supply exceeds demands, accompanied by decreased spending and a rise in unemployment, is _____ .

(c) Increasing governmental expenditures, lowering taxes, increasing governmental debt, lowering interest rates, and increasing the amount of money available for circulation represent _____
_____ .

(d) Decreasing governmental expenditures, raising taxes, reducing governmental debt, raising interest rates, and decreasing the amount of money available for circulation represent _____
_____ .

(e) The act which specifically pledges the federal government to assume responsibility for the economy, created the Council of Economic Advisers, and requires the president to submit annual economic reports to Congress is the _____ .

18.   (a) The term used to refer to the government programs of income taxes and welfare which work automatically to counter the effects of economic cycles is _____ .

(b) The increase of income taxes is accompanied by an automatic decrease in welfare payments during what economic condition? _____
_____

(c) The decrease of income taxes is accompanied by an automatic increase in welfare payments during what economic condition? _____

19.   The type of monetary policy imposed by the Federal Reserve Board (FRB) during an inflation, making it more difficult for banks to lend money and thus reducing inflationary pressures, is a _____
_____ .

20.   (a) The uncertainty of economic prediction, the "lag" between governmental action and its impact, the unpopularity of counterinflationary ac-

tions, frequent overreaction to short-run economic disturbances, simultaneous occurrence of inflation and recession, and the lack of effective coordination are all _____ .

(b) The congressional act passed to help stabilize the economy and to allow the president to impose direct wage and price controls is the _____

_____ .

21.   (a) The congressional act which is a vague statement condemning monopolies and restraint of trade and allows the court and the Justice Department great flexibility in antitrust policy is _____

_____ .

(b) The congressional act which attempted to define antitrust policy in general, and monopoly and restraint of trade in particular; prohibited specific business activities that interfered with competition; facilitated the bringing of suits by injured parties against businesses; specifically exempted labor unions from federal prosecution under the antitrust laws; and prohibited a corporation from acquiring the capital stock of another corporation where it would lessen competition is the _____ .

22.   (a) The type of business combination in which separate businesses engaged in the production or sale of the same articles are joined together is _____ .

(b) The type of business combination in which various stages in the production process from raw materials to marketing finished products are combined is _____ .

(c) The type of business combination in which totally different businesses operating in different industries are combined is a _____ .

23.   (a) The ICC, FTC, CAB, SEC, FPC, FCC, and AEC are all _____

_____ .

(b) A civil action to require businesses to stop engaging in prohibited activities is a _____ .

(c) The establishment of rules that govern rates, discriminatory practices, adequacy of service, control of entry into the industry, and unfair methods of competition for industries represents _____

_____ .

24.   (a) The congressional act which guarantees labor's right to organize into unions and its right to bargain collectively through union representatives is _____ .

(b) The term for the union's negotiating with the employer through union representatives is _____ .

(c) The term used to refer to the requiring of employers and unions to submit their differences to any government agency for binding decisions is _____ .

25.   The congressional act which placed severe restrictions on the activities of unions but reserved for labor all of the basic guarantees of the earlier Wagner Act was_____

26.   Identify the terms defined by the following statements:

(a) A man cannot be hired unless he is already a member of a union.

_____ .

(b) A person is required to join a union after his employment. _____

_____ .

(c) Certain laws give states the power to outlaw union shops. _____

_____

(d) Union members sometimes refuse to work with nonunion-made goods. _____

(e) The union attempts to win employer recognition for itself rather than another union through a strike. _____

(f) The union tries to cause an employer to pay persons for services which are not performed or are unnecessary. _____

27. (a) Deductions for interest payments, depreciation, business and professional expenses, state and local taxes, exemptions, and capital gains at different levels are _____ .

(b) The effect of taxation on the distribution of income has caused what type of change? _____

28. Increasing consolidation of economic enterprise into a small number of giant corporations, a system of interlocking directorates, and a corporate ownership system in which control blocks of stock are owned by financial institutions rather than private individuals are all _____

_____ .

29. (a) The administration and expending of American capital by managers of large corporations and financial institutions is referred to as the _____

_____

(b) Indulgence of the ideas that certain uses of power are "wrong" (contrary to the established interest and value system of the community) as a limitation on economic power is called the _____ .

30. (a) The armed forces, the Defense Department, military contractors, and congressmen who represent defense-oriented constituencies all compose the _____ .

(b) The view of the military-industrial complex as a conspiracy to promote war and imperialism is a _____ view.

(c) The view of the military-industrial complex as not dependent upon war or the threat of war for any significant proportion of its income or sales is the _____ view.

31. The gradual blurring of the distinction between private and public activity in the economy, the view that the military-industrial complex is part of a general merger of corporate and governmental enterprises into a giant "technostructure," and the view that market competition in America is gradually being replaced with corporate planning and governmental planning which come together on behalf of a consensus for stable planned growth are all ideas expressed in *The New Industrial State* by _____

Correct Responses

1. Decisions made by economic organizations (p. 102).

2. (a) National income accounting (p. 102); (b) Gross national product (p. 103); (c) Transfer payments (p. 103); (d) Components of the GNP (p. 103).

3. Land, labor, capital, and management (p. 103).

4.   Factors of production do not receive the full value of their output (p. 103).

5.   (a) Personal income (p. 103); (b) Disposable personal income (p. 105).

6.   (a) Real increase (p. 105); (b) Dollar increase (p. 105); (c) Constant dollars (p. 105); (d) 3 ½ percent (p. 106).

7.   Quality of life in American society (pp. 106 - 108).

8.   (a) Social indicators movement (p. 108); (b) Obstacles to the social indicators movement (p. 108).

9.   Economic system (p. 108).

10.   (a) Private enterprise system (pp. 108 - 110); (b) Market (p. 109); (c) Prices (pp. 109 - 110); (d) Profits (p. 110); (e) Willingness to pay (p. 110); (f) Ability to pay (p. 110); (g) Labor market (p. 110); (h) Competition (p. 110).

11.   Consumer demand, product supply, and competition (p. 110).

12.   (a) Monopolistic (p. 111); (b) Monopsonistic (p. 111); (c) Spillover effects (p. 111); (d) Mobile economy (p. 111).

13.   (a) Mixed economic system (p. 111); (b) Reasons for government interference in the free market (pp. 111 - 112).

14.   (a) Laissez-faire (classical) economics (pp. 112 - 113); (b) Traditional democracy and laissez-faire economics (p. 113).

15.   (a) Keynesian (mixed) economics (pp. 116 - 118); (b) Self-adaptability of the free enterprise system (pp. 116 - 118).

16.   (a) Fiscal policy (p. 117); (b) Monetary policy (p. 117); (c) Fiscal policy (p. 118).

17.   (a) Inflation (p. 118); (b) Depression (p. 118); (c) Fiscal and monetary policies to cure a depression (p. 119); (d) Fiscal and monetary policies to cure an inflation (p. 119); (e) Employment Act of 1946 (pp. 118 - 119).

18.   (a) Automatic stabilizers (p. 119); (b) Prosperity (p. 119); (c) Recession (p. 119).

19.   Tight money policy (p. 119).

20.   (a) Practical difficulties in governmental use of fiscal and monetary policy (p. 120); (b) Economic Stabilization Act of 1970 (p. 120).

21.   (a) Sherman Anti-Trust Act of 1890 (pp. 121 - 122); (b) Clayton Anti-Trust Act of 1914 (p. 122).

22.   (a) Horizontal business combination (p. 122); (b) Vertical business combination (p. 122); (c) Conglomerates (p. 122).

23.   (a) Independent regulatory commissions (pp. 122 - 123); (b) Cease and desist action (p. 123); (c) Legal powers of the independent regulatory commissions (p. 123).

24.   (a) National Labor Relations Act (Wagner Act) (pp. 123 - 124); (b) Collective bargaining (pp. 123 - 124); (c) Compulsory arbitration (p. 124).

25.   Labor-Management Relations Act of 1947 (Taft-Hartley Act) (pp. 124 - 125).

26.   (a) Closed shop (p. 124); (b) Union shop (p. 124 - 125); (c) Right-to-work laws (p. 125); (d) Secondary boycott (p. 125); (e) Jurisdictional strike (p. 125); (f) Featherbedding (p. 125).

27.   (a) Tax loopholes (p. 127); (b) Negligible change (p. 127).

28.   Factors contributing to the increasing concentration of corporate power (pp. 128, 130).

29. (a) Management technostructure (pp. 132 - 134); (b) Corporate conscience (pp. 133 - 134).

30. (a) Military-industrial complex (p. 135); (b) Radical view (p. 135); (c) Author's view (pp. 135 - 136).

31. John K. Galbraith (pp. 136 - 137).

KEY TERMS

national income accounts

gross national product (GNP)

business investment

financial transfers

government purchases for goods and
 services

transfer payments

national income

net national product

personal income

disposable personal income

inflation

real increase

dollar increase

constant dollars

social indicators

the economic system

private enterprise economy

market

prices

profits

consumer demands

product supply

willingness to pay

ability to pay

labor market

competition

monopolistic

monopsonistic

spillover effects

mobile economy

mixed economy

Wealth of Nations

Adam Smith

classical (laissez-faire) economics

mercantilism

John M. Keynes

fiscal policy

monetary policy

Employment Act of 1946

Council of Economic Advisers

deficit

automatic stabilizers

Federal Reserve Board

easy money

tight money

Economic Stabilization Act of 1970

Sherman Anti-Trust Act of 1890

Clayton Anti-Trust Act of 1914

horizontal business combinations

vertical business combinations

conglomerates

Interstate Commerce Commission

Federal Trade Commission

Truth-in-Packaging Act of 1966

Truth-in-Lending Act of 1968

CAB

SEC

FPC	right-to-work laws
FCC	secondary boycott
AEC	jurisdictional strike
"cease and desist" system	featherbedding
National Labor Relations Act (Wagner Act) of 1935	effective tax rate
	marginal tax rate
National Labor Relations Board	capital gains
collective bargaining	tax loopholes
compulsory arbitration	interlocking directorates
Labor-Management Relations Act (Taft-Hartley Act) of 1947	corporate ownership system
	corporate conscience
closed shop	military-industrial complex
union shop	technostructure

DISCUSSION QUESTIONS

1. Explain how economists compute the gross national product (GNP). Differentiate between "real" increases in the GNP and "dollar" increases in the GNP. What are the weaknesses of the GNP measure?

2. Within a free enterprise economy, discuss the role of:
    (a) The market
    (b) Consumer demands
    (c) Profits
    (d) Prices
    (e) Willingness to pay and ability to pay
    (f) Labor market
    (g) Competition

3. Suppose you are in a debate over the values of a free enterprise system and you must argue that a "mixed" economic system is better. What reasons for governmental interference with the economy would you stress?

4. Discuss the similarities between laissez-faire (classical) economics and a traditional democratic political system.

5. Suppose the United States were in an *inflationary* period and you were a Keynesian economist. In terms of Keynesian (mixed) economics, discuss the necessary action with regard to:
    (a) Fiscal policy
        (1) Governmental expenditures and purchases
        (2) Taxes
        (3) Government debt
    (b) Monetary policy
        (1) Availability of money and credit

(2) Interest rates
(c) How would the automatic stabilizers work?
(1) Federal income taxes
(2) Welfare and unemployment programs

Discuss the question if the United States were in a *recessional* period.

6. Choose four of the following congressional acts and explain how each represented an attempt by government to maintain competition in the economy:
(a) Sherman Anti-Trust Act of 1890
(b) Clayton Anti-Trust Act of 1914
(c) Truth-in-Packaging Act of 1966
(d) Truth-in-Lending Act of 1968
(e) National Labor Relations Act of 1935 (Wagner Act)
(f) Labor-Management Relations Act of 1947 (Taft-Hartley Act)

7. Discuss the reasons for the increasing concentration of corporate power. What effects have corporate planning and governmental planning had on the management of corporations and on competition?

SUGGESTED READINGS

GEORGE L. BACH, *Economics: An Introduction to Analysis and Policy*, 7th ed. (Englewood Cliffs, N.J.: Prentice-Hall, 1971).

CONGRESSIONAL QUARTERLY, *The Power of the Pentagon* (Washington: Congressional Quarterly, 1972).

JOHN KENNETH GALBRAITH, *The New Industrial State* (New York: Signet Books, 1968).

GABRIEL KOLKO, *Wealth and Power in America* (New York: Praeger, 1962).

C. JOSEPH PECHMAN, *Federal Tax Policy* (Washington: Brookings, 1968).

U.S. DEPARTMENT OF HEALTH, EDUCATION AND WELFARE, *Toward a Social Report* (Ann Arbor: University of Michigan Press, 1970).

CHAPTER 5

Power and Personality

PERFORMANCE OBJECTIVES

The student should be able to:

1. Define personality, characteristic, habitual, enduring, and organized.

2. Distinguish between personality and role.

3. Contrast clinical psychology with experimental psychology and with social psychology.

4. Define psychiatry, psychoanalysis, and socialization.

5. Identify the psychiatrist who developed the theory of psychoanalysis.

6. Identify the three major systems which compose personality, according to Freud.

7. Differentiate between reality anxiety, neurotic anxiety, and moral anxiety. Cite the processes by which an individual reduces anxiety. Define the defense mechanisms which may be employed to reduce anxiety and tension: repression, projection, reaction formation, and regression.

8. Identify the two instincts regarded by Freud as the most seriously repressed by society.

9. Identify and define the stages of personality development as seen by Freud.

10. Differentiate between anal-retentive personality characteristics and anal-expulsive personality characteristics.

11. Define Oedipus complex, castration anxiety, and latency period.

12. List the criticisms of Freudian theory.

13. Identify the goal of behavioral (stimulus-response) theory.

14. List and define the four requirements for the establishment of a linkage between a conditioned stimulus and a response.

15. Differentiate between a stimulus generalization and a stimulus discrimination.

16. Define counterconditioning.

17. Describe the various theories of how people think.

18. Explain how behavioral psychologists eliminate undesirable (dysfunctional) behaviors.

19. Explain the early influence of Gestalt psychologists on social psychology.

20. Define the socialization process.

21. Identify the psychologist responsible for developing the notion of roles to explain how the individual internalizes the expectations of others and acquires the values of society.

22. Outline Charles H. Cooley's "looking glass" self-system.

23. Explain how Kurt Lewin used the term *life space*.

24. Define these terms used by social psychologists: *integrated personality, personality disorganization, desocialization,* and *sensitivity group*.

25. Contrast the Freudian theory approach to power and personality with learning theory approach and the interpersonal-interaction theory approach.

26. Outline the relationship between human behavior and the concept of behavioral conditioning of B. F. Skinner.

27. Identify the five functional forms in which power occurs in an individual's life as defined by clinical psychologist Rollo May.

28. Compare and contrast the views of powerlessness and the "other-directedness" held by the clinical psychologist Rollo May and the social psychologist David Riesman.

29. Outline the major findings of *The Authoritarian Personality*. Define the F (fascism) Scale. List the characteristics of the authoritarian personality. List the sources of authoritarianism. Discuss the criticisms of *The Authoritarian Personality* and the F Scale. Define dogmatism.

POWER AND PERSONALITY

Individuals react toward power and authority in characteristic ways. In many different situations and over a relatively prolonged period of time, their responses to power and authority are fairly predictable. Some individuals regularly seek power and authority while others avoid it. Some individuals are submissive to authority, while others are habitually rebellious. Some individuals try to conform to the expectations of other people while others are guided by internalized standards. Some individuals feel powerless, helpless, and isolated; they believe they have little control over their own lives. Other individuals are self-assured and aggressive; they speak out at meetings, organize groups, and take over leadership positions. Some individuals are habitually suspicious of others, unwilling to compromise; they prefer simple, final, and forceful solutions

"I've been fired, Mr. Durslag, but **you** *have a nose like a potato."*
Drawing by Donald Reilly; © 1973 The New Yorker Magazine, Inc.

to complex problems. Some individuals are assertive, self-confident, and strong-willed while others are timid, submissive, and self-conscious. There are as many different ways of responding to power as there are types of personalities.

Personality is all of the characteristic ways of behaving which an individual exhibits; it is the enduring and organized sets of responses which an individual habitually makes when subjected to particular stimuli. By *characteristic* and *habitual* we mean that individuals tend to respond in a similar fashion to many separate situations. For example, their attitudes toward authority in general may affect their response to any number of different leaders, supervisors, directors, or other authority figures, in different situations. By *enduring* we mean that these characteristic ways of behaving may operate over a long time, perhaps through youth, young adulthood, and maturity. Attitudes toward authority in the home may carry over to the school, university, job, church, government, etc. By *organized* we mean that there are relationships between various elements of an individual's personality. A change in one element (let us say, a growing need for social approval) would bring about a change in another element (let us say, an increased willingness to conform to group norms). Thus, personality is not just a bundle of traits but an integrated *pattern* of responses.

It is important to distinguish the concept of "personality" from the concept of "role." A role is a pattern of expected behavior associated with a given position in society—as father, automobile worker, union member, church deacon, Little League baseball coach, etc. Occasionally it is difficult to distinguish role-determined from personality-determined behavior. Sometimes the only way to do so is to observe how a person behaves in a number of different roles. If he displays a similar characteristic—for instance, if he is an authoritarian—in all of his roles, then we can attribute this characteristic to *personality* rather than role.

Psychologists differ over the precise meaning of "personality." Psychologist Gordon Allport lists no less than 50 types of definitions.[1] Definitions tend to be linked to major theories or approaches to individual behavior—that is, to the major divisions within psychology itself.

Clinical psychology has to do with the treatment of psychological disorder. It is closely related to the medical practice of *psychiatry*—the diagnosis and treatment of mental illness. The clinician deals with real persons with real psychological problems. He enters the patient's world and concerns himself with the subjective human experience, including wishes, fears, anxieties, ambitions. Clinical psychology stresses therapy, ranging from chemical therapy and shock treatment to psychoanalysis. *Psychoanalysis* is a therapy which encourages the patient to think about himself—his problems, dreams, memories—so that he can gain insight into the causes of his own difficulties. Psychoanalysis enables patients to talk about early childhood experiences and thus to reveal unconscious motivations, emotions, and conflicts. Hence, the psychoanalytic approach to personality emphasizes childhood experiences and unconscious feelings as determining factors in personality development. Psychoanalysis relies heavily on the theoretical contributions of Sigmund Freud.

Experimental psychology is concerned with the scientific study of the behavioral responses of humans and animals to various stimuli. Experimental psychology focuses on observed behavior—it is frequently termed "behavioral psychology." Its setting is the academic laboratory, and rats and pigeons are frequent subjects of experimentation. There is an emphasis on careful observation, quantitative data, and statistical methods. Behavioral psychology relies heavily on *learning theory* (stimulus-response theory), which views all behavior as a product of learning or conditioning. Behavioral patterns are learned through a process whereby a stimulus evokes a response that is either rewarded or punished, and habits are formed. The behavioral approach to personality views personality as a pattern of learned, reinforced responses.

Social psychology is concerned with the individual's relationship with other individuals and groups. The social psychologist studies the whole person, the impact of his social world on him, the world of social interaction and group life, which constantly shapes and modifies his goals, perceptions, attitudes, and behavior. The social psychological approach to personality emphasizes the individual's socialization—the development of individual identity by interpersonal experiences, and the internalizing of the expectations of significant others.

Thus, to understand personality, we must examine several different theoretical approaches to this topic: psychoanalytic (Freudian) theory, learning (stimulus-response) theory, and interpersonal interaction theory.

SIGMUND FREUD AND PSYCHOANALYSIS

Perhaps no other scholar has had a greater impact on social sciences than the Viennese psychiatrist Sigmund Freud (1856 - 1939). Freud completed medical school at the University of Vienna in 1881. He would have preferred an academic position at a university, but discrimination against Jews forced him to enter private practice. Freud's interest in neurology led him to specialize in the treatment of nervous disorders; he studied hypnosis because a French neurologist, Jean Charcot, had learned that neurotic symptoms could be removed during hypnotic trance. He also collaborated with another Viennese physician, Joseph Breuer, who learned that some worries could be alleviated by having the patient talk about them.

In his initial treatment of neurotic patients, Freud used hypnosis. But soon he found that patients did not really need to be in a full hypnotic trance so long as they felt relaxed and uninhibited. He encouraged them to engage in free association—to say anything that came into their minds without regard to organization, logic, or embarrassment over socially unacceptable ideas. He wanted to make the patient's *unconscious* motives, drives, feelings, and anxieties *conscious* ones. The goal of psychoanalysis, as it was called, was to help patients attain insight or self-knowledge. Once this was achieved, the neurotic symptoms tended to disappear.

According to Freud, the personality is composed of three major systems: the *id*, the *ego*, and the *superego*. The *id* is the basic system of life instincts—hunger, thirst, sex, rest, pain avoidance, etc. The id is in close touch with the body's needs; these needs produce psychic energy which is experienced as uncomfortable states of tension. The id endeavors to reduce the tensions—it operates on the *pleasure* principle—but the id has no knowledge of objective reality. A newborn baby's personality is almost pure id. It seeks immediate gratification of bodily urges and has no knowledge of reality or morals.

The *ego* is the part of the personality that is in contact with objective reality. It directs the energies of the id toward real-world objects which are appropriate for the satisfaction of the urge and the reduction of tension. The ego operates on the *reality* principle, formulating plans for the satisfaction of needs, testing these plans, and deciding what needs will be satisfied first and in what manner. The ego exercises important executive functions, coordinating the sometimes conflicting desires of the id with the conditions of the external world.

The *superego*, the last part of the personality to be developed, is the internal representative of the values, standards, and morals that the child is taught. The superego is the *moral* arm of the personality and develops through rewards or punishments imposed upon the child by his parents. The superego decides what is right and wrong, rewarding the individual with feelings of pride or punishing

Sigmund Freud, founder of psychoanalysis and father of modern psychology. While many of his original theories have been subject to much criticism, his greatest contribution was a new insight into human behavior. *Wide World Photo*

him with feelings of guilt. It inhibits the impulses of the id, persuades the ego to direct energies toward moralistic goals rather than realistic ones, and strives for moral perfection.

"Light on the id, heavy on the super-ego."
Drawing by Mahood; ©1974 The New Yorker Magazine, Inc.

Anxiety is derived from several sources. The basic source is fear of real dangers in the external world—threats of pain and destruction. This is *reality anxiety*. Another source is the ego's fear that instincts will get out of control and make the person do something which will cause pain. This is *neurotic anxiety*. Finally, *moral anxiety* is the superego's fear of guilt. The function of anxiety is to warn the person of impending danger. Anxiety is a state of tension. Anxiety reduction is a drive like hunger or thirst or sex, but it is produced by psychological rather than physical conditions.

The separate components of the personality interact, and the interaction determines behavior. *Identification* is one process by which an individual reduces anxiety. He imitates characteristics of another person and incorporates them into his own personality. The child identifies with his parents because they appear to him to be all-powerful. A person may identify with another out of fear, believing that if he behaves like another powerful individual he will not be hurt. Identification is also important in the development of the superego, when the child incorporates the moral values of his parents into his own personality. Another process is *displacement*—when an original choice of an instinctual drive is blocked and another choice substituted for it. The substituted choice may involve less danger or guilt. But often it fails to reduce all of the tension produced by the drive. If a person builds up a large pool of undischarged tension by less-than-satisfying displacement, he may begin to show compulsive nervousness and restlessness. A displacement which substitutes a higher cultural activity for an instinctual drive is called a *sublimation*. Freud believed that sublimation of various instinctive drives was a great source of cultural achievement and civilization.

Freud believed that sex and aggression were the most severely repressed instincts. The availability of sexually-oriented publications creates the opportunity for the process of displacement — where an original choice of an instinctual drive is blocked out and replaced by a less dangerous, but also less satisfying, substitution. *Boston Globe Photo*

The personality may also employ *defense mechanisms* to reduce anxiety and tension. Defense mechanisms may operate unconsciously. Perhaps the most important is *repression:* The ego protects the individual from unbearable impulses by forcing them out of consciousness. This may occur when an impulse would endanger life, risk punishment, or risk feelings of guilt. But there are costs to repression. A severely repressed individual who has denied many strong impulses may suffer fatigue, nervousness, or depression. Repression can even interfere with the functioning of the body; sexual impotence can result from severely repressed sexual impulses. Repression and displacement may operate together: A son who has repressed his hostility toward his father may express displaced hostile feelings against symbols of authority.

Projection occurs when an individual attributes his own impulses to others in the external world because to admit his own impulses would produce too much anxiety or guilt. Instead of saying, "I hate him," one says, "He hates me." In this way an individual can express aggressive impulses toward others under the guise of defending himself against his enemies. *Reaction formation* is the replacement in the consciousness of an anxiety-producing impulse by its opposite. "I hate you" becomes "I love you," or vice versa. *Regression* is a mechanism whereby one reverses the process of maturity. When growing up entails responsibilities, frustrations, and anxieties, a person may regress to an earlier stage of development.

Freud never drew up a comprehensive list of instincts or needs. But he was convinced that of all of our many instincts, those of sex and aggression were the most seriously repressed by society. This repression begins with the newborn infant and extends through adulthood. If we feel hunger, we can immediately go out and buy a hamburger; but if we feel a sexual urge, it usually must be denied until an appropriate outlet is found. Aggressive impulses are also severely restricted. Thus, Freud's seeming emphasis on sex was not a product of his belief that this drive was any more powerful than others, but it was the most repressed and hence the source of many personality disorders.

Freud believed that an individual passed through a series of stages of *personality development*. The first stages were decisive. The newborn infant at the *oral stage* derives pleasure from sucking and eating. It is a passive and receptive stage which centers on oral gratification. In adulthood, oral characteristics including smoking, overeating, extreme dependence on others. Sarcasm and argumentativeness may be a displaced form of oral aggression or biting.

The *anal stage* centers about control of the sphincter and the tension reduction involved in the release of feces. When toilet training is introduced, the infant experiences his first external regulation of an instinctual pleasure. Overreaction to demands that relief be postponed may lead to *anal-retentive* personality characteristics. The individual becomes possessive, stingy, excessively orderly, interested in collections of various sorts, and frequently constipated. Excessive praise for producing feces on demand may lead to *anal-expulsive* characteristics—an excessive concern with creativity and productivity.

In the *phallic stage* the infant becomes aware of the pleasure to be derived from the genital organs. Autoerotic activity (masturbation) is quickly repressed by parents. Later the child (three to five years old) feels sexual attraction toward the parent of the opposite sex and hostile feelings toward the parent who appears as a love rival. According to Freud, every small boy goes through a period when he lusts after his mother and wishes his father were out of the way. (The term *Oedipus complex* comes from an ancient Greek play, *Oedipus Rex*, in which Oedipus unknowingly kills his own father and marries a woman who, he later finds out, is his mother.) These feelings produce various anxieties; for example, a *castration anxiety* is the fear that his father will retaliate by cutting off his offending organs. But usually the male child resolves his problem by eventually *identifying* with his father and replacing his dangerous sexual attraction to his mother with harmless tender affection. Freud believed that little girls may hold their mother responsible for the absence of a protruding penis. The girl's love for her father is mixed with a feeling of envy—"penis envy"—because he possesses something that she lacks.

Freud believed that every person is bisexual; each sex is attracted to members of the same sex as well as the opposite sex. However, homosexual impulses are repressed in most people. Bisexuality actually helps reduce the problems of the Oedipus complex because the boy does have some positive feelings for his father and the girl for her mother.

After age five or six the child enters a *latency* period, in which many of the early oral, anal, and phallic problems are repressed. Indeed, the repression of these early feelings is responsible for our loss of memory of early childhood and infancy. It is not until puberty that latent feelings are reawakened by physical maturation, and repression is again attempted.

The *genital stage* represents maturity in personality development. The gratification an individual receives from his own body pleasure as a child is redirected toward external love objects. The adolescent begins to love others not simply for selfish or narcissistic reasons. Earlier oral, anal, and phallic stages are fused into genital impulses; the personality gradually stabilizes with habitual displacements, sublimations, and identifications. The final organization of personality represents contributions from all four stages.

Perhaps no other social science theory has been subjected to such searching and bitter criticism as Freudian theory. The criticism ranges from charges that Freud was a "sex maniac" (Freud was a dedicated father and husband whose marriage lasted a lifetime; Freud's daughter, Anna, became a distinguished psychoanalyst herself) to more serious scientific reservations. One set of criticisms centers on psychoanalytic therapy: It is long, costly, and not always successful; drugs, shock treatment, and behavioral therapy frequently produce more complete results with less time and expense. Another problem: Freud's observations were based on abnormal, clinical cases rather than normal adults; most of his patients were middle-class Europeans; and he worked in a cultural period when sexual repression in society was much greater than it is today. All of these factors may have produced distortions in his theory.

A more pointed criticism is that Freudian theory is difficult to test scientifically. Freudian explanations proceed from observed behavior *back* to unconscious feelings and childhood experiences; but they do not permit predictions of future behavior from these factors. For example, Freudian theory might hypothesize that a boy who has a severe Oedipus complex and cannot "cut the apron strings" and identify with his father may cope with this problem by becoming a homosexual. But Freudian theory might also hypothesize that the same Oedipus complex could lead the boy to become a "lady-killer," with a string of sexual conquests to prove his masculinity to himself. A scientist can object that Freudian theory provides two completely different behaviors with the same explanation. It does not predict which of the two behaviors may result from an Oedipus complex. Hence it is "bad" scientific theory. Nevertheless, psychologist William McDougall concluded, "In my opinion Freud has, quite unquestionably, done more for the advancement of our understanding of human nature than any other man since Aristotle."[2]

BEHAVIORISM AND LEARNING THEORY

Behavioral psychology is heavily indebted to learning theory or, more precisely, stimulus-response (SR) theory. It is not an overstatement to say that rats and other animals have had more to do with shaping this theory than humans; SR theory grew out of experimental laboratory studies with animals. Academic psychology is based largely on SR theory; most college courses in psychology are oriented toward this approach. Behavioral psychology asserts that psychologists should study *behavior* employing the same scientific tests as other natural sciences. Behavioral psychologists discount Freudian notions about the mind or the personality, which cannot be directly observed.

The founder of modern stimulus-response theory is the famous Russian physiologist Ivan Petrovich Pavlov (1849 - 1936), who had already won a Nobel Prize for his studies of digestive glands before he undertook his landmark experiments with salivating dogs. Pavlov's early experiments established the notion of *conditioning*. If a bell is sounded just a moment before meat is placed in a dog's mouth, presently the dog will salivate merely upon hearing a bell even if the meat is not given. Dogs do not normally salivate at the sound of a bell, so such a response is a "conditioned response." The bell and the meat have become associated in the dog's mind by their occurring together—that is, their "contiguity."

The learning process is a bit more complex than it first appears. To establish a linkage between a conditioned stimulus and a response, there must be a *drive*, a *cue*, a *response*, and *reinforcement*. In simple terms, in order to learn, one must want something as a result of his action (reinforcement). There must first be a drive (hunger, thirst, pain, curiosity, etc.) in order for learning to occur. (A rat placed in a box with a wire grid floor can be given a drive if an electric current is sent pulsing through the grid floor.) A cue is a stimulus that guides the response of the organism; it may be visual (objects, colors, lights, designs, printed words) or auditory (bells, whistles, spoken words) or related to any of the other senses. (The electric shock can be accompanied by a buzzer.) Of course, before a response can be linked to a cue, a response must occur. Thus, a critical stage in the learning process is the production of the appropriate response. (A rat experiencing an electric shock and hearing the buzzer will make a variety of responses; eventually it may pull on the lever that turns off the current.) The particular response which satisfies the drive is likely to recur the next time the same situation is encountered. Learning (the establishment of an SR linkage) takes place gradually, not so much through "trial and error" as through trial and *success."* (Of course, the rat may not pull the lever immediately on the second trial; its first success was really an accident. After several shocking experiences, however, the rat learns to pull the lever right away to stop the current.)

The key to the learning process is the *reinforcement* of the appropriate behavior. Reinforcement occurs each time the behavior is accompanied by reduction in the drive. The cue itself will eventually elicit the same response as the original drive. (The rat will pull the lever when it hears the sound of the buzzer whether it is shocked or not.) Thus, a previously neutral stimulus becomes a "secondary drive," or a "conditioned stimulus," when the organism learns to respond in a particular way to it. (The rat now has learned to pull a lever at the sound of a buzzer.)

When a particular conditioned stimulus (the buzzer) gains the capacity to elicit a response because of its being associated with an unconditioned stimulus (electric shock), other stimuli which are similar to the conditioned stimuli also tend to produce the same response. (Any sound similar to a buzzer may cause the rat to pull the lever.) This is called *stimulus generalization.* A related idea is *response generalization:* A stimulus acquires the capacity to elicit not only the response that reduced the drive but also a number of similar responses. *Stimulus discrimination* occurs when an organism learns to distinguish between two somewhat similar cues and to behave differently according to which cue is presented.

The strength of the SR connection is a function of (1) the strength of the original drive, (2) the closeness of the drive reduction to the response, and (3) the number of consistently reinforced trials. (The combination of a strong shock, the quick elimination of the shock after the rat pulls the lever, and a large number of trials makes a well-trained rat.) Learned behavior can be eliminated by *counterconditioning.* (A rat that has learned to pull a lever at the sound of a buzzer can also unlearn this behavior, if a shock is continued even after it pulls the lever.)

Higher-order learning takes place when an organism establishes elaborate, complex, and abstract linkages between stimulus and response. Higher-order conditioning occurs, for example, when a child learns to associate the written word *bell* spelled on a card with the sound of a bell. Cues become stimuli which provoke a response, which in turn becomes a cue to still another response. Certainly *language* can be viewed as an abstract set of cues. By labeling and naming events, things, and experiences, the individual can increase his powers of stimulus generation and discrimination. For example, if he labels two completely different situations as "threatening," he may behave in the same manner in both situations. Or stimulus differentiation permits an individual to label two people "friend" and "enemy" and then respond differently toward each.

Thinking itself may be the tracing-out of elaborate and abstract series of linkages between cues and responses. We substitute mental cue-producing responses for overt behavior. It is possible through a series of cue-producing responses (thoughts) to begin at a goal situation and work backward to identify the correct instrumental response. This higher-order learning substitutes for the direct response. Indeed, in order to think, we must first learn to inhibit or delay direct responses, in order to give higher-order learning an opportunity to function.

In recent years, behavioral psychologists have come out of the laboratory to engage in some types of treatment for mental disorders. Behaviorists define disorders in terms of the undesirable behaviors which are exhibited. Behavioral psychologists seldom talk about oral or anal personalities or Oedipus complexes; they talk in terms of functional (desirable) and dysfunctional (undesirable) behaviors. They believe that neurotic behavior has been learned—generally by inconsistent use of rewards and punishments. (Hungry rats that are shocked when they pull a lever which previously produced food develop symptoms similar to "nervous breakdowns"!) Undesirable behaviors can be extinguished by withholding rewards or by punishment. Neurotic behavior can be unlearned by the same combination of principles by which it was taught. Behavioral psychotherapy establishes a set of conditions by which neurotic habits are unlearned and nonneurotic habits learned. The behavioral therapist is regarded as a kind of teacher and the patient as a learner. Thus, patients in mental hospitals may be rewarded for good behavior by tokens to be used to buy small luxuries. Or smokers can learn avoidance reaction by having thick, obnoxious cigarette smoke blown in their faces. Or bed wetters can unlearn their habit by sleeping on a wired blanket which produces a mild shock when it becomes wet. Even repression (viewed by the behaviorists as "learned non-thinking") can be overcome by forcing individuals to confront situations, events, or experiences they have repressed.

SOCIAL PSYCHOLOGY—
THE SELF IN RELATION TO OTHERS

Social psychology is primarily concerned with interpersonal interactions—how the individual interacts with others. The social psychologist studies the individual as a whole person, interacting with his environment, rather than particular responses, behaviors, or reflexes. Many social psychologists are critical of the "reductionism" of behavioral psychology—the tendency to reduce individual behavior to a series of stimulus-response linkages. Social psychology is strongly influenced by early "Gestalt" psychologists, who argued that the whole man is an entity which cannot be understood by breaking him into sensory elements. (The German word *Gestalt* means "whole," "pattern," or "configuration.")

Social psychologists view interpersonal interaction as the critical determinant of personality development. Indeed, an individual develops an awareness of *self* only by interacting with his environment. The newborn infant cannot distinguish his own body from the outer world. He acquires an identity—a sense of self—only by moving out into the world and relating to other people. As the infant observes and responds to his mother, she becomes a meaningful object bringing pleasure, frustration, pain, and so on. The infant becomes aware of himself by placing himself in relation to others. An infant who is totally ignored withdraws to a corner of his bed, does not talk or develop in any way, and withers away physiologically and psychologically. The emergence of self-identity requires interpersonal interaction.

The process by which an individual internalizes the values, attitudes, and judgments of others is called *socialization*. By interacting with others he comes to understand what is expected of him and internalizes these expectations as part of his personality. Psychologist George Herbert Mead conceived the notion of *roles* to explain how the individual internalizes the expectations of others and acquires the values of society. The essential process in the development of self is the individual's taking on the roles of others.

Years ago, psychologist Charles H. Cooley described the self as a system of ideas drawn from the social world. The "looking glass" self is a product of:

1. The individual's image of his appearance to others. Each of us tries to see how he is regarded by others—how his actions are viewed and interpreted by others.

2. The individual's image of the judgment of others. Each of us imagines how others are evaluating him.

3. The individual's self-feeling. Each of us reacts to his perceptions of others' judgments with feelings of pride, shame, guilt, self-esteem, self-hate, and so forth.

In short, our self-conception derives from interaction with others from infancy through adulthood.

Through interaction with his mother, the child learns that certain sounds—such as "Mama" and "Daddy"—gain him favorable attention. He begins to repeat these sounds because of the response they evoke in others, and hence he learns language. He also learns that the things he does are meaningful to those around him, and thus he develops a sense of *self*. Infants who are ignored fail to develop either language or self-identity. Later the small child at play tries on a variety of roles—"mother," "father," "fireman," "soldier"—and increases his self-realization in the process. Even such basic social roles as male and female may be viewed as a product of socialization rather than biology. Masculine and feminine traits develop through the child's internalization of expectations of others and through role-playing. Schools, games, and group ac-

Our self-conception derives from interaction with others as early as infancy and throughout adulthood. By trying on a variety of adult roles small children develop a sense of identity. *Eugene Richards Photo*

tivities provide more and more role-playing opportunities. Of course, not all of the "others" in one's life are equally influential in shaping self-identity; each person has some *significant others* whose judgments concern him more than the judgments of others. As socialization continues, knowledge of roles and attitudes of others become more generalized. The individual gradually unifies and consolidates the many roles he has played into a generalized self-conception. At this point the mature personality emerges.

But the self never stops changing. Every interpersonal interaction has an impact on self-identity. "It is perhaps fair to say that every time a man reacts to his environment he becomes a permanently changed man—be it ever so slightly."[3] Throughout life everyone is part of a social "field." The German social psychologist Kurt Lewin extends the idea of self to include the individual's interactions with a field of forces in social situations. Since the field is constantly changing, the individual's behavior is too. Lewin employed the term *life space* to refer to the characteristics of the environment which determine the behavior of an individual. The life space includes past as well as present social experiences. Even

TABLE 5-1. Some Interpersonal Response Traits*

Role Dispositions

Ascendance (social timidity). Defends his rights; does not mind being conspicuous; is not self-reticent; is self-assured; forcefully puts self forward.

Dominance (submissiveness). Assertive; self-confident; power-oriented; tough; strong-willed; order-giving or directive leader.

Social initiative (social passivity). Organizes groups; does not stay in background; makes suggestions at meetings; takes over leadership.

Independence (dependence). Prefers to do own planning, to work things out in own way; does not seek support or advice; emotionally self-sufficient.

Sociometric Dispositions

Accepting of others (rejecting of others). Nonjudgmental in attitude toward others; permissive; believing and trustful; overlooks weaknesses and sees best in others.

Sociability (unsociability). Participates in social affairs; likes to be with people; outgoing.

Friendliness (unfriendliness). Genial, warm; open and approachable; approaches other persons easily; forms many social relationships.

Sympathetic (unsympathetic). Concerned with the feelings and wants of others; displays kindly, generous behavior; defends underdog.

Expressive Dispositions

Competitiveness (noncompetitiveness). Sees every relationship as a contest—other people are rivals to be defeated; self-aggrandizing; noncooperative.

Aggressiveness (nonaggressiveness). Attacks others directly or indirectly; shows defiant resentment of authority; quarrelsome; negativistic.

Self-consciousness (social poise). Embarrassed when entering a room after others are seated; suffers excessively from stage fright; hesitates to volunteer in group discussions; bothered by people watching him at work; feels uncomfortable if different from others.

Exhibitionistic (self-effacing). Is given to excess and ostentation in behavior and dress; seeks recognition and applause; shows off and behaves queerly to attract attention.

*Opposite trait in parentheses.

a hermit carries with him into the wilderness memories of interpersonal relationships, which continue to influence his personality.

Over time, an individual acquires a distinctive pattern of interpersonal response traits—relatively consistent and stable dispositions to respond in a distinctive way toward others. These interpersonal response traits constitute the personality. They represent the sum of a person's socialization, his role experiences, his history of successes and failures with various interpersonal responses. Table 5-1 presents 12 interpersonal response traits.

Many social psychologists believe that interpersonal interaction theory provides a basis for the treatment of personality disorders. They define an "integrated personality" as one in which the individual plays fairly well-defined and stable roles, his roles are not incompatible or conflicting, and they are consistent with the values of the groups and culture in which he lives. Personality "disorganization" occurs when an individual finds himself in conflicting roles. Most people can handle mildly conflicting roles, such as being mother and office worker simultaneously; but serious role conflicts, such as an inability to fully assume either a male or a female identification, create deeper problems. Another source of personality "disorganization" may be an abrupt change in roles—for example, the loss of a job to a breadwinner, the loss of a wife or husband by a devoted spouse, a change from rural to urban living, even war and natural disaster. Failure to be adequately "socialized" in the first place is another recognized source of personality disorder—for example, the adult who exhibits childlike behavior, or the adolescent who cannot "find himself," that is, find a mature responsible role for himself in society. "Desocialization" occurs when an individual, encountering consistent defeat and frustration in interpersonal situations, withdraws from contacts with others. Note that social psychologists tend to view mental disorder in terms of the individual's relationship to his social environment—whether he is well adjusted and capable of functioning in a socially acceptable fashion.

One popular form of social psychological therapy is the "sensitivity" group. Individuals try to heighten their own self-awareness and self-consciousness by close interaction with others. The object is to help individuals see themselves through the eyes of others with whom they are interacting. Group therapy is also employed to create new group memberships, loyalties, and expectations, to bring social forces to bear on individuals to conform to new behavioral patterns—as in group therapy for alcoholics or drug addicts.

SEPARATE APPROACHES
TO POWER AND PERSONALITY

It is not surprising that variations among psychologists in approaches to personality are reflected in different interpretations of individual reactions to power and authority.

The Freudian approach to power relationships focuses upon the channeling and blocking of drives; the conflict among the id, ego, and superego; unconscious processes; and early childhood determinations of habitual responses to power and authority. The view of power and personality which emerges from this perspective is summarized by political scientist Harold Lasswell's early formulation:

The general formula for the developmental history of political man employs three terms:

$$p \mathrel{\}} d \mathrel{\}} r = P$$

where p equals private motives; d equals displacement onto a public object; r equals rationalization in terms of the public interest; P signifies the political man and } equals transformed into.[4]

Power motives—for example, a person's drive to dominate others, or his pleasure in leaving decision-making to others and accepting direction—are organized into the personality early in life. They are *displaced* onto general power and activity structures in society—for example, a person's desire to acquire powerful office or position, or his willingness to accept directions and orders of superiors. The real motives for the individual's public behavior are largely unconscious, so he *rationalizes* his behavior in terms of the public interest. Ideologists provide ready-made rationalizations for the exercise of power as well as submission to activity. Later in this chapter we will examine "the authoritarian personality" mainly within the framework provided by Freudian theory.

Learning theory approaches individual responses to power and activity in the familiar terms of behavioral conditioning: drive, cue, response, and reinforcement. Reinforced responses toward authority become habits through the process of conditioning, and unrewarded responses tend to be extinguished.

Stimulus generalization suggests that learned responses in particular power situations may be generalized into similar responses in many different power situations. It has been argued that the leadership of the Soviet Union has been heavily influenced by this approach to personality; Soviet leaders believe that through large-scale manipulation of rewards and punishments they can shape the personalities and behaviors of the populations under their control. In the next section we examine the ideas of behavioral psychologist B. F. Skinner for the control of human behavior in our own society.

Interpersonal interaction theory approaches power as an attribute of interpersonal relations. Through the process of socialization, the individual "internalizes" the expectations of significant others in his life. Without the ability to interact with others—to both exercise power over others and respond to their needs and desires—the individual loses his sense of significance and self-identity. Powerlessness, then, can be viewed as a threat to individual identity. Modern mass urban society—with its weakened family, community, religion, and social group ties—may increase the individual's sense of powerlessness. In the absence of meaningful social interaction, he searches for synthetic ties to replace the ones lost in the process of modernization. He becomes "other-directed," that is, decreasingly reliant on his own conscience and increasingly dependent upon other people for his ideas and actions. The other-directed person is easily manipulated by the mass media, by demagogic leaders, and by mass political movements. Later in this chapter we will describe the problems of "powerlessness and the other-directed man."

B. F. SKINNER
The Control of Human Behavior

Power is the capacity to control human behavior. What if behavioral science learns to control human behavior and develops a "behavioral technology" to do so? Who will apply this technology and for what purposes? Will the behavioral scientist acquire the ultimate power in society?

Behavioral psychologist B. F. Skinner believes that society can no longer afford individual freedom and self-determination.[5] He argues that human behavior must be controlled to ensure the survival of humanity and that *behavioral conditioning* must be employed on a massive scale to remold man and his culture. In the Skinnerian world men will be conditioned to be humanitarian rather than selfish, to refrain from polluting, from over-populating, from rioting, and from making war. Behavioral conditioning will create a utopian society of communal ownership, egalitarian relationships, and devotion to art, music, and literature. Outmoded ideas of individual freedom and self-determination will be discarded in favor of a scientifically designed culture which will condition men to be "good."

Skinner believes that the freedom and dignity of autonomous man are "illusions" anyhow. All behavior is determined by prior conditioning. The apparent freedom of man is merely inconspicuous control: A permissive government is simply relying on other sources of control—family, church, schools, values, ideologies. If people behave well without government control, it is because they are being controlled by these other agencies. But there is ample evidence—war, crime, poverty, racism, etc.—that existing control mechanisms are inadequate for survival. Behavioral conditioning replaces imperfect and haphazard control methods with a more effective technology of behavioral control. "Brainwashing" is attacked by scholars who otherwise support changing people's minds by less obvious control mechanisms. Yet according to Skinner, brainwashing is an effective means of accomplishing behavioral modification.

> A common technique is to build up a strong aversive condition, such as hunger or lack of sleep, and, by alleviating it, to reinforce any behavior which "shows a positive attitude" toward a political or religious system. A favorable "opinion" is built up simply by reinforcing favorable statements.[6]

Skinner believes that all attitudes are developed in this way; the only difference is that formal behavioral conditioning appears obvious and conspicuous.

Skinner developed his ideas through a lifetime of laboratory research on

B. F. Skinner

American behavioral psychologist B. F. Skinner has drawn a number of conclusions from his laboratory work leading to his belief that society and its members should be controlled by formal behavioral conditioning. *Boston Globe Photo*

behavioral conditioning. The long-famous "Skinner box" is a soundproof enclosure with a food dispenser that can be operated by a rat pressing a lever or a pigeon pecking at a bar. Skinner is convinced that human behavior can be scientifically controlled:

> I've had only one idea in my life—a true idée fixe. To put it as bluntly as possible—the idea of having my own way. "Control" expresses it. The control of human behavior. In my early experimental days it was a frenzied, selfish desire to dominate. I remember the rage I used to feel when a prediction went awry. I could have shouted at the subjects of my experiments, "Behave, damn you! Behave as you ought!"[7]

He pioneered in the development of teaching machines and programmed instruction, which employs conditioning principles in reinforcing correct answers with a printed statement that the student's response is correct.

Can behavioral conditioning be used on a massive scale? Skinner believes it

B. F. Skinner

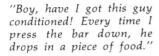

"Boy, have I got this guy conditioned! Every time I press the bar down, he drops in a piece of food."

Jester for Columbia University

can. Social science has been slowed, he thinks, because of its concentration on states of mind, feelings, and traits. "Unable to understand how or why the person we see behaves as he does, we attribute his behavior to the person inside." Mistakenly we believe that man "initiates, originates, and creates," and that man is autonomous. But in fact man's behavior is a product of conditioning. "Behavior is shaped and maintained by its consequences. Once this fact is recognized, we can formulate the interaction between the organism and environment in a much more comprehensive way." Behavior which operates on the environment to produce consequences ("operant behavior") can be modified by arranging environments in which specific consequences are contingent upon it. In short, according to Skinner, the environment can be designed so that "good" behavior is reinforced and "bad" behavior extinguished.

However, arranging effective reinforcements even in a laboratory setting is sometimes very complicated. It is far more complex in the real world. Skinner does not provide much specific information on how behavioral technology is to be employed. So the first problem with Skinner's world is that it may be unworkable.

Still more serious dilemmas of power are raised by Skinner's proposals. Who is to determine what is "good" and "bad" behavior? What standards will be used? Who decides what constitutes pleasure and pain and reward and punishment? In Skinner's utopia, immense power would be placed in the hands of the behavioral scientist who designs the culture. Skinner's utopia is benevolent but totalitarian. Can the behavioral scientist be trusted to always be "good"? How can his power be checked if he has full capacity to manipulate human behavior? Moreover, what kind of human beings would be produced under a system which manipulates behavior, choices, tastes, and desires? If we believe that man's freedom and dignity are essential components of his humanity, then behavioral conditioning on a massive scale is dehumanizing. Giving up freedom and dignity to achieve a secure, comfortable, unpolluted, egalitarian world may be too high a price to pay.

B. F. Skinner

POWERLESSNESS AND
THE "OTHER-DIRECTED" MAN

There is a common adage that "Power corrupts, and absolute power corrupts absolutely." It reflects our negative view of power, and our association of power with abuse. But the distinguished clinical psychologist Rollo May contends that power is a fundamental aspect of the life process. Indeed, he believes that *powerlessness* corrupts the human personality by robbing the individual of his sense of meaning and significance.

Rollo May's argument is that power occurs in an individual's life in five functional forms.[8] The first is the *power to be.* The word *power* comes from the Latin root meaning "to be able." The newborn infant must have the power to make others respond to his needs—he cries and waves his arms violently as signs of his discomfort. An infant who cannot get a response from others around him fails to develop as a separate personality. *Power as self-affirmation* is the recognition of one's own worth and significance in life. Some power is essential for self-esteem and self-belief. *Power as self-assertion* makes it clear who we are and what we believe. It gives us the potential to react to attack and protect ourselves from becoming victims. Power also occurs in everyone's life as *aggression*—thrusting out against a person or thing seen as an adversary. The constructive aspects of aggression include cutting through barriers to initiate relationships; confronting another person without the intent to hurt but in order to penetrate his consciousness; and actualizing one's own self in a hostile environment. The destructive side of aggression, of course, includes thrusting out to inflict injury and the taking of power simply to increase one's own range of control. Finally, power occurs as *violence.* May believes that violence is an attempt to exercise power. It may result from a failure at self-affirmation or self-assertion, or it may accompany aggression. Violence can be functional to the individual if there is no other way for him to assert his own significance in life.

It is May's belief that modern mass society impairs the individual's self-esteem and self-worth. The feeling of personal powerlessness is widespread.

> To admit our own individual feelings of powerlessness—that we cannot influence many people; that we count for little; that the values to which our parents devoted their lives are to us insubstantial and worthless; that we feel ourselves to be "faceless others," insignificant to other people and therefore not worth much to ourselves—this is indeed, difficult to admit.[9]

He believes that much irrational violence—riots, assassinations, senseless murders—is a product of feelings of powerlessness.

Social psychologist David Riesman has also expressed concern about the relative powerlessness of the modern man in mass society. Riesman identifies three broad social characters, in terms of the source of control over personal behavior: *tradition-directed,* *inner-directed,* and *other-directed.* (Social character is found in traditional societies, where obedience to the family and adherence to traditional ways of life are dominant values. Things that are old and long-established are considered good. Traditional norms are the dominant guide for individual behavior. Traditional societies existed in the Western world through the Middle Ages and still exist in many rural areas of the non-Western world.)

The inner-directed character is associated with the rise of Protestantism and capitalism. General values and norms are implanted in the child at an early age by parents. The mature, inner-directed adult has internalized these values and norms, and he uses them to guide his behavior throughout life, regardless of changing conditions or the values of others around him. The values of the inner-directed man in the Western world generally include respect for work and self-sufficiency, a desire for personal achievement and production, strong moral restraints on sexual behavior, devotion to family and children, the postponement and sacrifice of pleasure for future well-being, and emphasis on personal savings and the accumulation of wealth. But the important aspect of the inner-directed man is his internalized "gyroscope" for behavioral guidance. He is punished by feelings of guilt when he violates these inner norms.

Riesman believes that modern mass society, particularly twentieth-century urban America, is producing an *other-directed* character type. For the other-directed person, the point of social control lies *outside,* rather than inside, the individual. As parental control weakens, and family and church influences wane, the individual seeks guides for behavior in the approval of his peers—classmates, friends, groups, society at large. The other-directed person has few internal restraints upon his behavior, so he is guided primarily by what is fashionable, what is popular, what others are doing. Instead of guilt, he experiences anxiety when his behavior does not conform to group expectations. His parents want him to be popular, and even the school curriculum emphasizes getting along with others—"life adjustment." The mass media, the advertising industry, and the clothing, music, entertainment, and recreation industries reinforce pressures on youth to be fashionable, "hip," "with it." The other-directed adult cares more about what his friends and neighbors think than about what he wants for himself or his children. He is an organization man, seeking security in a large corporate or governmental bureaucracy. His values constantly shift as conditions change and social values fluctuate. He is more concerned with leisure and consumption than work and production, less "hung up" about sexual standards, more interested in the immediate "now" than in planning for the future, and oriented toward spending money rather than saving it.

The other-directed person is powerless in the face of group pressures and his own need for group approval. Conformity results from the need to belong and to be accepted by a group. Individual freedom and dignity and self-reliance are submerged in the necessity for conformity and social approval.

POWER AND PERSONALITY: A CASE STUDY

The Authoritarian Personality

Perhaps the most influential study of power, authority, and personality is the landmark volume entitled *The Authoritarian Personality*.[10] This study was undertaken after World War II by a group of psychologists who sought to identify the potentially antidemocratic individual—the individual whose personality structure renders him particularly susceptible to authoritarian appeals. The research was supported by the American Jewish Committee because of its interest in finding the causes of anti-Semitism and social prejudice. But the study identifies an entire "syndrome" of authoritarianism—an organized set of related attitudes.

The Authoritarian Personality study employed a variety of methodological tools to identify and explain authoritarianism: questionnaires, in-depth interviews, responses to pictures and inkblots, and psychiatric clinical observations. One of the tools to be developed was the F (fascism) Scale, now widely used by social scientists to identify authoritarianism. Part of the original F Scale is reproduced in Table 5-2. Persons who agree with all or most of the items in the F Scale are said to be authoritarian.

TABLE 5–2. **Questions from the F (Fascism) Scale**

---

a. *Conventionalism:* Rigid adherence to conventional, middle-class values.

    Obedience and respect for authority are the most important virtues children should learn.

    A person who has bad manners, habits, and breeding can hardly expect to get along with decent people.

b. *Authoritarian Submission:* Submissive, uncritical attitude toward idealized moral authorities of the ingroup.

    Obedience and respect for authority are the most important virtues children should learn.

    Young people sometimes get rebellious ideas, but as they grow up they ought to get over them and settle down.

    What this country needs most, more than laws and political programs, is a few courageous, tireless, devoted leaders in whom the people can put their faith.

TABLE 5–2. (Cont.)

c. *Authoritarian Aggression:*   Tendency to be on the lookout for, and to condemn, reject, and punish people who violate conventional values.

> A person who has bad manners, habits, and breeding can hardly expect to get along with decent people.
> What the youth needs most is strict discipline, rugged determination, and the will to work and fight for family and country.
> An insult to our honor should always be punished.
> If people would talk less and work more, everybody would be better off.
> Homosexuals are hardly better than criminals and ought to be severely punished.

d. *Anti-introception:*   Opposition to the subjective, the imaginative, the tender-minded.

> When a person has a problem or worry, it is best for him not to think about it, but to keep busy with more cheerful things.
> Nowadays more and more people are prying into matters that should remain personal and private.
> If people would talk less and work more, everybody would be better off.

e. *Superstition and Stereotypy:*   The belief in mystical determinants of the individual's fate; the disposition to think in rigid categories.

> Science has its place, but there are many important things that can never possibly be understood by the human mind.
> Every person should have complete faith in some supernatural power whose decisions he obeys without question.
> People can be divided into two distinct classes: the weak and the strong.

f. *Power and "Toughness":*   Preoccupation with the dominance-submission, strong-weak, leader-follower dimension; identification with power figures; overemphasis upon the conventionalized attributes of the ego; exaggerated assertion of strength and toughness.

> No weakness or difficulty can hold us back if we have enough will power.
> What the youth needs most is strict discipline, rugged determination, and the will to work and fight for family and country.
> People can be divided into two distinct classes: the weak and the strong.

g. *Destructiveness and Cynicism:*   Generalized hostility, vilification of the human.

> Human nature being what it is, there will always be war and conflict.
> Familiarity breeds contempt.

h. *Projectivity:*   The disposition to believe that wild and dangerous things go on in the world; the projection outwards of unconscious emotional impulses.

> Nowadays more and more poeple are prying into matters that should remain personal and private.
> The wild sex life of the old Greeks and Romans was tame compared to some of the goings-on in this country, even in places where people might least expect it.
> Most people don't realize how much our lives are controlled by plots hatched in secret places.

i. *Sex:*   Exaggerated concern with sexual "goings-on."

> Sex crimes, such as rape and attacks on children, deserve more than mere imprisonment, such criminals ought to be publicly whipped, or worse.
> The wild sex life of the old Greeks and Romans was tame compared to some of the goings-on in this country, even in places where people might least expect it.

Source: Abridgment of Table 7 (pp. 255–7) "The F (Fascism) Scale" in *The Authoritarian Personality* by T. W. Adorno et al. Copyright 1950 by The American Jewish Committee. Reprinted by permission of Harper & Row, Publishers, Inc.

The Authoritarian Personality

WHAT ARE THE CHARACTERISTICS OF THE AUTHORITARIAN PERSONALITY?

Dominant and Submissive. The central attitudes of authoritarianism are dominance and submission—dominance over subordinates in any power hierarchy and submissiveness toward superiors. The authoritarian is highly ambivalent in his attitudes toward authority. He is outwardly servile toward those he perceives as his superiors, but in fact he also harbors strong negative feelings toward them. He conceals this hate with the ego-defense of *reaction formation*—bending over backward in excessive praise of authority and admiration for the strong. His repressed rage toward his superiors is redirected into hostility toward the weak and inferior.

Power-Oriented. Authoritarians tend to think in power terms, to be acutely sensitive in any situation to questions of who dominates whom. The authoritarian is very uncomfortable when he does not know what the chain of command is. He needs to know whom he should obey and who should obey him.

Rigid. The authoritarian is "intolerant of ambiguity." He likes order and is made uncomfortable by disorder. When matters are complex, he imposes his own rigid categories on them. His thinking, therefore, is largely in *stereotypes*.

Admiring of Toughness and Strength. The authoritarian shows exaggerated concern with virility and strength. Feelings of personal weakness are covered with a facade of toughness. He is unusually preoccupied with masculine virtues, and he also stereotypes women as feminine and soft.

Conventional. The authoritarian is particularly sensitive to the prevailing standards of his own social group. He rigidly conforms to these standards himself and he is prepared to severely punish others who deviate from them. He is particularly upset by sexual deviations of any kind.

Anti-introceptive. The authoritarian is impatient with, and opposed to, the subjective and tender-minded. He is unimaginative and reluctant to acknowledge his own feelings and fantasies.

Cynical and Threat-Oriented. The authoritarian is cynical about the motives of others and generally pessimistic about human nature. He is disposed to believe that the world is a jungle and that various conspiracies exist to threaten him and his way of life.

Ethnocentric. The authoritarian views members of social groups other than his own as outsiders who are different, strange, unwholesome, and threatening. He holds an exalted opinion of his own group. He rejects outsiders and *projects* many of his own aggressive impulses on them. He places stereotyped labels on outsiders.

Superstitious. The authoritarian attributes much of what he does not understand in the world to fate or mysticism.

What are the sources of authoritarianism? Early childhood experiences with authority are cited as one probable cause of authoritarianism:

> When we consider the childhood situation . . . we find reports of a tendency toward rigid discipline on the part of the parents, with affection which is conditional rather than unconditional, i.e., dependent upon approved behavior on the part of the child. Related to this is a tendency apparent in families of prejudiced subjects to base interrelationships on rather clearly defined roles of dominance and submission. . . . Forced into a surface submission to parental authority, the child develops hostility and aggression which are poorly channelized. The displacement of a repressed antagonism toward authority may be one of the sources, and perhaps the principal source, of his antagonism toward outgroups.[11]

Children who have been socialized in warm, close, affectionate interpersonal relationships are less likely to have authoritarian attitudes than children who have been socialized in strict, rigid, punitive situations. This explanation is also consistent with interpersonal interaction theory.

The authoritarian syndrome can also be explained in the "classic" psychoanalytic pattern of sadomasochistic resolution of the Oedipus complex.[12] In this pattern, love for the mother is severely repressed, and hatred for the father is transformed through reaction formation into a strong identification with authority, masculinity, and toughness. The transformation is a difficult task that never succeeds completely. While part of the original hostility toward the father is transformed in security and pleasure in obedience and subordination, some of the hostility is left over as sadism, which seeks an outlet in aggressive behavior toward outgroups and subordinates. The authoritarian never perceives the ambivalence of his own view: blind submission to authority, yet a readiness to attack those who are deemed weak.

A great deal of research followed *The Authoritarian Personality* study, much of it using the F Scale to identify authoritarians and then observing related attitudes, environments, and behaviors. Some of the subsequent research on authoritarianism raised serious criticisms and reservations about the original work. First, it was observed that poorly educated persons tend to agree with F Scale statements more frequently than well-educated persons. This finding does not necessarily mean that a lack of education *causes* authoritarianism, but it does suggest that differences in F Scale scores may be a product of education and *not* personality development. Better-educated persons, whether they are authoritarian or not, simply know enough not to agree with the obviously biased statements on the F Scale.

Another problem is that the F Scale tests only for *right-wing* (fascist) authoritarianism and fails to identify *left-wing* authoritarianism. Yet there is ample evidence of exaggerated submission to authority in revolutionary and communist movements; aggression and sadism practiced by left-wing

TABLE 5-3. Questions from the Dogmatism Scale

In this complicated world of ours the only way we can know what's going on is to rely on leaders or experts who can be trusted.

Most people just don't know what's good for them.

Of all the different philosophies which exist in this world there is probably only one which is correct.

The highest form of government is a democracy and the highest form of democracy is a government run by those who are most intelligent.

The main thing in life is for a person to want to do something important.

I'd like it if I could find someone who would tell me how to solve my personal problems.

It is only when a person devotes himself to an ideal or cause that life becomes meaningful.

Most people just don't give a "damn" for others.

To compromise with our political opponents is dangerous because it usually leads to the betrayal of our own side.

While I don't like to admit this even to myself, my secret ambition is to become a great man, like Einstein, or Beethoven, or Shakespeare.

Even though freedom of speech for all groups is a worthwhile goal, it is unfortunately necessary to restrict the freedom of certain political groups.

It is better to be a dead hero than to be a live coward.

Source: V. C. Troldahl and F. A. Powell, " A Short-Form Dogmatism Scale," *Social Forces,* 44 (1965), 211–214.

authoritarians against the hated outgroup—the "bourgeoisie"; rigidity, toughness, and power-orientedness among revolutionaries; extreme cynicism toward society among leftists, as well as conspiratorial views about politics; and rigid conformity to stereotyped Marxist ideas. Unfortunately, the F test equates authoritarianism with only fascist ideas.

As a result of this problem, some researchers have attempted to develop a measure of dogmatism—the openness or closedness of the individual's belief system—which taps both right-wing and left-wing intolerance. Excerpts from one version of the D (dogmatism) Scale are shown in Table 5-3.

Another criticism is that authoritarianism is not really a complete syndrome; some of the component attitudes are found separately in individuals who do not exhibit other attitudes in the supposed syndrome. For example, ethnocentrism is frequently encountered in individuals who are not dominant-submissive. Ethnocentric attitudes may be acquired in a family or subculture which is otherwise warm and affectionate. A stable and loving individual may have stereotyped views of outgroups, and even harbor suspicion toward them, simply because he has been taught to do so. In other words, ethnocentrism may be part of a culture or subculture, rather than a personality characteristic. The same may be true of superstition, rigidity, and conventionalism.

Despite these reservations, *The Authoritarian Personality* remains one of the most important studies of the relationship between power and personality. It provides us with invaluable insight into the psychological mechanisms by which some individuals adjust themselves to power and authority.

NOTES

1.   Gordon Allport, *Personality* (New York: Holt, 1937), pp. 24 - 54.

2.   William McDougall, quoted in Gardner Lindzey (ed.), *Handbook of Social Psychology*, Vol. I (Reading, Mass.: Addison-Wesley, 1954), p. 144.

3.   David Krech, Richard S. Crutchfield, and Egerton L. Ballachey, *Individual in Society* (New York: McGraw-Hill, 1962), p. 103

4.   Harold Lasswell, *Psychopathology and Politics* (Chicago: University of Chicago Press, 1930), p. 262.

5.   B. F. Skinner, *Beyond Freedom and Dignity* (New York: Knopf, 1971).

6.   Ibid., p. 96.

7.   *Time*, September 20, 1971, p. 47.

8.   Rollo May, *Power and Innocence* (New York: Norton, 1972).

9.   Ibid., p. 21.

10.   T. W. Adorno, Else Frenkel-Brunswik, Daniel J. Levinson, and R. Nevitt Sanford, *The Authoritarian Personality* (New York: Harper, 1950).

11.   Ibid., p. 482.

12.   Ibid., pp. 759 - 772.

TESTING YOUR PERFORMANCE

Note to the Student.   The following questions are to test how well you achieved the Performance Objectives identified for you at the beginning of this chapter. The correct answers are supplied, accompanied by corresponding pages for you to review if you have answered incorrectly. The questions are coordinated numerically with the Performance Objectives at the beginning of the chapter. This exercise will assist you in determining the type of questions you have the most difficulty in answering (discussion, identification, explanation, definition, etc.) and will prepare you for test questions likely to be asked by your instructor.

1.   (a) All of the characteristic ways of behaving which an individual exhibits and the enduring and organized sets of responses which an individual habitually makes when subjected to particular stimuli make up _____
_____ .

(b) Individuals tending to respond in a similar fashion to many separate situations are acting in ways that are _____ .

(c) Characteristic ways of behaving that operate over long periods of time are _____ .

(d) Relationships between various elements of an individual's personality so that a change in one characteristic brings about a change in another characteristic are said to be _____ .

2. (a) A pattern of expected behavior associated with a given position in society is a _____ .

(b) The pattern behavior of a person in a number of different roles is attributable to his _____ .

3. (a) The type of psychology which has to do with the treatment of psychological disorder and in which the psychologist enters the patient's world and concerns himself with subjective human experience is _____ .

(b) The type of psychology which is concerned with the scientific study of the behavioral responses of humans and animals to various stimuli and focuses on observed behavior is _____ .

(c) The type of psychology which is concerned with the individual's relationship with other individuals and groups is _____ .

4. (a) The medical practice which diagnoses and treats mental illness is _____ .

(b) Therapy which encourages the patient to think about himself—his problems, dreams, memories—so that he can gain insight into the causes of his own difficulties is _____ .

(c) The development of individual identity by interpersonal experiences with other persons, and the internalizing of the expectations of significant others is _____ .

5. The psychiatrist who developed the theory of psychoanalysis was _____ .

6. (a) According to Freud, the three major systems which compose personality are the _____ .

(b) The basic system of life instincts is the _____ .

(c) The system operating on the reality principle—formulating plans for the satisfaction of needs, testing these plans, and deciding what needs will be satisfied first and in what manner—is the _____ .

(d) The moral arm of the personality, representative of the values, standards, and morals that the child is taught, is the _____ .

7. Identify the type of anxiety defined by the following items:

(a) Fear of the real dangers in the external world—threats of pain and destruction. _____

(b) The ego's fear that instincts will get out of control and make the person do something which will cause pain. _____

(c) The superego's fear of guilt. _____

Identify the following processes by which an individual reduces anxiety:

(d) Imitating characteristics of another person and incorporating them into his own personality. _____

(e) Substituting another choice for an original choice of an instinctive drive which is blocked. _____

(f) Substituting a higher cultural activity for an instinctual drive. _____

Identify the following defense mechanisms employed by the personality to reduce anxiety and tension:

(g) The ego's protecting the individual from unbearable impulses by forcing them out of consciousness. _____

(h) An individual's attributing his own impulses to others in the external world because to admit his own impulses would produce too much anxiety or guilt. _____

(i) The replacement in the consciousness of an anxiety-producing impulse by its opposite. _____

(j) The mechanism whereby an individual reverses the process of maturity. _____

8.   The two instincts regarded by Freud as the most seriously repressed by society are _____ .

9.   Identify the following Freudian stages of personality development:

(a) The passive and receptive stage which centers on oral gratification. _____

(b) The stage centering about control of the sphincter and the tension reduction involved in the release of feces. _____

(c) The stage in which an infant becomes aware of the pleasure to be derived from the genital organs. _____

(d) The stage, representing maturity, in which the gratification an individual receives from his own body pleasure as a child is redirected toward external love objects. _____

10.   Identify the type of personality described by the following characteristics:

(a) Possessive, stingy, excessively orderly, interested in collections of various sorts, frequently constipated. _____

(b) Excessive concern with creativity and productivity. _____
_____

11.   (a) The term used for every small boy going through a period when he lusts after his mother and wishes his father were out of the way is _____
_____ .

(b) The fear that his father will retaliate by cutting off his offending organs is _____ .

(c) A period entered by a child after age five or six in which many of the early oral, anal, and phallic problems are repressed is the _____
_____

12.   Sex mania of the author; length, cost, and lack of success of psychoanalytic therapy; observations in a time period when cultural repression in society was great; and difficulties of being able to test it scientifically and therefore limiting the theory's predictability are all _____
_____ .

13.   Studying of behavior employing the same scientific tests other natural sciences use is the goal of _____
_____ .

14.   Identify the following requirements for the establishment of a linkage between a conditioned stimulus and a response:

(a) Hunger, thirst, pain, curiosity. _____

(b) A stimulus that guides the response of the organism. _____

(c) A critical stage which satisfies the drive and is likely to recur the next time the same situation is encountered. _____

(d) Occurs each time the behavior is accompanied by reduction in the drive. _____

15. (a) When a particular conditioned stimulus gains the capacity to elicit a response because of its being associated with an unconditioned stimulus, and other stimuli which are similar to the conditioned stimuli also tend to produce the same response, this is called _____ .

(b) When an organism learns to distinguish between two somewhat similar cues and to behave differently according to which cue is presented, this is called _____ .

16. Elimination of learned behavior (unlearning) is known as the process of _____ .

17. Tracing out elaborate and abstract series of linkages between cues and responses, and learning to inhibit or delay direct responses in order to give higher-order learning an opportunity to function are _____ .

18. Behavioral psychologists eliminate undesirable (dysfunctional) behavior by withholding rewards or by punishment. The type of therapy that establishes a set of conditions by which neurotic habits may be unlearned and nonneurotic habits learned is _____ .

19. Social psychology was heavily influenced by some early psychologists, who argued that the whole man is an entity which cannot be understood by breaking him into sensory elements, known as _____ psychologists.

20. The process by which an individual internalizes the values, attitudes, and judgments of others is called _____ .

21. The psychologist responsible for developing the notion of roles to explain how the individual internalizes the expectations of others and acquires the values of society was _____ .

22. The individual's image of his appearance to others, his image of the judgment of others, and his self-feeling were used by psychologist Charles H. Cooley to describe the self as a system of ideas drawn from the social world, or the _____ self.

23. The term used by Kurt Lewin to refer to the characteristics of the environment which determined the behavior of an individual and include his past as well as his present social experiences is _____ .

24. (a) The type of personality identified by social psychologists as one in which the individual plays fairly well-defined and stable roles (not incompatible or conflicting, and consistent with the values of the groups and culture in which he lives) is _____ .

(b) The term used to describe the condition that occurs when an individual finds himself in conflicting roles is _____ .

(c) The term used to describe the process that occurs when an individual who encounters consistent defeat and frustration in interpersonal situations withdraws from contacts with others is _____ .

(d) A popular form of social psychological therapy in which individuals try to heighten their own self-awareness and self-consciousness by close interaction with others is _____ .

25. Identify the theory that approaches power and personality by:

(a) Focusing upon the channeling and blocking of drives, the conflict among the id, ego, and superego, unconscious processes, and early childhood determinations of the individual's habitual responses to power and authority. _____

(b) Looking at the behavioral conditioning processes of drive, cue, response, and reinforcement. _____

(c) Looking at interpersonal relations and the process of socialization. _____

26.   The behavioral psychologist who argues that human behavior must be controlled to ensure the survival of humanity, and that behavioral conditioning must be employed on a massive scale to remold man and his culture, is _____ .

27.   Identify the following functional forms in which power occurs in an individual's life as identified by Rollo May:

(a) Power to make others respond to his needs. _____

(b) Recognition of one's own worth and significance in life. _____

(c) Making it clear who you are and what you believe. _____

(d) Thrusting out against a person or thing seen as an adversary. _____

(e) Attempt to exercise power resulting from a failure at self-affirmation or self-assertion, or possibly accompanying aggression. _____

28.   (a) The clinical psychologist who expressed the belief that modern mass society impairs the individual's self-esteem and self-worth and that the feeling of personal powerlessness is widespread is _____ .

(b) The social psychologist who expressed concern about the relative powerlessness of the modern man in mass society and who identified three broad social characters in terms of the source of control over their behavior (tradition-directed, inner-directed, and other-directed) is _____

29.   (a) The study which identified the potentially antidemocratic individual—the individual whose personality structure renders him particularly susceptible to authoritarian appeals—was _____ .

(b) The scale widely used by social scientists to identify authoritarianism is the _____ .

(c) Dominant and submissive; power-oriented, rigid, admiring of toughness and strength, conventional, anti-introceptive, cynical and threat-oriented, ethnocentric, and superstitious are all _____ .

(d) Early childhood experiences with authority, and the psychoanalytic pattern of sadomasochistic resolution of the Oedipus complex are both _____ .

(e) The possibility that differences in F Scale scores may be a product of education, *not* personality development, and the failure to identify left-wing authoritarianism are _____ .

(f) The measure which attempted to tap both right-wing and left-wing intolerance (the closedness or openness of an individual's belief system) is the _____ .

Correct Responses

1. (a) Personality (p. 150); (b) Characteristic and habitual (p. 150); (c) Enduring (p. 150); (d) Organized (p. 150).

2. (a) Role (p. 150); (b) Personality (p. 151).

3. (a) Clinical psychology (p. 151); (b) Experimental psychology (p. 151); (c) Social psychology (p. 151).

4. (a) Psychiatry (p. 151); (b) Psychoanalysis (p. 151); (c) Socialization (p. 151).

5. Sigmund Freud (p. 152).

6. (a) Id, ego, and superego (p. 152); (b) Id (p. 152); (c) Ego (p. 152); (d) Superego (pp. 152 - 153).

7. (a) Reality anxiety (p. 154); (b) Neurotic anxiety (p. 154); (c) Moral anxiety (p. 154); (d) Identification (p. 154); (e) Displacement (p. 154); (f) Sublimation (p. 154); (g) Repression (p. 155); (h) Projection (p. 155); (i) Reaction formation (p. 155); (j) Regression (pp. 155 - 156).

8. Sex and aggression (p. 156).

9. (a) Oral stage (p. 156); (b) Anal stage (p. 156); (c) Phallic stage (p. 156); (d) Genital stage (p. 157).

10. (a) Anal-retentive (p. 156); (b) Anal-expulsive (p. 156).

11. (a) Opedipus complex (p. 156); (b) Castration anxiety (p. 156); (c) Latency period (p. 157).

12. Criticisms of Freudian theory (pp. 157 - 158).

13. Behavioral (stimulus-response) theory (p. 158).

14. (a) Drive (p. 158); (b) Cue (p. 158); (c) Response (p. 158); (d) Reinforcement (p. 159).

15. (a) Stimulus generalization (p. 159); (b) Stimulus discrimination (p. 159).

16. Counterconditioning (p. 159).

17. Theories of how people think (pp. 159 - 160).

18. Psychotherapy (p. 160).

19. Gestalt (p. 160).

20. Socialization (p. 161).

21. George Herbert Mead (p. 161).

22. "Looking glass" self (p. 161).

23. Life space (p. 162).

24. (a) Integrated personality (p. 163); (b) Personality disorganization (pp. 163 - 164); (c) Desocialization (p. 164); (d) Sensitivity group (p. 164).

25. (a) Freudian theory (p. 164); (b) Learning theory (p. 164); (c) Interpersonal-interaction theory (p. 165).

26. B. F. Skinner (pp. 166 - 168).

27. (a) Power to be (p. 169); (b) Power as self-affirmation (p. 169); (c) Power as self-assertion (p. 169); (d) Aggression (p. 169); (e) Violence (p. 169).

28. (a) Rollo May (p. 169); (b) David Riesman (pp. 169 - 170).

29. (a) *The Authoritarian Personality* (p. 171); (b) F (fascism) Scale (p. 171); (c) Characteristics of the authoritarian personality (pp. 171 - 173); (d) Sources of authoritarianism (p. 174); (e) Criticisms of *The Authoritariian Personality* and the F Scale (pp. 174 - 175); (f) D (dogmatism) Scale (p. 175).

KEY TERMS

personality

role

clinical psychology

psychiatry

psychoanalysis

experimental psychology (behavioral psychology)

learning theory

social psychology

socialization

psychoanalytic (Freudian) theory

learning (stimulus-response) theory

interpersonal-interaction theory

free association

id

ego

superego

pleasure principle

reality principle

moral

reality anxiety

neurotic anxiety

moral anxiety

identification

displacement

sublimation

defense mechanisms

repression

projection

reaction formation

personality development

oral stage

anal stage

anal-retentive

anal-expulsive

phallic stage

Oedipus complex

castration anxiety

"penis envy"

latency period

genital stage

Sigmund Freud

Ivan Pavlov

conditioning

drive

cue

response

reinforcement

learning

secondary drive (conditioned stimulus)

stimulus generalization

response generalization

stimulus discrimination

counterconditioning

functional behaviors

dysfunctional behaviors

psychotherapy

interpersonal interactions

Gestalt

significant others

social field

life space

integrated personality

personality disorganization

desocialization

sensitivity group

other-directed

behavioral conditioning

Skinner box

operant behavior

power to be

power as self-affirmation

power as self-assertion

aggression

violence

tradition-directed

inner-directed

stereotypes

dogmatism

The Authoritarian Personality

DISCUSSION QUESTIONS

1. Differentiate between the concept of personality and the concept of role.

2. You have decided to become a psychologist and are faced with the task of deciding which *type* of psychology you wish to specialize in. Choose *one* of the following types and discuss the theory of psychology which accompanies it as well as the areas of concentration and methods utilized:
   (a) Clinical (Freudian) psychology
   (b) Experimental (behavioral) psychology
   (c) Social (interpersonal-interaction) psychology

3. Discuss the following components of Freudian (psychoanalytic) theory:
   (a) The three major systems composing the personality (id, ego, and superego)
   (b) The types of anxiety (reality, neurotic, and moral)
   (c) The processes of interaction (identification, displacement, sublimation)
   (d) Defense mechanisms to reduce anxiety and tension (repression, projection, reaction formation, and regression)
   (e) Stages of personality development (oral, anal, phallic, latency period, genital)

   What are the criticisms of Freudian theory?

4. Discuss the following components of learning (stimulus-response) theory:
   (a) Conditioning
   (b) The learning process: drive, cue, response, reinforcement
   (c) Counterconditioning
   (d) Thinking

5.   Discuss the following components of interpersonal-interaction theory:
(a) Socialization
(b) Social field/life space
(c) Integrated personality
(d) Personality disorganization
(e) Desocialization
(f) Sensitivity groups

6.   Choose one of the personality theories and explain how it interprets individual reactions to power and authority:
(a) Freudian (psychoanalytic) theory
(b) Learning (stimulus-response) theory
(c) Interpersonal-interaction theory

7.   Choose one of the following psychologists and discuss his theory and findings:
(a) B. F. Skinner: behavioral conditioning
(b) Rollo May: five functional forms of power: power to be; power as self-affirmation; power as self-assertion; aggression; and violence
(c) David Riesman: tradition-directed, inner-directed, and other-directed social characters

SUGGESTED READINGS

T. W. Adorno et al., *The Authoritarian Personality* (New York: Harper, 1950).

Calvin S. Hall, *A Primer of Freudian Psychology* (Cleveland: World Publishing, 1954).

Calvin S. Hall and Gardner Lindzey, *Theories of Personality*, 2nd ed. (New York: Wiley, 1970).

David Krech, Richard S. Crutchfield, and Egerton L. Ballachey, *Individual in Society: A Textbook of Social Psychology* (New York: McGraw-Hill, 1962).

Harold Laasswell, *Psychopathology and Politics* (Chicago: University of Chicago Press, 1930).

Rollo, May, *Power and Innocence* (New York: Norton, 1972).

David Riesman, *The Lonely Crowd* (New Haven, Conn.: Yale University Press, 1961).

B. F. Skinner, *Beyond Freedom and Dignity* (New York: Knopf, 1971).

CHAPTER 6

Power and Government

PERFORMANCE OBJECTIVES

The student should be able to:

1.   Name the two distinguishing factors of the power of government.

2.   Contrast totalitarianism and constitutionalism.

3.   Identify the English political philosopher who expounded the idea of natural law and constitutional government in *Essay Concerning Human Understanding* and *Two Treatises on Civil Government*. Define natural rights. Define social contract. List the primary features of constitutional government as expounded by Locke.

4.   Contrast Jeffersonian descriptions of inalienable rights of individuals with those of Locke.

5.   Compare and contrast the ideal meanings of democracy with the procedural meanings of democracy.

6.   Identify the basic values underlying classic democracy.

7.   Trace the notion of equality from the Founding Fathers to the present.

8.   Define republican government and limited government.

9.   Differentiate between expressed (delegated) powers and implied powers. List the powers expressly given to the national government and to Congress.

10.   Cite the constitutional clause in Section 8 of Article I which became the basis for much of the ensuing expansion of the powers of the national government.

11.   List the restrictions placed on the powers of the states by the U.S. Constitution.

185

12.   Contrast a federal political system with a unitary political system and a confederation of states.

13.   Cite the constitutional amendment which "reserves" to the states the power to protect and advance the public health, safety, welfare, or morals.

14.   Describe how the federal government has vastly expanded its power over states and communities by the use of grants-in-aid. Define guidelines.

15.   Identify the power which enables the national government to exercise important powers in areas originally "reserved" to the states.

16.   Contrast the good effects of federal aid and guidelines with the bad effects.

17.   Define separation of powers. Cite the French writer whose *Spirit of the Laws* political textbook inspired the Founding Fathers. Identify the intentions of the Founding Fathers regarding a system of separated powers in the national government. Identify *The Federalist* papers.

18.   Compare and contrast the constituencies, terms, and checks and balances of each of the four major decision-making bodies of the national government as construed by the Founding Fathers.

19.   Define the concept of judicial review. Cite the U.S. Supreme Court case which established this precedent and the chief justice of the Supreme Court who argued for it.

20.   List the factors contributing to the increased powers of the president in the twentieth century.

21.   List the five "psychological functions of the presidency" as observed by Fred Greenstein.

22.   Identify the role of Congress. List the constitutional powers of Congress.

23.   Identify the role of the courts. Explain why the Founding Fathers allowed decisions of the president and Congress to be set aside by the federal courts. Contrast the Supreme Court of the 1930s with the Warren Court of the 1960s.

24.   Identify the primary form of political participation. Identify the two decisions an individual must make regarding voting.

25.   List and describe the provisions of the amendments and congressional acts which circumscribe voting laws in the states.

26.   Describe the function of the party label. Describe the functions of political parties. Contrast American political parties with European political parties.

27.   List and discuss the three ways of discerning the difference between the Democratic and the Republican parties.

28.   Identify the single most important factor influencing voter decisions. Identify where it is primarily acquired.

29.   Describe the conditions which prompt elites to resort to repressive measures as discussed in "Watergate and the Resignation of Richard Nixon."

Differentiate between the Watergate break-in and repressive tactics and activities of previous administrations.

30.   Define executive privilege. Identify the Supreme Court case which established the power of the courts to review the actions of other branches of government. Identify the Supreme Court's ruling regarding a president's right of executive privilege in *The United States* v. *Richard M. Nixon.*

POWER AND GOVERNMENT

A distinguished American political scientist, Harold Lasswell, defined "Politics" as "Who Gets What, When, How." "The study of politics," he said, "is the study of influence and the influential. The influential are those who get the most of what there is to get. . . . Those who get the most are the *elite*; the rest are *mass*." He went on to define political science as "the shaping and sharing of power."

Admittedly, Lasswell's definition of political science is very broad. Indeed, if we accept Lasswell's definition of political science as *the study of power*, then political science includes cultural, economic, social, and personal power relationships—topics we have already discussed in anthropology, economics, sociology, and psychology.

Although many political scientists have accepted Lasswell's challenge to study power in all of its forms in society, most limit the definition of political science to *the study of government and politics*.

What distinguishes *governmental* power from the power of other institutions, groups, and individuals? The power of government, unlike that in other institutions in society, is distinguished by (1) the legitimate use of physical force and (2) coverage of the whole society rather than only segments of it. Because government decisions extend to the whole of society, and because only government can legitimately use physical force, government has the primary responsibility for maintaining order and for resolving differences that arise *between* segments of society. Thus, government must regulate conflict by establishing and enforcing general rules by which conflict is to be carried on in society, by arranging compromises and balancing interests, and by imposing settlements that the parties in the dispute must accept. In other words, government lays down the "rules of the game" in conflict and competition between individuals, organizations, and institutions within society.

THE STUDY OF POLITICAL SYSTEMS

Political scientists ever since Plato have constructed ideal political systems—notions of what a *good* "polity" should be like. Today we refer to efforts to devise *good* political systems as *political philosophy.* Political philosophy concerns itself with political norms and values—criteria for judging the "rightness" or "wrongness" of governmental structures and actions. In Chapter 8 we will discuss political ideologies—liberalism, conservatism, communism, socialism, and fascism—and examine philosophies more closely.

Political science also concerns itself with describing *the structure of political systems.* Schemes for classifying political systems are as old as the study of politics itself. Aristotle, for example, produced a classification based on two criteria: (1) the number of citizens who could participate in making rules—one, few, or many; and (2) whether the rulers governed in "the common interest" or in their own selfish interest.

Aristotle's Classification of Governments

Number of Persons Who Ruled	Interests Served	
	Common	*Selfish*
One	Monarchy	Tyranny
Few	Aristocracy	Oligarchy
Many	Polity	Democracy

Aristotle's classification system shows six types of governments. Note that Aristotle believed that "democracy" was a corrupt form of government in which the masses pursued their selfish interests at the expense of the common good. Not until the nineteenth century did the word *democracy* come to have positive connotation.

The German social and political scientist Max Weber also classified political systems, but he focused on their source of "legitimacy." He suggested that the authority of governmental leaders can be based on:

1. Tradition: where legitimacy rests on established beliefs in the sanctity of authority and the moral need to obey leaders.
2. Charisma: where legitimacy rests on the personal heroic qualities of a particular leader.
3. Legality: where legitimacy is based on a commitment to constitutional rules which bind both leaders and the people.

Weber identified these types of authority in a variety of political systems.

Many modern political scientists have attempted to improve on Aristotle's and Weber's simple typologies. For example, two Yale political scientists applied a statistical technique known as factor analysis to 68 measured characteristics of 115 countries and "inductively derived" seven major *factors* which distinguish political systems:[1]

1. Access to political participation
   Authoritarian *Limited*
   Democratic *Open*
2. Differentiation of separate political institutions
   Modern *Modern System*
   Undeveloped *A Big Cheif rules all*
3. Consensus about rules governing political systems
   Governmental stability
   Instability, "personalism"
4. Sectionalism
   Western
   Non-Western
5. Legitimation
   Bureaucratic, rule-oriented, developed ideology
   Traditional, personality-oriented, authoritarianism
6. Patterns of interest groupings
   Two-party systems
   Multi-party systems
7. Executive leadership
   Strong
   Weak

Political scientists are also concerned with *the political processes and behaviors among individuals and groups.* The study of political processes and behaviors goes beyond the study of political philosophy and ideology and the study of political structures. It asks how voters, interest groups, parties, legislators, executives, bureaucrats, judges, and other political actors behave and why. Behavioral political scientists study the way individuals acquire political values and attitudes and how these values and attitudes shape their political activity; why people vote as they do or choose not to vote at all; how and why interest groups are formed and what influence they have on governments; how and why city councilmen, state legislators, and congressmen vote as they do on pieces of legislation; what motivates the actions of mayors, governors, and presidents, and what influences the decisions of judges; what the attitudes and functions of political parties are before and after elections; and so on.

But political philosophy and ideology, the structure of governments, and the behavior of political figures can seldom be studied separately. Discovering how these important areas of study interact is necessary to produce a better understanding of power in society. In our examination of power and government in this chapter we will first take up the political philosophies which are influential in shaping American government and politics; then consider how power is structured in American government; and finally describe political processes and behaviors in Congress, the presidency, the courts, voters, and political parties. We will conclude with a case study illustrating the conflict between elite consensus and the presidential power in the Watergate affair.

JOHN LOCKE *and* Constitutionalism

The potential power of governments has worried men for a long time. Indeed, since the earliest recorded history, men have attempted to limit the powers of government, to set standards of legitimate authority, and to prevent the arbitrary use of governmental power. Of course, not all men or societies share the belief that government power should be limited. Totalitarianism is a belief that the state should be orderly, harmonious, and unified in purpose and values, and that the power of government should be unlimited and all-embracing. In a totalitarian state, government exercises unlimited authority in all segments of life—the economy, education, the church, the family, etc.

Constitutionalism is the belief that government power should be limited and controlled. A fundamental ideal of constitutionalism—"a government of laws and not of men"—suggests that those who exercise governmental authority are restricted in their use of it by a higher law. A constitution governs government. A constitution describes the offices and agencies of government, defines their prerogatives, prescribes how they should function, sets limits on the authority of government, and protects the freedoms of individual citizens. In other words, a constitution defines what governmental authority can and cannot do. A constitution should not be subject to change by the ordinary acts of government officials; change should come only through a process of general public consent. Most importantly, a constitution must truly limit and control the exercise of authority by government; the so-called constitutions of totalitarian states which merely describe government offices and agencies but do not actually limit their powers are not genuine constitutions.

In the eighteenth century the notion of constitutionalism was associated with the idea of a higher natural law. *Natural law* is based on the nature of man and society: It is immutable and it provides the standards and guidelines for governmental institutions and human law. Natural law binds both rulers and the ruled. The natural law includes natural rights possessed by all men; these rights are not derived from, or subject to, government but derive from the nature of man himself and have an independent and unchanging existence. The natural law limits governments; more importantly, it limits the power of majorities over individuals. Thus, natural law deprives even majorities of the power to violate the inalienable rights of individuals to life, liberty, and property.

A famous exponent of the idea of natural law and constitutional government was the English political philosopher John Locke (1632 - 1704). Perhaps more than anyone else, Locke inspired the political thought of our nation's Founding Fathers in that critical period of American history in which the new nation won its independence and established its constitution. Locke's ideas are written into both the Declaration of Independence and the Constitution of the United States. His writings, particularly his *Essay Concerning Human Understanding*

John Locke

and his *Two Treatises on Civil Government* were widely read in early America and even plagiarized in part by Thomas Jefferson in the Declaration of Independence.

According to Locke, men are essentially rational beings, capable of self-government and able to participate in political decision-making. Locke believed that men formed a contract among themselves to establish a government in order to better protect their natural rights, maintain peace, and protect themselves from foreign invasion. The *social contract* which established government made for safe and peaceful living and for the secure enjoyment of one's life, liberty, and property. Thus the ultimate legitimacy of government derived from a contract among the people themselves and not from gods or kings. It was based upon the consent of the governed. The people agreed to be governed in order to safeguard their individual rights.

Since government was instituted as a contract to secure the rights of men, government itself could not violate individual rights. If government did so, it would dissolve the contract establishing it. Revolution, then, was justified if government was not serving the purpose for which it had been set up. However, according to Locke, revolution was justified only after a long period of abuses by government, not over every little mismanagement.

Six primary features of constitutional government were expounded by Locke: (1) The authority of government must be limited by the purposes and ends for which government is instituted, that is, preservation and protection of the natural rights of the individual; (2) government must conform to the law of nature and cannot violate the inalienable rights to life, liberty, and property; (3) laws must have the expressed or implied consent of the governed; (4) laws must apply equally to all; (5) laws must not be arbitrary or oppressive; and (6) taxes must not be levied without the consent of the people or their representatives.

Thomas Jefferson eloquently expressed Lockean ideals in the Declaration of Independence:

> We hold these truths to be self-evident, that all men are created equal, that they are endowed by their Creator with certain unalienable rights, that among these are life, liberty, and the pursuit of happiness. That to secure these rights, governments are instituted among men, deriving their just powers from the consent of the governed. That whenever any form of government becomes destructive of these ends, it is the right of the people to alter or to abolish it, and to institute new government, laying its foundation on such principles and organizing its powers in such form, as to them shall seem most likely to effect their safety and happiness.

Notice that Jefferson varied slightly from Locke in his description of inalienable rights. While Locke had affirmed the right of the individual to "life, liberty, and *property*," Jefferson substituted the more general idea in his famous formulation of the right to "life, liberty, and the *pursuit of happiness*."

John Locke

THE MEANING OF DEMOCRACY

Ideally, democracy means individual participation in the decisions that affect one's life. In traditional democratic theory, popular participation has been valued as an opportunity for individual self-development. Responsibility for the governing of one's own conduct develops one's character, self-reliance, intelligence, and moral judgment—in short, one's dignity. Even if a benevolent king could govern in the public interest, he would be rejected by the classic democrat. The argument for citizen participation in public affairs is based not upon the policy outcomes it would produce but on the belief that such involvement is essential to the full development of human capacities.

Procedurally, popular participation was to be achieved through majority rule and respect for the rights of minorities. Self-development means self-government, and self-government can be accomplished only by encouraging each individual to contribute to the creation of public policy and by resolving conflicts over public policy through majority rule. Minorities who had had the opportunity to influence policy but whose views had not succeeded in winning majority support would accept the decisions of majorities. In return, majorities would permit minorities to openly attempt to win majority support for their views. Freedom of speech and press, freedom to dissent, and freedom to form opposition parties and organizations are essential to ensure meaningful individual participation. This freedom of expression is also necessary for ascertaining what the majority views really are.

The underlying value of democracy is individual dignity. Man, by virtue of his existence, is entitled to life, liberty, and the pursuit of happiness. Implicit in the democratic notion of freedom is the commitment that governmental activity and social control over the individual be kept to a minimum; hence the removal of as many external restrictions, controls, and regulations on the individual as is consistent with the freedom of his fellow citizens.

Another vital aspect of classic democracy is a belief in the equality of all people. The Declaration of Independence expresses the conviction that "all men are created equal." Even the Founding Fathers believed in equality for all men *before the law*, notwithstanding the circumstances of the accused. A man was not to be judged by social position, economic class, creed, or race. Many early democrats also believed in *political equality* (equal access of individuals to political influence), that is, equal opportunity to influence public policy. Political equality is expressed in the concept of "one man, one vote."

Over time, the notion of equality has also come to include *equality of opportunity* in all aspects of American life—social, educational, and economic, as well as political, and encompassing employment, housing, recreation, and public accommodations. Each person has as much opportunity to develop his individual capacities to their natural limits as any other person.

In summary, democratic thinking involves the following ideas:

1. Popular participation in the decisions that shape the lives of individuals in a society.
2. Government by majority rule, with recognition of the rights of minorities to try to become majorities. These rights include the freedoms of speech, press, assembly, and petition and the freedom to dissent, to form opposition parties, and to run for public office.
3. A commitment to individual dignity and the preservation of the liberal values of liberty and property.
4. A commitment to equal opportunity for all to develop their individual capacities.

POWER IN THE AMERICAN CONSTITUTION

The Founding Fathers—those 55 men who met in the summer of 1787 in Philadelphia to establish a new American national government—shared the same philosophy of government. They agreed with Locke that the fundamental purpose of government was the protection of liberty and property. They believed in government by the consent of the governed. They believed that the origin of government is an implied contract among men: Men pledged allegiance and obedience to government in return for the protection of their natural rights, the maintenance of peace, and protection from foreign invasion. They believed that the ultimate legitimacy of government (that is, "sovereignty") rested with the people themselves, and not with kings. *But* they also feared the "tyranny of the majority"—the tendency of the masses to use their majority position to capture powers of government and use these powers to attack individual rights, particularly rights of *property*. Their greatest fear was not that a *minority* would seize control of government and trample property rights but that a *majority* would do so.

The Founding Fathers believed in *republican government*, by which they meant representative, responsible, and nonhereditary government. But they did not mean mass democracy with direct participation by people in decision-making. Rather, they expected the masses to consent to be governed by men of principle and property out of recognition of their abilities, talents, and education. Many of the Founding Fathers felt that men of wealth and property had a greater "stake in society" than the masses and were therefore more entitled to govern. In their opinion the masses should have only a limited part in the selection of government leaders.

The Founding Fathers believed in *limited government*. Government should be designed so it would not become a threat to liberty or property. Not only should the government be limited by the Constitution in the powers that it can exercise, but the government itself should be so constructed as to prevent the concentration of power. Power should be divided among separate bodies of the government, capable of checking each other in the event that any one branch should pose a threat to liberty or property.

Finally, the Founding Fathers regarded a *strong national government* as a safer repository of power than state and local governments. State and local governments, they thought, were more vulnerable to takeover by propertyless masses than a national government. Thus at this period in American history, men of property supported a strong national government while most champions of the common people supported strong state and local governments.

The compromises that took place in the Constitutional Convention in 1787 were relatively unimportant in comparison to the consensus among the Founding Fathers on fundamentals. Consensus in this elite group in 1787 was profoundly conservative in that it wished to preserve the status quo in the distribution of power and property in America. At the same time, that consensus was radical in comparison with the beliefs of other elites in the world. Most governments adhered to the principle of hereditary monarchy—and a privileged nobility—while American elites were committed to republicanism. Other elites asserted the divine right of kings while American elites talked about government by the consent of the governed. American elites believed in the equality of man with respect to his inalienable rights while the elites of Europe rationalized and defended a rigid caste system.

POWERS OF THE NATIONAL GOVERNMENT

The Constitution delegates authority to the national government. The Founding Fathers tried to implement Locke's idea of limiting government by granting to the national government *only* certain expressed powers (sometimes called "delegated powers"), together with powers which might reasonably be implied from the expressed powers. Article I, Section 8, of the Constitution provides a fairly lengthy list of specific powers which are expressly delegated to Congress. They are the foundation stones of the national power.

The national government is given the power to *declare war and make peace*. Congress is authorized to raise and support armies and to provide a navy. It can define and punish piracy and other international offenses. The president is made commander in chief of the armed forces and given power to make treaties with the consent of the Senate and give or withhold diplomatic recognition ("send and receive ambassadors"). These significant foreign and military powers are expressive of the most urgent of the drives to produce a powerful national government—the drive to provide defense against common enemies.[2]

A second group of powers expressly delegated to Congress prepared the way for the economic and commercial unity and stability of the nation. Congress is authorized to *regulate commerce* among the states, with foreign nations, and with the Indian tribes. It is authorized to coin money, to make uniform rules for bankruptcy, and to borrow money. By way of aiding economic and social development, Congress is authorized to establish post offices and post roads, to provide for patents and copyrights, and to fix standards of weights and measures. (For a listing of the national powers, see Table 6-1.)

TABLE 6-1. The Constitutional Distribution of Powers

National Powers

Military affairs and defense

Provide for the common defense (I-8)
Declare war (I-8)
Raise and support armies (I-8)
Provide and maintain a navy (I-8)
Define and punish piracies (I-8)
Define and punish offenses against the law of nations (I-8)
Make rules for the regulation of military and naval forces (I-8)
Provide for calling forth the militia to execute laws, suppress insurrections, and repel invasions (I-8)
Provide for organizing, arming, and disciplining militia (I-8)
Declare the punishment of treason (III-3)

Economic matters

Regulate commerce with foreign nations, among the several states, and with Indian tribes (I-8)
Establish uniform laws on bankruptcy (I-8)
Coin money and regulate its value (I-8)
Regulate value of foreign coin (I-8)
Fix standards of weights and measures (I-8)
Provide for patents and copyrights (I-8)
Establish post offices and post roads (I-8)

Taxing powers

Levy taxes (I-8)
Contract and pay debts (I-8)

Governmental organization

Constitute tribunals inferior to Supreme Court (I-8, III-1)
Exercise exclusive legislative power over the seat of government and over certain military installations (I-8)
Admit new states (IV-3)
Dispose of and regulate territory or property of the United States (IV-3)
Make rules for appointments (II-2)

Implied powers

Make necessary and proper laws for carrying expressed powers into execution (I-8)

Restrictions on National Power

TABLE 6–1. (Cont.)

Economic matters

No preference to ports of any state (I-9)

No tax or duty on articles exported from any state (I-9)

Fiscal matters

No direct tax except by apportionment among states on population bases (I-9), now superseded as to income tax (Amendment XVI)

No money to be drawn from Treasury except by appropriation (I-9)

Social classes

No title of nobility to be granted (I-9)

Civil and political rights

Congress not to establish religion or prohibit free exercise of religion (Amendment I)

Congress not to abridge freedom of speech, press, assembly, or right of petition (Amendment I)

Right to bear arms protected (Amendment II)

Restriction on quartering of soldiers in private homes (Amendment III)

No unreasonable searches or seizures (Amendment IV)

Guarantees of fair trials (Amendment V, Amendment VI, Amendment VII)

No excessive bail or cruel or unusual punishments (Amendment VIII)

No taking of life, liberty, or property without due process (Amendment V)

Voting not to be denied because of race, color, previous servitude (Amendment XV),
or sex (Amendment XIX), or age if 18 or over (Amendment XXVI)

Voting not to be denied because of nonpayment of any tax (Amendment XXIV)

Suspension of habeas corpus limited (I-9)

Limits on State Power

Foreign affairs

States may not enter into treaties, alliances, or confederation (I-10)

No compact with a foreign state, except by congressional consent (I-10)

Military affairs

No letters of marque and reprisal (I-10)

No standing military forces in peace without congressional consent (I-10)

No engagement in war, without congressional consent, except in imminent danger or when
invaded (I-10)

Economic matters

No legal tender other than gold or silver coin (I-10)

No separate state coinage (I-10)

No impairment of the obligation of contracts (I-10)

No emission of bills of credit (I-10)

No levying of import or export duties, except reasonable inspection fees, without consent
of Congress (I-10)

Civil and political rights

No slavery (Amendment XIII)

No bills of attainder (I-10)

No ex post facto laws (I-10)

No denial of life, liberty, or property by state without due process of law (Amendment
XIV)

No denial by state of the equal protection of the laws (Amendment XIV)

TABLE 6-1. (Cont.)

No abridgment by state of privileges and immunities of national citizenship (Amendment XIV)

No abridgment of voting rights because of race, color, or previous condition of servitude (Amendment XV)

No abridgment of voting rights because of sex (Amendment XIX)

No poll or other taxes required for voting in federal elections (Amendment XXIV)

Social restrictions

No titles of nobility (I-10)

General restrictions

Federal law supreme (VI)

No payment of debts for rebellion against United States or for emancipated slaves (Amendment XIV)

The national government is also given power to *tax and spend* for the common defense and general welfare. Congress can tax and spend for any purpose —education, welfare, housing, agriculture, business, urban affairs, manpower, etc.

At the end of Article I, Section 8, the Constitution makers added, in paragraph 18, the *necessary and proper clause*, which became the basis for much of the ensuing expansion of the powers of the national government: The Congress shall have power

> To make all laws which shall be necessary and proper for carrying into execution the foregoing powers [those mentioned in Article I, Sec. 8], and all other powers vested by this Constitution in the Government of the United States, or in any department or officer thereof.

The last part of this clause makes clear that Congress has powers that may be implied from any of the expressly delegated powers in the Constitution.

The federal government is restricted in many ways by the Constitution, largely in the interest of protecting individual rights. These restrictions are analyzed in detail in Chapter 11.

The powers granted to the national government are accompanied by certain *restrictions* on the powers of the states, which serve to reinforce the grant of authority to the national government. These restrictions are listed in Table 6-1, but let us observe generally that the restrictions on the states take them completely out of the field of foreign affairs and partly out of military matters. In addition, the activities of the states in the economic sphere are sharply limited.

States may not enter into relations with foreign states. They cannot make treaties or agreements (unless Congress consents) with other countries. In short, they have no foreign policy. Similarly, although the states have never completely given up their armies (they retain the state militia and the National Guard, with congressional consent), the national government can control these armies; and they have certainly become less significant than they once were. In the economic sphere, the states cannot coin money or create any new legal tender for payment of debts. In addition, the states cannot impair the obligation of contracts and, hence, cannot pass laws which invalidate private agreements. In effect, a limit is placed on changing the rules of the economic game. Finally, states may not levy import and export duties.

THE GROWTH OF POWER IN WASHINGTON

The Constitution divides power between two separate authorities, the nation and the states, each of which can directly enforce their own laws on individuals through their own courts. This arrangement is known as *federalism*. In a disputed area, only the Constitution can determine whose authority is legitimate. American federalism differs from a "unitary" political system in that the central government has no legal authority to determine, alter, or abolish the power of the states. At the same time, American federalism differs from a confederation of states, in which the national government is dependent upon its states for power. The American system shares authority and power constitutionally and practically.

Debate over state versus national power can never be removed from the political context in which it takes place. Interests that are dominant in national politics assert the supremacy of the national government and extol the virtues of national regulation. In contrast, interests that are weak in national politics but dominate politics in one or more states emphasize the preservation of the rights of states. For example, states' rights were vigorously defended in the 1950s and 1960s by southern state leaders seeking to maintain the segregation of the races. In contrast, civil rights groups appealed to the national government for support in their fight against state and local policies, and succeeded—in *Brown* v. *The Board of Education of Topeka* in 1954, the Civil Rights Act of 1964, the Voting Rights Act of 1965, and the Fair Housing Act of 1968—in moving the national government to overrule the segregationist policies of state and local governments.

The Constitution, in the Tenth Amendment, "reserves" to the states the power to protect and advance the public health, safety, welfare, or morals. Presumably this means that the national government may enact no laws dealing *directly* with housing, streets, zoning, schools, health, police protection, crime, and so on. However, the national government may *tax* or *borrow* or *spend money* to contribute to the general welfare. The federal government has vastly expanded its power over states and communities by the provision of *grants-in-aid*. During the Great Depression of the 1930s it used its taxing and spending powers in a wide variety of areas formerly reserved to states and communities.

A bread line was a typical sight in the Depression of the 1930's. To combat resulting problems, the federal government initiated many new grant-in-aid programs during this period. *Wide World Photo*

Grant-in-aid programs were initiated for public assistance, unemployment compensation, employment services, child welfare, public housing, urban renewal, highway construction, and vocational education and rehabilitation. The inadequacy of state and local revenue systems contributed significantly to the increase of national power in states and communities. Federal grants-in-aid to state and local governments have grown rapidly in recent years. Today federal grant money accounts for over one-sixth of all state and local government revenue.

Whenever the national government contributes financially to state or local programs, the state or local officials are left with less discretion than they would have otherwise. Federal grants-in-aid are invariably accompanied by congressional standards or "guidelines" that must be adhered to if states and communities are to receive their federal money. Often Congress delegates to federal agencies the power to establish the conditions attached to grants. Federal standards are designed to ensure compliance with national minimum standards, but they are bound to annoy state and local leaders. Sometimes protests from state and local leaders are loud enough to induce Congress to yield to the view of sub-elites.

States or communities can reject federal grants-in-aid if they do not wish to meet federal standards, and some have done so. But it is difficult to resist the pressure to accept federal money. They are "bribed" by the temptation of much-needed funds, and they are "blackmailed" by the thought that the other states and communities will get the money if they do not, although the money was contributed in part by federal taxation of their own citizens.

In short, through the power to tax and spend for the general welfare and through the conditions attached to grants-in-aid, the national government exercises important powers in areas originally "reserved" to the states. Of course, federal grants-in-aid have enabled many states and communities to provide necessary and desirable services that they could not otherwise have afforded, and federal guidelines have often improved standards of administration, personnel policies, and fiscal practices in states and communities. Further, federal guidelines have helped to ensure that states and communities will not engage in racial discrimination in federally aided programs. However, many commentators are genuinely apprehensive that states and communities have surrendered many of their powers to the national government in return for federal money. They argue that the role of states and communities in the American federal system has been weakened by federal grant-in-aid programs and the conditions which are attached to them, because the centralization of power in Washington and the increased role of the national government in state and community affairs limit the powers of the state and local elites.

THE SEPARATION OF POWERS

The system of separated powers in the national government—separate legislative, executive, and judicial branches—was intended by the Founding Fathers as a bulwark against majoritarianism and an additional safeguard for liberty. The doctrine of separation of legislative, executive, and judicial powers derived from the French writer Montesquieu, whose *Spirit of the Laws* was a political textbook for these eighteenth-century statesmen. *The Federalist* paper No. 51 expresses the logic of the checks and balances system:

> Ambition must be made to counteract ambition. . . . It may be a reflection on human nature, that such devices should be necessary to control the abuses of government. But what is government itself, but the greatest of all reflections on human nature? If men were angels, no government would be necessary. If angels were to govern men, neither external nor internal controls on government would be necessary. In framing a government which is to be administered by men over men, the great difficulty lies in this: you must first enable the government to control the governed; and in the next place oblige it to control itself.[3]

The separation of powers concept is expressed in the opening sentences of the first three articles of the Constitution: "All legislative powers herein granted shall be invested in the Congress of the United States. . . . The Executive power shall be vested in a president of the United States of America. . . . The judicial power of the United States shall be vested in one Supreme Court and in such inferior courts as the Congress may from time to time ordain and establish." If this system divides responsibility and makes it difficult for the masses to hold government accountable for public policy, then it is achieving one of the purposes intended by the Founding Fathers.

Originally, each of the four major decision-making bodies of the national government was to be chosen by different constituencies—the House by the voters in the several states, the Senate by the state legislatures, the president by electors chosen by the states, and the judiciary by the president and the Senate. Note that in the Constitution of 1787 only one of these four governing institutions—the House of Representatives—was to be directly elected by the people. There was no direct popular participation in the selection of president, senators, or judges. These arrangements indicate that the Founding Fathers did not fully trust the masses in the selection of governing officials. However, by the early 1800s, presidential electors began the practice of running for their posts as "pledged" to cast their votes for one party and candidate or another. This permitted popular participation in the selection of the president by enabling voters to choose between electors pledged to particular candidates. The same practice holds today: Voters in presidential elections actually cast their votes for slates of electors pledged to one candidate or another. It was not until the Seventeenth Amendment was added to the Constitution in 1913 that the people won the opportunity to participate directly in the election of U.S. senators. Thus, today three of the four governing bodies of the national government are popularly elected. Only the Supreme Court and federal judiciary remain free from direct popular control.

The Founding Fathers also made a sharp differentiation in the terms of these decision-making bodies, so that a complete renewal of government by popular vote at one stroke is impossible. The House is chosen for two years; the Senate is chosen for six, but not in one election, for one-third of the senators complete their terms every two years. The president is chosen every four years, but judges of the Supreme Court hold office for life. Thus the people are restrained from working immediate havoc through direct elections; they must wait years in order to make their will felt in all of the decision-making bodies of the national government.

Moreover, each of these decision-making bodies possesses important *checks and balances* over the decisions of the others. No bill can become law without the approval of both the House and the Senate. The president shares in legislative power through his veto and his responsibility to "give to the Congress information of the State of the Union, and recommend to their consideration such measures as he shall judge necessary and expedient." He can also convene sessions of Congress. But the appointing power of the president is shared by the Senate; so is his treaty-making power. Also, Congress can override executive vetoes. The president must execute the laws, but in order to do so he must rely upon executive departments, and these must be created by Congress. Moreover, the executive branch cannot spend money that has not been appropriated by Congress. Thus, the concept of "separation of powers" is really misnamed, for what we are really talking about is a sharing, not a separating, of power; each branch participates in the activities of every other branch.

Even the Supreme Court, which was created by the Constitution, must be appointed by the president with the consent of the Senate, and Congress may prescribe the number of judges. More importantly, Congress must create lower and intermediate courts, establish the number of judges, fix the jurisdiction of lower federal courts, and make "exceptions" to the appellate jurisdiction of the Supreme Court.

Perhaps the keystone of the system of checks and balances is the idea of *judicial review*, an original contribution by the Founding Fathers to the science of government. In the case of *Marbury* v. *Madison* in 1803, Chief Justice John Marshall argued convincingly that the Founding Fathers intended the Supreme Court to have the power of invalidating not only state laws and constitutions but also any laws of Congress that came in conflict with the Constitution of the United States. Marshall reasoned (1) that the "judicial power" was given to the Supreme Court, (2) that historically the judicial power included the power to interpret the meaning of the law, (3) that the supremacy clause made the Constitution the "supreme law of the land," (4) that laws of the United States should be made "in pursuance thereof," (5) that judges are sworn to uphold the Constitution, and (6) that judges must therefore declare void any legislative act that the feel conflicts with the Constitution. Thus, the Supreme Court stands as the final defender of the fundamental principles agreed upon by the Founding Fathers against the encroachments of popularly elected legislatures.

PRESIDENTIAL POWER

The president does not command American elites, but he stands in a central position in the elite structure. The responsibility for the initiation of public policy falls principally upon him and his staff and executive departments. He has a strong incentive to fulfill this obligation, for in the eyes of a large segment of the American public the president is responsible for everything that happens in the nation during his term of office, whether or not he has the authority or the capacity to do anything about it.

Through the power of policy initiation alone, the president has considerable impact on American elites. He sets the agenda for public decision-making. His programs are presented to Congress in various presidential messages and in his budget, and he thereby largely determines what the business of Congress will be in any session. Few major undertakings get off the ground without presidential initiation; the president frames the issues, determines their context, and decides their timing.

On the whole, presidents of the twentieth century have exercised greater power and initiative than those of the nineteenth century, partly because of America's greater involvement in world affairs and the constant increase in the importance of military and foreign policy. The Constitution gives the president unmistakable and far-reaching powers in foreign and military affairs: He is authorized to send and receive ambassadors and to make treaties (with the advice and consent of the Senate) and is made commander in chief of the armed forces. In effect, these powers put him in almost exclusive control over foreign and military policy in the nation.

A second factor contributing to the power of the president in the twentieth century has been the growth of the executive branch, which he heads. The federal bureaucracy has become a giant power structure, and the president's constitutional powers as chief executive place him at the top of this structure. The Constitution gives the president broad, albeit vague, powers to "take care that the laws be faithfully executed" and to "require the opinion, in writing, of the principal officer of each of the executive departments upon any subject relating to the duties of their respective offices." By this clause the president has general executive authority over the 2.5 million civilian employees of the federal bureaucracy. Moreover, he has the right to appoint (and generally the right to remove) the principal officers of the executive branch of government (the Senate consenting). A major addition to his constitutional authority over the executive branch came in the Budget and Accounting Act of 1921, in which Congress vested in the president the control of the initiation and execution of the federal budget. Budgetary control is a major weapon in the hands of the president, for it can mean the life or death of an administrative agency. While it is true that Congress must appropriate all monies spent by executive departments, nonetheless, the president has responsibility for formulating the budget. Congress may cut a presidential budget request and even appropriate more than the president asks for a particular agency or program, but by far the greatest portion of the president's budget is accepted by Congress.

The third reason for the importance of the presidency in the twentieth century can be traced to technological improvements in the mass media and the strengthening of the role of the president as party leader and molder of public opinion. Television brings the president directly in contact with the masses, and the masses have an attachment to him which is unlike their attachment to any other public official or symbol of government. Fred I. Greenstein has classified the "psychological functions of the presidency":[4] First, the president "simplifies perception of government and politics" by serving as "the main cognitive 'handle' for providing busy citizens with some sense of what their government is doing." Second, the president provides "an outlet for emotional expression" through public interest in his and his family's private and public life. Third, the president is a "symbol of unity" and of nationhood (as the national shock and grief over the death of a president clearly reveals). Fourth, the president provides the masses with a "vicarious means of taking political action," in the sense that he can act decisively and effectively while they cannot do so. Finally, the president is a "symbol of social stability," in that he provides the masses with a feeling of security and guidance. Thus, for the masses, the president is the most visible elite member.

TABLE 6-2.   Formal Presidential Powers

Chief administrator

Implement policy—"take care that laws be faithfully executed."
Supervise executive branch of government.
Appoint and remove policy officials.
Prepare executive budget.

Chief legislator

Initiate policy—"give to the Congress information of the State of the Union and recommend to their consideration such measures as he shall judge necessary and expedient."
Veto legislation passed by Congress.
Convene special sessions of Congress "on extraordinary occasions."

Party leader

Control national party organization.
Control federal patronage.
Influence (not control) state and local parties through prestige.

Chief diplomat

Make treaties ("with the advice and consent of Senate").
Make executive agreements.
Exercise power of diplomatic recognition—"to send and receive ambassadors."
Represent the nation as chief of state.

Commander-in-chief

Command U.S. armed forces—"the President shall be Commander-in-Chief of the Army and the Navy."
Appoint military officials.
Initiate war.
Use broad war powers.

The president has many sources of formal power (see Table 6-2); he is chief administrator, chief diplomat, commander in chief, chief of state, party leader, and voice of the people. But despite the great powers of the office, no president can monopolize policy-making. The president functions within an established elite system, and he can exercise power only within its framework. The choices available to him are limited to those alternatives for which he can mobilize elite support. He cannot act outside existing consensus in the elite, outside of the "rules of the game."

THE POWER OF CONGRESS

What are the powers of Congress in the American political system? Policy proposals are initiated outside Congress; Congress's role is to respond to proposals from the president, executive agencies, and interest groups. Congress does not merely ratify or "rubber-stamp" decisions; it plays an independent role in the policy-making process. But this role is essentially a deliberative one, in which Congress accepts, modifies, or rejects the policies initiated by others. For example, the national budget, perhaps the single most important policy document, is written by the executive branch and modified by the president before it is submitted to Congress. Congress may make further modifications, but it does not formulate the budget. Of course, Congress is a critical screen through which appropriations and revenue measures must pass. But sophisticated lawmakers are aware that they function as *arbiters* rather than *initiators* of public policy. As Robert Dahl explains:

> The Congress no longer expects to originate measures but to pass, veto, or modify laws proposed by the Chief Executive. It is the President, not the Congress, who determines the content and substance of the legislation with which Congress deals. The President is now the motor of the system; the Congress applies the brakes. The President gives what forward movement there is in the system; his is the force of thrust and innovation. The Congress is the force of inertia—a force, it should be said, that means not only restraint, but stability in politics.[5]

From a constitutional point of view, of course, the potential for power in Congress is very great. Article I empowers Congress to levy taxes, to borrow and spend money, to regulate interstate commerce, to establish a national money supply, to establish a post office, to declare war, to raise and support an army and navy, to establish a court system, and to pass all laws "necessary and proper" to implement these powers. Congress may also propose amendments to the Constitution or call a convention to do so. Congress admits new states. In the event that no candidate receives a majority of votes in the electoral college, the House of Representatives may select the president. The Senate "advises and consents" to treaties and approves presidential nominations to executive and judicial posts. The House has the power to impeach, and the Senate to try, any officer of the United States government, including the president. Congress may also conduct investigations, discipline its own members, and regulate its internal affairs.

Yet despite these extensive formal powers, Congress is only one component of America's elite system. Many important decisions, particularly in foreign and military affairs, are made without the direct participation of Congress. The president may commit Congress and the nation to a foreign policy or military action that Congress cannot prevent or reverse. For example, Congress could do little more than appropriate the necessary funds for the Korean War and the Vietnam War. Often congressional leaders are told of a major foreign policy decision only moments before it is announced on national television.

Congress is more influential in domestic than in foreign and military affairs. It is much freer to reject presidential proposals in business, labor, agriculture, education, welfare, urban affairs, civil rights, taxation, and appropriations. Congressional committees share with the president control over executive agencies dealing with domestic affairs. For example, the Office of Education, the Social Security Administration, the Housing Assistance Administration, the Department of Agriculture, the Office of Economic Opportunity—all must go to Congress for needed legislation and appropriations. Congressional committees can exercise power in domestic affairs by giving or withholding the appropriations and the legislation wanted by these executive agencies.

THE POWER OF COURTS

The Founding Fathers viewed the federal courts as the final bulwark against mass threats to principle and property. In *The Federalist* paper No. 78, Hamilton wrote:

> By a límited Constitution I understand one which contains certain specified exceptions to the legislative authority; such, for instance, as that it shall pass no bills of attainder, no ex post facto laws, and the like. Limitations of this kind can be preserved in practice no other way than through the medium of courts of justice, whose duty it is to declare all acts contrary to the manifest tenor of the Constitution void. Without this, all the reservations of particular rights or privileges would amount to nothing.

Since *Marbury* v. *Madison,* the federal courts have struck down more than 80 laws of Congress and uncounted state laws that they believed conflicted with the Constitution. Judicial review and the right to interpret the meaning and decide the application of law are great sources of power for judges. Some of the nation's most improtant policy decisions have been made by courts rather than by executive or legislative bodies. In recent years, federal courts have taken the lead in eliminating segregation in public life, ensuring the separation of church and state, defining relationships between individuals and law enforcers, and guaranteeing individual voters equal voice in government. Courts are an integral component of America's governmental elite system, for sooner or later most important policy questions are brought before them.

The undemocratic nature of judicial power has long been recognized in American politics. Nine Supreme Court justices—who are not elected to office, whose terms are for life, and who can be removed only for "high crimes and misdemeanors"—possess the power to void the acts of popularly elected presidents, Congresses, governors, and state legislators. The decision of the Founding Fathers to grant federal courts the power of judicial review of *state* decisions—as expressed in Article VI, that the Constitution and the laws and treaties of the national government are the supreme law of the land, "anything in the Constitution or laws of any state to the contrary notwithstanding"—is easy to understand. Federal court power over state decisions is probably essential in maintaining national unity, for 50 different state interpretations of the meaning of the United States Constitution or of the laws and treaties of Congress would create unimaginable confusion. Thus, the power of federal judicial review over state constitutions, laws, and court decisions is seldom questioned.

However, at the national level, why should the views of an appointed court about the meaning of the Constitution prevail over the views of an elected Congress and president? Congressmen and presidents are sworn to uphold the Constitution, and it can reasonably be assumed that they do not pass laws they believe to be *un*constitutional. Since laws must be approved by majorities of those voting in both houses and must have the president's formal approval, why should the Founding Fathers have allowed the decisions of these bodies to be set aside by federal courts?

The answer appears to be that the Founding Fathers distrusted both popular majorities and elected officials who might be influenced by popular majorities. They believed that government should be limited so that it could not attack principle and property, whether to do so was the will of the majority or not. So the courts were deliberately insulated against popular majorities; to ensure their independence, judges were not to be elected, but appointed for life terms. Originally, it was expected that they would be appointed by a president who was not even directly elected himself and confirmed by a Senate that was not directly elected. Only in this way, the writers of the Constitution believed, would they be sufficiently protected from the masses to permit them to judge courageously and responsibly.

The Supreme Court is best understood as an elite institution, rather than as a "conservative" or "liberal" institution. During the 1930s, the Supreme Court was a bastion of conservatism; it attacked the economic programs of the New Deal and clung to the earlier elite philosophy of rugged individualism. In recent years, the Court has been criticized as too liberal in its orientation toward racial equality, church-state relations, and individual rights before the law. The apparent paradox can be understood if we view the Court as an exponent of the dominant elite philosophy, rather than as an unchanging liberal or conservative element in national politics. When the dominant elite philosophy was rugged individualism, the Court reflected this fact, just as it reflects a liberal philosophy today. Of course, owing to the insulation of the Court even from other elites, through life terms and independence from the executive and legislative branches, there is a *time lag* between changes in elite philosophy and the Court decisions reflecting these changes. For example, Franklin D. Roosevelt became president in 1933, but the Supreme Court did not generally approve New Deal legislation until after 1937.

A liberal concern for the underprivileged in America by the Supreme Court, under the leadership of Chief Justice Earl Warren, was reflected in the development of civil rights law. The Court firmly insisted that no person in America should be denied equal protection of the law. It defended the right of Negroes to vote, to attend integrated schools, and to receive justice in the courts; it upheld the power of Congress to protect Negroes from being discriminated against in public accommodations, employment, voting, and housing. It ruled that discrimination against any group of voters by state legislatures in the apportioning of election districts was unconstitutional. It protected religious minorities (and the nonreligious) from laws establishing official prayers and religious ceremonies in public schools. It protected defendants in criminal cases from self-incrimination through ignorance of their rights, through the subtlety of law enforcement officials in extracting confessions, or through lack of legal counsel.

The elevation of Warren Burger as chief justice by Richard Nixon in 1969 did not significantly alter the commitments of the Court to end racial segregation under law, ensure equality in representation, and maintain separation of church and state. Contrary to popular expectations, the Supreme Court, with four Nixon appointees, has continued to uphold these fundamental commitments of the nation's elite. The Burger Court extended the doctrine of *Brown* v. *Board of Education of Topeka* to uphold court-ordered busing of children to end racial imbalance in schools with a history of racial segregation under law (i.e., southern schools). The Burger Court struck down state payments to church schools to pay for nonreligious instruction. Only in the area of rights of criminal defendants has the Burger Court altered the direction of Warren Court holdings. But even here the Burger Court has not reversed earlier declarations of the rights of criminal defendants; it has merely failed to extend them further.

Perhaps the most sweeping declaration of individual liberty in the Supreme Court's history was the assertion, by the Burger Court, of the constitutional right of women to have abortions in the first three months of pregnancy. The ultimate impact of this decision on society—on population growth, the environment, and

U.S. Supreme Court Chief Justice Warren Burger, in striking contrast to his bewigged British colleagues, attends an American Bar association convention in London. The Burger court, while slightly more conservative than its predecessor, the Warren court, has still made many liberal decisions including those in the area of court-ordered busing and abortion. *United Press International Photo*

the role of women in society—may be as far-reaching as that of any decision ever rendered by the Court. Certainly this decision clearly indicates that the Supreme Court continues to be a powerful institution capable of affecting the lives of all Americans.

Recognizing the elitist character of the U.S. Supreme Court, Professor John P. Roche once described the Court as

> . . . a Platonic graft on a democratic process—a group of wise men insulated from the people who have the task of injecting truth serum into the body politic, of acting as an institutional chaperone to insure that the sovereign populace and its elected representatives do not act unwisely.[6]

POLITICAL BEHAVIOR IN AMERICA

Popular participation in the political system is the very definition of democracy. Individuals in a democracy may run for public office; participate in marches and demonstrations; make financial contributions to political candidates or causes; attend political meetings, speeches, and rallies; write letters to public officials or newspapers; belong to organizations that support or oppose particular candidates or take stands on public issues; wear a political button or place a bumper sticker on their car; attempt to influence friends while discussing candidates or issues; vote in elections; or merely follow an issue or campaign in the mass media. This list of activities constitutes a ranking of the forms of political participation, in inverse order of their frequency. Those activities at the beginning of the list require greater expenditure of time and energy and greater personal commitment and consequently are engaged in by far fewer people than the activities at the end of the list. Less than 1 percent of the American adult population run for public office. Only about 5 percent are ever active in political parties and campaigns, and only about 10 percent make financial contributions. About 60 percent will vote in a presidential election, but fully one-third of the population are politically apathetic: They do not vote, and they are largely unaware of and indifferent to the political life of the nation.[7]

Voting is the primary form of popular participation in a democracy, and voter participation is highly valued in American political theory. Popular control of government—the control of leaders by followers—is supposed to be accomplished through the electoral process. Voting requires an individual to make not one but two decisions: He must choose whether he will cast his vote at all; and if he decides to vote, he must choose between rival parties or candidates. Both decisions are equally important; decisions about whether or not to vote can clearly influence the outcome of elections.

Most Americans seem to have confidence in the electoral process. A majority of Americans regularly exercise their right to vote in presidential elections, and by doing so they are indicating that they feel they have some stake in the outcome of these elections and can personally influence the outcome. Nevertheless, nonvoting is widespread. While presidential elections inspire about 60 percent of the adult population to vote, congressional elections bring out less than one-half of the population. Yet in these "off-year" contests the nation chooses all of its U.S. representatives, one-third of its U.S. senators, and about one-half of its governors. Local government elections—for mayor, councilmen, school board, etc.—frequently attract only one-quarter or one-third of eligible voters.

Before 1970 only 3 of the 50 states permitted persons 18 to 21 years of age to vote: Georgia, Kentucky, and Alaska. All the rest, in the exercise of their constitutional responsibility to determine the qualifications of "electors," had set the voting age at 21. The movement for 18-year-old voting had received its original impetus in Georgia in 1944 under the leadership of Governor Ellis Arnall, who argued successfully that 18-year-olds were then being called upon to fight and die for their country in World War II and therefore deserved to have a voice in the conduct of government. But this argument failed to convince adult voters or leaders in other states; qualifications for military service were not regarded as the same as qualifications for rational decision-making in elections. In state after state, voters rejected state constitutional amendments designed to extend the vote to 18-year-olds. But in 1970 Congress passed and sent to the

A significant stride in allowing blacks full participation in the process of government was accomplished with the passage of the Voting Rights Act of 1965. Here black and white voters line up at the polls in Little Rock, Arkansas. *Wide World Photo*

states the Twenty-sixth Amendment to the Constitution extending voting rights to all persons over 18 years of age in all federal, state, and local elections. The legislatures of three-fourths of the states promptly ratified the amendment.

Voting laws in the states are now heavily circumscribed by national authority:

Fifteenth Amendment—No denial of voting because of race.

Nineteenth Amendment—No denial of voting because of sex.

Twenty-fourth Amendment—No poll taxes in federal elections.

Twenty-sixth Amendment—No denial of voting to persons 18 or over.

Civil Rights Act of 1964—No discrimination in the application of voter registration laws.

Voting Rights Act of 1965—Attorney general may replace local voting officials with federal examiners on evidence of voter discrimination in southern states.

Voting Rights Act of 1970—No denial of voting to persons 18 or over; no residency requirements in national elections; no literacy tests.

The states, however, continue to administer and finance national, state, and local elections. All but four states (Alaska, Arkansas, North Dakota, and Texas) have established a system of voting registration. Presumably, registration helps to prevent fraud and multiple voting in elections.

DEMOCRATS AND REPUBLICANS
—WHAT'S THE DIFFERENCE?

Democracy is ultimately based on majority rule, and one function of political parties is to put the majority together. Political parties organize voters for effective political expression at the polls. Voters, in turn, use party labels to help them identify the general political viewpoints of the candidates.

Because American parties are necessarily rather loose coalitions of interests, they do not command the total loyalty of every officeholder elected under a party's banner. The fact that a candidate runs under a Republican or Democratic label does not clearly indicate where he will stand on every public issue. Even so, these coalitions do have considerable cohesion and historical continuity. The party label discloses the coalition of interests and the policy views a candidate has generally associated himself with, and at least the party label tells more about a candidate's politics than would a strange name on the ballot with no party affiliation attached.

Especially in two-party systems such as we have in the United States, parties also limit the choice of candidates for public office and thus relieve voters of the task of choosing from among dozens of contending candidates on election day. This preliminary selecting and narrowing of candidates, by conventions and primary elections, is indispensable in a large society.

Political parties help to define the major problems and issues confronting society. In attempting to win a majority of the voters, parties inform the public about the issues facing the nation. The comparisons made by parties during political campaigns have an important educational value: Voters come to "know" the opposing candidates for public office, and problems of national interest are spotlighted.

Finally, the party *out* of office performs an important function for democratic government by criticizing officeholders. Moreover, the very existence of a recognized party *outside* government helps to make criticism of government legitimate and effective.

It is sometimes argued that there are few significant differences between the two main American parties. It is not uncommon in European nations to find totalitarian parties competing with democratic parties, fascists with communists, capitalist parties with socialist parties, Catholic parties with secular parties, and so on. In contrast, in America both Republican and Democratic parties accept and strongly support constitutional government, with separation of powers, federalism, and judicial review. The policies of both parties reflect the same general cultural values. In addition, both parties compete for a majority in the electorate and therefore tend to take moderate stands that will encompass the views of the largest number of voters.

If it were true that the American parties offered *no* real alternatives to the

"Good day sir, . . . Unlike my thoughtless opponent, who is running an impersonal TV Radio campaign . . ."

Paul Szep, The Boston Globe

voters, then effective popular control of government through elections would be impossible. This is exactly what Marxist critics charge about American democracy—that there are no differences between the American parties and no choices open to the American people.

However, within the context of American political experience, the Democratic and Republican parties can be clearly differentiated. There are at least three ways in which to discern the differences: (1) by examining differences in the coalitions of voters supporting each party; (2) by examining differences in the policy views of the leaders in each party; and (3) by examining differences in the voting records of the congressmen of each party.

In ascertaining party differences according to support from different groups of voters, we must note first that major groups are seldom *wholly* within one party or the other. For example, in presidential elections all major social groups divide their votes between the parties (see Table 6-3). Yet differences between the parties are revealed in the proportions of votes given by each major group to each party. Thus, the Democratic party receives a disproportionate amount of support from Catholics, Jews, Negroes, lower educational and income groups, younger people, blue-collar workers, union members, and big-city residents. The Republican party receives disproportionate support from Protestants, whites, higher educational and income groups, older people, professionals and managers, white-collar workers, nonunion members, and rural and small-town residents.

The second way of discerning Democratic and Republican party differences involves an examination of the political opinions of the leaders and voters of each party. Political scientist Herbert J. McClosky made a study of party

TABLE 6-3. Voting Behavior of Major American Social
Groups in Presidential Elections

| | 1964 | | 1968 | | | 1972 | |
	Dem. LBJ	Rep. Goldwater	Dem. HHH	Rep. Nixon	Ind. Wallace	Dem. McG.	Rep. Nixon
National total	61.3	39.7	43.0	43.4	13.6	38.0	62.0
Race							
White	59	41	38	47	15	32	68
Nonwhite	94	6	85	12	3	87	13
Education							
College	52	48	37	54	9	37	63
High school	62	38	42	43	15	34	66
Grade school	66	34	52	33	15	49	51
Occupation							
Prof. and							
business	54	46	34	56	10	31	69
White collar	57	43	41	47	12	36	64
Manual	71	29	50	35	15	43	57
Age							
Under 30	64	36	47	38	15	48	52
30–49	63	37	44	41	15	33	67
50 and older	59	41	41	47	12	36	64
Religion							
Protestant	55	45	35	49	16	30	70
Catholic	76	24	59	33	8	48	52

Source: Table constructed from data in the Gallup Opinion Index, February 1974.

differences by presenting a series of policy questions to over 3,000 delegates to
the Democratic and Republican national conventions. He found substantial
differences of opinion between Democrats and Republicans on important public
issues, including public ownership of natural resources, government regulation
of the economy, equalitarianism and human welfare, tax policy, and foreign
policy. On the basis of this research, McClosky concludes:

Although it has received wide currency, especially among Europeans, the belief
that the two American parties are identical in principle and doctrine has little foundation in fact. Examination of the opinions of Democratic and Republican leaders
shows them to be distinct communities of co-believers who diverge sharply on
many important issues. Their disagreements, furthermore, conform to an image
familiar to many observers and are generally consistent with differences turned up
by studies of congressional roll calls. . . . [They] grow out of their group identification and support—out of the managerial, proprietary, and high-status connections
of the one, and the labor, minority, low-status, and intellectual connections of the
other. . . . Democratic leaders typically display the stronger urge to elevate the
lowborn, the uneducated, the deprived minorities, and the poor in general; they

are also more disposed to employ the nation's collective power to advance humanitarian and social welfare goals (e.g., social security, immigration, racial integration, a higher minimum wage, and public education). They are more critical of wealth and big business and more eager to bring them under regulation. Theirs is the greater faith in the wisdom of using legislation for redistributing the national product and for furnishing social services on a wide scale. Of the two groups of leaders, the Democrats are more "progressively" oriented toward social reform and experimentation. The Republican leaders, while not uniformly differentiated from their opponents, subscribe in greater measure to the symbols and practices of individualism, *laissez-faire*, and national independence. They prefer to overcome humanity's misfortunes by relying upon personal effort, private incentives, frugality, hard work, responsibility, self-denial (for both men and government), and the strengthening rather than the diminution of the economic and status distinctions that are the "natural" rewards of the differences in human character and fortunes.[8]

The third indication of party differences in America is the roll-call voting behavior of Democratic and Republican congressmen on controversial issues. Although members of the same party in Congress often have serious and lasting disagreements over important issues, it is possible to show that the *centers of gravity* of the two parties are rather widely separated in many issue areas, including government regulation of the economy, labor legislation, education and welfare programs, and foreign affairs. Table 6-4 shows the division of Democrats and Republicans in the House and Senate on selected key votes. Party differences in Congress can also be distinguished by the degree of support each party gives to the president. An important function of the congressional parties is the support or opposition given the president, depending on which party he heads. Analysis of congressional voting records indicates that the parties do, in fact, perform this function. The Democrats generally supported the recommendations of the Democratic president Lyndon Johnson, and the Republicans were generally critical of his recommendations; Democratic congressmen tended to vote against the recommendations of Republican President Richard Nixon more often than Republican congressmen.

Voters usually think of themselves as Democrats or Republicans, and this party identification is the single most important factor in voter decisions. Candidates and issues, two other bases of voter decisions, are influential in elections, but they do not provide the solid core of millions of party supporters who will vote for the party's nominee no matter who he is. This is particularly pertinent because the vast majority of candidates who appear on the ballot are unknown to the voter, especially candidates for the more obscure offices—those of county commissioner, city councilman, registrar of deeds, auditor general, and so on.

People who identify themselves as Democrats outnumber those who identify themselves as Republicans by as much as two to one in national samples. Thus, if the Republican party is to win an election, it must nominate candidates who

TABLE 6–4. Party Divisions on Selected Key Votes in Congress

	House Votes			
	Republicans		Democrats	
	Yes	No	Yes	No
Medicare (1965)	65	73	249	42
Establish Department of Housing and Urban				
Development (1965)	9	118	208	66
Federal aid to education (1965)	35	96	228	57
Wider cities programs (1966)	16	81	162	60
Rat control in cities (1967)	22	148	154	59
Anticivic grants to states (1967)	172	4	84	143
Turn over poverty program to states (1970)	103	63	60	168
Override Nixon's veto of labor-welfare funds	27	156	199	35

	Senate Votes			
	Republicans		Democrats	
	Yes	No	Yes	No
Medicare (1965)	13	14	55	7
Repeal Taft-Hartley "right-to-work"				
provisions (1965)	5	26	40	21
Reduction in spending 5% across all items (1965)	26	5	17	41
Nomination of Abe Fortas for chief justice of				
Supreme Court (1968)	10	24	35	19
Antiballistic missile (ABM) system (1970)	29	14	21	36

Source: *Congressional Quarterly,* various issues, 1965–1970.

can attract Democratic voters, as Eisenhower and Nixon were able to do but as Goldwater failed to do. However, the Republican party's electoral hopes are aided by the fact that its adherents—higher education, higher income, white-collar groups—tend to vote more often than the Democrats.

Americans acquire their party identification much as they acquire most of their other values and attitudes: at home. National samples generally show that voters' preferences tend to correspond with those of their parents. This inclination does not necessarily represent blind or shallow thinking. Children get most of their values through their parents, and it would be inconsistent if their political values did not match what they were taught in the home.

POWER TO THE PEOPLE?

Are governmental elites really accountable to the people? Can the people influence the direction of public policy through participation in parties and elections? How "democratic" is the American political system?

In a "pure democracy" every citizen would help decide every policy which affected his life. But in a large complex society it is a practical impossibility to have every issue placed before the American voter on a referendum. Perhaps the closest thing to a "pure democracy" ever to occur on our shores was the old New England town meeting, in which all citizens came together regularly to act as a town legislature. But this is certainly not a feasible option in a society of 210 million people. So the question arises as to whether America's system of parties and elections is really an effective means of popular participation in policy-making.

Political scientists have long acknowledged that America is not a pure democracy. As Harold Lasswell wrote in 1952, "The discovery that in all large-scale societies the decisions at any given time are typically in the hands of a small number of people" confirms a basic fact: "Government is always government by the few, whether in the name of the few, the one, or the many."[9] But many political scientists contend that "the people" can still influence the course of events in America because:

1. There is competition between multiple elites, and this competition results in a checking and balancing of different interests in society; no simple elite dominates society.

2. Voters can influence public policy by choosing between competing elites in elections.

3. Individuals are forced to form new interest groups and to pressure parties and government officials for changes in the laws.

These ideas form the basis of modern *pluralism*—the belief that democratic values can be preserved in a system of multiple competing elites, voters can exercise meaningful choices in elections, and new elites can gain access to power by forming interest groups.

Critics of pluralism have argued that this system does not always work to ensure democracy. First, elites do not really compete over the fundamental character of American society—the free enterprise system, private property, individual liberty, opposition to communism and fascism, the promotion of economic growth. The major domestic programs of "the liberal establishment"—social security, the tax structure, the welfare system, avoidance of depression, the fight against poverty, reduction of racial conflict, government regulation of public utilities—have been supported by most segments of American leadership. The same is true in foreign policy, with most leaders agreeing on a strong national defense, international involvement, and communist containment. Generally, Democrats and Republicans, liberals and conservatives, "hawks" and "doves" argue over the *means* of accomplishing national goals, rather than the goals themselves.

Second, critics of pluralism argue that voters cannot exercise a meaningful choice in elections if competing candidates do not offer clear policy choices, if they deliberately obscure their intentions, or if they try to straddle the important issues. They also note that many, perhaps most, voters cast their vote according to traditional party loyalties or candidate "images" and TV personalities, and *not* on the basis of careful consideration of their policy positions. Thus elections determine *personnel* (who occupies public office) but not *policy* (what public officials do once they are in office).

Finally, critics of pluralism contend that many individuals find it difficult to have their voices heard in government. The most powerful interest groups—the groups with the greatest unity, organization, skill, money, and access to public officials—are not representative of "the common man." Only recently have poor people, blacks, and consumers found effective interest group representation in Washington. Today many "middle Americans"—white, working class, middle income, taxpaying Americans—feel that they have little say in government. Even when citizens join interest groups and pay dues, they often have scant control over the leaders of these groups; for example, individual union members may feel they have almost no influence with the leadership of the AFL-CIO, or individual blacks may believe they cannot really affect the leadership of the NAACP, and so on.

Despite these problems, however, there is ample evidence that voters do *influence* the behavior of government officials. Elections may not enable the masses to exercise power over policy directly, but they enable those who vote to affect the conduct of elected officials indirectly. Elections give voters the opportunity to express themselves about the conduct of public officials who *have* been in power. People can vote *against* officeholders whose policies they know they do not like. Research by political scientists has revealed that many voters cast votes *against* rather than *for* political candidates.

Elected public officials—from presidents and congressmen to governors, state legislators, mayors, and councilmen—are *influenced* by the knowledge that voters can pass judgment on their past behavior in office. Political scientist Gerald Pomper contends that because "politicians might be affected by the voters in the next election, they regulate their conduct appropriately."[10]

Competitive elections may not permit masses to decide what should be done on public issues, but elections do encourage governing elites to consider the welfare of the masses in their decision-making.

> The existence of the vote does not make politicians better as individuals; it simply forces them to give greater consideration to the demands of enfranchised and sizable groups, who hold a weapon of potentially great force. . . . The ability to punish politicians is probably the most important weapon available to citizens. It is direct, authoritative, and free from official control.[11]

While individual voters may not consciously consider policy issues in casting their votes, many express their own group identification when talking about candidates or parties. "The Democrats are better for working people." "The

Republicans keep us out of wars." "The Democrats help black people." "The Democrats give away too much of the taxpayer's money," etc. Political scientist V. O. Key, Jr., argues that these vague associations between parties and interests in the minds of many voters represent some degree of rationality in voter choice.[12] Voters may not know the details of policy questions confronting the nation, but they do identify the parties and candidates who they think best represent their group interests.

Elections also protect individuals and groups from official abuse. Long ago the English political philosopher John Stuart Mill wrote, "Men, as well as women, do not need political rights in order that they might govern, but in order that they not be misgoverned."[13] The long history of efforts to ensure black voting rights in the southern states indicates that many Americans believed that if blacks could secure access to the polls they could better protect themselves from official discrimination. Although the success of the voting rights movement has not succeeded in eliminating racism in America, it has nonetheless helped blacks achieve significant political power, notably in the southern states. Blacks now serve in every southern state legislature, and few southern politicians make direct racist appeals any more, partly out of respect for the voting power of their black constituents.

In summary, the American people exercise considerable influence over their government. But there are many obstacles to direct citizen control over public policy.

POWER AND GOVERNMENT: A CASE STUDY

Watergate and the Resignation of Richard Nixon

The president does not stand above America's elites but among them. Election to the nation's highest office—even by an overwhelming majority—does not entitle the president to govern. It only gives him the opportunity to engage in consultation, accommodation, and compromise with other elites. Richard Nixon's forced resignation from the presidency was not merely a product of specific misdeeds or improprieties associated with Watergate. It also grew out of his general isolation from established elites, his failure to cooperate with Congress and the courts, and his disregard of general "rules of the game."

Watergate and the Resignation of Richard Nixon

President Nixon claimed that his critics blew up a petty incident—the Watergate break-in—out of all proportion to its importance. And indeed the burglary of a party headquarters is trivial compared to ending the Vietnam War, or reopening relations with China, or securing the SALT agreement to limit nuclear arsenals, or the Middle East crisis. But Watergate's importance grew as the president escalated his defense, challenged the powers of other elites, attacked the powerful television networks, asserted his own authority, and offended Congress, the courts, and even loyal members of his own party.

The Origins of Watergate. Threats to democracy can originate from elites as well as masses, even democratically elected elites. Elite repression frequently appears in response to mass unrest—riots, demonstrations, extremism, violence, and threats of violence. These mass activities generate fear and insecurity among men of power, who respond by curtailing liberties and strengthening "national security." Dissenters come under official suspicion and surveillance, the news media are cut off from their sources or censored, free speech is curtailed, political activists are jailed, and police and security forces are strengthened, usually in the name of "law and order."

The origins of Watergate are found in the climate of mass unrest of the late 1960s and early 1970s which seemed to threaten the security of the nation. A decade of disorder began with the assassination of President John F. Kennedy in 1963, to be followed by the assassinations of Martin Luther King, Jr., and Robert F. Kennedy in 1968 and the attempted assassination of George C. Wallace in 1972. Mass demonstrations and civil disobedience were developed and refined as political tactics by various mass movements. Humiliation and defeat in a prolonged and fruitless military effort in Vietnam undermined the legitimacy of the government. The Democratic National Convention in Chicago in 1968 featured violent antiwar protests outside the convention hall, and police responded with counterviolence of their own. College protest activity, which had been relatively restrained for most of the decade, became increasingly violence-prone in the 1970s. In May 1970, National Guardsmen were sent to Kent State University after the ROTC building had been set afire as a protest against the U.S. operations in Cambodia. When students defied an order to disperse, some Guardsmen fired their weapons; four students were killed and nine were wounded. In that same month, campus protest activity closed down many of the nation's leading universities. More than 60,000 persons, mostly students, assembled in Washington for antiwar demonstrations. In 1971, the *New York Times* and the *Washington Post* published the so-called Pentagon Papers, which had been taken from the files of the Department of Defense by a former Defense Department adviser, Daniel Ellsberg. The president and his senior advisers were convinced that this important elite—the influential newsmakers—had acted outside the established "rules of the game" in their effort to end the war quickly.

Watergate and the Resignation of Richard Nixon

Thus by the early 1970s all of the conditions for elite repression existed: (1) racial unrest and violence; (2) the approval and encouragement of violence in the form of mass protest; (3) defeat and humiliation in war; (4) counterelite violence, including bombing and arson; (5) attacks from the press which went beyond the "rules of the game." The Watergate affair provides an illustration of the response of national elites to these conditions, and their tendency to resort to repressive measures when threatened. It may be psychologically comforting to believe that the "White House horrors" are unique and unprecedented in American history, and that the Nixon administration is the only administration that has ever resorted to repression in times of crisis. But this is not the case. Repressive behavior is typical of elites when they perceive threats to the political system—witness the Alien and Sedition Acts in the administration of John Adams; the suspension of due process rights by Abraham Lincoln during the Civil War; the "red scare" roundup of suspected "Bolsheviks" in the administration of Woodrow Wilson; the mass internment of thousands of Japanese-Americans by the Roosevelt administration in World War II; and the "loyalty and security" programs of the Truman and Eisenhower administrations, with their persecution of suspected communists and "fellow travelers." Most of the actions revealed in the Watergate hearings—wiretapping, monitoring of the mail, checking of tax returns, surveillance of suspected subversives, infiltration of radical organizations, "surreptitious entry" (burglary), and so forth—have been long-standing practices of federal security agencies. What is different about Watergate is that some of them were used against the national Democratic party headquarters located in the Watergate office complex in Washington, D.C., during the 1972 presidential elections. Repressive tactics applied in "national security" cases were common in Democratic as well as Republican administrations in the past. But for one segment of the nation's established leadership to use such tactics against another segment is to violate the fundamental "rules of the game."

The "Plumbers" at Work.   To deal with the increasingly troublesome radical protest activity of the late 1960s and early 1970s, and particularly to halt damaging leaks of secret government information to a hostile press, the president convened an interagency committee composed of the directors of the FBI, the CIA, the Defense Intelligence Agency, and the National Security Council Agency. This group considered a report calling for: (1) intensified electronic surveillance of both domestic security threats and foreign diplomats; (2) monitoring of American citizens using international communications facilities; (3) increased legal and illegal opening and reading of mail; (4) more informants on college campuses; (5) the lifting of restrictions on "surreptitious entry" (burglary); (6) the establishment of an interagency group on domestic intelligence. The president approved a plan, but later FBI Director J. Edgar Hoover objected to it—not because he opposed such measures but because the

Watergate and the Resignation of Richard Nixon

FBI was not given exclusive control of the program. Hoover's opposition resulted in the formal withdrawal of the plan.

However, the White House still believed that the political system was endangered by disruptive and subversive elements, that disloyal members of the administration were leaking government secrets to the press, and that "extraordinary" measures were required to protect the government. A Special Investigations Unit was created within the White House—known as "The Plumbers" because it was supposed to stop leaks of secret government information. The unit was placed under the supervision of John Ehrlichman and his assistant Egil Krogh. The Plumbers unit soon included ex-CIA agent and author of spy novels E. Howard Hunt, Jr., and former FBI agent G. Gordon Liddy. The Plumbers unit worked independently of the FBI and the CIA (although it received occasional assistance from the CIA) and reported directly to John Ehrlichman. It undertook a variety of activities—later referred to as "White House horrors"—including: the investigation of Daniel Ellsberg and the burglary of his psychiatrist's office to learn more about his motives in releasing the Pentagon Papers; the investigation (and later forgery) of the record of the events surrounding the assassination of South Vietnam's President Diem during the administration of John F. Kennedy; the investigation of national security leaks which affected the U.S. negotiating position in the SALT talks; and other undisclosed domestic and foreign intelligence activities. Later John Ehrlichman strongly defended the actions of the Plumbers unit before the Senate Watergate Committee as necessary to protect national security.

The Watergate Break-in.　　The Watergate break-in itself—burglarizing and wiretapping of the Democratic National Headquarters—was an outgrowth of earlier undercover activities by members of the Plumbers unit. The work of the Plumbers had tapered off by the end of 1971, and Hunt and Liddy found new jobs with the president's reelection campaign organization, the Committee to Re-elect the President (CREEP), headed by former Attorney General John M. Mitchell. The "security coordinator" for CREEP was James W. McCord, Jr., who had been an FBI and CIA agent. It was easy for Hunt, McCord, and Liddy to confuse threats to national security with threats to the reelection of the incumbent president, and to employ well-known "national security" tactics, including bugging and burglary, against the president's opponents. On the night of June 17, 1972, five men were arrested in the offices of the Democratic National Committee with burglary and wiretapping tools: James W. McCord and Bernard L. Barker and three Cuban exiles. Later a grand jury charged these five men, together with Hunt and Liddy, with burglary and wiretapping; at a trial in January 1973 all seven were convicted. But U.S. District Court Judge John J. Sirica believed that the defendants were covering up for whoever had ordered and paid for the bugging and break-in. The *Washington Post* reported

Watergate and the Resignation of Richard Nixon

"It's for you."   Paul Szep, The Boston Globe

that the defendants were under pressure to plead guilty, that they were still being paid by an unnamed source, and that they had been promised a cash settlement and executive clemency if they went to jail and remained silent. Judge Sirica threatened the defendants with heavy sentences, and soon McCord broke and told of secret payments and a cover-up.

The Cover-up. It was probably not the political embarrassment of the Watergate break-in that led the White House to attempt a cover-up (news of the burglary did not seriously affect the president's reelection campaign, and he was reelected overwhelmingly in November 1972, five months *after* the break-in). Instead the White House seemed concerned over exposure of the whole series of repressive acts undertaken earlier by the Plumbers. The great blunder of the Watergate operation was that certain individuals who were involved in the petty political burglary of the National Democratic Headquarters—Liddy, Hunt, and McCord—had previously served with the Special Investigations Unit of the White House and the CIA. The Watergate burglary mixed partisan politics with national security affairs. The president attempted to limit the Watergate investigation to the partisan political act of the break-in of the Democratic National Headquarters, to protect his close associates, and to prevent exposure of the repressive measures taken by the White House over several years.

Watergate and the Resignation of Richard Nixon

The U.S. Senate formed a Special Select Committee on Campaign Activities—the so-called Watergate Committee—headed by Senator Sam J. Ervin to delve into Watergate and related activities. The national press, led by the prestigious *Washington Post*, which had always been hostile to Richard Nixon, began its own "investigative reporting" and, in cooperation with the major television networks, launched a series of damaging stories involving former Attorney General John Mitchell, White House chief of staff H. R. Haldeman, and White House adviser John Ehrlichman. Rumors of a White House cover-up, including secret payments of money to the Watergate burglars and promises of executive clemency, were reported nightly on the national television networks.

In March 1973 the president announced the resignation of his two top aides, Haldeman and Ehrlichman, and at the same time dismissed White House counsel John Dean, who, although deeply involved in the cover-up itself, had been secretly giving information to the FBI and Senate Watergate investigators regarding the cover-up.

The President's Use of "Executive Privilege."　President Nixon might have been able to stay in office and weather the Watergate storm if he had publicly repented his own actions, assisted in the Watergate investigation in Congress, and cooperated with Attorney General Elliot Richardson and (the first) Special Prosecutor Archibald Cox. But it was Nixon's style to confront crisis directly, to avoid surrender, to test his own strength of character against adversity. His gut instinct in a crisis was to "fight like hell" rather than to bargain, accommodate, and compromise. James David Barber believes that such political figures eventually become rigid:

> Such a President will, eventually, freeze around some adamant stand—as did Wilson in the League of Nations fight, Hoover in refusing relief to Americans during the Depression, and Johnson in the Vietnam escalation. Increasingly, as his stance rigidifies, he will see compromise as surrender, justify his cause as sacred, plunge into intense and lonely effort, and concentrate his enmity on specific enemies he thinks are conspiring against him.[14]

As the Watergate affair broadened and intensified, Nixon increasingly viewed it as a test of his strength and character; he perceived a conspiracy of liberal opponents in Congress and the news media to reverse the 1972 election outcome; he became rigid in his stance on executive privilege—that is, in withholding tapes, documents, and information. He came to believe he was defending the presidency itself.

When the Senate Watergate Committee learned that the president regularly taped conversations in the Oval Office, it (and later the special prosecutor) issued subpoenas for tapes which would prove or disprove charges by John Dean

Watergate and the Resignation of Richard Nixon

and others of a cover-up. In response, President Nixon argued that the constitutional separation of powers permits the president to withhold information from both the Congress and the courts. He relied on the doctrine of "executive privilege"—the assertion of the right of the president to keep information, documents, or testimony from either the Congress or the courts if in the opinion of the president it is necessary to do so in the interest of national security or the proper functioning of the executive. He was not acting without precedent in his refusal to cooperate with Congress and the courts in his assertion of executive privilege. Indeed, executive privilege was first invoked against Congress by George Washington in 1796 and employed by many presidents to withhold information from Congress; and it was once invoked by Thomas Jefferson in 1807 to withhold information from the Supreme Court. The claim of executive privilege has been made relative not only to information affecting national security and international diplomacy but to all communications between presidents and their own advisers and cabinet members. Presumably, the doctrine of executive privilege ensures that advisers can be completely candid in their conversations with the president. President Nixon used the doctrine of executive privilege to prevent Watergate-related tapes of presidential conversations from becoming available both to Congress and to the courts.

Eventually, however, the dispute over the Watergate tapes reached the Supreme Court in the important decision of *The United States* v. *Richard M. Nixon*. The Court denied the president the power to withhold subpoenaed information from the courts under the doctrine of executive privilege when such information was essential to a criminal investigation. The Supreme Court reaffirmed *Marbury* v. *Madison* (1803) establishing the power of the courts to review the actions of other branches of the government. The Court recognized the principle of executive privilege but denied that it applied to criminal cases or that the president could refuse judges access to information in order to determine for themselves whether such information applied to criminal cases.

The Impeachment Movement.   The movement to impeach Richard Nixon began in earnest after Attorney General Elliot Richardson resigned and Special Prosecutor Archibald Cox was fired. The story of Richardson and Cox illustrates very clearly the necessity of the president's accommodating established elites. As the Watergate scandal broadened in early 1973, and after the president dismissed Haldeman and Ehrlichman from the White House, the president seemed to reach an understanding with congressional leadership about the handling of the case. He would appoint Elliot Richardson as attorney general, who would appoint Harvard Professor Archibald Cox as special prosecutor, and Cox would have complete independence in conducting his investigations of Watergate. This pledge was made to the Senate during confirmation hearings on Richardson's appointment as attorney general. But when Cox was installed in office, he

Watergate and the Resignation of Richard Nixon

quickly recruited a staff of liberal attorneys and expanded his investigative activities until Nixon began to suspect that Cox was engaged in a conspiracy to
destroy him. When Nixon appeared to reach an agreement with Senate
Watergate Committee Chairman Sam Ervin to provide transcripts of certain
taped conversations and to allow Senator John Stennis to verify the transcripts
by listening to the tapes, Cox objected and insisted on obtaining the tapes
himself. Cox cited the original promise to give him full independence in pursuing his investigation. Attorney General Richardson backed up his old Harvard Law School professor. Nixon acted abruptly in "the Saturday night
massacre" to dismiss Cox and precipitate the resignation of Richardson.

In firing Cox and forcing Richardson out, President Nixon made a serious
error. He not only broke a solemn pledge made to the Congress, but more importantly he cut his last ties with liberals inside and outside of his own party. He
further isolated himself from established leaders.

Nonetheless, movement to impeach Richard Nixon could not win strong support among Democrats in Congress and the influential news media as long as
Spiro Agnew was vice-president. Agnew was considered even more offensive to
liberals and newsmen than Nixon. It was politically essential that Agnew be
removed from the vice-presidency before any serious impeachment movement
could be launched against Nixon. But removing Agnew turned out to be a
relatively easy task. Early in his career Agnew had served as Baltimore County
executive and then governor of Maryland. Baltimore County politics had long
been notorious for its corruption. Rumors of Agnew's early involvement in corrupt local politics had circulated in Washington cocktail parties for many years.
The Justice Department, under pressure from the national news media, obtained indictments against Vice-President Agnew for accepting money from
government contractors and failing to report it on his income tax returns. Agnew
pleaded no contest in court to the charge of tax fraud, resigned from office, and
was given a suspended sentence. The president appointed Gerald R. Ford,
Republican minority leader in the House of Representatives and a popular
figure in the Congress, to the vice-presidency. Perhaps President Nixon hoped
that the popular Ford would prove an asset in congressional relations in the up-
coming impeachment fight. But the removal of Agnew opened the way for
direct frontal attack on Nixon as president.

President Nixon publicly released the transcripts of the subpoenaed White
House tapes in a national television broadcast in which he urged the public to
read the tapes in their entirety rather than as single excerpts. Nixon contended
that the tapes proved his innocence of any prior knowledge of the Watergate
break-in or any participation in the cover-up. One of the key tapes recorded a
meeting between President Nixon and John Dean on March 21, 1973. Dean told
the president that "a cancer is growing on the presidency," referring to the fact
that the Watergate scandal had grown to such large proportions that the cover-

Watergate and the Resignation of Richard Nixon

up was breaking down. Dean told the president that McCord had already implicated several staff members of the Committee to Re-elect the President. More importantly, Hunt was blackmailing the White House for immediate payment of $120,000 plus pledges of immediate financial payoffs and executive clemency after conviction. Dean and the president estimated that eventual payoffs to everyone to keep silent would amount to a million dollars or more. The conversations on the tapes are rambling and inconclusive, and subject to varied interpretations. The most common interpretation is that President Nixon approved an immediate payoff to Hunt but declined to promise him clemency. The tape's importance, however, rested not so much on its suggestion of Nixon's complicity in obstruction of justice as on the tone and quality of Nixon's leadership. In many taped conversations, Nixon appeared more concerned with narrow and self-serving political interests than with legal or moral questions.

The Judiciary Committee of the House of Representatives, chaired by Representative Peter Rodino of New Jersey, was convened in the spring of 1974 to consider a series of articles of impeachment against President Nixon. The release of the tapes failed to persuade this committee of Nixon's innocence. Indeed, the opposite occurred; the tapes were used by the president's opponents in Congress and the news media to convince the majority of the committee of Nixon's culpability. Three articles of impeachment were passed by the committee. Article One accused the president of obstructing justice in the Watergate investigation. Article Two accused the president of misusing his executive power and disregarding his constitutional duties to take care that the laws be faithfully executed, specifically in establishing the Plumbers unit and approving its activities. Article Three accused the president of refusing to cooperate with the congressional investigation and disobeying its subpoenas. Two of the articles of impeachment were passed by the predominantly Democratic Judiciary Committee and sent to the floor of the House of Representatives.

However, before the House of Representatives could take up these articles of impeachment, Nixon released another tape which damaged his case beyond repair. It was a tape of a meeting between the president and H. R. Haldeman, June 23, 1972, five days after the Watergate break-in. The president withheld this tape until ordered by the Supreme Court to release it to the special prosecutor. The president also acknowledged that he had withheld this evidence even from his own attorney. The tape suggests that the president himself ordered the cover-up of the Watergate affair and tried to restrict the FBI's investigation by implying CIA involvement. With its release, all Republican minority members of the Judiciary Committee who had supported the president publicly announced that they had changed their minds and would vote for impeachment when the articles reached the floor of the House of Representatives. Shortly thereafter, Nixon was informed by congressional leaders of his own party

Watergate and the Resignation of Richard Nixon

—including Senate Minority Leader Hugh Scott, House Minority Leader John Rhodes, and Senator Barry Goldwater—that impeachment by majority of the House and removal from office by two-thirds of the Senate was assured.

On August 9, 1974, President Nixon resigned his office—the first president of the United States ever to do so. Gerald R. Ford was sworn in as president. On September 8, 1974, President Gerald Ford pardoned former President Richard Nixon "for all offenses against the United States which he, Richard Nixon, has committed or may have committed or taken part in" during his presidency. In accepting the pardon, Nixon expressed remorse over Watergate and acknowledged grave errors of judgment, but he did not admit personal guilt. Despite intensive questioning by the press and Congress, President Ford maintained that his purpose in granting the pardon was to end "bitter controversy and divisive national debate" and "to firmly shut and seal this book" on Watergate.

Summary.   The president must govern the nation within the boundaries of elite consensus. Voters may determine who will be president, but elites determine what he can do in office. It is ironic that Richard Nixon saw himself as a tribune of the people—"the great silent majority"—pitting himself against the liberal establishment that was not popularly elected and did not reflect grassroots sentiments. Nixon believed that he understood "middle America," and he probably did. But in the end, elites in Congress and in the news media were able to turn middle America against him. In six months in 1973, Richard Nixon suffered one of the steepest plunges in public opinion approval rating ever recorded by a president. Richard Nixon failed to understand that even landslide victories at the polls are meaningless if the president cannot win the confidence of the Congress, the press, and other segments of the nation's leadership. Popular majorities may elect the president, but they do not permit him to govern in disregard of traditional "rules of the game."

NOTES

1.   Philip M. Gregg and Arthur S. Banks, "Dimensions of Political Systems," *American Political Science Review*, 59 (September 1965), 602 - 614.

2.   William M. Riker, *Federalism: Origin, Operation, Significance* (Boston: Little, Brown, 1964), pp. 17 - 20.

3.   *The Federalist* papers were a series of essays by James Madison, Alexander Hamilton, and John Jay, written in 1787 and 1788 to explain and defend the new Constitution during the struggle over its ratification (*The Federalist*, New York: Modern Library, 1937).

4.   Fred I. Greenstein, "The Psychological Functions of the Presidency for Citizens," in Elmer E. Cornwell (ed.), *The American Presidency: Vital Center* (Chicago: Scott, Foresman, 1966), pp. 30 - 36.

Watergate and the Resignation of Richard Nixon

5.   Robert Dahl, *Pluralist Democracy in the United States* (Chicago: Rand McNally, 1967), p. 136.

6.   John P. Roche, *Courts and Rights*, 2nd ed. (New York: Random House, 1966), pp. 121 - 122.

7.   See Lester Milbrath, *Political Participation: How and Why Do People Get Involved in Politics?* (Chicago: Rand McNally, 1965), pp. 19, 21.

8.   Herbert J. McClosky et al., "Issue Conflict and Consensus Among Party Leaders and Followers," *American Political Science Review*, 54 (June 1960), 425 - 426.

9.   Harold Lasswell and Daniel Lerner, *The Comparative Study of Elites* (Stanford, Calif.: Stanford University Press, 1952), p. 7.

10.   Gerald Pomper, *Elections in America: Control and Influence in Democratic Politics* (New York: Dodd, Mead, 1968), p. 254.

11.   Ibid., pp. 254 - 255.

12.   V. O. Key, Jr., *The Responsible Electorate* (Cambridge, Mass.: Harvard University Press, 1960).

13.   John Stuart Mill, *Considerations on Representative Government* (Chicago: Regnery, Gateway edition, 1962), p. 144.

14.   James David Barber, "Tone-Deaf in the Oval Office," *Saturday Review/World*, January 12, 1974, p. 14.

TESTING YOUR PERFORMANCE

Note to the Student.   The following questions are to test how well you achieved the Performance Objectives identified for you at the beginning of this chapter. The correct answers are supplied, accompanied by corresponding pages for you to review if you have answered incorrectly. The questions are coordinated numerically with the Performance Objectives at the beginning of the chapter. This exercise will assist you in determining the type of questions you have the most difficulty in answering (discussion, identification, explanation, definition, etc.) and will prepare you for test questions likely to be asked by your instructor.

1.   The legitimate use of physical force and the coverage of the whole of society rather than only segments of society are _____

_____ .

2.   (a) A belief that the state should be orderly, harmonious, and unified in purpose and values, and that the power of government should be unlimited and all-embracing is _____ .

(b) The belief that governmental power should be limited and controlled, suggesting that those who exercise governmental authority are limited in their use of authority by a higher law, is _____ .

3.   (a) The English political philosopher who discussed the idea of natural law and constitutional government in *Essay Concerning Human Understanding* and *Two Treatises on Civil Government* was _____ .

(b) Rights that are not derived from, or subject to, government but that derive from the nature of man himself and have an independent and unchanging existence are _____.

(c) The term used for a contract formed among men themselves to establish a government in order to better protect their natural rights, to maintain peace, and to protect themselves from foreign invasion is _____.

(d) John Locke identified the preservation and protection of the natural rights of the individual; the conformity of government to the law of nature and the inalienable rights to life, liberty, and property; the necessity of laws having the expressed or implied consent of the governed; equal application of laws to all; prohibition of arbitrary or oppressive laws; and the prohibition of taxation without the consent of the people or their representatives as _____.

4. (a) John Locke identified the inalienable rights of individuals as _____.

(b) Thomas Jefferson identified the inalienable rights of individuals as _____.

5. (a) Individual participation in the decisions that affect one's life exemplifies which meaning of democracy? _____

(b) The achievement of popular participation through majority rule and respect for the rights of minorities exemplifies which meaning of democracy?
_____

6. Beliefs in individual dignity and the equality of all men are the basic values underlying what kind of democracy? _____

7. Equality for all men before the law, political equality, and equality of opportunity encompassing education, employment, housing, recreation, and public accommodations represent _____.

8. (a) The term used by the Founding Fathers for representative, responsible, and nonhereditary government is _____.

(b) The term used for the idea that the government itself should be constructed so as to prevent the concentration of power is _____.

9. (a) The types of national government powers found in the Constitution itself are _____.

(b) The types of national government powers not explicitly listed in the Constitution but capable of being inferred from those that are listed are _____.

(c) The power to declare war and make peace, powers to prepare the way for the economic and commercial unity and stability of the nation, and the power to tax and spend for the common defense and general welfare are all _____.

10. The constitutional clause in Section 8 of Article I which became the basis for much of the ensuing expansion of the powers of the national government is _____.

11. Prohibitions against entering into relations with foreign states, coining money, creating any new legal tender for payment of debts, impairing obliga-

tions of contracts (passing laws which invalidate private agreements) are all ___
.

12. (a) A political system in which power is divided between two separate authorities (the nation and the states), each directly enforcing their own laws on individuals through their own courts is a _____
_____ .

(b) A political system in which the central government has legal authority to determine, alter, or abolish the power of the states is a _____
_____ .

(c) A political system in which the national government is dependent upon the states for power is a _____ .

13. The constitutional amendment which "reserves" to the states the power to protect and advance the public health, safety, welfare, or morals is the _____
_____ .

14. (a) The increase of federal spending in federal programs coupled with the inadequacy of state and local revenue systems contributed significantly to the increase of national power in states and communities. This federal spending occurred through use of _____ .

(b) Congressional standards accompanying federal grants-in-aid that must be adhered to if states and communities are to receive their federal money are called _____ .

15. The power which enables the national government to exercise important powers in areas originally "reserved" to the states is the _____
_____ .

16. (a) Enabling the states to provide necessary and desirable services they could not have afforded and helping to ensure that states and communities will not engage in racial discrimination in federally funded programs are both ___
_____ .

(b) The surrendering of powers to the national government in return for federal money, and the weakening of the role of states and communities in the American federal system are argued to be _____
_____ .

17. (a) The distributing of power to separate legislative, executive, and judicial branches, intended by the Founding Fathers as a bulwark against majoritarianism and an additional safeguard for liberty, is _____
_____ .

(b) The French writer whose *Spirit of the Laws* political textbook inspired the Founding Fathers was _____ .

(c) A series of essays by James Madison, Alexander Hamilton, and John Jay written to explain and defend the new U.S. Constitution during the struggle over its ratification was _____ .

18. Identify the four major decision-making bodies of the national government as conceived by the Founding Fathers:

(a) Chosen by the votes in each state; for two-year terms; must approve a bill for it to become law; can help override the president's veto; can help prescribe the number of judges and the jurisdiction of lower courts and make "exceptions" to the appellate jurisdiction of the Supreme Court. _____
.

(b) Chosen by the state legislatures; for six-year terms; must approve a bill for it to become law; can help override the president's veto; approves presidential treaties; can help prescribe the number of judges and the jurisdiction of lower courts and make "exceptions" to the appellate jurisdiction of the Supreme Court. _____

(c) Chosen by electors chosen by the states; for a four-year term; veto power over legislation; State of the Union address to Congress; can convene sessions of Congress; appointment power; treaty-making power; appoints justices of the Supreme Court. _____

(d) Chosen by the president and the Senate; for a life term; interprets the laws made by Congress. _____

19.   (a) The power of the U.S. Supreme Court to invalidate state laws and constitutions and congressional laws conflicting with the U.S. Constitution is

_____ .

(b) The U.S. Supreme Court case which established the precedent of judicial review was _____ .

(c) The chief justice of the U.S. Supreme Court who argued for judicial review was _____ .

20.   America's greater involvement in world affairs and the constant increase in the importance of military and foreign policy, the growth of the federal executive bureaucracy, and technological improvements in the mass media and the strengthening of the role of the president as party leader and molder of mass opinion are all _____

_____ .

21.   Simplifying the perception of government and politics by serving as the main cognitive handle for providing busy citizens with some sense of what their government is doing; providing an outlet for emotional expression through public interest in his and his family's private and public life; being a symbol of unity and nationhood; providing the masses with a vicarious means of taking political action in the sense that he can act decisively and effectively while they cannot do so; and being a symbol of social stability by providing the masses with a feeling of security and guidance were all classified by Fred Greenstein as _____

_____ .

22.   (a) Responding to proposals from the president, executive agencies, and interest groups by deliberating, and accepting, modifying, or rejecting the policies initiated by others is the role of _____ .

(b) Levying taxes, borrowing and spending money, regulating interstate and foreign commerce, coining money, declaring war, maintaining armies and navies, passing laws necessary and proper to carry out these duties, and admitting new states are all _____ .

23.   (a) Serving as the final bulwark against mass threats to principle and property is the role of the _____ .

(b) The reason the Founding Fathers allowed decisions of the president and Congress to be set aside by federal courts was _____

_____ .

(c) The Supreme Court which acted as the bastion of conservatism, attacked the economic program of the New Deal, and expressed the elite philosophy of rugged individualism was the _____ .

(d) The Supreme Court which was concerned for the underprivileged in America and had a liberal orientation toward equality of the law, church-state relations, and individual rights before the law was the _____

_____ .

24. (a) The primary form of political participation is _____ .
    (b) The two decisions an individual must make regarding voting are

_____ .

25. Identify the following amendments which circumscribed voting laws in the states:
    (a) No denial of voting because of race. _____

_____

    (b) No denial of voting because of sex. _____

_____

    (c) No poll taxes in federal elections. _____

_____

    (d) No denial of voting to persons 18 or over. _____

_____

    Identify the following congressional acts which circumscribed voting laws in the states:
    (e) No discrimination in the application of voter registration laws. __

_____

    (f) Attorney general may replace local voting officials with federal examiners on evidence of voter discrimination in southern states. _____

_____

    (g) No denial of voting to persons 18 or over, no residency requirements in national elections and no literacy tests. _____

_____

26. (a) Disclosing the coalition of interests and the policy views a candidate has generally associated himself with is the role of the _____ .
    (b) Limiting the choice of candidates for public office, helping to define the major problems and issues confronting society, and making criticisms of government legitimate and effective are all _____

_____ .

    (c) The political party system in which totalitarian parties compete with democratic parties, Fascists compete with Communists, and capitalist parties compete with socialist parties is the _____ .
    (d) The political party system in which the two main parties both accept and strongly support constitutional government, their policies reflect the same cultural values, and both tend to take moderate stands that will encompass the views of the largest number of voters is the _____

_____ .

27. Examining differences in the coalitions of voters supporting each party, examining differences in the policy views of the leaders in each party, and examining differences in the voting records of the congressmen of each party are three ways of _____

_____ .

28. (a) The single most important factor influencing voter decisions is _____

_____ .

    (b) Party identification is primarily acquired from an individual's _____

_____ .

29. (a) Racial unrest and violence, the approval and encouragement of violence in the form of mass protest, defeat and humiliation in war, counterelite violence, and attacks from the press which went beyond the established "rules of the game" are all _____

_____ .

(b) The Watergate break-in differed from repressive activities of previous presidential administrations such as the Alien and Sedition Acts of the John Adams administration or the "loyalty and security" programs of the Truman and Eisenhower administrations by using repressive tactics against

30. (a) The right of the president to withhold information, documents, or testimony from either the Congress or the courts if, in the opinion of the president, it is necessary to do so in the interest of national security or the proper functioning of the executive is _____ .

(b) The Supreme Court case which established the power of the courts to review the actions of other branches of government was _____ _____ .

(c) The Supreme Court in *The United States* v. *Richard M. Nixon* restricted the president's power of executive privilege by denying that it applied to _____ cases or that the president could refuse judges access to information in order to determine for themselves whether such information applied to _____ cases.

Correct Responses

1. Distinguishing factors of governmental power (p. 187).

2. (a) Totalitarianism (p. 190); (b) Constitutionalism (p. 190).

3. (a) John Locke (pp. 190 - 191); (b) Natural rights (p. 190); (c) Social contract (p. 191); (d) Primary features of constitutional government (p. 191).

4. (a) Life, liberty, and property (p. 191); (b) Life, liberty, and the pursuit of happiness (p. 191).

5. (a) Ideal meaning (p. 192); (b) Procedural meaning (p. 193).

6. Classic democracy (p. 192).

7. Ideas about equality in America (p. 192).

8. (a) Republican government (p. 193); (b) Limited government (pp. 193 - 194).

9. (a) Expressed (delegated) powers (p. 194); (b) Implied Powers (p. 194); (c) Powers expressly given to the national government and to Congress (pp. 194 - 197).

10. Necessary and proper clause (p. 197).

11. Constitutional restrictions on states' powers (pp. 197 - 198).

12. (a) Federal political system (p. 198); (b) Unitary political system (p. 198); (c) Confederation (p. 198).

13. Tenth Amendment (p. 198).

14. (a) Grants-in-aid (p. 198); (b) Guidelines (p. 199).

15. Power to tax and spend for the general welfare (p. 200).

16. (a) Good effects of federal aid (p. 200); (b) Bad effects of federal aid (p. 200).

17. (a) Separation of powers (p. 200); (b) Montesquieu (p. 200); (c) *The Federalist papers* (p. 200).

18.　(a) House of Representatives (pp. 201 - 202); (b) Senate (pp. 201 - 202); (c) President (pp. 201 - 202); (d) Supreme Court (pp. 201 - 202).

19.　(a) Judicial review (p. 202); (b) *Marbury* v. *Madison* (p. 202); (c) John Marshall (p. 202).

20.　Factors contributing to the increased powers of the president in the twentieth century (pp. 203 - 204).

21.　The psychological functions of the presidency (p. 204).

22.　(a) Congress (p. 205); (b) Constitutional powers of Congress (p. 205).

23.　(a) Federal courts (p. 206); (b) Distrust of both popular majorities and elected officials influenced by them (p. 207); (c) Supreme Court of the 1930s (pp. 207 - 208); (d) Warren Court of the 1960s (p. 208).

24.　(a) Voting (p. 210); (b) Whether to vote and whom to vote for (p. 210).

25.　(a) Fifteenth Amendment (p. 211); (b) Nineteenth Amendment (p. 211); (c) Twenty-fourth Amendment (p. 211); (d) Twenty-sixth Amendment (p. 211); (e) Civil Rights Act of 1964 (p. 211); (f) Voting Rights Act of 1965 (p. 211); (g) Voting Rights Act of 1970 (p. 211).

26.　(a) Party label (p. 212); (b) Functions of political parties (p. 212); (c) European political party system (p. 212); (d) American political party system (p. 212).

27.　Discerning the difference between the Democratic and Republican parties (pp. 213 - 215).

28.　(a) Party identification (p. 215); (b) Parents (p. 216).

29.　(a) Conditions prompting elites to resort to repressive measures (p. 221); (b) Another segment of the nations established leadership (p. 221).

30.　(a) Executive privilege (p. 225); (b) *Marbury* v. *Madison* (p. 225); (c) Criminal (p. 225).

KEY TERMS

political philosophy

totalitarianism

constitutionalism

natural law

Essay Concerning Human Understanding

Two Treatises on Civil Government

John Locke

social contract

equality before the law

political equality

equality of opportunity

sovereignty

tyranny of the majority

republican government

limited government

expressed (delegated) powers

implied powers

necessary and proper clause

federalism

unitary political system

confederation of states

Brown v. *Board of Education of Topeka*, 1954

Civil Rights Act of 1964

Voting Rights Act of 1965

Fair Housing Act of 1968

grants-in-aid

federal guidelines

separation of powers

The Federalist papers

checks and balances

judicial review

Marbury v. *Madison*, 1803

Budget and Accounting Act of 1921

The Federalist, Number 78

national supremacy clause

Twenty-sixth Amendment

Voting Rights Act of 1970

The Pentagon Papers

executive privilege

criminal cases

United States v. *Richard M. Nixon*

DISCUSSION QUESTIONS

1. Contrast totalitarianism and constitutionalism.

2. Discuss the meaning of democracy:
   (a) Ideal meaning
   (b) Procedural meaning
   (c) Values

3. Discuss the reasons why the Founding Fathers favored:
   (a) Republican government
   (b) Limited government
   (c) Strong national government
   (d) Necessary and proper clause
   (e) Congressional power to declare war and make peace
   (f) Congressional power to regulate commerce
   (g) Congressional power to tax and spend for the common defense and general welfare
   (h) Restrictions on the powers of states
   (i) A system of separated powers

4. Contrast expressed (delegated) powers and implied powers.

5. Compare and contrast authority in the following types of political systems:
   (a) Unitary
   (b) Federal
   (c) Confederation of states

6. The federal government has vastly expanded its power over states and communities by use of *grants-in-aid*. Discuss:
   (a) How and why they began
   (b) Guidelines
   (c) Good effects (advantages)
   (d) Bad effects (disadvantages)

7. Contrast presidential power, congressional power, and judicial power with regard to:
    (a) Roles
    (b) Contributing factors to the expansion or decreasing of power
    (c) Effects of public opinion on each
    (d) Primary areas of decision-making

8. Discuss participation and nonparticipation in democracy:
    (a) Who participates?
    (b) What are the possible ways of participating (activities to participate in)? Which are most common?
    (c) Which amendments and congressional acts have been passed to remove obstacles to citizen participation through voting?

9. Discuss the American political party system:
    (a) The functions political parties and the party label perform for the voter
    (b) In comparison with European political party systems
    (c) Ways of discerning differences between them
    (d) Factors affecting a voter's party participation

SUGGESTED READINGS

PETER BACHRACH, *The Theory of Democratic Elitism* (Boston: Little, Brown, 1967).

STUART G. BROWN, *The American Presidency* (New York: Macmillan, 1966).

THOMAS R. DYE and HARMON ZIEGLER, *The Irony of Democracy: An Uncommon Introduction to American Politics* (Belmont, Calif.: Wadsworth, 1969).

SAMUEL KRISLOV, *The Supreme Court in the Political Process* (New York: Macmillan, 1965).

LESTER W. MILBRATH, *Political Participation* (Chicago: Rand McNally, 1965).

NEW YORK TIMES, *The Pentagon Papers* (New York: New York Times, 1971).

NELSON W. POLSBY and AARON B. WILDAVSKY, *Presidential Elections: Strategies in American Politics* (New York: Scribner, 1968).

GERALD M. POMPER, *Elections in America* (New York: Dodd, Mead, 1968).

CLINTON ROSSITER, *1787: The Grand Convention* (New York: Macmillan, 1966).

FRANK J. SORAUF, *Party Politics in America* (Boston: Little, Brown, 1972).

CHAPTER 7

Power and History

PERFORMANCE OBJECTIVES

The student should be able to:

1. Define history from two perspectives.

2. Describe the necessary bias of all historians.

3. Compare and contrast the theories of history as derived by Hegel, Marx, Spengler, and Toynbee.

4. Contrast the *"great man" explanation* of history with the *institutional explanation,* with Frederick Jackson Turner's *western frontier explanation,* and with Richard Hofstadter's *incrementalism explanation.*

5. Outline the findings of Charles Beard in *An Economic Interpretation of the Constitution.* Describe the method he used to study history. Cite the most important enumerated power that enabled the national government to end its dependence upon the states. Trace the reasoning of the Founding Fathers regarding other national governmental powers.

6. List the criticisms of Beard's interpretation of history.

7. Compare and contrast Beard and Frederick Jackson Turner's interpretations of the significant events in American history.

8. Contrast the interests and economics of northern elites with those of southern elites. Describe how the Missouri Compromise of 1820, the Compromise of 1850, and the Kansas-Nebraska Act of 1854 sought to keep American elites united.

9. Identify the areas of agreement between northern and southern elites. Describe how Lincoln's Emancipation Proclamation was a *conservative action* rather than a revolutionary action.

10. Identify the importance of the Civil War for America's power structure. Explain how the philosophy of the social Darwinists fitted the new industrial elite. Describe the effects the industrialists had on Congress.

238

11. Contrast the "rugged individualism" elite of pre-Depression days with the "liberal establishment" elite of the New Deal era. Identify the U.S. president responsible for ushering in a new era in American elite philosophy.

12. Outline and contrast the earlier historical interpretation of the black experience in America during the Reconstruction era with the more recent interpretation by historian C. Vann Woodward.

HISTORY AND SOCIAL SCIENCE

Can history inform the social sciences about the nature and uses of power in society? The purpose of this chapter is not to teach American history but rather to examine the work of historians to see what contribution they can make to our understanding of power.

History really has two meanings: History may refer to all past human actions and events, or it may refer to the recording, narrating, and interpreting of these events by historians. History includes the discovery of facts about past events, as well as the interpretation of these events. Many historians contend that their primary responsibility is the disclosure of facts about the past: the accurate presentation of what actually happened, unbiased by interpretive theories or philosophies.

But however carefully the historian tries to avoid bias, he cannot report *all* the facts of human history. Facts do not select and arrange themselves. The historian must select and organize facts which are worthy of interest, and this process involves personal judgment of what is important about the past. The historian's judgment about the past is affected by present conditions and by his own feelings about the future. So the past is continually reinterpreted by each generation of historians. History is "an unending dialogue" between the present and the past; it is "what one age finds worthy of note in another."

Yet most historians view their task primarily as one of determining and reporting what happened. They leave it to other social scientists to explain why men behave as they do. This division of labor between history and social science does not always work out. In selecting and organizing their facts historians must consider the causes of wars and revolutions, the reasons for the rise and fall of civilizations, the consequences of great events and ideas. They cannot marshal their facts without some notion of interrelations among human events. Since they must consider what forces have operated to shape the past, they become involved in economics, sociology, psychology, anthropology, and political science. Historian Henry Steele Commager has observed, "No self-respecting modern historian is content merely with recording what happened; he wants to explain why it happened."[1] Thus, history and social science are intimately related.

What is fact

THEORIES OF HISTORY:
HEGEL, MARX, SPENGLER, TOYNBEE

Some historians have claimed to perceive patterns in the course of human events. From these patterns they have developed theories of history which enable them to interpret great historical movements over time and even predict the flow of future events. Many other historians condemn theories of history as illusions; they deny that there are any universal patterns in man's history. But the temptation to construct theories has attracted many scholars to the task.

For example, the German philosopher Hegel believed that the history of man was explained by the development of human ideals. Every society expressed some ideal in the form of its politics, social life, family life, religion, art, etc. This historical evolution occurs in a "dialectical" fashion: each idea (thesis) contains within itself its own contradiction (antithesis), and the conflict gives rise to a new and higher ideal (synthesis). The dialectical process occurs in civilizations as well as men's minds. Hegel believed that historical change was the result of the growth of ideas and that culture was the expression or embodiment of the ideas.

Marx agreed with Hegel on the dialectic of history but differed profoundly over the moving force in the process. To Hegel the moving force of history was ideological whereas Marx was convinced it was material—the mode of production. According to Marx, history is determined by the mode of production:

> The materialist conception of history starts from the proposition that the production of the means to support human life, and, next to production, the exchange of things produced, is the basis of all social structure, that in every society that has appeared in history, the manner in which wealth is distributed, and society divided into classes or orders, is dependent upon what is produced, how it is produced, and how the products are exchanged. From this point of view, the final causes of all social changes and political revolutions are to be sought, not in men's brains, not in man's better insight into external truth and justice, but in changes in the modes of production and exchange.[2]

Both Hegel and Marx believed in the inevitability of progress. Hegel was an idealist and Marx a materialist, but both believed in continuous human progress over time.

The twentieth century has brought war, death, and destruction to human civilization on a scale unprecedented in any previous era of human history. Hence it is difficult to maintain optimism and faith in the historical progress of mankind. Theories of history which stressed continuous human progress have given way to more cyclical theories—encompassing the decay and death of civilizations as well as their birth and growth.

Oswald Spengler's the *Decline of the West* presents a theory of history in which cultures pass through four cycles: springtime, summer, autumn, and winter. Each great civilization lives about a thousand years and follows the same cyclical course. During the springtime of a culture, new myths and values are created which inspire philosophy, science, politics, religion, and art. During its summer, the culture spreads its influence and realizes the full potential of its values and myths; in this period it builds its great architecture and develops its science and mathematics. The autumn brings a questioning of old values and myths. Social cohesion begins to break down, and there is a growth of rationalism and individualism. While this is a creative period for new ideas and philosophies, nonetheless, the initial spirit that inspired the culture fades, old values are lost, and the civilization dies.

Spengler described the rise and fall of eight great cultures: Egypt, Babylonia, India, China, the Maya culture, Greek and Roman civilization, the Arabian culture, and western Europe. Our own Western culture, begun about the year 1000, is declining and approaching death. In this decline, old elites and old values are overthrown in the name of reason, and above all in the name of "the people." Mass rule has replaced the ordered society.

Another important history of the rise and fall of civilizations is Arnold Toynbee's *Study of History.* Toynbee also perceived a cyclical pattern in the rise and fall of great cultures, but he saw more overall progress than Spengler. Each succeeding civilization can learn from the experiences, values, and myths of earlier civilizations; therefore each succeeding civilization is a little richer in culture than the one preceding it. Toynbee described 21 civilizations. Each went through similar stages of growth, maturation, breakdown, and disintegration. Toynbee agreed with Spengler that our own civilization is passing into a period of decline and disintegration.

According to Toynbee, great civilizations emerge as successful, adaptive response to great challenges. The initial challenge is one of overcoming the physical environment, but later challenges may include outside invasion, or industrialization, or revolution. The challenges must be rigorous enough to spur men to surmount them but not so severe as to overcome a civilization. The best type of challenge is one that evokes an adaptive and creative response. Frequently this response is a dynamic new religion, and new religions often form the foundations of new civilizations.

Toynbee did not accept the idea that civilizations must follow a preordained life cycle and age and die in the fashion of an organism. Instead, civilizations decline when they finally confront a challenge they cannot meet. Disintegration occurs when a civilization loses its adaptive power, its self-determination, its creative leaders. No longer able to cope with the next great challenge, it splits into warring factions and disintegrates in a "time of troubles."

Interesting as those theories may seem, for the most part contemporary American historians avoid overarching theories of history. They search for explanations, but not in terms of grand generalities or laws or theories of history. A quotation from the preface of H. A. L. Fisher's *History of Europe* has become something of a classic in expressing the contemporary disillusionment with theories of history:

> One intellectual excitement has been denied me. Men wiser and more learned than I have discovered in history a plot, a rhythm, a pre-determined pattern. These harmonies are concealed from me. I can see only one emergency following upon another as wave follows upon wave; only one great fact with respect to which, since it is unique, there can be no generalizations; only one safe rule for the historian: that he should recognize in the development of human destinies the play of the contingent and the unforeseen.[3]

POWER, CHANGE, AND THE AMERICAN EXPERIENCE

There is a great temptation to romanticize national history. Many national histories are self-congratulating, patriotic exercises. Many historical biographies paint their subjects as larger-than-life figures, free of the foibles of common men, who shape the course of events themselves rather than merely respond to the world in which they live. National leaders of the past—Washington, Jefferson, Jackson, Lincoln—are portrayed as noble men, superior in character and wisdom to today's politicians. Even with the myth of the cherry tree discarded, generations of historians have looked with awe upon the gallery of national heroes from George Washington through Abraham Lincoln to Franklin D. Roosevelt as almost superhuman individuals who saved the nation.

Some national histories do not rely on "great man" explanations but instead emphasize the origin and growth of governmental institutions. Democracy is traced from its ancient Greek beginnings, through English constitutional development, to the colonies and the American constitutional system. Frequently these national histories reinforce reverence for existing political and governmental institutions. Some are written more to support than to explain America.

In the 1890s historian Frederick Jackson Turner argued that the main influence on American history was not the development of political institutions from English or Greek origins, or even the actions of "great men," but the impact of the western frontier upon American society. As historians explained (and occasionally exaggerated) Turner's thesis, they wrote new and even more nationalistic sagas of the American expansion. They hailed western settlement, the Indian wars, the development of transportation and communication, and the rugged individualism of the heroic democratic frontiersman.

But historians have also been critical of American institutions. At the beginning of the twentieth century the reform politicians and the muckraking jour-

A wagon train assembles at a Missouri River port to begin the 2000 mile trek across the western frontier. In 1893 Frederick Jackson Turner postulated his famous frontier thesis that American political institutions were a unique result of the nation's frontier experience. *Courtesy of the Boston Public Library*

nalists brought a new iconoclasm to the scene. The Progressive era was critical of the malfunctioning of many governmental institutions which had become sacred over time—and even of the Olympian position of the Founding Fathers. In 1913 Charles A. Beard created an uproar by suggesting that economic motives played a part in leading the Founding Fathers to write the Constitution.

Nevertheless, for the most part the quest for the American past has been carried on in a spirit of sentiment and nostalgia, rather than critical analysis. Historical novels, fictionalized biographies, pictorial collections, books on American regions all appeal to our fondness for looking back to what we believe was a better era. Americans have a peculiar longing to recapture the past, to try to recover what seems to have been lost.

Our own bias about the importance of power in society leads us to focus attention on *changing sources of power over time* in American history, and the characteristics of men and groups who have acquired power. We shall contend that the Constitution itself, and the national government which it established, reflected the beliefs, values, and interests of the men of power—the elite—of the new republic. Truly to understand the Constitution it is necessary to investigate the political interests of the Founding Fathers and the historical circumstances surrounding the Philadelphia Convention in 1787.

Power structures change over time. To understand power in society we have to explore the historical development of power relationships. Any society, in order to maintain stability and avoid revolution, must provide opportunities for talented and ambitious individuals to acquire power. As new sources of wealth were opened in an expanding economy, power in America shifted to those groups and individuals who acquired the new economic resources. Western expansion and settlement, industrialization, immigration, urbanization, technological innovation, and new sources of wealth all create new bases of power and new power holders.

But power in America has changed slowly, without any serious break in the ideas and values underlying the American political and economic system. The nation has never experienced a true revolution, in which national leadership is formally replaced by groups or individuals who do not share the values of the system itself. Instead, changes have been slow and incremental. New national leaders have generally accepted the national consensus about private enterprise, limited government, and individualism.

Historian Richard Hofstadter argues effectively that many accounts of the American past overemphasize the political differences in every era:

> The fierceness of the political struggles has often been misleading; for the range of vision embraced by the primary contestants in the major parties has always been bounded by the horizons of property and enterprise. However much at odds on specific issues, the major political traditions have shared a belief in the rights of property, the philosophy of economic individualism, the value of competition; they have accepted the economic virtues of capitalist culture as necessary qualities of man. Even when some property right has been challenged—as it was by followers of Jefferson and Jackson—in the name of the rights of man or the rights of the community, the challenge, when translated into practical policy, has actually been urged on behalf of some other kind of property.
>
> The sanctity of private property, the right of the individual to dispose of and invest it, the value of opportunity, and the natural evolution of self-interest and self-assertion, within broad legal limits, into a beneficent social order have been staple tenets of the central faith in American political ideologies; these conceptions have been shared in large part by men as diverse as Jefferson, Jackson, Lincoln, Cleveland, Bryan, Wilson, and Hoover.[4]

Over the years, America's political leadership has been essentially conservative. Whatever the popular label of the American political and economic system—Federalist, Democrat, Whig, Republican, Progressive, Conservative, or Liberal—American leaders have remained committed to the same values and ideas that motivated the Founding Fathers. While it is true that major changes in public policy and in the structure of American government have taken place over two centuries, these changes have been *incremental* rather than revolutionary.

CHARLES BEARD and the Economic Interpretation of the Constitution

Charles Beard, historian and political scientist, has provided the most controversial historical interpretation of the origin of American national government in his landmark book *An Economic Interpretation of the Constitution*. Not
all historians agree with Beard's interpretation—particularly his emphasis on
economic forces—but all concede that it is a milestone in understanding the
American Constitution. From an analysis of the economic interests of the
Founding Fathers Beard drew the following conclusions:

> The movement for the Constitution of the United States was originated and
> carried through principally by four groups of personalty interests which had been
> adversely affected under the Articles of Confederation: money, public securities,
> manufactures, and trade and shipping.
>
> The first firm steps toward the formation of the Constitution were taken by a
> small and active group of men immediately interested through their personal
> possessions in the outcome of their labors.
>
> No popular vote was taken directly or indirectly on the proposition to call the
> Convention which drafted the Constitution.
>
> A large propertyless mass was, under the prevailing suffrage qualifications, ex-
> cluded at the outset from participation (through representatives) in the work of
> framing the Constitution.
>
> The members of the Philadelphia Convention which drafted the Constitution
> were, with a few exceptions, immediately, directly, and personally interested in,
> and derived economic advantages from, the establishment of the new system.
>
> The Constitution was essentially an economic document based upon the concept
> that the fundamental private rights of property are anterior to government and
> morally beyond the reach of popular majorities.
>
> The major portion of the members of the Convention are on record as recogniz-
> ing the claim of property to a special and defensive position in the Constitution.[5]

Beard argued that to understand the Constitution we must understand the
economic interests of the national elite which included the writers of the
document:

> Did the men who formulated the fundamental law of the land possess the kinds of
> property which were immediately and directly increased in value or made more
> secure by the results of their labors in Philadelphia? Did they have money at in-
> terest [loans outstanding]? Did they own public securities [government bonds]?
> Did they hold Western lands for appreciation? Were they interested in shipping
> and manufactures? [6]

Beard was *not* charging that the Founding Fathers wrote the Constitution ex-

Charles Beard

While the rhetoric of the Founding Fathers portrayed America as a society without the marked class distinctions of Europe, in reality this was not quite true, as this woodcut of an early nineteenth century dinner suggests. In his *Economic Interpretation of the Constitution* Charles Beard showed how the drafting of the Constitution was affected by the upper class economic interest of its authors. *The Bettmann Archive*

clusively for their own benefit. But he argued that they personally benefited immediately from its adoption, and they did not act only "under the guidance of abstract principles of political science." Beard closely studied old unpublished financial records of the U.S. Treasury Department and the personal letters and financial accounts of the 55 delegates to the Philadelphia Convention. Table 7-1 summarizes his findings of the financial interests of the Founding Fathers. Then Beard turned to an examination of the Constitution itself, *in the original form in which it emerged from the Convention,* to observe the relationship between economic interests and political power. There are 17 specific grants of power to Congress in Article I, Section 8, followed by a general grant of power to make "all laws which shall be necessary and proper for carrying into execution the foregoing powers." The first and perhaps the most important enumerated power is the power to "lay and collect taxes, duties, imposts, and excises." The *taxing power* is, of course, the basis of all other powers, and it enabled the national government to end its dependence upon the states. The taxing power was essential to the holders of public securities, particularly when it was combined with the provision in Article VI that "All debts contracted and engagements entered into before the adoption of this Constitution shall be as valid against the United

Charles Beard

States under this Constitution as under the Confederation." This meant that the national government would be obliged to pay off all those investors who held bonds of the United States, and the taxing power would give the national government the ability to do so on its own.

Congress was also given the power to "regulate commerce with foreign nations, and among the several States." The *interstate commerce clause*, together with the provision in Article I, Section 9, prohibiting the states from taxing exports, created a free trade area over the 13 states. In *The Federalist*, No. 11, Hamilton describes the advantages of this arrangement for American merchants:

> The speculative trader will at once perceive the force of these observations and will acknowledge that the aggregate balance of the commerce of the United States would bid fair to be much more favorable than that of the thirteen states without union or with partial unions.

Following the power to tax and spend, to borrow money, and to regulate commerce in Article I, there is a series of *specific powers designed to enable Congress to protect money and property*. Congress is given the power to make bankruptcy laws, to coin money and regulate its value, to fix standards of weights and measures, to punish counterfeiting, to establish post offices and post roads, to pass copyright and patent laws to protect authors and inventors, and to punish piracies and felonies committed on the high seas. Each of these powers is a specific asset to bankers, investors, merchants, authors, inventors, and shippers. Obviously, the Founding Fathers felt that giving Congress control over currency and credit in America would result in better protection for financial interests than would leaving this essential responsibility to the states. Likewise, control over communication and transportation ("post offices and post roads") was believed to be too essential to trade and commerce to be left to the states.

All of the other powers in Article I deal with *military affairs*—raising and supporting armies, organizing, training, and calling upon the state militia, declaring war, suppressing insurrections, and repelling invasions. These powers in Article I, together with the provisions in Article II making the president the commander in chief of the army and navy and of the state militia when called into the federal service, and the power of the president to make treaties with the advice and consent of the Senate and to send and receive ambassadors, all combined to centralize diplomatic and military affairs at the national level. The centralization of diplomatic-military power is confirmed in Article I, Section 10, in which the states are specifically prohibited from entering into treaties with foreign nations, maintaining ships of war, or engaging in war unless actually invaded. It is clear that the Founding Fathers had little confidence in the state

Charles Beard

TABLE 7-1. Founding Fathers Classified by Known Economic Interests

| Public Security Interests | | Real Estate and |
Major	Minor	Land Speculation
Baldwin	Bassett	Blount
Blair	Blount	Dayton
Clymer	Brearley	Few
Dayton	Broom	FitzSimons
Ellsworth	Butler	Franklin
FitzSimons	Carroll	Gerry
Gerry	Few	Gilman
Gilman	Hamilton	Gorham
Gorham	L. Martin	Hamilton
Jenifer	Mason	Mason
Johnson	Mercer	R. Morris
King	Mifflin	Washington
Langdon	Read	Williamson
Lansing	Spaight	Wilson
Livingston	Wilson	
McClurg	Wythe	
R. Morris		
C. C. Pinckney		
C. Pinckney		
Randolph		
Sherman		
Strong		
Washington		
Williamson		

militia, particularly when it was under state control. Moreover, if western settlers were to be protected from the Indians, and if the British were to be persuaded to give up their forts in Ohio and open the way to American westward expansion, the national government could not rely upon state militia but must instead have an army of its own. Similarly, a strong navy was essential to the protection of American commerce on the seas (the first significant naval action under the new government was against the piracy of the Barbary States). Thus, a national army and navy were not so much for protection against invasion (for many years the national government would continue to rely primarily upon state militia for this purpose), but rather for the protection and promotion of its commercial and territorial ambitions.

Protection against domestic insurrection also appealed to the southern slaveholders' deep-seated fear of a slave revolt. The Constitution permitted Congress to outlaw the *importation of slaves* after the year 1808. But most of the southern planters were more interested in protecting their existing property and slaves than they were in extending the slave trade, and the Constitution provided an explicit advantage to slaveholders in Article IV, Section 2:

Charles Beard

Lending and Investments	Mercantile, Manufacturing and Shipping	Planters and Slaveholders
Bassett	Broom	Butler
Broom	Clymer	Davie
Butler	Ellsworth	Jenifer
Carroll	FitzSimons	A. Martin
Clymer	Gerry	L. Martin
Davie	King	Mason
Dickinson	Langdon	Mercer
Ellsworth	McHenry	C. C. Pinckney
Few	Mifflin	C. Pinckney
FitzSimons	G. Morris	Randolph
Franklin	R. Morris	Read
Gilman		Rutledge
Ingersoll		Spaight
Johnson		Washington
King		Wythe
Langdon		
Mason		
McHenry		
C. C. Pinckney		
C. Pinckney		
Randolph		
Read		
Washington		
Williamson		

No person held to service or labor in one State, under the laws thereof, escaping into another, shall, in consequence of any law or regulation therein, be discharged from such service or labor, but shall be delivered up on claim of the party to whom such service or labor may be due.

This was an extremely valuable protection for one of the most important forms of property in America at the time. The slave trade lapsed after 20 years, but slavery as a domestic institution was better safeguarded under the new Constitution than under the Articles of Confederation.

The *restrictions placed upon state legislatures* by the Constitution also provided protection to economic elites in the new nation. States were not allowed to coin money, issue paper money, or pass legal tender laws that would make any money other than gold or silver coin tender in the payments of debts. This restriction would prevent the states from issuing cheap paper money, which could be used by debtors to pay off their creditors with less valuable currency.

The Constitution also forbids states to pass any law "impairing the obligation

Charles Beard

of contracts." The structure of business relations in a free enterprise economy depends upon government enforcement of private contracts, and it is essential to economic elites that the government be prevented from relieving persons from their obligations to contracts. If state legislatures could relieve debtors of their contractual obligations, or relieve indentured servants from their obligations to their masters, or prevent creditors from foreclosing on mortgages, or declare moratoriums on debt, or otherwise interfere with business obligations, the interests of investors, merchants, and creditors would be seriously damaged.

Historians disagree with Beard's emphasis on the economic motives of the Founding Fathers. For example: "The Constitution was adopted in a society which was fundamentally democratic, not undemocratic; and it was adopted by people who were primarily middle-class property owners, especially farmers who owned realty, not just by the owners of personalty."[7] And: "The Constitution was not just an economic document, although economic factors were undoubtedly important. Since most of the people were middle-class and had private property, practically everybody was interested in the protection of property."[8] Moreover, in the struggle over ratification it is clear that men of prestige, reputation, and property can be found on both sides of the question of accepting the new Constitution. Influential "Anti-Federalists" deplored the undemocratic features of the Constitution, and their criticism about the omission of a Bill of Rights led directly to the inclusion of the first ten amendments. Supporters of the Constitution were forced to retreat from their demand for unconditional ratification and they agreed to add a Bill of Rights as amendments as soon as the first Congress was convened under the Constitution.

FREDERICK JACKSON TURNER
AND THE RISE OF THE WEST

Power relationships change over time. Industrialization, urbanization, technological change, and new sources of wealth create new bases of power and new power holders. The governmental structure of society must provide for changes in the distribution of power or suffer the threat of instability and even revolution. The political system must provide for the "circulation of elites" as new bases of power and new power holders emerge in society.

According to historian Frederick Jackson Turner, "The rise of the New West was the most significant fact in American history.[9] Certainly the American West had a profound impact on the political system of the new nation. People went west because of the vast wealth of fertile lands that awaited them there; nowhere else in the world could one acquire wealth so quickly. Because aristocratic families of the eastern seaboard seldom had reason to migrate

Charles Beard

One of the significant aspects of the economic boom in the West was the sale of land. This picture portrays the first real estate office in Minneapolis in 1857. *Minnesota Historical Society*

westward, the western settlers were mainly middle or lower class immigrants. With hard work and good fortune, a penniless migrant could become a rich plantation owner or cattle rancher in a single generation. Thus, the West meant rapid upward social mobility.

New elites arose in the West and had to be assimilated into America's governing circles. This assimilation had a profound effect on the character of America's elites. No one exemplifies the new entrants better than Andrew Jackson. Jackson's victory in the presidential election of 1828 was not a victory of the common man over the propertied classes but a victory of the new western elites over established Republican leadership in the East. It forced the established elites to recognize the growing importance of the West and to open their ranks to the new rich who were settled west of the Alleghenies.

Since Jackson was a favorite of the people, it was easy for him to believe in the wisdom of the common man. But "Jacksonian democracy" was by no means a philosophy of leveling equalitarianism. The ideal of the frontier society was the self-made man, and wealth and power won by competitive skill were much admired. What offended the frontiersmen was wealth and power obtained through special privilege. They believed in a *natural aristocracy*, rather than an aristocracy by birth, education, or special privilege. It was *not* absolute equality that Jacksonians demanded but a more open elite system—a greater opportunity for the rising middle class to acquire wealth and influence through competition.

In their struggle to open America's elite system, the Jacksonians appealed to mass sentiment. Jackson's humble beginnings, his image as a self-made man, his military adventures, his frontier experience, and his rough, brawling style endeared him to the masses. As beneficiaries of popular support, the new elites of the West developed a strong faith in the wisdom and justice of popular decisions. All of the new western states that entered the Union granted universal white male suffrage, and gradually the older states fell into step. Rising elites, themselves often less than a generation away from the masses, saw in a widened electorate a chance for personal advancement that they could never have achieved under the old regime. Therefore, the Jacksonians became noisy and effective advocates of the principle that all men should have the right to vote and that no restrictions should be placed upon officeholding. They also launched a successful attack upon the congressional caucus system on nominating presidential candidates. Having been defeated in Congress in 1824, Jackson wished to sever Congress from the nominating process. In 1832, when the Democrats held their first national convention, Andrew Jackson was renominated by acclamation.

Jacksonian democracy also brought changes in the method of selecting presidential electors. The Constitution left to the various state legislatures the right to decide how presidential electors should be chosen, and in most cases the legislatures themselves chose the electors. But after 1832 all states elected their presidential electors by popular vote. In most states the people voted for electors who were listed under the name of their party and their candidate.

THE CIVIL WAR AND ELITE CLEAVAGE

Social scientists can gain insight into societal conflict and the breakdown of elite consensus through the study of history—particularly the Civil War period. America's elites were in substantial agreement about the character and direction of the new nation during its first 60 years. In the 1850s, however, the role of blacks in American society—the most divisive issue in the history of American politics—became an urgent question that drove a wedge between elites and ultimately led to the nation's bloodiest war. The political system was unequal to the task of negotiating a peaceful settlement to the problem of slavery because America's elites were themselves deeply divided over the question.

It was the white elites and not the white masses of the South who had an interest in the slave and cotton culture. On the eve of the Civil War probably not more than 400,000 southern families—approximately one in four—held slaves. And many of these families held only one or two slaves each. The number of great planters—men who owned 50 or more slaves and large holdings of land—was probably not more than 7,000. Yet the views of these men dominated southern politics.

The northern elites consisted in merchants and manufacturers who depended upon free labor. However, northern elites had no direct interest in the abolition of slavery in the South. Some northern manufacturers were making good profits from southern trade, and with higher tariffs they stood a chance to make even better profits. Abolitionist activities imperiled trade relations between North and South and were often looked upon with irritation even in northern social circles. But both northern and southern elites realized that control of the West was the key to future dominance of the nation. Northern elites wanted a West composed of small farmers who produced food and raw materials for the industrial and commercial East and provided a market for eastern goods. Southern planters feared the voting power of a West composed of small farmers and wanted western lands for the expansion of the cotton and slave culture. Cotton ate up the land and, because it required continuous cultivation and monotonous rounds of simple tasks, was suited to slave labor. Thus, to protect the cotton economy, it was essential to protect slavery in the West. This conflict over western land eventually precipitated the Civil War.

Yet despite such differences, the underlying consensus of American elites was so great that compromise after compromise was devised to maintain unity. In the Missouri Compromise of 1820, the land in the Louisiana Purchase exclusive of Missouri was divided between free territory and slave territory at 36° 30′; and Maine and Missouri were admitted as free and slave states, respectively. After the war with Mexico, the elaborate Compromise of 1850 caused one of the greatest debates in American legislative history, with Senators Henry Clay, Daniel Webster, John C. Calhoun, Salmon P. Chase, Steven A. Douglas, Jefferson Davis, Alexander H. Stephens, Robert Toombs, William H. Seward, and Thaddeus Stevens all participating. Cleavage within the elite was apparent, but it was not yet so divisive as to split the nation. A compromise was achieved, providing for the admission of California as a free state; for the creation of two new territories, New Mexico and Utah, out of the Mexican cession; for a drastic fugitive slave law to satisfy southern planters; and for the prohibition of the slave trade in the District of Columbia. Even the Kansas-Nebraska Act of 1854 was intended to be a compromise; each new territory was supposed to decide for itself whether it should be slave or free, the expectation being that Nebraska would vote free and Kansas slave. But gradually the spirit of compromise gave way to divergence and conflict.

Beginning in 1856, proslavery and antislavery forces fought it out in "bleeding Kansas." Senator Charles Sumner of Massachusetts delivered a condemnation of slavery in the Senate and was beaten almost to death on the Senate floor by Congressman Preston Brooks of South Carolina. Intemperate

While the single greatest result of the Civil War was the abolition of slavery, Lincoln's original intent was to preserve the Union. This Thomas Nast wood engraving from *Harper's Weekly* depicts a battle as seen by the reserve troops on December 27, 1862. *Courtesy of the Boston Public Library, Print Department*

language in the Senate became commonplace, with frequent threats of secession, violence, and civil war. In 1857 a southern-dominated Supreme Court decided, in *Dred Scot* v. *Sanford*,[10] that the Missouri Compromise was unconstitutional because Congress had no authority to forbid slavery in any territory. Slave property, said Chief Justice Roger B. Taney, was as much protected by the Constitution as was any other kind of property. In 1859 John Brown and his followers raided the United States arsenal at Harper's Ferry, as a first step to freeing the slaves of Virginia by force. Brown was captured by Virginia militia under the command of Colonel Robert E. Lee, tried for treason, found guilty, and executed. Southerners believed that Northerners had tried to incite the horror of slave insurrection, while Northerners believed that Brown died a martyr.

Yet historian Richard Hofstadter observes that even in the midst of this disastrous conflict one finds extensive evidence of attempts to maintain consensus among the elite. There were many genuine efforts at compromise and conciliation. Abraham Lincoln never attacked slavery in the South; his exclusive concern was to halt the spread of slavery in the western territories. He wrote in 1845: "I hold it a paramount duty of us in the free states, due to the union of the states, and perhaps to liberty itself (paradox though it may seem), to let the slavery of the other states alone."[11] Throughout his political career he consistently held this position. On the other hand, with regard to the western territories, he said: "The whole nation is interested that the best use shall be made of these territories. We want them for homes and free white people. This they cannot be, to any considerable extent, if slavery shall be planted within them."[12] In short, Lincoln wanted the western territories to be tied economically and culturally to the northern system. As for Lincoln's racial views, as late as 1858 he said:

> I will say, then, that I am not, nor ever have been, in favor of bringing about in any way the social and political equality of the white and black races: that I am not, nor ever have been, in favor of making voters or jurors of negroes, nor of qualifying them to hold office, nor to intermarry with white people. . . .
>
> And inasmuch as they cannot so live, while they do remain together there must be the position of superior and inferior, and I as much as any other man am in favor of having the superior position assigned to the white race.[13]

Hofstadter believes that Lincoln's political posture was essentially *conservative:* He wished to preserve the long-established order and consensus that had protected American principles and property rights so successfully in the past. He was *not* an abolitionist, and he did *not* seek the destruction of the southern elites or the rearrangement of the South's social fabric. His goal was to bring the South back into the Union, to restore orderly government, and to establish the principle that the states cannot resist national authority with force. At the beginning of the Civil War Lincoln knew that a great part of conservative northern opinion was willing to fight for the Union but might refuse to support a war to free Negroes. Lincoln's great political skill was his ability to gather all of the issues of the Civil War into one single overriding theme—the preservation of the Union. On the other hand, he was bitterly attacked throughout the war by radical Republicans who thought that he had "no anti-slavery instincts."

As the war continued and casualties mounted, opinion in the North became increasingly bitter toward southern slave owners. Many Republicans joined the abolitionists in calling for emancipation of the slaves simply to punish the "rebels." They knew that the power of the South was based on the labor of slaves. Lincoln also knew that if he proclaimed to the world that the war was being fought to free the slaves there would be less danger of foreign intervention. Yet even in late summer 1862 Lincoln wrote:

> My paramount object in this struggle is to save the Union. If I could save the Union without freeing any slaves, I would do it; if I could save it by freeing some and leaving others alone, I would also do that. I shall do less whenever I shall believe what I am doing hurts the cause, and I shall do more whenever I believe doing more will help the cause. I shall adopt new views as fast as they shall appear to be true views.[14]

Finally, on September 22, 1862, Lincoln issued his preliminary Emancipation Proclamation. Claiming his right as commander in chief of the army and navy, he promised that "On the first day of January, . . . 1863, all persons held as slaves within any State, or designated part of a State, the people whereof shall then be in rebellion against the United States, shall be then, thenceforward, and forever free." Thus one of the great steps forward in human freedom in this nation, the Emancipation Proclamation, did not come about as a result of demands by the people, and certainly not a result of demands by the slaves themselves. Historian Richard Hofstadter contends that it was a political and military action by the president for the sake of helping to preserve the Union. It was not a revolutionary action but a conservative one.

POWER AND THE INDUSTRIAL REVOLUTION

The importance of the Civil War for America's power structure lay in the commanding position that the new industrial capitalists won during the course of the struggle. Even before 1860, northern industry had been altering the course of American life; the economic transformation of the United States from an agricultural to an industrial nation reached the crescendo of a revolution in the second half of the nineteenth century. Canals and steam railroads had been opening up new markets for the growing industrial cities of the East. The rise of corporations and of stock markets for the accumulation of capital upset old-fashioned ideas about property. The introduction of machinery in factories revolutionized the conditions of labor and made the masses dependent upon industrial capitalists for their livelihood. Civil War profits compounded the capital of the industrialists and placed them in a position to dominate the economic life of the nation. Moreover, when the southern planters were removed from the national scene, the government in Washington became the exclusive domain of the new industrial leaders.

The new industrial elite found a new philosophy to justify its political and economic dominance. Drawing an analogy from Darwinian biology, Herbert Spencer undertook to demonstrate that, just as an elite was selected in nature through evolution, so also society would near perfection as it allowed natural social elites to be selected by free competition. Spencer hailed the accumulation of new industrial wealth as a sign of "the survival of the fittest." The "social Darwinists" found in the law of survival of the fittest an admirable defense for the emergence of a ruthless ruling elite, an elite which defined its own self-interest more narrowly, perhaps, than any other in American history. It was a philosophy that permitted the conditions of the masses to decline to the lowest depths in American history.

After the Civil War, industrialists became more prominent in Congress than they had ever been. They had little trouble in voting high tariffs and hard

THE COMFORT SPEED AND SAFETY AFFORDED PATRONS OF THE CHICAGO GREAT WESTERN RAILWAY MAKE TRAVEL A LUXURY. F.H.LORD General Passenger & Ticket Agt Chicago. THE MAPLE LEAF ROUTE

Improved means of transportation provided the foundation for the growth of the industrial revolution in America; and the railroad was the most significant improvement. This advertisement for a Chicago Great Western Railway luxury train shows the level which this development reached in a relatively short period of time. *The Bettmann Archive*

money, both of which heightened profits. Very little effective regulatory legislation was permitted to reach the floor of Congress. After 1881 the Senate came under the spell of Nelson Aldrich, son-in-law of John D. Rockefeller, who controlled Standard Oil. Aldrich served 30 years in the Senate. He believed that geographical representation in that body was old-fashioned and openly advocated a Senate manned officially by representatives from the great business "constituencies"—steel, coal, copper, railroads, banks, textiles, and so on.

The corporate form of business facilitated the amassing of capital by limiting the liability of capitalists to their actual investments and thereby keeping their personal fortunes safe in the event of misfortunes to their companies. The corporate form also encouraged risk-taking in the expansion of industrial capital through the stock market. "Wall Street," the address of the nation's busiest security market—the New York Stock Exchange—became a synonym for industrial capitalism. The markets for corporation stocks provided a vast and ready money source for new enterprises or for the enlargement and consolidation of old firms.

Typical of the great entrepreneurs of industrial capitalism was John D.

Perhaps more than anyone else, John D. Rockefeller typified the great capitalist entrepreneurs of the nineteenth century. In less than 30 years he singlehandedly created an almost total monopoly over the production and distribution of oil in America. *Wide World Photo*

Rockefeller. By the end of the Civil War, Rockefeller had accumulated a modest fortune of $50,000 in wholesale grain and meat. In 1865, with extraordinary good judgment, he invested his money in the wholly new petroleum business. He backed one of the first oil refineries in the nation and continually reinvested his profits in his business. In 1867, he and two partners—H. M. Flagler and F. W. Harkness—founded the Standard Oil Company of Ohio, which in that year refined 4 percent of the nation's output. By 1872, with monopoly as his goal, he had acquired 20 of the 25 refineries in Cleveland and was laying plans that within a decade would bring him into control of over 90 percent of the oil refineries of the country. Rockefeller bought up pipelines, warehouses, and factories and was able to force the railroad to grant him rebates. In 1882 he formed a giant trust, the Standard Oil Company, with a multitude of affiliates. Thereafter, the Standard Oil Company became a prototype of American monopolies. As Rockefeller himself put it: "The day of combination is here to stay. Individualism has gone, never to return."

There were two major components to Franklin D. Roosevelt's New Deal. The first was the creation of federally funded grant-in-aid programs. The personal nature of the second component, his famous fireside chats, was in marked contrast to the impersonal bureaucratic nature of the first.
From Stefan Lorant's *The Glorious Burden*

THE NEW DEAL AND THE EMERGENCE OF "THE LIBERAL ESTABLISHMENT"

Herbert Hoover was the last great advocate of the rugged individualism of the old order. The economic collapse of the Great Depression undermined the faith of both the elite and the nonelite in the idea of "social Darwinism." Following the stock market crash of October 1929, and in spite of assurances by the elite that prosperity lay "just around the corner," the American economy virtually stopped. Prices dropped sharply, factories closed, real estate values declined, new construction practically ceased, banks went under, wages were cut drastically, unemployment figures mounted, and welfare rolls swelled.

The election of Franklin Delano Roosevelt to the presidency in 1932 ushered in a new era in American elite philosophy. The Great Depression did not bring about a revolution; it did not result in the emergence of new elites; but it did have important impact on the thinking of America's governing circles. The economic disaster that had befallen the nation caused the elites to consider the need for economic reform. The Great Depression also reinforced the notion that elites must acquire a greater public responsibility. The victories of fascism in Germany and communism in the Soviet Union and the growing restlessness of the masses in America made it plain that reform and regard for the public welfare were essential to the continued maintenance of the American political system and the dominant place of the elite in it.

Roosevelt sought to elaborate a New Deal philosophy that would permit government to devote much more attention to the public welfare than did the philosophy of Hoover's somewhat discredited "rugged individualism." The New Deal was not a revolutionary system but rather a necessary reform of the capitalist system.

In the New Deal, American elites accepted the principle that the entire community, through the agency of the national government, had a responsibility for mass welfare. Roosevelt's second inaugural address called attention to "one third of a nation, ill housed, ill clad, ill nourished." Roosevelt succeeded in saving the existing system of private capitalism and avoiding the threats to the established order of fascism, socialism, communism, and other radical movements.

Historian Richard Hofstadter comments on Roosevelt's liberal, public-regarding philosophy:

> At the beginning of his career he took to the patrician reform thought of the progressive era and accepted a social outlook that can best be summed up in the phrase "noblesse oblige." He had a penchant for public service, personal philanthropy, and harmless manifestos against dishonesty in government; he displayed a broad easy-going tolerance, a genuine liking for all sorts of people; he loved to exercise his charm in political and social situations.[15]

Roosevelt's personal philosophy was soon to become the prevailing ethos of the new liberal establishment.

Thus, liberalism in America today is a product of elite response to economic depression at home and the rising threats of fascism and communism abroad. Its historical origin can be traced to elite efforts to *preserve* the existing political and economic system through reform. This historical perspective on the liberal tradition enables social scientists to better understand the origins of change and reform within society.

POWER AND HISTORY: A CASE STUDY

Reconstruction and Black History

The ideal history, completely objective and dispassionate, is really an illusion. Consciously or unconsciously, all historians are biased. There is bias in their choice of subject, in their selection of material, in their organization and presentation of the material, and, inevitably, in their interpretation of it. Our own interest in power biases our view of the American experience. Charles A. Beard, whose account of the Constitutional Convention was biased by his interest in economic forces, concluded that the only honorable course for a historian to follow is to frankly acknowledge his "frame of reference"—that is, his bias. Yet this is a difficult thing to do, because we are not always aware of our own biases.

Let us consider the case of the historical interpretation of black experience in America, particularly in the Reconstruction era following the Civil War. Only a few years ago historians viewed the Reconstruction Congress as vindictive and sinful. The period as a whole was considered destructive, oppressive, and corrupt. Military rule was imposed upon the South. "Carpetbaggers" and "scallywags" confiscated the property of helpless Southerners and retarded the economic progress of the South for decades. Maladministration and corruption in the federal government were portrayed as being greater than ever before in American history. The role of blacks in the Reconstruction years was regarded with ridicule: It was implied that the blacks were pushed into positions of authority by spiteful military rules in order to humiliate proud southern whites. The accomplishments of blacks during this period were overlooked. Finally, it was suggested that the separation of the races—segregation—was the "normal" pattern of southern life. The belief was fostered that blacks and whites in the South had never known any other pattern of life than slavery and segregation.

A new awareness of black history in recent years has resulted in a thoroughgoing reinterpretation of the Reconstruction era. Historian C. Vann Woodward's work, among others, led the way in bringing new light to this important period. Woodward recorded the progress of blacks during Reconstruction, described the good-faith efforts of the Reconstruction Congress to secure equality for black Americans, and explained the reimposition of segregation in terms of class conflict among whites.

When the radical Republicans (as opposed to the moderate faction within the party) gained control of Congress in 1867, blacks momentarily seemed destined to attain their full rights as United States citizens. Under military rule southern states adopted new constitutions that awarded the vote and other civil liberties to Negroes. Black men were elected to state legislatures and to the U.S. Congress. In 1865 nearly 10 percent of all federal troops were black. The literacy rate among blacks rose rapidly as hundreds of schools set up by the federal government's Freedmen's Bureau began providing education for ex-slaves.[16]

The first black actually to serve in Congress was Hiram R. Revels of Mississippi, who in 1870 took over the Senate seat previously held by Confederate President Jefferson Davis. In all, 22 southern blacks served in Congress between 1870 and 1901. All were elected as Republicans; 13 were former slaves. Many of these men made substantial contributions to Reconstruction policy. Robert B.

Elliott of South Carolina won national fame when he delivered a two-hour speech on behalf of the Civil Rights Act of 1875. The last black congressman under Reconstruction from the South was George H. White of North Carolina, who finally left the Congress in 1901.

The accomplishments of the Reconstruction Congress were considerable. Even before the radical Republicans gained control, the Thirteenth Amendment had become part of the Constitution. But it was the Fourteenth and Fifteenth Amendments and the important Civil Rights Act of 1875 which attempted to secure a place in America for the black man equal to that of his white neighbor. The wording of the Fourteenth Amendment was explicit:

> No State shall make or enforce any law which shall abridge the privileges or immunities of citizens of the United States; nor shall any State deprive any person of life, liberty, or property, without due process of law; nor deny to any person within its jurisdiction the equal protection of the laws.

The Civil Rights Act of 1875 declared that all persons were entitled to the full and equal enjoyment of all public accommodations—inns, public conveniences, theaters, and other places of public amusement. In this act the Reconstruction Congress committed the nation to a policy of nondiscrimination in all aspects of public life.

Between 1865 and the early 1880s the success of the civil rights movement was reflected in the great prevalence of Negro voting throughout the South, the ascendance of many blacks to federal and state offices, and the almost equal treatment afforded Negroes in theaters, restaurants, hotels, and public transportation facilities. But by 1877 support for Reconstruction policies began to crumble. In what has been described as the "Compromise of 1877," the national government agreed to end military occupation of the South, thereby giving up its efforts to rearrange southern society and lending tacit approval to white supremacy in that region. In return, the southern states pledged their support for the Union, accepted national supremacy, and permitted the Republican candidate, Rutherford B. Hayes, to assume the presidency following the much-disputed election of 1876 in which his opponent, Samuel Tilden, had received a majority of the popular vote.

The withdrawal of federal troops from the South in 1877 did not bring about an instant change in the status of the black man. Southern blacks voted in large numbers well into the 1880s and 1890s. Certainly we do not mean to suggest that discrimination was nonexistent during this period. Perhaps the most debilitating of all segregation—that in the public schools—appeared immediately after the Civil War under the beneficent sanction of Reconstruction authorities. Yet segregation in its full-blown Jim Crow form took shape only gradually, and largely as the result of political and economic conflicts that divided southern whites.

Reconstruction and Black History

Segregation was closely associated with the rise of populism—a movement purporting to represent the interests of the common people—in the South. Interestingly, the earliest southern populists adopted a style of equalitarianism and attempted to enlist blacks in a coalition of white and black poor people against their common economic oppressors. However, they soon came to realize that this strategy was bound to fail since racial prejudice was greatest among the depressed lower economic classes to whom their appeal was directed. These were the classes most subject to deep-rooted fears of the black man. Conservatives, realizing that the populists had erred in their strategy, were able to discredit the early populists by fanning the flames of racial hatred, thus driving a wedge between poor blacks and poor whites. Alarmed by the populists' successes in the 1880s and 1890s (especially after the formation of the Populist party in 1891), the conservatives soon raised the cries of "Negro domination" and "white supremacy," thereby galvanizing the racial fears of southern whites of all classes. The planters of the rich lowland counties needed an issue—even better, a scapegoat—to oppose the growing influence of white farmers from the mountainous counties. Soon the Populists realized that they would have to disassociate themselves from blacks and adopt the white supremacy position.

The first objective of the white supremacy movement was to disenfranchise blacks. The standard devices developed for achieving this feat were the literacy test, the poll tax, the white primary, and various forms of intimidation. Following the disenfranchisement of blacks, the white supremacy movement established segregation and discrimination as public policy by the adoption of a large number of Jim Crow laws, designed to prevent the mingling of whites and blacks (Jim Crow was a stereotype Negro in a nineteenth-century song-and-dance show). Between 1900 and 1910, laws were adopted by southern state legislatures requiring segregation of the races in streetcars, in hospitals, in prisons, in orphanages, and in homes for the aged and indigent. A New Orleans ordinance decreed that white and black prostitutes confine their activities to separate districts. In 1913 the federal government itself adopted policies that segregated the races in federal office buildings, cafeterias, and rest-room facilities. Social policy followed (indeed, exceeded) public policy. Little signs reading "White Only" or "Colored" appeared everywhere, with or without the approbation of law.

Many early histories of Reconstruction paid little attention to blacks' response to the imposition of segregation. But there were at least three distinct types of response: (1) accommodation and acceptance of a subordinate position in society, (2) participation in the formation of a black protest movement, and (3) migration out of the South to avoid some of the consequences of white supremacy.

The foremost black advocate of accommodation to segregation was the well-known black educator Booker T. Washington. Washington enjoyed wide pop-

Booker T. Washington felt that increased civil and political rights would be a hollow victory for black people, and that improvement of their economic condition was far more important. Accordingly, he founded Tuskegee Institute, which emphasized vocational training as the antidote to black poverty. *Wide World Photo*

ularity among both white and black Americans. He was an adviser to two presidents (Theodore Roosevelt and William Howard Taft) and was highly respected by white philanthropists and government officials. In his famous Cotton States' Exposition speech in Atlanta in 1895, Washington assured whites that blacks were prepared to accept a separate position in society:

> As we have proved our loyalty to you in the past, in nursing your children, watching by the sickbed of your mothers and fathers, and often following them with tear-dimmed eyes to their graves, so in the future, in our humble way, we shall stand by you. . . . In all things that are purely social we can be as separate as the fingers, yet one as the hand in all things essential to mutual progress.[17]

Booker T. Washington's hopes for black America lay in a program of self-help through education. He himself had attended Hampton Institute in Virginia, where the curriculum centered around practical trades for blacks. Washington obtained some white philanthropic support in establishing his own Tuskegee Institute in Tuskegee, Alabama, in 1881. His first students helped build the

Reconstruction and Black History

George Washington Carver was Tuskegee Institute's best known faculty member. His biggest contribution was research into a variety of uses for southern crops. *Culver Pictures*

school. Training at Tuskegee emphasized immediately useful vocations such as farming, preaching, and blacksmithing. Washington urged his students to stay in the South, to acquire land, and to build homes, thereby helping to eliminate ignorance and poverty among their fellow blacks. One of Tuskegee's outstanding faculty members was George Washington Carver, who researched and developed uses for southern crops. Other privately and publicly endowed black colleges were founded that later developed into major universities, including Fisk and Howard (both started by the Freedmen's Bureau), and Atlanta, Hampton, and Southern.

While Washington was urging blacks to make the best of segregation, a small band of Negroes were organizing themselves behind a declaration of Negro resistance and protest that would later rewrite American public policy. The leader of this group was W. E. B. Du Bois, a brilliant historian and sociologist at Atlanta University. In 1905 Du Bois and a few other black intellectuals meeting in Niagara Falls, Canada, drew up a black platform intended to "assail the ears" and sear the consciences of white Americans. In rejecting moderation and compromise, the Niagara statement proclaimed: "We refuse to allow the impression to remain that the Negro American assents to inferiority, is submissive under oppression and apologetic before insults." The platform listed the major injustices

In contrast to Booker T. Washington, educator W. E. B. Du Bois emphasized civil rights as the primary tool for improving conditions for black Americans. He was instrumental in the founding of the NAACP in 1909. *Wide World Photo*

perpetrated against Negroes since Reconstruction: the loss of voting rights, the imposition of Jim Crow laws and segregated public schools, the denial of equal job opportunities, the permitting of inhumane conditions in southern prisons, the exclusion of blacks from West Point and Annapolis, and the failure on the part of the federal government to enforce the Fourteenth and Fifteenth Amendments. Out of the Niagara meeting came the idea for a nationwide organization dedicated to fighting for blacks, and on 12 February 1909, the one hundredth anniversary of Abraham Lincoln's birth, the National Association for the Advancement of Colored People (NAACP) was founded.[18]

Du Bois himself was on the original board of directors of the NAACP. But a majority of the board consisted of white liberals. In the years to follow, most of the financial support and policy guidance for the association was provided by whites rather than blacks. However, Du Bois was the NAACP's first director of research and the editor of its magazine, *Crisis*. The NAACP began a long and eventually successful campaign to establish black rights through legal action. Over the years hundreds of court cases were brought at the local, state, and federal court levels on behalf of blacks denied their constitutional rights.

World War I provided an opportunity for restive blacks in the South to escape the worst abuses of white supremacy by migrating en masse to northern cities. In the years 1916 - 1918, an estimated half-million blacks moved to the North to fill the labor shortage caused by the war effort. Most migrating blacks arrived in northern big cities only to find more poverty and segregation. But at least they could vote and attend better schools, and they were not obliged to step off the sidewalk into the gutter when a white man approached.

The progressive "ghettoization" of black Americans—their migration from the rural South to the urban North and their increasing concentration in central-city ghettos—had profound political as well as social implications. The ghetto provided an environment conducive to collective mass action. Even as early as 1928, the black residents of Chicago were able to elect one of their own to the House of Representatives. The election of Oscar de Priest, the first Negro congressman from the North, signaled a new turn in American urban politics by announcing to white politicians that the black vote in northern cities would have to be reckoned with. The black ghettos would soon provide an important element in a new political coalition that was about to take form, namely, the Democratic party of Franklin Delano Roosevelt.

The increasing concentration of blacks in northern ghettos in large politically competitive "swing" states provided black voters with new political power—not only to support the Democratic party coalition in national politics but also to elect black men to local public office. Today black mayors serve, or have served, in cities as diverse as Los Angeles, Cleveland, Gary, Atlanta, and Newark. Thus, "revisionist" history helps social scientists to understand how blacks coped with segregation and emerged from this experience with new power, unity, and purpose.

NOTES

1. Henry Steele Commager, *The Study of History* (Columbus, Ohio: Merrill, 1965), p. 79.

2. F. Engels, *Socialism, Utopian and Scientific* (1892), Introduction.

3. H. A. L. Fisher, *A History of Europe* (Boston: Houghton Mifflin, 1935), Preface.

4. Richard Hofstadter, *The American Political Tradition and the Men Who Made It* (New York: Vintage Books, 1956), p. viii.

5. Charles Beard, *An Economic Interpretation of the Constitution* (New York: Macmillan, 1913), pp. 324 - 325.

6. Ibid., p. 73.

7. Robert E. Brown, *Charles Beard and the Constitution* (Princeton, N.J.: Princeton University Press, 1956), p. 200.

8. Ibid.

9. Frederick Jackson Turner, "The West and American Ideals," in *The Frontier in American History* (New York: Holt, 1921).

10. *Dred Scott* v. *Sanford,* 19 Howard 393 (1857).

11. Richard Hofstadter, *The American Political Tradition* (New York: Knopf, 1948), p. 109.

12. Ibid., p. 113.

13. Ibid., p. 116.

14. Ibid., pp. 132 - 133.

15. Ibid., pp. 323 - 324.

16. For a general history of Reconstruction politics, see C. Vann Woodward, *Reunion and Reaction* (Boston: Little, Brown, 1951); also see C. Vann Woodward, *The Strange Career of Jim Crow* (New York: Oxford University Press, 1957).

17. Quoted in Henry Steele Commager (ed.), *The Struggle for Racial Equality: A Documentary Record* (New York: Harper & Row, 1967), p. 19.

18. Ibid.

TESTING YOUR PERFORMANCE

Note to the Student.   The following questions are to test how well you achieved the Performance Objectives identified for you at the beginning of this chapter. The correct answers are supplied, accompanied by corresponding pages for you to review if you have answered incorrectly. The questions are coordinated numerically with the Performance Objectives at the beginning of the chapter. This exercise will assist you in determining the type of questions you have the most difficulty in answering (discussion, identification, explanation, definition, etc.) and will prepare you for test questions likely to be asked by your instructor.

1.   The reference to all past human actions and events, and the reference to the recording, narrating, and interpreting of these events are two definitions of _____ .

2.   The necessary personal selection and organization of facts which are worthy of interest, a personal judgment of what is important about the past, the effect of present conditions, and the person's feelings about the future result in the necessary and unavoidable _____ .

3.   Identify the historian who derived each of the following theories of history:

(a) Belief that the history of man was explained by the development of human ideals; that historical evolution occurs in a dialectical fashion—each idea (thesis) contains within itself its own contradiction (antithesis), and this conflict gives rise to a new and higher ideal (synthesis)—and that the moving force of history is ideological. _____

(b) Belief that history is determined by the mode of production, belief in the dialectic of history, and belief in the inevitability of progress through materialism. _____

(c) Belief in the cyclical nature of cultures in history: springtime, summer, autumn, and winter; belief that each great civilization lives about a thousand years and follows the same cyclical course; belief that in the decline of a civilization old elites and old values are overthrown in the name of reason and in the name of "the people." _____

(d) Belief in the cyclical nature of cultures accompanied by belief that each succeeding civilization can learn from the experiences, values, and myths of earlier civilizations (therefore each is a little richer in culture than the one preceding it); belief that great civilizations emerge as successful, adaptive response to great challenges and that disintegration occurs when a civilization loses its adaptive power, its self-determination, and its creative leaders. _____

4. Identify the following explanations of history:

(a) The explanation through historical biographies, which portrays leaders of the past as larger than life figures who shaped the course of events themselves rather than merely responding to the world in which they lived. _____

(b) The explanation emphasizing the origin and growth of governmental institutions, which often reinforces reverence for existing political and governmental institutions. _____

(c) The explanation used by Frederick Jackson Turner, which argued that the main influence on American history was the impact of the western frontier upon American society. _____

(d) The explanation used by Richard Hofstadter which stresses that power in America has changed slowly without any serious breaks in the ideas and values underlying the American political and economic system, and that, over the years, America's political leadership has been essentially conservative.

5. (a) The movement for a constitution to replace the Articles of Confederation was conducted primarily by four interest groups (money, public securities, manufactures, and trade and shipping) that had been adversely affected by the Articles; no popular vote was taken either directly or indirectly on whether to call a constitutional convention; the propertyless mass did not participate in writing the Constitution; and the authors of the Constitution were interested in, and derived economic advantages from, the establishment of the new system. All of these were conclusions found in what famous historical work?

(b) In an effort to understand the Constitution, a study of economic interests of the national elite which included the writers of the document, and a study of the old unpublished financial records of the U.S. Treasury Department, the personal letters and financial accounts of the 55 delegates to the Philadelphia Convention, and the original form of the Constitution as it emerged from the convention are components of _____ .

(c) The most important enumerated power that enabled the national government to end its dependence upon the states was the _____ .

(d) The power given to Congress to regulate commerce with foreign nations and among the several states was found in what constitutional clause?

(e) The Founding Fathers felt that better protection for financial interests would be provided by giving Congress powers to _____ _____ , rather than by leaving it to the states.

(f) To protect western settlers from the Indians and to open the way to American westward expansion; and to protect American commerce on the seas; and to protect the commercial and territorial ambitions of the Founding Fathers —all were reasons for giving the national government the power to _____ _____ .

(g) Since slavery as a domestic institution was better safeguarded under the new Constitution than under the Articles and provided an explicit advantage to slaveholders who were interested in protecting their *existing* property and slaves, there was no objection to giving Congress the power to _____ _____ .

(h) Protection to economic elites, provided by the Constitution's preventing the states from issuing cheap paper money which could be used by debtors to pay off their creditors with less valuable currency, was ensured by constitutional _____ .

(i) The interests of investors, merchants, and creditors would have been seriously damaged if state legislatures could have interfered with business obligations; therefore, the Constitution prevented states from passing any law _____ .

6. The contention that most of the people were middle class and had private property and consequently were interested in the protection of property; the finding of men of prestige, reputation, and property on *both* sides of the question of accepting the new Constitution; and the retreat of the supporters of the Constitution from their demand for unconditional ratification by agreeing to later add a Bill of Rights are all used as _____ _____ .

7. The historian who saw the rise of the New West as the most significant fact in American history—which brought about rapid upward social mobility, caused a successful assimilation of new elites into America's governing circles symbolized by Andrew Jackson's election as president, and resulted in this new elite's support by the public and its strong faith in the wisdom and justice of popular decisions—was _____ .

8. (a) Merchants and manufacturers dependent upon free labor, having no direct interest in the abolition of slavery, and favoring a West composed of small farmers to produce food and raw materials for the industrial and commercial East and to provide a market for eastern goods made up the _____ _____ .

(b) Those who had an interest in the slave and cotton culture, and who wanted western lands for the expansion of the cotton and slave culture made up the _____ .

(c) Both northern and southern elites realized that the key to future dominance of the nation was _____ .

(d) The compromise which divided land in the Louisiana Purchase exclusive of Missouri between free territory and slave territory at 36° 30′ and admitted Maine and Missouri as free and slave states, respectively, was the _____ .

(e) The compromise which provided for the admission of California as a free state, for the creation of two new territories, New Mexico and Utah, for a drastic fugitive slave law to satisfy southern planters, and for prohibition of the slave trade in the District of Columbia was the _____

_____ .

(f) The compromise act which provided that each territory decide for itself whether it should be slave or free, with the expectation that Nebraska would vote free and Kansas slave, was the _____

_____ .

9. (a) Continued devotion to the principles of constitutional government and private property were _____

_____ .

(b) The fact that the goal was not the destruction of the southern elites or the rearrangement of the South's social fabric; the gathering of all the issues into the single theme of preservation of the Union to avoid foreign intervention; and the fact that it did *not* come about as a result of demands by the people or by the slaves themselves are all indicators of the _____

_____ .

10. (a) The commanding position that the new industrial capitalists won during the course of the struggle evidenced the _____

_____ .

(b) The new industrial elite adopted the philosophy that society would near perfection as it allowed natural social elites to be selected by free competition. This philosophy is known as _____ .

(c) Voting in high tariffs and hard money, blocking any effective regulatory legislation, and maintaining that the Senate should be manned officially by representatives from big business were all _____

_____ .

11. (a) The elite of pre-Depression days which stressed the "rich getting richer" and ignored the plight of the masses was the _____

_____ .

(b) The elite of the New Deal era which accepted the principle that reform and regard for the public welfare were essential to the continued maintenance of the American political system and their dominant place in it was the

_____ .

(c) The U.S. president who was responsible for ushering in a new era in American elite philosophy was _____ .

12. Identify the following interpretations of the black experience in America during the Reconstruction era:

(a) A view of the Reconstruction Congress as vindictive and sinful; of the Reconstruction period of the American South as destructive, oppressive, and corrupt; of the role of blacks as unimportant; and of segregation as the "normal" pattern of southern life. _____

(b) A view of the progressiveness of blacks during the Reconstruction period; a recognition of the efforts of the Reconstruction Congress to secure equality for black Americans; and an explanation of the reimposition of segregation in terms of class conflict among whites. _____

_____ .

Correct Responses

1. History (p. 239).

2. Bias of all historians (p. 239).

3. (a) Hegel (p. 240); (b) Marx (p. 240); (c) Spengler (pp. 240 - 241); (d) Toynbee (p. 241).

4. (a) "Great man" explanation (p. 242); (b) Institutional explanation (p. 242); (c) Western frontier explanation (p. 242); (d) Incrementalism explanation (p. 244).

5. (a) Charles Beard's *An Economic Interpretation of the Constitution* (p. 245); (b) Beard's method of studying history (p. 246); (c) Taxing power (p. 246); (d) Interstate commerce clause (p. 247); (e) Protect money and property (p. 247); (f) Raise an army and navy (pp. 247 - 248); (g) Outlaw the importation of slaves after 1808 (p. 248); (h) Restrictions upon state legislatures (p. 249); (i) Impairing the obligation of contracts (pp. 249 - 250).

6. Criticisms of Beard's interpretation of history (p. 250).

7. Frederick Jackson Turner (pp. 250 - 251).

8. (a) Northern elites (p. 253); (b) Southern elites (p. 253); (c) Control of the West (p. 253); (d) Missouri Compromise of 1820 (p. 253); (e) Compromise of 1850 (p. 253); (f) Kansas-Nebraska Act of 1854 (p. 253).

9. (a) Areas of agreement between northern and southern elites (p. 253); (b) Conservativeness of the Emancipation Proclamation (pp. 255 - 256).

10. (a) Importance of the Civil War for America's power structure (p. 256); (b) Social Darwinism (p. 256); (c) Effects of the industrialists on Congress (pp. 256 - 257).

11. (a) "Rugged individualism" elite (pp. 259 - 260); (b) "Liberal establishment" elite (p. 260); (c) Franklin Delano Roosevelt (p. 259).

12. Earlier interpretations (p. 261); (b) C. Vann Woodward's interpretation (p. 261).

KEY TERMS

history

dialectical

thesis

antithesis

synthesis

"great man" explanation

An Economic Interpretation of the Constitution

Charles Beard

enumerated powers

taxing power

interstate commerce clause

obligation of contracts clause

supremacy clause of Article VI

Frederick Jackson Turner

The Rise of the West

Jacksonian democracy

natural aristocracy

Missouri Compromise of 1820

Compromise of 1850

Kansas-Nebraska Act of 1854

Dred Scott v. *Sanford,* 1857

Emancipation Proclamation

social Darwinists

Wall Street

Thirteenth Amendment

Fourteenth Amendment

Fifteenth Amendment

Civil Rights Act of 1875

Compromise of 1877

segregation

white supremacy movement

National Association for the Advancement of Colored People (NAACP)

"ghettoization"

DISCUSSION QUESTIONS

1.　Choose two of the following historians and discuss their theories of history:
    (a) Hegel
    (b) Marx
    (c) Spengler
    (d) Toynbee

2.　Contrast the following ways of studying or interpreting history. Mention the strengths and weaknesses of each.
    (a) "Great man" explanation
    (b) "Institutional" explanation
    (c) "Incremental" explanation

3.　Discuss how Charles Beard interpreted each of the following constitutional powers as being economically advantageous to the Founding Fathers:
    (a) Taxing power
    (b) Interstate commerce clause
    (c) Congressional powers to protect money and property
    (d) Power to raise an army and a navy
    (e) Outlawing the importation of slaves
    (f) Restrictions upon state legislatures
    (g) Prevention of laws impairing obligation of contracts
    (h) Supremacy clause of Article VI
What are the criticisms of Beard's theory?

4.　Discuss the following impacts of the rise of the New West as interpreted by the historian Frederick Jackson Turner:
    (a) Rapid upward social mobility
    (b) Andrew Jackson's election to the presidency; Jacksonian democracy with its emphasis on popular participation in decision-making
    (c) The opening of the elite system

5. Contrast American elite philosophy in the following time periods of American history:
   (a) Civil War
   (b) Industrial revolution
   (c) New Deal

6. Show how different historical interpretations of the same historical events can radically differ by contrasting earlier interpretations of the Reconstruction era and the Reconstruction Congress with the more recent interpretation of the same by historian C. Vann Woodward.

SUGGESTED READINGS

CHARLES BEARD, *An Economic Interpretation of the Constitution* (New York: Macmillan, 1913).

ROBERT E. BROWN, *Charles Beard and the Constitution* (Princeton, N.J.: Princeton University Press, 1956).

JOHN P. DAVIS (ed.), *The American Negro Reference Book* (Englewood Cliffs, N.J.: Prentice-Hall, 1966).

JOHN HOPE FRANKLIN, *From Slavery to Freedom, A History of American Negroes* (New York: Knopf, 1956).

PIETOR GEYL, ARNOLD J. TOYNBEE, and PITIRIM A. SOROKIN, *The Pattern of the Past: Can We Determine It?* (New York: Greenwood Press, 1968).

RICHARD HOFSTADTER, *The American Political Tradition* (New York: Vintage Books, 1956).

MICHAEL E. MURRAY, *Modern Philosophy of History* (The Hague: Nijhoff, 1970).

RONALD H. NASH (ed.), *Ideas of History* (New York: Dutton, 1969).

CLINTON ROSSITER, *1787: The Grand Convention* (New York: Macmillan, 1966).

MORTON GABRIEL WHITE, *Foundations of Historical Knowledge* (New York: Harper & Row, 1965).

C. VANN WOODWARD, *The Strange Career of Jim Crow* (New York: Oxford University Press, 1957).

PART THREE

The Uses of Power

CHAPTER 8

Power and Ideology

PERFORMANCE OBJECTIVES

The student should be able to:

1. Define ideology. Describe how power and ideology are related.

2. List the ways in which ideologies control people's behavior.

3. Discuss the common characteristics of the modern ideologies.

4. Compare and contrast classical liberalism and modern liberalism.

5. Describe how laissez-faire economics and classical liberal democracy are closely related.

6. Cite the author who is associated with modern conservatism. Compare and contrast classical liberalism and modern conservatism.

7. Define Burkean representation.

8. Describe fascism as an ideology. Identify the goals of the fascist state. Identify the power structure of the fascist regime.

9. Trace the development of communism and socialism.

10. Cite the philosopher who made socialism an effective ideology and a successful political movement. Identify *The Communist Manifesto* and *Das Kapital.*

11. Define and discuss the basic ideas of Marxian communism: economic determinism, dialectical materialism, the class struggle, the theory of surplus value, the inevitability of revolution, and the dictatorship of the proletariat.

12. Differentiate between egalitarianism and socialism. Compare and contrast communism and socialism.

13. Cite the spokesman for "revisionism" who revised many of the Marxian ideas and contributed to the break between communism and socialism. List the components of communism rejected by this man.

14. Describe the ideological justification for contemporary radicalism as seen by Herbert Marcuse. Outline the characteristics of contemporary radicalism.

15.   Identify what became a contributing factor to radicalism in America.

16.   Contrast Marxism and Leninism. Identify what Lenin saw as the key to a successful revolution. Describe Lenin's theory of imperialism. Explain why Lenin and Stalin decided to create "communism in one country."

17.   Outline or summarize the more serious flaws in Marxism.

18.   Describe the problems involved with comparing ideologies.

THE POWER OF IDEAS

Ideas have power. People are coerced by ideas—beliefs, symbols, doctrines—more than they ever realize. Indeed, whole societies are shaped by systems of ideas which we frequently refer to as "ideologies." An ideology is an integrated system of ideas that provide society and its members with rationalizations for a way of life, guides for evaluating "rightness" and "wrongness," and emotional impulses to action. Power and ideology are intimately related. Ideology rationalizes and justifies the exercise of power. By providing a justification for power, ideology itself becomes a source of control over people. Without the added legitimacy provided by ideology, power holders would be confronted by an aroused populace who strongly resented what they regarded as the naked power exercised over them. Nothing could be more dangerous to the stability of a power system. Yet the very ideology that legitimizes power also governs the conduct of power holders. Once an ideology is deeply rooted in a society, power holders themselves are bound by it if they wish to retain power.

Ideologies control people's behavior in several ways. (1) Ideologies affect perception. Ideas influence what men "see" in the world around them. Ideologies frequently describe the character of man in society; they help us become aware of certain aspects of society but often impair our ability to see other aspects. Ideologies may distort and oversimplify in their effort to provide a unified and coherent account of society. (2) Ideologies rationalize and justify a way of life and hence provide legitimacy for the structure of society. An ideology may justify the status quo, or it may provide a rationale for change, or even for revolution. (3) Ideologies provide normative standards to determine "rightness" and "wrongness" in the affairs of society. Ideologies generally have a strong moral component. Occasionally, they even function as "religions"—complete with prophets (Marx), scriptures (the Communist Manifesto), saints (Lenin, Stalin, Mao), and visions of utopia (communist revolution). (4) Ideologies provide motivation for social and political action. They give their followers a motive to act to improve world conditions. Ideologies can "convert" individuals to a particular social or political movement and arouse them to action.

THE AGE OF IDEOLOGY

Ideas have always moved men. The Crusades of the Middle Ages, the Reformation and Counter-Reformation, and the great religious wars of centuries past are sufficient evidence that ideas can produce wide-ranging consequences. But modern ideologies differ somewhat from those of the past. The nineteenth and twentieth centuries are sometimes referred to as "the age of ideology." Despite their quarrels, modern ideologies—capitalism, liberalism, socialism, communism, fascism—share several important characteristics:

1. Modern ideologies are typically utopian. Their vision is not of a blissful life hereafter or an other-worldly Kingdom of God, but rather of a perfect life on earth. Such a vision stands in marked contrast to earlier periods of history, in which the conditions of human existence were largely taken for granted. The usual expectation was that people would go on living much as their fathers and grandfathers had done. Utopia was reserved for life in the hereafter. Doubtlessly the utopianism of modern ideology is a product of revolutionary scientific and technological advances over the last two centuries and the industrial revolution; the rapid improvements in living conditions inspired men to believe that life on earth could be perfected. Their minds were diverted from heavenly concerns toward the improvement of life here and now.

2. Modern ideologies are typically optimistic about human progress. In an age of technological progress, it is easy to conclude that the steady improvement of human welfare is not only possible but inevitable. Frequently ideologies are presented as "the wave of the future." Supporters of various modern ideologies believe that they possess the ultimate "truth" and that they will achieve the ultimate "victory."

3. Modern ideologies are typically oversimplifications. Oversimplification is both their strength and their weakness. They inspire habits of thinking in terms of "we" and "they," "friend" and "enemy." The more committed one is to an ideology, the more likely he is to view his opponents as sinister and to look upon political disagreement as a struggle between the forces of good and the forces of evil.

It is difficult to summarize a modern ideology in a few brief paragraphs. The risk of oversimplification is great. And since ideologies themselves are oversimplifications, the problem is compounded. Moreover, ideologies are constantly changing. When old utopian hopes are disappointed, they are frequently revised or replaced by new ones. New ideologies compete with older ones in various stages of revision. To unravel the ideological forces operating in society at any given time is a highly complex affair. With these warnings in mind, however, let us consider some of the major ideologies that influence our contemporary world.

CLASSICAL LIBERALISM: THE LEAST GOVERNMENT IS THE BEST GOVERNMENT

Both "classical liberalism" and "modern liberalism" assert the worth and dignity of the individual. They both emphasize the rational ability of man to determine his own destiny, and they reject ideas, practices, and institutions that submerge the individual into a larger whole and deprive him of his essential dignity. Liberalism grew out of eighteenth-century Enlightenment or Age of Reason, in which great philosophers, such as Voltaire, Locke, Rousseau, Adam Smith, and Thomas Jefferson, affirmed their faith in reason, virtue, and common sense. Liberalism originated as an attack upon hereditary prerogatives and distinctions of a feudal society, the monarchy, the privileged aristocracy, the state-established church, and the restrictions on individual freedom associated with the feudal order. Classical liberalism and modern liberalism differ in important ways on how the freedom and dignity of the individual should be preserved. But both classical and modern liberals agree that the "fundamental assumption is the worth and dignity and creative capacity of the individual."[1]

Classical liberalism helped motivate America's Founding Fathers to declare their independence from England, to write the American Constitution, and to establish the Republic. It rationalized their actions and provided ideological legitimacy for the new nation. John Locke, the English political philosopher whose writings most influenced America's Founding Fathers, argued that even in a "state of nature"—that is, a world in which there were no governments—an individual possesses inalienable rights to life, liberty, and property. Locke spoke of a "natural law," or moral principle, which guaranteed to every man these rights. They were not given to the individual by government, and no government may legitimately take them away. Locke believed that the very purpose of government was to protect individual liberty. Men form a "social contract" with one another in establishing a government to help protect their rights; they agree to accept governmental authority in order to better protect life, liberty, and property. Implicit in the social contract and the liberal notion of freedom is the belief that governmental activity and social control over the individual should be kept to a minimum. This involves a removal of as many external restrictions on the individual as is consistent with the freedom of his fellow citizens.

Classical liberalism included a belief in "limited government." Since government is formed by the consent of the governed to protect individual liberty, it logically follows that government cannot violate the rights it was established to protect.

Classical liberalism also asserted the value of popular participation in government as an opportunity for individual self-development. Procedurally, classical liberalism held that popular participation was to be achieved through majority rule and respect for the rights of minorities. Minorities, who have had the oppor-

LF Dignity of Man
LF Natural Law & Reason
LF Limited Government
LF x Equality of Opportunity
LF ∧ Popular participation
Republican Govt.

"Look, Son, I'm a far-right conservative and you're a far-left radical. O.K.? So let's you and me go out and beat up some liberals."

Drawing by W. Miller; © 1971 The New Yorker Magazine, Inc.

tunity to influence policy but whose views have not succeeded in winning majority support, must accept the decision of the majority. In return, the majority would permit minorities to openly attempt to win majority support for their views. Freedom of speech and press, freedom to dissent, and freedom to form opposition parties and organizations not only are "natural rights" but are essential to ensure meaningful participation in government. Thus, the procedural requirements for self-government and the underlying ethics of liberal democracy are linked: Freedom of speech, press, religion, and political activity can be defended as natural God-given rights essential to human dignity, and they can also be defended as necessary for ensuring individual participation in government and ascertaining what the majority views really are.

Classical liberalism, however, did not place unlimited confidence in the ability of the masses to make public policy. Most classical liberals believed in "republican government." They were opposed to hereditary monarchies and a privileged aristocracy. But they did not support mass democracy, with direct participation by the people in decision-making. The classical liberals believed that the role of the masses was to select competent leaders and turn men out of office who did not govern in a wise and virtuous fashion. But they did not believe that the masses themselves should decide questions of public policy.

Classical liberalism also affirmed the equality of all men. The Declaration of Independence expressed the conviction that "all men are created equal." The Founding Fathers believed in equality for all *before the law* notwithstanding the accused's circumstances. Over time, the notion of equality has also come to include equality of *opportunity* in all aspects of life—social, educational, and economic. Each person should have an equal chance to develop his individual capacities to their natural limits; there should be no artificial barriers to personal advancement. It is important to remember, however, that classical liberalism has always stressed *equality of opportunity* and not *absolute equality*. Thomas Jefferson recognized a "natural aristocracy" of talent, ambition, and industry, and classical liberals have always accepted inequalities that are a product of individual merit and hard work. Absolute equality, or "leveling," is *not* a part of classical liberalism.

Finally, classical liberalism, as a *political* ideology, is closely related to capitalism as an *economic* ideology. The economic version of liberal freedom is the freedom to make contracts, to trade, to bargain for one's services, to move from job to job, to start one's own business, and so forth. Laissez-faire economics and classical liberal democracy are closely related as economic and political systems. Laissez-faire economics stresses individual rationality in economic matters; freedom of choice in working, producing, buying, and selling; and limited government intervention in economic affairs. Liberal democracy emphasizes individual rationality in voter choice; freedom of speech, press, and political activity; and limitations on governmental power over individual liberty. In liberal politics the individual is free to speak out, to form political parties, and to vote as he pleases—to pursue his political interest as he thinks best. In liberal economics, the individual is free to find work, to start businesses, and to spend his money as he pleases—to pursue his economic interest as he thinks best. The role of government is restricted to protecting private property, enforcing contracts, and performing only those functions and services which cannot be performed by the private market.

MODERN LIBERALISM: POWER TO "DO GOOD"

Modern liberalism rationalizes and justifies much of the growth of governmental power in America in the twentieth century. Modern liberalism retains the fundamental commitment to individualism, civil liberties, and faith in reason and virtue. But it emphasizes the importance of social and economic security of a whole population as a prerequisite to individual self-realization and self-development. Classical liberalism looked with suspicion on the state as a potential source of "interference" with personal freedom. But modern liberalism looks upon the power of government as a positive force to be used to contribute to the elimination of social and economic conditions that adversely affect people's lives and impede their self-development. The modern liberal approves of the use of governmental power to ensure the general social welfare and to correct the perceived ills of society.

Modern liberals believe they can change people's lives through the exercise of governmental power: end discrimination, abolish poverty, eliminate slums, ensure employment, uplift the poor, eliminate sicknesses, educate the masses, and instill humanitarian values in everyone. The prevailing impulse is to *do good*, to perform public services, and to assist the least fortunate in society, particularly the poor and the black. Modern liberalism is impatient with what it sees as slow progress through individual initiative and private enterprise toward the solution of socioeconomic problems, so it seeks to use the power of the national government to find immediate and comprehensive "solutions" to society's troubles.

Modern liberalism is frequently critical of certain aspects of capitalism, but it proposes to "reform" capitalism rather than replace it with socialism. Modern liberalism continues to recognize the individual's right to own private property, but it imposes on the property owner social and economic obligations that are designed to reduce capitalism's hardships. It assumes that business will be privately owned, but subject to considerable governmental regulation. Thus, the government intervenes to ensure fair labor standards, minimum wages, healthy working conditions, consumer protection, and so forth. Modern liberalism stresses the utility of government fiscal policies—taxing and spending—for maintaining full employment and economic stability. Modern liberals are committed to a significant enlargement of the public (governmental) sector of society—in matters having to do with education, welfare, housing, recreation facilities, transportation, urban renewal, medicine, employment, child care, etc. Modern liberalism envisions a larger role for government in the future—setting new goals, managing the economy, meeting popular wants, and drastically redirecting national resources away from private wants toward public needs.

Modern liberalism places much greater emphasis on the value of "equality" than does classical liberalism. Classical liberalism stressed the value of *equality of opportunity:* The individual should be free to make the most of his talents and skills; but differences in wealth or power that arose as a product of differences in talent, initiative, risk-taking, and skill were accepted as natural. In contrast, modern liberalism contends that individual dignity and equality of opportunity depend in some measure upon reduction of absolute inequality in society. Modern liberals believe that true equality of opportunity cannot be achieved where there are significant numbers of people suffering from hunger, remediable illness, or extreme hardships in the conditions of life. They believe that the existence of opportunities to "rise" in employment, housing, education, and the like depends upon a certain degree of *absolute equality*. Thus, modern liberalism supports government efforts to reduce extreme inequalities in society.

Govt. is a positive force   Popular participation
Dignity of the Individual   Republician form of Govt.
Natural Laws & rules of Nature   Absolute Equality

CONSERVATISM: THE INSIGHTS
OF EDMUND BURKE

In America today, "conservatism" is associated with classical liberalism. Conservatives in this country retain the early liberal commitment to individual freedom from government controls; maximum personal liberty; reliance upon individual initiative and effort for self-development, rather than governmental programs and projects; a free enterprise economy with a minimum of governmental intervention; and rewards for initiative, skill, risk, and hard work, in contrast to government-imposed "leveling" of income. These views are consistent with the early *liberalism* of Locke, Jefferson, and the nation's Founding Fathers. The result, of course, is a confusion of ideological labels: Conservatives today charge modern liberals with abandoning the principles of individualism, limited government, and free enterprise, and today's conservatives claim to be the true "liberals" in society.

Modern conservatism does indeed incorporate much of classical liberalism, but conservatism also has a distinct ideological tradition of its own. Indeed, conservatism had its origins in reaction to the excesses of early liberalism, particularly the radical liberalism of the French Revolution. The first important statement of modern conservatism is found in Edmund Burke's assessment of French liberalism, *Reflections on the Revolution in France,* written in 1790.

Conservatism is not as optimistic as liberalism about human nature. Traditionally, conservatives doubted the supposed wisdom, virtue, and humaneness of the masses; conservatives were unwilling to place supreme confidence in the rational capacities of the masses. Conservatives realized that human nature includes elements of irrationality, intolerance, extremism, ignorance, prejudice, and violence. Thus they were more likely to place their faith in law and tradition than in the popular emotions of mass movement. Edmund Burke recognized selfish and irrational motives of men. He believed that without law or tradition men would exist in a jungle of violence, terror, and chaos—a jungle in which only the most powerful would survive by cunning, deceit, and violence. If law and tradition were discredited and exclusive reliance placed upon rationality, the fabric that holds society together would be weakened. Without the protection of law and tradition, men and societies are vulnerable to terror and violence. The absence of law does not mean freedom, but rather exposure to the tyranny of terrorism and violence.

Conservatives doubt the ability of governmental planners to solve all of society's problems. Edmund Burke believed that reason was a valuable and distinctive human gift, but he challenged the views of liberals that the answers to every human problem were already at hand or could easily be discovered. In Burke's eyes, this was unpardonable conceit, and he was convinced that the intellectual arrogance of liberal reformers could lead society into chaos. Conservatives since

Burke have doubted the rational powers of governmental bureaucracies. They tend to think that societies are held together not exclusively by government programs and policies but also by traditional morality and force of habit, and that the progress of civilization depends as much on the maintenance of social order as on governmental planning.

Conservatism sets forth an evolutionary view of social progress. Burke believed that real progress in society was the outcome of continuous social change over a prolonged period of time. Revolutionary change is far more likely to set back society than to improve it. But over time, men can experiment in small ways with incremental changes, and continued from generation to generation this process of evolutionary change leads to a progressive improvement in the condition of humanity. No government possesses the wisdom to resolve all problems, but the cumulative experience of society does produce certain workable arrangements for the amelioration of social ills. Gradual progress is possible, but only if men do not destroy the painfully acquired wisdom of the past in favor of new untried utopian solutions that jeopardize the well-being of society.

Conservatives hold that man is a rational being, but he is also a victim of passion. Irrational drives and impulses—hatred, prejudice, intolerance, violence—are constantly at war with rational judgment and humane feelings. Without the guidance of law, tradition, and morality, man would soon come to grief by the unruliness of his passion, destroying both himself and others in pursuit of selfish gain. Rationalism is far from a sufficient guide to action; law, tradition, and morality are also needed for the realization of human purposes. Left to his own instincts, without the benefit of the accumulated wisdom of ages, and without institutions to channel and modify his aggressive instincts, man will degenerate to savagery. Strong institutions—family, church, and even government—are needed to repress selfish and irrational impulses of individuals and to inculcate civilized ways of life.

Conservatives believe in government by the consent of the governed, but they are skeptical of the ability of the masses to decide public policy questions themselves. Edmund Burke believed in *representative* government: The masses should elect wise and virtuous men to govern them, and the masses should have the power to replace leaders who misgovern them. But Burke did not believe that the masses themselves should handle public policy matters. Representatives were elected to use their own best judgment in deciding public issues; they should not become slaves of public opinion. To subject leaders to the caprice of public opinion was to invite anarchy. Thus today the term *Burkean representation* refers to the willingness of an elected representative to ignore public opinion and settle public issues in the light of his own judgment about what is best for society. While Burke did not trust in the wisdom of the masses, he was only slightly more trustful of the wisdom of political leaders. The only real hope for preserving civilization, he felt, lay in the wisdom of tradition and experience.

FASCISM: THE SUPREMACY
OF RACE AND NATION

Fascism is an ideology that asserts the supremacy of the nation or race over the interests of individuals or classes. In the words of Benito Mussolini, "Everything for the state; nothing against the state; nothing outside of the state." The state is the embodiment of a unifying, ethical "ideal" that stands above the materialistic class interest of a Marxist or the selfish individualism of the liberals. Fascism is presented as a form of lofty idealism—"a religious conception in which man is seen in immanent relation to a higher law, an objective will, that transcends a particular individual and raises him to conscious membership in a spiritual society."

Fascism perceives the state as not merely a governmental bureaucracy but the organic life of a whole people. According to Mussolini, "The Italian nation is an organism having ends, life, and means of action superior to those of the separate individuals or groups of individuals which compose it." In *Mein Kampf*, written prior to his assumption of power, Adolf Hitler added to the concept of an organic state, with his idea of the *Volk* (people) in which race and nation are united.

> The highest purpose of the volkish State is the care for the preservation of those racial primal elements which, supplying culture, create the beauty and dignity of a higher humanity. We, as Aryans, are therefore able to imagine a state only to be the living organism of a nationality which not only safeguards the preservation of that nationality, but which, by a further training of its spiritual and ideal abilities, leads it to the highest freedom.[2]

The central ideal of the *Volk*, then, is that of a racial folk or an "organic people" with a life, will, and purpose of its own.

The goal of the fascist state is not the welfare of the mass of people but the development of a superior type of human being. The goal is the cultivation of the best qualities of a people—bravery, courage, creativeness, genius, intelligence, and strength. Fascism values the superior individual who rises out of the mire of mass mediocrity—and the superior nation that rises above the vast ant-hill of mankind. If life is a struggle for existence in which the fittest survive, then strength is the ultimate virtue and weakness is a fault. Good is that which survives and wins; bad is that which fails. Socialism, communism, and democracy mean the worship of mediocrity and the hatred of excellence; not the superior man but the majority man becomes the ideal and the model; everyone comes to resemble everyone else. These ideologies submerge what is best and noble in the people. All of this degrades the race and contradicts the theory of evolution. In contrast, fascism admires heroism in individuals and nations. War frequently brings out the best in a nation: unity, bravery, strength, and courage.

Benito Mussolini speaking in Italy. A major component of Fascism was its embodiment in a single powerful leader; and a major component of that leadership was public oratory. *United Press International Photo*

Fascism asserts the superiority of "will" over "reason." The great deeds of history were performed not by reason but by heroic will. Peoples are preserved not by rational thought but by racial intuition. They rise to greatness when their will to power surmounts physical and world handicaps. Happiness is a poor motive in comparison with heroism, self-sacrifice, duty, and discipline. This irrationalism derives from a belief that life is too difficult, too complex, and too changeable to be reduced to a rational formula—that nature is driven by many forces, as yet unknown to science, that can only be understood by intuition and genius. The one universal law is that of the survival of the fittest. The fascist hero is the opposite of the democratic egalitarian. He lives dangerously and is prepared to meet disaster. He does not wish to be mediocre, but instead superior in everything he does. He creates his own rules and tramples down the opposition.

Politically, fascism offers itself as a merger of nationalism and socialism. Prior to World War II, fascism in Italy and in Germany put itself forward as a socialist regime adopted to national purposes. The party of Adolf Hitler was the National Socialist Party or "Nazi" Party.

Since the nation is an organic whole, the economy ought to be cooperative

Leader —— individual
State
Organic organ
Pragmatic ideology

rather than competitive. Every class and every interest ought to work together for the good of the nation. Thus, national socialism was designed to appeal not only to the working class but also to the lower middle class—the small shopkeepers and salaried employees—who suffer from inflation and depression and who are fearful of the prospect of being degraded to the ranks of the proletariat, a fate that Marxism had promised them. A program of national socialism involves complete control of the national economy by the national government in the national interest. Against the rights of liberty or equality, national socialism established the duties of service, devotion, and discipline. As an extreme form of nationalism, fascism identified internationalism with cowardice and lack of honor. Indeed, fascism depended for its driving force upon sentiments of national patriotism.

The power structure of a fascist regime is totalitarian. The unity of the fascist state requires "one people, one party, one leader." The fascist believes that a natural, superior, self-made leadership will emerge to provide intelligence and direction to the nation. The Nazi elite emerges from political combat as the fittest and most deserving of political survival; there is no interest in mass vote

In Germany Adolph Hitler's Nazi party brought about the rise of Fascism. Here Hitler reviews a unit of the German army in Warsaw a few days after the German blitzkreig subdued Poland. *Wide World Photo*

The full name of the Nazi party was the National Socialist Party. Nationalism was inculcated at an early age as this picture of the Hitler Youth Movement suggests. *Wide World Photo*

counting. A Nazi leadership represents *das Volk* simply by embodying more clearly and explicitly its will to power. At the head of the fascist elite is the leader—*Il Duce* in Italy or *Der Fuehrer* in Germany—in whose name everything is done, who is said to be "responsible" for all, but whose acts can nowhere be called into question. The leader is neither a scholar nor a theorist, but a charismatic man of action. Fascism strives for a "totality of power" in which all sectors of society—education, labor, art, science—are incorporated into the state and serve the purposes of the state. No sphere of social activity is free from national scrutiny and control. All of society's resources are viewed as resources of the state.

MARXISM: "WORKERS OF THE WORLD, UNITE"

Liberalism represented an eighteenth-century revolt against the aristocracy of a feudal system. Socialism represents a nineteenth-century revolt against the privileged wealth of a capitalist system. Communism is a particularly violent strain of the larger ideological movement termed *socialism*. Both socialism and communism arose out of the industrial revolution and the social evils it generated. Even though the industrial revolution led to a rapid rise in standards of living in western Europe, what impressed many early observers of this revolution was the economic inequalities it engendered. Throughout much of the nineteenth century, the only beneficiaries of the new industrialism seemed to be the successful manufacturers, bankers, merchants, and speculators, and the lot of the slum-dwelling working classes showed little improvement. This was a bitter disappointment to the humanitarian hopes of many who had earlier embraced liberalism in the expectation that the rewards of economic progress would be shared by everyone. It appeared that liberalism and capitalism had simply substituted an aristocracy of wealth for an aristocracy of birth.

The first stirrings of socialism date back to the days of the French Revolution itself. Although the majority of French revolutionists were liberals whose aim it was to establish *equality of opportunity,* there were already a few who wished to establish *absolute equality* of wealth and income. The rise of Napoleon appeared to check the growth of socialism for a time, but a number of "utopian" socialists continued to develop schemes to replace the free market system with cooperative, egalitarian communities. Much of this effort was directed toward founding small communistic communities that were self-sufficient and organized on a cooperative basis, with profits from labor distributed equally among the members of the community. This socialism was mild and philanthropic; it was neither political nor violent. Utopian socialism and communal living never amounted to a strong political movement or a full-fledged ideology. The man who finally made socialism an effective ideology and a successful political movement was Karl Marx.

Like many socialists, Karl Marx (1818 - 1883) was an upper middle class intellectual, who was educated at the University of Berlin and began his career as a professor of philosophy. When his radicalism barred academic advancement, he turned to journalism and moved to Paris. There he met Friedrich Engels, a wealthy young intellectual who supported Marx financially and collaborated with him on many of his writings. It was Marx's humanitarian sympathy for industrial workers, not his personal experience in a factory, that led him to devote his activities to the cause of the working classes. Marx's first important work, *The Condition of the Working Class in England* (1844), was a protest against the sufferings and inequities of the working classes in the industrial revolution. The *Communist Manifesto* (1848) was a political pamphlet—short, concise, and full of striking phrases. It provided an ideology to what before had been no more than scattered protest against injustices. The *Manifesto* set forth the key ideas of Marxism which would be developed twenty years later in great detail in a lengthy work, *Das Kapital.*

Let us summarize the basic ideas of Marxian communism: economic determinism, dialectical materialism, the class struggle, the theory of surplus value, the inevitability of revolution, and the dictatorship of the proletariat.

Lenin (center) was a contributor to communism both as an intellectual theorist and as a practicing revolutionary. Here he addresses a May Day rally in Red Square in 1918. *Culver Pictures.*

Economic Determinism.   Communism believes that economic arrangements in society, or "modes of production," are basic to all the rest of society. The mode of production determines the class structure, the political system, religion, education, family life, law, and even art and literature. The mode of production determines the basic social structure of society, and the rest is simply "superstructure," which is molded by the prevailing economic arrangements. For example, the economic structure of feudalism creates a class structure of a privileged aristocracy and a suffering serfdom. The economic structure of capitalism creates a class structure of a wealthy *bourgeoisie* (a property-owning class of capitalists) who control the government and exercise power over the *proletariat* (the propertyless workers).

Dialectical Materialism.   Marx borrowed the idea of the "dialectic" from his former teacher, the German philosopher Hegel. Hegel used this word to refer to a process whereby ideas are first advanced (thesis), then challenged by contradictory ideas (antithesis), and then combined into a higher idea (synthesis), containing elements of each. Hegel argued that the dialectic of ideas determined the historic development of social institutions. While Hegel was an idealist who believed that ideas shaped history, Marx was a materialist who believed that economic arrangements or modes of production shaped society.

bourgeoisie vs proletariat
Haves vs Have nots

The dialectic of Marx, therefore, involved modes of production rather than ideas in any given economy. There is a ruling class which by virtue of its monopoly over the mode of production is able to dominate a whole society. Yet, great as the power of the ruling class may be, it is basically unstable because new modes of production are developed, leading to new forms of economic organizations and new classes arising to challenge the monopoly of the older ruling class. History is determined by dialectical materialism: The established mode of production with its ruling class is a thesis, and new emerging modes of production and new classes are the antithesis—the source of social change and revolution. Marx believed that the old aristocracy had been successfully challenged by liberal capitalism because the mode of production had changed from agriculture to industrialism. In the French Revolution, the new class of capitalists had broken the regime of their former rulers, the aristocrats, whose power had been based upon the ownership of land. As strong as they appeared, however, the material dialectic of history was moving on, and capitalism was producing its own antithesis—the factory workers or "proletariat."

The Class Struggle.   The first sentence of the *Communist Manifesto* exclaims: "The history of all hitherto existing society is the history of class struggles." These class struggles are created by the mode of production; the class that owns the mode of production is in the dominant position and exploits the other classes. Such exploitation creates antagonism, which gradually increases until it bursts into revolution. The means of production in the Middle Ages was land, and the aristocracy that owned the land controlled government and society. The industrial revolution created a new class, the bourgeoisie, which rose to importance because it owned the means of production—money, machines, and factories. But just as the aristocracy was supplanted by the bourgeoisie, so the bourgeoisie will in the course of time be superseded by the proletariat. The capitalist exploits the worker to the point where the worker is forced to revolt against his oppressors and overthrow a capitalist state.

The Theory of Surplus Value.   According to Marx, labor is the only source of value. Labor is the one thing common to all commodities and gives each commodity its value. As Marx put it, "All wealth is due to labor, and therefore, to the laborer, all wealth is due." Although the laborer deserves the full value of the commodity he makes, under capitalism he receives only a small part of it, just enough for his subsistence. The rest, which Marx called "surplus," is taken by the capitalist for his own enrichment. Thus the capitalist system is a gigantic scheme for exploiting the worker by confiscating the surplus value he has created. The practical solution, of course, is to make it impossible for capitalists to exploit workers by establishing "collective ownership of all means of production, distribution, and exchange." In other words, the proletarian must

The thrust of communism in the Soviet Union has been to create an industrial society from an agrarian one. The conversion, however, has also required increased mechanization of Soviet agriculture. Here winter wheat is harvested on a collective farm. *United Press International Photo*

eliminate the capitalist and own all of the tools of production, distribution, and exchange himself, so that the surplus value will not flow to the capitalist.

The Inevitability of Revolution.   Not only did Marx predict the coming of the proletariat revolution; he also sought to show that such a revolution was inevitable. According to the *Communist Manifesto*, "What the bourgeoisie produces, above all, is its own grave-diggers. Its fall and the victory of the proletariat are equally inevitable." As each capitalist tries to maximize his profit, the rich become richer and the poor become poorer. Moreover, competition squeezes out small capitalists, and ownership is gradually concentrated in the hands of fewer and fewer capitalists. As exploitation increases, and as more petty capitalists are forced into the ranks of the proletariat, both the strength and the antagonism of the proletariat increase. The proletariat develops a working class consciousness and ultimately rises up against the exploiters. As capitalists drive wages down to maximize profits, capitalism becomes plagued by a series of crises or depressions, each one worse than the one before. As wages are forced ever lower, capitalists soon cannot sell their products because of the low purchasing power of the proletariat, and depression follows. Further, as capitalists introduce more machinery, the demand for labor declines, and unemployment rises. The result of these internal contradictions in capitalism is a great deal of human misery, which eventually explodes in revolution. Thus, in his drive for profit, the capitalist really digs his own grave by bringing the revolution ever closer.

The Dictatorship of the Proletariat.   Although Marx claimed that the coming of the revolution is inevitable, he nonetheless urged the workers to organize for revolutionary action. The *Communist Manifesto* closes with the words, "The proletarians have nothing to lose but their chains. They have a world to win. Working men of all countries, unite!" The capitalists will never peacefully give up their ruling position. Only a violent revolution will place the proletarians in power. When the proletarians come to power, they, like ruling classes before them, will set up a state of their own—a dictatorship of the proletariat—to protect their class interests. Unlike governments of the past, however, which served oppressive minorities, the proletariat dictatorship will be a government by and for the great majority of workers. It will seize the property of the capitalist majority and place ownership of the modes of production in the hands of the proletariat. The bourgeoisie will be eliminated as a class.

Communism and the Withering Away of the State.   Since class differences depend upon ownership of the modes of production, the result of common ownership will be a one-class or "classless" society. Since the purpose of government is to assist the ruling class in exploiting and oppressing other classes, once a classless society is established the government will have no purpose and will gradually "wither away." In the early stages of the revolution the rule of distribution will be "from each according to his ability, to each according to his work." But after the victory of communism and the establishment of a full classless society, the rule of distribution will be "from each according to his ability, to each according to his need." After the elimination of classes, society will be peaceful and cooperative, and there will no longer be any need for coercion. Government and its coercive powers will disappear forever.

SOCIALISM: FROM PRIVATE ENTERPRISE TO PUBLIC OWNERSHIP

There is a bewildering variety of definitions of socialism. Communists employ the term as a label for societies that have experienced successful communist revolutions and are in the process of developing a communist society. Occasionally critics of government welfare programs in the United States label as "socialist" any program or policy that restricts free enterprise in any way. Socialism is also frequently confused with egalitarianism—governmental efforts to achieve absolute equality or "leveling" of wealth or income. But fundamentally, *socialism means public ownership of the means of production, distribution, and service.* Socialists agree on one point: Private property in land, buildings, factories, and stores must be transformed into social or collective property. The idea of collective ownership is the core of socialism.

Socialism shares with communism a condemnation of the capitalist system as exploitive of the working classes. Communists and socialists agree on the evils of industrial capitalism—the exploitation of labor, the concentration of wealth, the insensitivity of the profit motive to human needs, insecurities and sufferings brought on by the business cycle, the conflict of class interests, and the propensity of capitalist nations to involve themselves in war. In short, most socialists agree on the criticisms of the capitalist system set forth by Marx.

Socialists are committed to the democratic process as a means of replacing capitalism with collective ownership of economic enterprise. They generally reject the desirability of revolution as a way to replace capitalism and instead advocate peaceful constitutional roads to socialism. Moreover, socialists have rejected the idea of a socialist "dictatorship"; they contend that the goal of socialism is a free society embodying the democratic principles of freedom of speech, press, assembly, association, and political activity. They frequently claim that socialism in the economic sector of society is essential to achieving democracy and equality in the political sector of society. In other words, they believe that true democracy cannot be achieved until wealth is widely distributed and the means of production are commonly owned. Wealth must be redistributed in such a way as to make it possible for all persons to share in the benefits created by society. This means a transfer of ownership of all substantial economic holdings to the government. But the transfer must be accomplished in a democratic fashion, rather than by force or violence; and a socialist society must be governed as a true democracy.

Socialists are generally committed to an evolutionary approach to the achievement of common ownership of an economic enterprise. They reject the necessity of violent revolution or civil war. They are prepared for a gradual evolutionary restructuring of society—a restructuring that can take place within the framework of liberal democratic traditions.

Socialists are ready to cooperate with liberal parties in order to achieve improvements in the conditions of the working classes—to mitigate the conditions of the impoverished, maintain full employment, regulate economic cycles, extend social security, eliminate discrimination, and expand educational and cultural opportunities for the masses. Unlike communists, they envision a gradual change from private to public ownership of property. Thus, socialists may begin by "nationalizing" the railroads, the steel industry, the automobile industry, privately owned public utilities, or other specific segments of the economy. Nationalization involves governmental seizure of these industries from private owners, perhaps accompanied by some form of compensation. Many socialists realize that support for collective ownership must not rest exclusively on a single class. Socialists have learned through hard experience that their programs have to have the approval of a wide segment of the public, and not merely the working class.

Socialism is egalitarian. Socialists would reduce or eliminate inequalities in the distribution of wealth or income. Socialism attempts to achieve *absolute equality*, rather than merely *equality of opportunity*, which is the goal of liberals.

Modern socialism grew out of revisions of basic Marxian doctrines in western European nations in the twentieth century. One of the most prominent spokesmen for "revisionism" was Edward Bernstein (1850 - 1932), who revised many Marxian ideas and contributed to the break between communism and socialism. Bernstein rejected the prediction that capitalism would inevitably collapse as a result of its own internal contradictions. He realized that capitalism would not produce the widespread economic misery that would compel workers to rise up in revolution. The only way to achieve socialism, he contended, would be through organized political activity within the democratic constitutional process. Moreover, he argued that capitalist society did indeed provide the working classes with opportunities for effective political action. He realized that socialist parties could be organized to function within the existing political systems of western European nations. Bernstein also rejected Marx's prediction that the rich must get richer and the poor poorer. He believed that through party activity, governmental reforms, and trade union activity, including collective bargaining with employers, the standard of living of the workers could be vastly improved without the necessity for revolution. Finally, he urged that socialism reject the communist notion of a political dictatorship by the working class and devote its energies to the welfare of all groups in society.

THE "NEW LEFT" IN AMERICA

The "New Left" in America covers a wide spectrum from reformers, to socialists, to violent revolutionaries. It is linked to a subculture or "counter-culture" that deliberately and flamboyantly rejects familiar American middle class ways of life. Much of the New Left movement is devoid of a coherent ideology. However, the writings of philosopher Herbert Marcuse provide contemporary American radicalism with whatever ideological justification it possesses.

The radicalism of Marcuse begins with a sweeping condemnation of contemporary society as a highly industrialized, bureaucratized machine, in which human nature is twisted and destroyed in the competitive values and institutions that it encounters. American society with its capitalist ethos is the most materialist and bureaucratized of all societies, but Marcuse considers his critique to be almost equally applicable to socialist nations such as the Soviet Union. Marcuse is primarily concerned with the quality of man's life and spirit, and he sees advanced technological society as destructive of human characteristics. Marcuse believes that the present ruinous use of technology is ironic, because for the first time in history man possesses the opportunity to satisfy all of his material needs with relatively little work, leaving him free to live a full, free, and creative life. The struggle against scarcity is over, and people are free to develop in a true humanistic fashion. When life's sustaining resources were scarce, human beings were violent and competitive, lacking attitudes of human solidarity and cooperativeness, but now they could really become more humane.

Only a radical restructuring of social and economic institutions will succeed in liberating people for humanistic, cooperative lifestyles. The existing institutions have conditioned man to be materialistic, competitive, and violent. He has been transformed into a "one-dimensional man" in whom genuine humanistic values are repressed. In other words, institutions have thoroughly distorted human nature. The implication is that they have corrupted men, and without them life would be loving, cooperative, and compassionate. The problem of social change is truly monumental because the values and institutions of American society are deeply rooted. Since most people are not aware of the fact that they are "one-dimensional," the first step in social change is making people aware of their misery—that is, "consciousness raising."

Bureaucracy, rationality, efficiency, and productivity are dehumanizing ideas that grow out of technology and materialism. Bureaucracies, both in socialist governments and in capitalist corporations, are insensitive to human needs. But the American capitalist system is the worst of all. Profitability rather than humanistic values remain the criterion of decision-making in the economy, and this is the reason for poverty and misery, despite material abundance. Bureaucracies being unresponsive, individuals feel powerless to change their condition in life.

Radicalism views American society as a huge, brutal, irrational machine that operates in terms of efficiency and profitability—diverted from human purposes. Contemporary radicals think of modern liberals as being hypocritical in their attempts to reform the system; only a general revolution and radical restructuring of institutions will succeed in ending war, racism, poverty, and alienation. Contemporary radicals are not necessarily committed to work for change within the existing framework of society; many endorse extralegal and sometimes violent alternatives as the only means of dealing with a system they regard as violent itself. The emphasis in contemporary radicalism is on negative goals: destroying institutions—governments, corporations, universities, the military, etc.—which are bureaucratic and unattentive to human needs. Radicals are vague about the kind of society they want to replace the present one after the revolution. But radical writings imply that the new society will be humanistic rather than materialistic and spontaneous rather than bureaucratic; popular participation in the spirit of solidarity and brotherhood will replace the bargaining and compromising and competition characteristic of contemporary society.

In the new society, based on the principles of cooperation and brotherhood rather than competition, love will overcome materialism. This new society will be organized not to foster technological or material progress but to develop human qualities. The New Left is not explicitly socialist because socialism implies large unresponsive state bureaucracies. However, the New Left emphasizes the need for collectivist control over the economic resources of society and popular participation in decisions about the use of these resources. "Participatory democracy" must replace bureaucratization and centralization in decision-making. Participatory democracy does not involve elections, bargains, or compromises but has to do with group interaction in the spirit of solidarity and brotherhood with a view toward developing consensus. It is not merely a way of registering individual preferences and deciding issues by majority rule but a group process in which individuals are qualitatively transformed into a whole community with a shared purpose. Participatory democracy will bring men out of isolation and powerlessness into solidarity and control. Institutions should not be governed from the top down but by the individuals who compose them. Participatory democracy should extend to work, school, neighborhood, prison, welfare recipients, etc. Thus, besides political institutions, all major societal institutions must be restructured to meet the criteria for participatory democracy.

Other characteristics of contemporary radicalism include:
—emphasis on the community rather than the individual;
—the superiority of sensory experience over rational knowledge;
—stress on cooperation rather than competition;
—emphasis on naturalness (rejection of makeup, bras, suits, ties, etc.);
—concern with self-knowledge, introspection, and self-discovery;
—and the rejection of rationality and objectivity in finding truth, with emphasis on direct experience and involvement.

Radicalism does not have a clear comprehensive theory of social change. Certainly radicals do not accept the necessity of "working within the system," believing as they do that present institutions are inflexible and incapable of transformation. But it is not clear how the revolution will come about. Contemporary radicalism has yet to find a mass base on which to found a revolution; most radicals are upper middle class intellectuals and students. They know they must form coalitions with broader based groups in society. Yet the New Left is fragmented over such questions as the role of black people in the movement, the organizational potential of the working class, and the ethics of violence. Radical meetings are frequently endless debates over such questions as: Is violence or nonviolence the better revolutionary tactic? With whom and under what conditions should coalitions be formed? How should popular current issues be ex-

Opposition to the Vietnam War served as a catalyst for the growth of a more generalized American radical movement. Antiwar demonstrations were common in the late 1960's and early 1970's. *Boston Globe Photo*

ploited—the Vietnam War, civil rights, poverty, for instance? Should radicals cooperate with liberals? Is the youth culture with its interest in drugs, pop music, and communal living a source of social change or a cop-out from the revolutionary struggle?

The Vietnam War was a contributing force to the growth of radicalism in America in the late 1960s and early 1970s. As the war grew in intensity, so did the New Left; but as the war subsided, radicalism declined, particularly on America's campuses. The war was regarded as a "mistake" by most Americans, but it especially inflamed middle class, idealistic young people who regarded it as immoral and unjust. It cast a shadow over their postcollege plans and produced some guilt over the knowledge that lower class youth were being drafted to fight while more favored middle class youth remained on campus. More importantly, the humiliation of national leadership in Vietnam called into question the whole range of societal values and institutions—American resistance to communistic expansion, the military-industrial complex, and mindless governmental bureaucracies. If the nation's leaders (the older generation) could be so disastrously mistaken about Vietnam, they could also be mistaken about many other values in American life. Hence, for many students, opposition to the war in Vietnam grew into a sweeping criticism of American society in general and then into radicalism as an ideology. However, U.S. disengagement from the war, the end of the draft, and perhaps even the Twenty-sixth Amendment to the Constitution giving 18- to 21-year-olds the right to vote and participate directly in the political system seemed to contribute to the decline of radicalism on the campus in the 1970s.

POWER AND IDEOLOGY: A CASE STUDY

Marxism-Leninism in the Soviet Union

The task fell to Nikolai Lenin to reinterpret Marxism as a revolutionary ideology, to carry out a successful communist revolution, and to construct a communist state in the Soviet Union after the 1917 Revolution. Lenin contributed a great deal to communist ideology—so much so that contemporary communist ideology is frequently referred to as "Marxism-Leninism."

From the Russian standpoint in 1917, Marxism was a discouraging doctrine because its hopes for the future were based on conditions that were supposed to emerge in the later stages of industrialism. Marx believed that the communist revolution would occur when capitalism itself produced a class of factory workers that would be large enough to overcome its capitalist rulers. But this theory did not apply in pre-World War II Russia, which was still a semifeudal society of peasants and landlords, with only a small number of factory workers and an even smaller number of capitalists. Lenin, however, believed that Russia could skip the capitalist stage of revolution and move directly from a feudal order to a communist society. His belief was based upon the decay of the Russian state after decades of inefficient despotism under the czarist regime. To Lenin the Russian political system appeared so weak that it could be destroyed by a relatively small, disciplined, hard-core group of professional revolutionaries.

The Totalitarian Party.   According to Lenin, the key to a successful revolution was the creation of a new and revolutionary type of totalitarian political party composed of militant professional revolutionaries. This party would be organized and trained like an army to obey the commands of superior officers. While western European socialist parties were gathering millions of supporters in relatively democratic organizations, Lenin constructed a small, exclusive, well-disciplined, elitist party. First he described such a party in an early pamphlet, entitled *What Is to Be Done;* then he proceeded to organize it. Under his skilled leadership, the Communist Party of the Soviet Union became the first modern totalitarian party.

Lenin could justify the creation of a highly disciplined party elite on the basis of Marx's ambiguous attitudes toward democracy. Marx's idea of a "dictatorship of the proletariat," and his phrase the "vanguard of the proletariat," seemed to suggest an elitist view of the revolutionary process. Lenin seized upon these and amplified them into an elitist and totalitarian notion of a communist party. According to Lenin, the Communist Party is the true "vanguard of the proletariat"—the most advanced and class-conscious sector of the proletariat, which has an exclusive right to act as spokesman for the proletariat as a whole and to exercise the dictatorial powers of the proletariat over the rest of society. There is no need to ask who speaks for the masses, or even who speaks for the proletariat; the Communist Party *is* the voice of the proletariat and it can legitimately exercise dictatorial powers in the name of the proletariat.

The Theory of Imperialism.   Lenin also tried to come to grips with two dilemmas: Why were capitalist societies still flourishing in the twentieth century, contrary to Marx's prediction? Why was the condition of the working classes improving, rather than deteriorating? Lenin's *Imperialism* was an attempt to answer these embarrassing questions. According to Lenin, when advanced capitalist countries were unable to find home markets for their products because of depressed worker income, they were obliged to turn outward and to seize colonial markets. This maneuver enabled them, for the time being at least, to expand without forcing the wages of their own workers down to a level of subsistence. By "exporting poverty abroad" they managed to keep their own workers relatively prosperous, thus delaying the development of true proletariat class consciousness in their own country. Lenin believed that the whole world was being divided into exploiters and exploited, with backward nations providing the surplus labor for more advanced nations. To shore up the shaky foundations of capitalism, capitalist nations were obliged to continually strive for fresh colonial markets. Of course, they were thus brought into bitter conflict with one another in their attempt to expand their respective empires. The final state of capitalism, therefore, would assume the form of imperialist warfare as rival capitalist nations engaged in a struggle to control colonial markets. To Lenin, World War I was proof that this advanced stage of capitalist decay had been reached and the worldwide capitalist system was ready for destruction. The idea of worldwide imperialism and exploitation also helped to explain why revolutionary activities in economically backward regions could be successful despite the absence of industrial capitalism. Since the inhabitants of these regions were the most cruelly exploited of all the world's workers, the revolution need not begin in the industrial heartland but would arise at the colonial periphery.

Communism in One Country.   After Lenin came to power in the Soviet Union, he found himself no longer in the position of revolutionary leader; he was the leader of a nation. Should the Soviet Union direct its energies toward immediate worldwide revolution, as envisioned by Marx? Or should it avoid confrontation with the Western world until it became a strong and self-sufficient nation? Gradually abandoning the original hopes for an immediate world revolution, Lenin and Stalin, his successor, turned to the task of creating "communism in one country." With the Communist Party more firmly and centrally disciplined than ever, the Soviet leaders turned to the achievement of rapid industrialization through a series of five-year plans designed to convert a backward agrarian country into a modern industrial nation. The sweeping industrialization, brought about by repression and terror of a totalitarian regime, came at great cost to the people. The Stalinist period saw brutality, oppression, imprisonment, purges, and murders—later officially admitted by the Soviet leaders. The Soviet regime held down the production of consumer goods in order to concentrate on development of heavy industry. As costly and ruthless as it was, the effect of this policy was the modernization of the Russian economy in the course of a single generation. In part, the ideology of communism made it possible to call upon the people for tremendous sacrifices for the good of the communist state.

Neither Marx nor Lenin proved successful as a political prophet. The state never "withered away" in communist Russia. Indeed, to maintain the communist government a massive structure of coercion—informants, secret police, official terrorism, and a giant prison system—was erected. (The brutality of the system is described by Nobel Prize-winning author and former Soviet political prisoner Aleksandr Solzhenitzyn in *The Gulag Archipelago*.) At the same time, the overall goal of world revolution, while never abandoned by the Soviet leadership, was compromised by the "realities" of world power. Particularly after the death of Stalin, the Soviet Union gradually restored its ties with the Western world. Among the factors that improved relations between ideologically opposed powers were: the unspeakable implications of nuclear weapons, creating a balance of terror and providing both sides with a reason to limit conflict; a gradual rise in the standard of living in the Soviet Union and a relaxation of forced industrialization; and the threat of an increasingly powerful Communist China on the eastern border of the U.S.S.R., compelling the Soviet leadership to seek support against a militant revolutionary rival.

The U.S.S.R. deviated from earlier interpretations of Marxism-Leninism in other ways. More and more, the Soviets have turned to the "principle of

material interest"—larger rewards for better labor and management performance—indicating that they are realistic enough to accept a capitalist notion
when it is in their interest to do so. Another change involves greater decentralization in industry, along with less reliance on centralized state direction. A
related development is the growing difficulty of centralized Kremlin rule by a
Communist Party apparatus that finds it hard to control the increasingly
sophisticated managerial and professional elite required in an advanced
technological society. Finally, there has been some decline in terrorism since the
Stalinist period, although the Soviet leadership has proved that it can oscillate
easily between cruel orthodoxy and relaxed experimentation as fits its purposes.

Despite these changes, Marxist-Leninist ideology still plays a very important
role in the Soviet Union today. There is no lack of interest in the continuing in-
doctrination of the citizenry in Marxism-Leninism—in schools, factories, collective farms, universities, the military, and social organizations.

Marxism as a political ideology has reshaped the modern world. More than
half of the world's population live under political regimes which call themselves
"communist" or "socialist." Yet Marxism as a scientific approach to understanding history and society is clearly inadequate. Let us summarize some of the more
serious flaws in Marxism:

1. Capitalism has given the American people the world's highest standard of
living—a standard of living that is clearly the envy of people living under
socialist and communist regimes. Capitalism does *not* inevitably depress the
condition of workers. On the contrary, workers in America own their own
homes, automobiles, appliances, and other material luxuries, and the middle
class has grown rather than diminished over time. Industrial workers in modern
capitalist nations have received larger and larger shares of national income, and
standards of living have increased rapidly. Labor under capitalism is *not* becoming progressively miserable and downtrodden.

2. Governments in capitalist nations have responded to the pressures of
organized labor and the masses of voters to provide a wide variety of health,
education, and welfare programs. It is difficult to argue that America's national
leadership has reflected only the interest of a ruling capitalist class, in view of
vast government programs and expenditures for social security, welfare, fair
labor standards, protection for union organizations, public education, and so
forth. Furthermore, these programs have been financed on a progressive income
tax structure that takes a larger proportion of the income of high-income persons
in taxation than low-income persons. In short, there are many examples of
government programs and policies in capitalist nations that conflict with the interests of capitalists.

3. Capitalist nations have more complex social structures than the simple
bourgeois-proletariat distinction of Marxism. There are many crosscutting
social, political, economic, religious, and racial interests and allegiances in a

Marxism-Leninism in the Soviet Union

modern industrial society. For example, Marx assumed that the interest of farm populations would be the same as those of factory workers, but in most nations farm populations have resisted communism. In America, industrial workers have been neither class-conscious nor revolutionary. Ironically, support for Marxism is greater among upper middle class intellectuals than among industrial workers.

4. Marxism does not recognize the difference between dictatorship and democracy. The idea of a "dictatorship of the proletariat" justifies suppression, terrorism, violence, purges, imprisonment, and murder when directed against "enemies of the people." After the revolution has occurred, and the proletariat has emerged victorious, there is no reason for political parties, or opposition candidates, or dissent of any kind. In a communist society only the party of the working class—the Communist Party—is permitted to exist.

5. Marxism predicts the "withering away" of the state in a communist society, but in fact communist governments have become giant bureaucracies which oversee every aspect of life and society.

COMPARING IDEOLOGIES

There is always some risk of oversimplification and misinterpretation when we try to compare ideologies. Ideologies have different kinds of emotional appeals, different interpretations of life, different origins and histories, and different strategies and tactics for changing society. Nevertheless, it is sometimes helpful to step back and gain a broad perspective on the various ideologies competing for our attention

One standard framework for comparison recognizes that major ideologies have both *political* and *economic* components. Politically, they may be either totalitarian or democratic; economically, they may stress either private enterprise or public (government) enterprise. Using these political and economic dimensions, we can construct a two-by-two arrangement with four separate cells as shown in Figure 8-1. This enables us to classify fascism, communism, liberalism (classical and modern), and socialism. Fascism and communism are totalitarian political systems—neither permits civil liberties, opposition parties

		Economic System	
		Private Enterprise	Public Enterprise
Political System	Totalitarian	Fascism	Communism
	Democratic	Liberalism	Socialism

FIGURE 8-1.

Marxism-Leninism in the Soviet Union

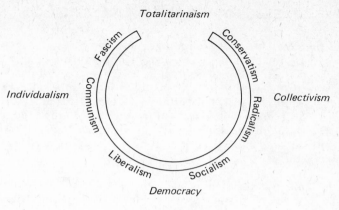

FIGURE 8-2.

or candidates, or political dissent. However, they differ in that fascism allows private ownership (so long as it serves the state), while communism insists on government ownership of the means of production. Liberalism and socialism are democratic political ideologies, but they differ over the question of private versus public ownership of the means of production.

Frequently ideologies are compared along a "left-right" dimension. During the years following the French Revolution (1789), the most radical, equalitarian, and violent members of the French National Assembly sat on the left of the chamber, while the right side was occupied by liberals and moderates. Today we continue to use the terms *right-wing* and *left-wing* to describe political factions. We think of the extreme right as fascist and the right wing as composed of conservatives and classical liberals. The extreme left is communist and radical, while the left wing is socialist. The left-right dimension is misleading, however, because extreme right and extreme left share totalitarian views—they both view democratic procedures as weak or corrupt and they favor dictatorship of one kind or another.

A more complex scheme for classifying ideologies is presented in Figure 8-2. The principal dimensions for this classification are (1) individualism versus collectivism and (2) totalitarianism versus democracy.

NOTES

1. Carl Becker, *Modern Democracy* (New Haven, Conn.: Yale University Press, 1941), p. 27.

2. Adolf Hitler, *Mein Kampf* (New York: Reynal and Hitchcock, 1939), p. 595.

TESTING YOUR PERFORMANCE

Note to the Student. The following questions are to test how well you achieved the Performance Objectives identified for you at the beginning of this chapter. The correct answers are supplied, accompanied by corresponding pages for you to review if you have answered incorrectly. The questions are coordinated numerically with the Performance Objectives at the beginning of the chapter. This exercise will assist you in determining the type of questions you have the most difficulty in answering (discussion, identification, explanation, definition, etc.) and will prepare you for test questions likely to be asked by your instructor.

1.   (a) An integrated system of ideas that provide society and its members with rationalizations for a way of life, guides for evaluating "rightness" and "wrongness," and emotional impulses to action is an _____ .
   (b) Power and ideology are intimately related. Ideology rationalizes and justifies the exercise of _____ .
2.   The affecting of perception, the rationalization and justification of a way of life and the provision of legitimacy for the structure of society, the providing of normative standards to determine "rightness" and "wrongness" in the affairs of society, and the provision of motivation for social and political action are all ways in which _____ .
3.   Utopianism, optimism about human progress, and oversimplification are the _____ .
4.   (a) The assertion of the worth and dignity of the individual, the emphasizing of the rational ability of man to determine his own destiny, and the rejection of ideas, practices, and institutions that submerge the individual into a larger whole and deprive him of his essential dignity are _____
_____ .
   (b) The type of liberalism which believes that man has a right to life, liberty, and property guaranteed by "natural law," believes in limited government, asserts the value of popular participation in government as an opportunity for individual self-development through majority rule and respect for minority rights, and believes in the equality of all men (equality of opportunity) is _____ .
   (c) The type of liberalism that emphasizes the importance of social and economic security of a whole population as a prerequisite to individual self-realization and self-development, looks upon the power of government as a positive force to eliminate social and economic conditions which adversely affect people's lives and impede their self-development, and contends that individual dignity and equality of opportunity depend in some measure upon reduction of absolute inequality in society, is _____ .
5.   The type of economics, closely related to classical liberal democracy, that stresses individual rationality in economic matters, freedom of choice in working, producing, buying, and selling, and limited government intervention in economic affairs is _____ .
6.   (a) The author who is associated with modern conservatism is _____
_____ .
   (b) The ideology that doubts the ability of governmental planners to solve

all of society's problems, sets forth an evolutionary view of social progress, holds that man is a rational being but also a victim of passion, stresses the need for strong institutions to repress selfish and irrational impulses of individuals, and believes in government by the consent of the governed but is skeptical of the ability of the masses to decide public policy questions themselves is _____ .

7. The willingness of an elected representative to ignore public opinion and settle public issues in the light of his own judgment about what is best for society is referred to as _____ .

8. (a) The ideology that asserts the supremacy of the nation or race over the interests of individuals or classes and perceives the state as not merely a governmental bureaucracy but the organic life of a whole people is _____ .

(b) The development of a superior type of human being and the cultivation of the best qualities of a people (bravery, courage, creativeness, genius, intelligence, and strength) are the _____ .

(c) The power structure of a fascist regime is _____ .

9. (a) The ideology that represents a nineteenth-century revolt against the privileged wealth of a capitalist system, arose out of the industrial revolution and the social evils generated by it, and goes back to the days of the French Revolution and the establishment of cooperative, egalitarian communities is

_____ .

(b) The ideology that is a particularly violent strain of the larger ideological movement termed socialism is _____ .

10. (a) The philosopher who made socialism an effective ideology and a succesful political movement was _____ .

(b) The short, concise pamphlet, full of striking phrases, that provided an ideology to what before had been only a scattered protest against injustices was

_____ .

(c) Marx's lengthy work discussing in detail the basic ideas of Marxian communism was _____ .

11. Identify the following basic ideas of Marxian communism:

(a) The belief that economic arrangements in society, or the "modes of production," are basic to all the rest of society. _____

_____

(b) The established mode of production with its ruling class is a thesis, and new emerging modes of production and new classes are the antithesis— the source of social change and revolution. _____

(c) The class that owns the mode of production is in the dominant position and exploits the other classes, creating antagonism, which gradually increases until it bursts into revolution. _____

(d) The laborer deserves the full value of the commodity he makes, but under capitalism, he receives only a small part of it, and the rest is taken by capitalists for their own enrichment. _____

(e) "What the bourgeoisie produces, above all, is its own grave-diggers. Its fall and the victory of the proletariat are equally inevitable." _____

_____

(f) When the proletarians come to power, they, like ruling classes before them, will set up a state of their own to protect their class interests. _____

_____

(g) Once a classless society is established the government will have no purpose and will gradually _____

12.   (a) The ideology that is a revolutionary interpretation of Marxism, and whose founder believed that Russia would skip the capitalist stage of revolution and move directly from a feudal order to a communist society, is _____

(b) The creation of a new and revolutionary type of totalitarian political party composed of militant professional revolutionaries was _____

(c) Lenin's belief that the whole world was being divided into exploiters and exploited, with backward nations providing the surplus labor for more advanced nations was the _____.

(d) Caught in the dilemma of whether to direct its energies toward immediate worldwide revolution or to avoid confrontation with the Western world until it became a strong and self-sufficient nation, Lenin and Stalin finally decided to turn to the task of creating _____.

13.   (a) Government efforts to achieve absolute equality or "leveling" of wealth or income are known as _____.

(b) Public (collective) ownership of the means of production, distribution, and service is _____.

(c) Condemnation of the capitalist system as exploitive of the working classes, and disagreement over the rapidity of change from private to public ownership of property represent the similarity and dissimilarity between which two ideologies? _____

14.   (a) The spokesman for "revisionism" who revised many of the Marxian ideas and contributed to the break between communism and socialism was __ _____.

(b) The prediction that capitalism would inevitably collapse as a result of its own internal contradictions, the prediction that the rich must of necessity get richer and the poor poorer, and the notion of a political dictatorship by the working class are all _____.

15.   (a) A sweeping condemnation of contemporary society as a highly industrialized, bureaucratized machine in which human nature is twisted and destroyed in the competitive values and institutions that it encounters, and the argument that only a radical restructuring of society's social and economic institutions will succeed in liberating people for humanistic, cooperative lifestyles (an ideological justification for contemporary radicalism) were made by _____ _____.

(b) The "ideology" viewing society as a huge, brutal, irrational machine operating in terms of efficiency and profitability and pushing for a general revolution and radical restructuring of institutions, implying that the new society will be humanistic rather than materialistic and spontaneous rather than bureaucratic and will be based on the principles of cooperation and brotherhood rather than competition, is _____.

16.   One of the contributing forces to radicalism in America in the late 1960s and early 1970s was the _____.

17.   Capitalism's provision of the highest standard of living, its improving of the condition of workers, the increasing of the size of the middle class, governmental provision of a wide variety of health, education, and welfare pro-

grams, the existence of many crosscutting social, political, economic, religious, and racial interests and allegiances in a modern industrial society, greater support for Marxism among upper class intellectuals than among industrial workers, and the fact that communist governments have become giant bureaucracies instead of withering away are all examples of _____
_____ .

18.   A risk of oversimplification and misinterpretation due to different kinds of emotional appeals, different interpretations of life, different origins and histories, different strategies and tactics for changing society, the existence of both political and economic components, and misleading use of the left-right dimension are all _____
_____ .

Correct Responses

1.   (a) Ideology (p. 278); (b) Power (p. 278).

2.   Ideologies control people's behavior (p. 278).

3.   Common characteristics of modern ideologies (p. 279).

4.   (a) Common beliefs of classical liberalism and modern liberalism (p. 280); (b) Classical liberalism (pp. 280 - 282); (c) Modern liberalism (pp. 282 - 283).

5.   Laissez-faire economics (p. 282).

6.   (a) Edmund Burke (p. 284); (b) Conservatism (pp. 284 - 285).

7.   Burkean representation (p. 285).

8.   (a) Fascism (p. 286); (b) Goals of the fascist state (p. 286); (c) Totalitarian (p. 288).

9.   (a) Socialism (pp. 289 - 290); (b) Communism (p. 289).

10.   (a) Karl Marx (p. 290); (b) *The Communist Manifesto* (p. 290); (c) *Das Kapital* (p. 290).

11.   (a) Economic determinism (p. 291); (b) Dialectical materialism (pp. 291 - 292); (c) The class struggle (p. 292); (d) Theory of surplus value (pp. 292 - 293); (e) The inevitability of revolution (p. 293); (f) Dictatorship of the proletariat (p. 294); (g) "Wither away" (p. 294).

12.   (a) Egalitarianism (p. 294); (b) Socialism (p. 294); (c) Communism and socialism (p. 295).

13.   (a) Edward Bernstein (p. 296); (b) Components of communism rejected by Bernstein (p. 296).

14.   (a) Herbert Marcuse (pp. 296 - 297); (b) Contemporary radicalism (pp. 297 - 298).

15.   Vietnam War (p. 299).

16.   Serious flaws in Marxism (pp. 303 - 304).

17.   Problems involved with comparing ideologies (pp. 304 - 305).

18.   (a) Leninism (p. 300); (b) Lenin's key to a successful revolution (p. 300); (c) Theory of imperialism (pp. 301 - 302); (d) Communism in one country (p. 302).

KEY TERMS

ideologies

utopianism

classical liberalism

modern liberalism

Enlightenment (Age of Reason)

natural law

state of nature

John Locke

social contract

limited government

the right of revolution

republican government

leveling

laissez-faire economics

positive freedom

conservatism

Edmund Burke

representative government

Burkean representation

Marxism

equality of opportunity

absolute equality

The Communist Manifesto

Das Kapital

economic determinism

modes of production

bourgeoisie

proletariat

dialectical materialism

class struggle

theory of surplus value

class society

Marxism-Leninism

vanguard of the proletariat

theory of imperialism

egalitarianism

socialism

nationalization

Edward Bernstein

fascism

organic state

Herbert Marcuse

participatory democracy

The New Left

DISCUSSION QUESTIONS

1.   Discuss ideologies:
    (a) How they control the behavior of men
    (b) Characteristics of modern ideologies

2. Compare and contrast classical liberalism, modern liberalism, and conservatism with regard to their emphases on:
    (a) Freedom
    (b) Role of the state (government)
    (c) Concern for social problems
    (d) Progress
    (e) Capitalism
    (f) Elite philosophy
    (g) Equality

3. Discuss the basic values of Marxian communism:
    (a) Economic determinism
    (b) Dialectical materialism
    (c) The class struggle
    (d) The theory of surplus value
    (e) The inevitability of revolution
    (f) The dictatorship of the proletariat
    (g) The withering away of the state

4. Discuss Leninism:
    (a) Differences with Marxism
    (b) The totalitarian party
    (c) The theory of imperialism
    (d) Communism in one country

5. Discuss the serious flaws in Marxism.

6. Compare and contrast socialism and communism with regard to:
    (a) Ownership of the means of production, distribution, and service
    (b) Condemnation of the capitalist system
    (c) Desirability of revolution
    (d) The idea of a dictatorship by the working class

7. Discuss the ideology of fascism:
    (a) The role of the state
    (b) The relationship of persons and the state
    (c) Its goals
    (d) Heroic will
    (e) Power structure
    (f) Economics

8. Discuss "radicalism" as an "ideology":
    (a) Ideological characteristics (as seen by Herbert Marcuse)
    (b) Ideological weaknesses

SUGGESTED READINGS

Daniel Bell, *The End of Ideology* (Glencoe, Ill : Free Press, 1960).

William F. Buckley, *Up from Liberalism* (New York: McDowell and Obstensky, 1959).

John Bunzel, *Anti-Politics in America* (New York: Random House, 1967).

MILTON FRIEDMAN, *Capitalism and Freedom* (Chicago: University of Chicago Press, 1962).

BARRY M. GOLDWATER, *The Conscience of a Conservative* (New York: Macfadden-Bartell, 1964).

JEFF GREENFIELD and JACK NEWFIELD, *A Populist Manifesto* (New York: Praeger, 1972).

LEWIS HARTZ, *The Liberal Tradition in America* (New York: Harcourt, Brace & World, 1955).

HERBERT MARCUSE, *One-Dimensional Man* (Boston: Beacon, 1964).

C. WRIGHT MILLS, *The Marxists* (New York: Delta Books, 1962).

STUDENTS FOR A DEMOCRATIC SOCIETY, *The Port Huron Statement* (Chicago: Students for a Democratic Society, 1966).

CHAPTER 9

Black Power and Racial Equality

PERFORMANCE OBJECTIVES

The student should be able to:

1.   Identify the initial goal (first step) in the struggle for equality in America. Identify the constitutional amendment and the clause upon which the civil rights movement is based.

2.   Contrast the rulings in *Plessy* v. *Ferguson* and *Brown* v. *Board of Education of Topeka, Kansas.*

3.   Give the reasons why the U.S. Supreme Court has little formal power at its disposal.

4.   List some of the resistance devices used by the southern states between 1954 and 1964 to avoid desegregation.

5.   Define *de facto* segregation.

6.   Outline the basic provisions of the Civil Rights Act of 1964.

7.   List the new techniques invented by the civil rights movement to enable minorities to acquire power and influence in American society.

8.   Cite the individual who was one of the nation's leading exponent of non-violent protest and founder of the Southern Christian Leadership Conference (SCLC).

9.   Discuss the effect of the participation of the mass media on nonviolent direct action.

10.   Outline the basic provisions of the Voting Rights Act of 1965 and the Civil Rights Act of 1968.

11.   Discuss the problems posed by nonviolent direct action.

313

12.   Describe the cycle at work in the ghettos which contributes to feelings of powerlessness among ghetto residents.

13.   Compare powerlessness in black ghettos with the "colonies" of an earlier era.

14.   Trace the development of the black power movement from a slogan to a program of political action.

15.   Explain why black militants reject integration.

16.   Identify the political party to which most black voters are heavily committed.

17.   Discuss what benefits black political activity has provided for blacks. Identify the strategy that is most effective in providing for black political power.

18.   Explain the relationship between *de facto* segregation and the "neighborhood school" concept.

19.   Outline the ruling of the Supreme Court in the case of *Swann* v. *Charlotte, Mecklenburg Board of Education.*

20.   Differentiate between *de facto* segregation in northern cities and *de facto* segregation in southern cities.

21.   Discuss the arguments for busing and the arguments against busing.

THE CIVIL RIGHTS MOVEMENT: ENDING LAWFUL DISCRIMINATION

The initial goal in the struggle for equality in America was the elimination of direct legal segregation. First, discrimination and segregation practiced by governments had to be prohibited, particularly in voting and public education. Then direct discrimination in all segments of American life, private as well as public—in transportation, theaters, parks, stores, restaurants, businesses, employment, and housing—came under attack. It is important to understand, however, that the elimination of direct lawful discrimination does not in itself ensure *equality.* The civil rights laws of the national government did not affect conditions of equality in America as directly as we might suppose. The problem of racial inequality—inequality between blacks and whites in income, health, housing, employment, education, and so on—is more than a problem of direct legal discrimination. Nevertheless, the first important step toward equality was the elimination of *lawful* segregation.

Led by Roy Wilkins, executive director of the National Association for the Advancement of Colored People, and Thurgood Marshall, chief counsel for the NAACP (who was later to become the first black Supreme Court justice), the newly emerging civil rights movement of the 1950s pressed for a court decision that direct lawful segregation violated the guarantee of "equal protection of

"Now, Charles, tell me all about the black experience."

Drawing by Wm. Hamilton; © 1973 The New Yorker Magazine, Inc.

laws" of the Fourteenth Amendment. For over half a century the courts had upheld laws *separating* the races so long as black and white facilities pretended to be equal in tangible respects, based on *Plessy* v. *Ferguson*. But the civil rights movement sought a complete reversal of this "separate but equal" interpretation of the Fourteenth Amendment; it wanted a decision that laws *separating* the races were unconstitutional.

The civil rights groups chose to bring suit for desegregation in Topeka, Kansas, where segregated black and white schools were equal with respect to buildings, curricula, qualifications and salaries of teachers, and other material factors. The object was to prevent the Court from ordering the admission of a black person because tangible facilities were not equal, and to force the Court to review the doctrine of segregation itself.

On May 17, 1954, the Court rendered its decision in *Brown* v. *Board of Education of Topeka, Kansas:*

Segregation of white and colored children in public schools has a detrimental effect upon the colored children. The impact is greater when it has the sanction of law, for the policy of separating the races is usually interpreted as denoting the inferiority of the Negro group. A form of inferiority affects the motivation of a child to learn. Segregation with the sanction of law, therefore, has a tendency to retard the educational and mental development of Negro children and to deprive them of some of the benefits they would receive in a racially integrated school system. Whatever may have been the extent of psychological knowledge of the time of *Plessy* v. *Ferguson,* this finding is amply supported by modern authority. Any language in *Plessy* v. *Ferguson* contrary to this source is rejected.[1]

Brown v. *Board of Education of Topeka, Kansas* marked the beginning of a new era in American politics. The *Brown* decision gave official legitimacy to the aspirations of the black people. It encouraged them to believe that they could achieve power within the constitutional framework. It raised their levels of expectations and inspired them to insist upon their full constitutional rights. This turning point in the power of black people in America was the product of a patient, reasoned, and legalistic approach to racial problems.

Of course the battle over segregation was just beginning in 1954. While segregation in any state-supported institution after 1954 was unconstitutional, it would remain a part of American life, regardless of its constitutionality, until effective *power* was brought to bear to end it. The Supreme Court, by virtue of the system of federalism and the separation of powers, has little formal power at its disposal. Congress, the president, state governors and legislators, and even occasional mobs of people, have more direct power at their disposal than the federal judiciary. The Supreme Court must rely largely on other branches of the federal government, on the states, and on private citizens to implement the law of the land. Yet in 1954 the practice of segregation was widespread and deeply ingrained in American life. Seventeen states required the segregation of the races in public schools,[2] and four additional states authorized segregation upon the option of the local school boards.[3] Moreover, the Congress of the United States required segregation of the races in the public schools of the District of Columbia.

The Supreme Court did not order immediate nationwide desegregation but instead turned over responsibility for desegregation to state and local authorities under the supervision of federal district court. The six border states with segregated school systems—Delaware, Kentucky, Maryland, Missouri, Oklahoma, West Virginia—together with the school districts in Kansas, Arizona, and New Mexico which operated segregated schools, chose not to resist desegregation formally. The District of Columbia also desegregated public schools the year following the Supreme Court's decision. But resistance to school desegregation was the choice of the 11 states of the old Confederacy. This resistance lasted more than 15 years. The refusal of a school district to desegregate until it was faced with a federal court injunction was the most common form of delay. Other schemes included state payments of private school tuition in lieu of providing public schools, the amending of compulsory attendance laws to provide that no child shall be required to attend an integrated school, and the use of pupil placement laws to avoid or minimize the extent of desegregation. Pupil placement laws, which guaranteed "freedom of choice," were the most successful of the delaying tactics. Black and white school children were permitted to indicate their choice of schools, and southern school authorities relied on the fact that most blacks and most whites selected the schools that they had previously attended—that is, segregated schools. Not until the late 1960s did federal courts decline to accept such plans from local school authorities as "good faith" implementation of desegregation. Finally, state officials themselves—including Governor George C. Wallace of Alabama —attempted to prevent desegregation on the grounds that it would endanger public safety. Violence flared in a number of southern communities; federal troops were used to desegregate Central High School in Little Rock, Arkansas, in 1957 and the University of Mississippi in 1962.

Resistance to desegregation was quite successful during the period from 1954 to 1964. Only about 2 percent of the black school children in the 11 southern states were attending integrated schools ten years after *Brown* v. *Board of Education of Topeka, Kansas.* But in the Civil Rights Act of 1964, Congress finally entered the civil rights field in support of Court efforts to achieve desegregation. Among other things, the act provided that every federal department or agency must take steps to end segregation in all departments or programs receiving federal financial assistance. The U.S. Office of Education was authorized to issue administrative orders or "guidelines" to eliminate segregation in schools receiving federal aid; schools which did not meet segregation guidelines faced termination of financial assistance from the federal government. Thus, in addition to Court orders requiring desegregation, school districts also faced federal guidelines and the loss of federal revenues. In 1969 the last legal justification for delay in implementing school desegregation collapsed when the Supreme Court rejected a request by Mississippi school officials for delay. The Court declared that every school district was obliged to end dual school systems "at once" and "now and hereafter" operate only unitary schools. The effect of the decision—15 years after the original *Brown* case—was to eliminate any further legal justification for continuation of segregation in public schools.

By 1970 southern school desegregation had proceeded to the point at which more black children were attending integrated schools in the South than in the North. Direct lawful segregation in southern schools had largely been eliminated. But even as the impact of segregation by law in the South was diminishing, more Americans came to realize the continuing impact of *de facto* segregation in northern cities. *De facto* segregation occurs when schools are predominantly white or black as a result of segregated housing patterns and neighborhood schools rather than direct lawful discrimination. If the issue is posed as one of "racial isolation," then by 1970 the efforts of federal courts and executive agencies to erase the last vestiges of segregation by law had so reduced racial isolation in the South that it was less than racial isolation in the North. Moreover, events in Boston, Massachusetts, Pontiac, Michigan, and other northern cities stemming from efforts to end racial isolation have produced disorder and violence, reminiscent of those involved in early desegregation efforts in the South.

THE CIVIL RIGHTS ACT OF 1964

As long as the civil rights movement was combating *governmental* discrimination, it could employ the U.S. Constitution as a weapon in its arsenal. Since the Supreme Court and the federal judiciary were charged with the responsibility of interpreting the Constitution, the civil rights movement could concentrate on judicial action to accomplish its objective of preventing governmental discrimination. But the Constitution has considerably less bearing upon the activities of private individuals than do the laws passed by Congress and the various states. Thus, when the civil rights movement turned its attention to combating *private* discrimination, it had to carry its fight into the legislative branch of government. The federal courts could help restrict discrimination by state and local governments and school authorities, but only Congress could restrict discrimination practiced by private owners of restaurants, hotels, and motels, private employers, and other individuals who were not government officials.

Prior to 1964 Congress had been content to let other agencies, including the president and the courts, struggle with the problem of civil rights. Yet Congress could not long ignore the nation's most pressing domestic issue. The civil rights movement had stepped up its protests and demonstrations and was attracting worldwide attention with organized sit-ins, freedom rides, picketing campaigns, boycotts, and mass marches. The mass media vividly portrayed the animosity of segregationists and helped to convince millions of Americans of the need for national legislation. After the massive "March on Washington" in August 1963, President Kennedy asked Congress for the most comprehensive civil rights legislation it had ever considered. After Kennedy's assassination, President Johnson brought heavy pressure upon Congress to pass the bill as a tribute to the late president. Everett M. Dirksen of Illinois, Republican leader in the Senate, provided Johnson with the bipartisan support needed to overcome a southern filibuster. The Civil Rights Act of 1964 finally passed both houses of Congress by better than a two-thirds vote and with the overwhelming support of both Republican and Democratic Congressmen. It can be ranked with the Emancipation Proclamation, the Fourteenth Amendment, and *Brown* v. *Board of Education* as one of the most important steps toward full equality for the Negro in America.

The act provides that:

1.   It is unlawful to apply unequal standards in voter registration procedures or to deny registration for irrelevant errors or omissions on records or applications. Literacy tests must be in writing and a sixth-grade education is a presumption of literacy.

2.   It is unlawful to discriminate or segregate persons on the grounds of race, color, religion, or natural origin in any place of public accommodation, including hotels, motels, restaurants, movies, theaters, sports arenas, entertainment houses, and other places offering to serve the public. This prohibition extends to all establishments whose operations affect interstate commerce or whose discriminatory practices are supported by state action. Private clubs are specifically exempted.

3.   The Attorney General shall undertake civil action on behalf of any person denied equal access to a public accommodation. If the proprietor continues to discriminate, he may be held in contempt of court and subjected to preemptory fines or imprisonment without trial by jury. (This mode of enforcement gave proprietors an opportunity to adjust to the new law without being punished, and it also avoided the possibility that southern juries would refuse to convict violators of the act.)

4.   The Attorney General shall undertake civil actions on behalf of persons attempting the orderly desegregation of public schools.

5.   The U.S. Commission on Civil Rights, first established by the Civil Rights Act of 1957, shall be empowered (1) to investigate deprivations of the right to vote, (2) to collect and to study information regarding discrimination in America, and (3) to make reports to the President and Congress as necessary.

6.   Each federal department and agency shall take appropriate action to end discrimination in all programs or activities receiving federal financial assistance in any form. These actions may include the termination of assistance.

7.   It shall be unlawful for any firm or labor union employing or representing twenty-five or more persons to discriminate against any individual in any fashion because of his race, color, religion, sex, or natural origins; an Equal Employment Opportunity Commission shall be established to enforce this provision by investigation, conference, conciliation, or civil action in federal court.

The Civil Rights Act of 1964 was truly a new emancipation for southern blacks. Enforcement proved to be no real difficulty. Southern businessmen seemed almost to welcome the excuse of a federal directive to open their facilities to black customers. A few isolated communities attempted to evade the law by turning their theaters and public swimming pools into "private clubs." Atlanta restaurant owner Lester Maddox closed his restaurant in the face of federal contempt charges arising out of his highly publicized refusal to obey the new law; his defiance won him sufficient popularity among Georgia's segregationists to propel him to the governor's chair in that state in 1966. But Maddox was an exception. The prevailing attitude of the white South was to accept the end of segregation.

MARTIN LUTHER KING, JR., and the Power of Protest

The civil rights movement invented new techniques for minorities to gain power and influence in American society. Mass protest is a technique by which groups seek to obtain a bargaining position for themselves that can induce desired concessions from established power holders. It is a means of acquiring a bargaining leverage for those who would otherwise be powerless. The protest may challenge established groups by threatening their reputations (where they might be harmed by unfavorable publicity), their economic position (where they might be hurt by a boycott), their peace and quiet (where noise and disruption might upset their daily activities), or their security (where violence or the threat of violence is involved).

The protest technique appeals to powerless minorities who have little to bargain with except their promise *not* to protest. Once the protest has begun—or even before it has begun if the *threat* of protest is made credible—the minority can promise not to protest in exchange for the desired concessions. Perhaps more importantly, mass protest frequently motivates members of established elites who have the political resources the protesters lack to enter the political arena on behalf of the protesters.

The nation's leading exponent of nonviolent protest was Dr. Martin Luther King, Jr. Indeed, King's contributions to the development of a philosophy of nonviolent, direct-action protest on behalf of blacks won him international acclaim and the Nobel Peace Prize in 1964. King first came to national prominence in 1955 when he was only 25 years old; he led a year-long bus boycott in Montgomery, Alabama, to protest discrimination in seating on public buses. In 1957 he formed the Southern Christian Leadership Conference (SCLC) to provide encouragement and leadership to the growing nonviolent protest movement in the South.

In 1963 a group of Alabama clergymen petitioned Martin Luther King, Jr., to call off mass demonstrations in Birmingham, Alabama. King, who had been arrested in the demonstrations, replied in his famous "Letter from Birmingham Jail":

> You may well ask, "Why direct action? Why sit-ins, marches, etc.? Isn't negotiation a better path?" You are exactly right in your call for negotiation. Indeed, this is the purpose of direct action. Nonviolent direct action seeks to create such a crisis and establish such creative tension that a community that has constantly refused to negotiate is forced to confront the issue. It seeks to so dramatize the issue that it can no longer be ignored. . . .
>
> You express a great deal of anxiety over our willingness to break laws. . . . One may well ask, "How can you advocate breaking some laws and obeying others?"

Martin Luther King, Jr.

Two Nobel Peace Prize winners, Dr. Martin Luther King, Jr., and Dr. Ralph Bunche, lead a civil rights march through Montgomery, Alabama. This scene was repeated over and over again in the 1960's. *Wide World Photo*

The answer is found in the fact that there are *unjust* laws. I would be the first to advocate obeying just laws. One has not only a legal but a moral responsibility to obey just laws. Conversely, one has a moral responsibility to disobey unjust laws. . . .

In no sense do I advocate evading or defying the law as the rabid segregationist would do. This would lead to anarchy. One who breaks an unjust law must do it *openly, lovingly* (not hatefully as the white mothers did in New Orleans when they were seen on television screaming "nigger, nigger, nigger") and with a willingness to accept the penalty. I submit that an individual who breaks a law that conscience tells him is unjust, and willingly accepts the penalty by staying in jail to arouse the conscience of the community over its injustice, is in reality expressing the very highest respect for law.[4]

Nonviolent direct action is a technique requiring direct mass action against laws regarded as unjust, rather than court litigation, political campaigning, voting, or other conventional forms of democratic political activity. Mass demonstrations, sit-ins, and other nonviolent direct-action tactics usually result in violations of state and local laws. For example, persons remaining at a segregated lunch counter after the owner orders them to leave are usually violating trespass laws. Marching in the street frequently entails the obstruction of traffic and results in charges of "disorderly conduct" or "parading without a

Martin Luther King, Jr.

permit." Mass demonstrations often involve "disturbing the peace" or refusing to obey the lawful orders of a police officer. Even though these tactics are non-violent, they did entail disobedience to civil law.

Civil disobedience is not new to American politics. Its practitioners have played an important role in American history, from the patriots who participated in the Boston Tea Party, to the abolitionists who hid runaway slaves, to the suffragists who paraded and demonstrated for women's rights, to the labor organizers who picketed to form the nation's major industrial unions, to the civil rights marchers of recent years. Civil disobedience is a political tactic of minorities. (Since majorities can more easily change laws through conventional political activity, they seldom have to disobey them.) It is also a tactic attractive to groups wishing to change the social status quo significantly and quickly.

The political purpose of nonviolent direct action and civil disobedience is to call attention or "to bear witness" to the existence of injustices. Only laws regarded as unjust are broken, and they are broken openly without hatred or violence. Punishment is actively sought rather than avoided since punishment will further emphasize the injustices of the law. The object of nonviolent civil disobedience is to stir the conscience of an apathetic majority and to win support for measures that will eliminate the injustices. By accepting punishment for the violation of an unjust law, the person practicing civil disobedience demonstrates his sincerity. He hopes to shame the majority and to make it ask itself how far it will go to protect the status quo.

Clearly the participation of the mass news media, particularly television, contributes immeasurably to the success of nonviolent direct action. Breaking the law makes news; dissemination of the news calls the attention of the public to the existence of unjust laws or practices; the public's sympathy is won when injustices are spotlighted; the willingness of the demonstrators to accept punishment provides evidence of their sincerity; and the whole drama lays the groundwork for changing unjust laws and practices. Cruelty or violence directed against the demonstrators by policemen or other defenders of the status quo plays into the hands of the demonstrators by stressing the injustices they were experiencing.

Nonviolent Direct Action and Social Change.   Perhaps the most dramatic application of nonviolent direct action occurred in Birmingham, Alabama, in the spring of 1963. Under the direction of Martin Luther King, Jr., the SCLC chose Birmingham as a major site for desegregation demonstrations during the centennial year of the Emancipation Proclamation. Birmingham was by its own description the "Heart of Dixie"; it was the most rigidly segregated large city in the United States. King believed that if segregation could be successfully challenged in Birmingham, it might begin to crumble throughout the South. Thousands of black people, including school children, staged protest marches in Birmingham from 2 to 7 May. In response, policemen and firemen under the

Martin Luther King, Jr.

Over 200,000 people jammed the Lincoln Memorial area on August 28, 1963 to hear Martin Luther King, Jr., recite the famous "I have a dream" speech. This "March on Washington" was an important factor in eventual passage of the Civil Rights Act of 1964. *Wide World Photo*

direction of Police Chief "Bull" Connor attacked the demonstrators with fire hoses, cattle prods, and police dogs—all in clear view of national television cameras. Pictures of police brutality were flashed throughout the nation and the world, doubtless touching the consciences of many white Americans. The demonstrators conducted themselves in a nonviolent fashion. Thousands were dragged off to jail, including Martin Luther King, Jr. (It was at this time that King wrote his "Letter from Birmingham Jail," explaining and defending nonviolent direct action.)

The most massive application of nonviolent direct action was the great "March on Washington" in August 1963, during which more than 200,000 black

Martin Luther King, Jr.

and white marchers converged on the nation's capital. The march ended in a
formal program at the Lincoln Memorial in which Martin Luther King, Jr.,
delivered his most eloquent appeal, entitled "I Have a Dream."

> I still have a dream. It is a dream deeply rooted in the American dream. I have a
> dream that one day this nation will rise up and live out the true meaning of its
> creed: "We hold these truths to be self-evident, that all men are created equal."

Another very significant application of nonviolent direct action occurred in
Alabama in the spring of 1965 during the SCLC-organized march from Selma to
Montgomery to protest voting inequities. The Selma marchers convinced
Congress that its earlier legislation was inadequate to the task of securely
quaranteeing the right to vote for all Americans. In response to the march,
Congress enacted the Voting Rights Act of 1965, which threatened federal intervention in local voting matters to a degree never before attempted. The act
authorized the attorney general, upon evidence of voter discrimination in
southern states, to replace local registrars with federal examiners, who were
authorized to abolish literacy tests, to waive poll taxes, and to register voters under simplified federal procedures. The impact of the Voting Rights Act of 1965
can be observed in increased black voter registration figures in the South and
the election of blacks to state legislatures in every southern state and to many
city and county offices as well.

White racial violence in the early 1960s contributed to the success of the nonviolent direct-action movement in winning the nation's sympathy and support.
Murders and bombings shocked and disgusted whites in both the North and the
South. In 1963 Medgar Evers, NAACP state chairman from Mississippi, was
shot to death by a sniper as he entered his Jackson home. In that same year a
bomb killed four black girls attending Sunday school in Birmingham, Alabama.
In 1964 three young men (Michael Schwerner and Andrew Goodman, both
white, and James Chaney, a black) were murdered in Philadelphia, Mississippi,
while working on a civil rights project in education and voter registration. In
1965 a black educator from Washington, D.C., Lemuel Penn, was murdered as
he drove through Athens, Georgia, while returning from military duty as a
reserve officer.

On 4 April 1968 Martin Luther King, Jr., was shot and killed by a white man
in Memphis, Tennessee. The murder of the nation's leading advocate of nonviolence was a tragedy affecting all Americans. Prior to his death, King had cam-
paigned in Chicago and other northern cities for an end to "*de facto*
segregation" of blacks in ghettos and the passage of fair housing legislation
prohibiting discrimination in the sale or rental of houses and apartments. But
King appeared to be having less success in achieving this goal than in his
previous efforts to effect change. "Fair housing" legislation had consistently

failed in Congress; there was no mention of discrimination in housing even in the comprehensive Civil Rights Act of 1964; and the prospects of a national fair housing law were unpromising at the beginning of 1968. With the assassination of Martin Luther King, Jr., however, the mood of the nation and of Congress changed dramatically. Many people came to feel that Congress should pass a fair housing law as a tribute to the slain civil rights leader. The Civil Rights Act of 1968 prohibited the following forms of discrimination:

> Refusal to sell or rent a dwelling to any person because of his race, color, religion, or national origin.
> Discrimination against a person in the terms, conditions, or privileges of the sale or rental of a dwelling.
> Indicating a preference or discriminating on the basis of race, color, religion, or national origin in advertising the sale or rental of a dwelling.

Risks of Nonviolent Direct Action.   Despite its successes, nonviolent direct action does pose problems. This tactic is capable of arousing extreme passions on either side of an issue and exciting and provoking masses to act without thinking, perhaps ultimately making disrespect for the law a commonplace attitude. If undertaken too frequently or directed against laws or practices that are not really serious injustices, it may have the effect of alienating the majority, whose sympathies are so essential to the success of the movement. A favorable outcome can be achieved by actions that arouse the conscience of a majority against injustice or that discomfort a majority to the point at which it is willing to grant the demands of the minority rather than experience further discomfort. But actions that provoke hostility or a demagogic reaction from the majority merely reduce the opportunities for progress.

Even in a *nonviolent* movement the risk of violence is always great. Though violence on the part of policemen or counterdemonstrators can assist in achieving the movement's objective, violence by demonstrators usually has the opposite effect. Unfortunately, mass followers do not always fully understand or appreciate the distinction between nonviolent demonstrations directed against injustice, and rioting, looting, and violence directed against society itself.

Finally, while nonviolent direct action may be effective against direct discrimination, or an obvious injustice, this strategy is less successful against very subtle discrimination or *de facto* segregation. Few Americans approve of direct discrimination or cruelty against a nonviolent minority, and direct-action tactics that spotlight such injustice can arouse the conscience of the white majority. But the white majority is less likely to become conscience-stricken over subtle forms of discrimination or *de facto* segregation or inequalities not immediately the product of direct discrimination.

Martin Luther King, Jr.

POWERLESSNESS IN THE GHETTO

White Americans can understand the unfairness of legal discrimination, and the majority agree that such discrimination is inconsistent with the norms of a democratic society. Yet, though the *legal* foundations of segregation have collapsed, the *actual* disparity between blacks and whites in terms of income, employment, housing, and other economic conditions has not changed greatly. Though the victories of the civil rights movement were immensely important, they are primarily *symbolic* gains rather than *real* changes in the conditions under which most blacks live in America. Increasingly the problem of inequality is being posed as one of differences in the "life chances" of blacks and whites. Figures can only suggest the bare outline of a black's life chances in American society (see Table 9-1). The income of the black family is only two-thirds that of the average white family. One-third of all black families have annual incomes below the government's "poverty line." Home ownership is greater among whites than blacks. The black unemployment rate is twice as high as that for whites. The average black acquires less education than the average white. Blacks are far less likely than whites to hold prestigious white-collar jobs in professional, managerial, clerical, or sales work. They hold few skilled craft jobs in industry but are concentrated rather in semiskilled, service, and laboring positions. Black women not only have more children but have them earlier than white women, and bearing too many children too early usually complicates the parents' lives, making it difficult for them to finish school or to save money. Thus, a cycle is at work in the ghettos: Low education levels produce low income levels, which prevent parents from moving out of the ghettos, which deprives children of educational opportunities—and so the cycle repeats.

The ghetto is peopled primarily by lower class black masses. Individual blacks who have attained middle class status are generally more acceptable to whites than are blacks living in the ghettos. Whites feel that they can communicate with the black middle class but not with the black masses. They regard blacks at the top of the social pyramid as living examples of what the determined or talented Negro can accomplish in a democratic capitalist society.

In addition to poverty, family disorganization, and inequality, the ghetto harbors various social pathologies. Crime and delinquency, mental illness, and drug addiction haunt America's ghettos. By and large the victims of these social pathologies are the ghetto residents themselves. Blacks are the principal victims of lawlessness in America; they are more likely than whites to be preyed upon by criminals. According to FBI crime statistics, blacks (11 percent of the population) account for 28 percent of all criminal arrests. In all major categories of offenses, the rate of arrests for blacks is higher than that for whites. Assuming that arrests are a rough indicator of the number of crimes committed, the black crime rate is apparently more than twice the proportion of blacks in the total population.

TABLE 9-1. Black-White Life Chances, 1970

	Black	*White*
Median family income	$6,191	$ 9,794
Percent of families with incomes under $3,000	20	8
Percent of families with incomes over $10,000	24	49
Poverty percentage	34	10
Median income, men 25–54		
Less than 8 years	$3,922	$ 5,509
High school 4 years	6,192	8,829
College 4 years	8,669	12,354
Unemployment rate (%)	8.2	4.5
Occupation, males (%)		
Professional, managerial	13	30
Clerical, sales	9	13
Craftsmen	14	21
Operatives	28	19
Service	13	6
Laborer	18	6
Farm	6	5
Education, persons 25–34 (%)		
Males completing high school	54.0	79.0
Females completing high school	58.0	76.0
Males completing college	5.8	10.9
Females completing college	6.4	12.3
Home ownership (%)	42	65
Infant mortality rate		
(per 1,000 live births)	34.6	19.2
Female-headed families (%)	26.8	9.1
Fertility rate		
(births per 1,000 women 15–44)	115	82
Voter participation		
(% reported they voted)	44	56

Source: Bureau of the Census, *The Social and Economic Status of Negroes in the United States 1970,* Current Population Reports, Series P-23, No. 38.

Blacks comprise about 40 percent of all persons confined in state prisons, a proportion significantly higher than the black arrest rate. They also constitute a disproportionate share of the drug addicts in the United States. Sociologist Alphonso Pinkney summarized the reasons that social deviance is disproportionately common among blacks:

(1) In the United States black people occupy a separate and subordinate economic and social position which leads to frustration. Their frustrations are usually displaced in acts of aggression against fellow Negroes, thus leading to a higher proportion of intraracial criminal acts. (2) As Myrdal has demonstrated, the caste system under which black people live operates in such a way as to prevent them from identifying with the society and the law. The very legal system itself is

One cause for the disproportionate share of social deviance among American blacks is that they are forced to live in dilapidated sections of cities. Ghetto areas are characterized by crime, poverty, poor housing, poor health conditions, and a generally lower quality of life. *Eugene Richards Photo*

manipulated to discriminate against black people. (3) Black persons, far more than white persons, are forced to live in deteriorated sections of cities. These areas are characterized by widespread social disorganization in terms of criminal values, as well as poverty, poor housing, restrictions on settlement, and limited outlets for recreation and employment. "Out of these and similar conditions arise elements conducive to greater criminality, as well as other forms of pathology, among the Negro population." (4) The high crime rate among black people is partially a function of their reaction to having their means to success blocked by discriminatory behavior. "Crime may thus be utilized as a means of escape, ego enhancement, expression of aggression, or upward mobility. . . ." (5) Black people are overrepresented in the lower class, and recorded crime tends to be concentrated in this class.[5]

Powerlessness in black ghettos is reflected in a comparison of ghettos with the "colonies" of an earlier era. Ghetto residents feel that they have little control over the institutions in their own communities; businesses, schools, welfare agencies, the police, and most other important agencies are controlled from the outside. Often the agents of these institutions—the store managers, clerks, teachers, welfare workers, and policemen—are whites who live outside of the ghetto. Thus, the important institutions of the ghetto are staffed and controlled almost entirely by outsiders; hence the analogy with colonialism. Sociologist Kenneth Clark writes:

> The dark ghetto's invisible walls have been erected by the white society, by those who have power, both to confine those who have *no* power and to perpetuate their powerlessness. The dark ghettos are social, political, educational, and—above all—economic colonies. Their inhabitants are subject peoples, victims of the greed, cruelty, insensitivity, guilt, and fear of their masters.[6]

In analyzing urban riots, the National Advisory Commission on Civil Disorders also referred to powerlessness, this time as a contributing cause to both urban social disorders and the rise of militant mass movements:

> Many Negroes have come to believe that they are being exploited politically and economically by the white "power structure." Negroes, like people in poverty everywhere, in fact lack the channels of communication, influence and appeal that traditionally have been available to ethnic minorities within the city and which enabled them—unburdened by color—to scale the walls of the white ghettos in an earlier era. The frustrations of powerlessness have led some to the conviction that there is no effective alternative to violence as a means of expression and redress, as a way of "moving the system." More generally, the result is alienation and hostility toward the institutions of law and government and the white society which controls them. This is reflected in the reach toward radical consciousness and solidarity reflected in the slogan "Black Power."[7]

Thus, the ghetto provides an environment that encourages appeals to racial consciousness, black solidarity, and black power. Feelings of powerlessness, alienation, and hostility toward white society can easily be exploited by political movements that reject traditional democratic methods and integrationist goals while asserting the coming of "black power" and black separatism.

THE BLACK POWER MOVEMENT

Black power began not as a program of political action but simply as a slogan.[8] The meaning of this slogan has been widely debated, and there is really no concise definition of what black power means as a political program. However, it is possible to identify several recurrent themes in militant black politics.

In a book entitled *Black Power: The Politics of Liberation in America*, Stokely Carmichael and Charles V. Hamilton write:

> Black Power . . . is a call for black people in this country to unite, to recognize their heritage, to build a sense of community. It is a call for black people to begin to

define their own goals, to lead their own organizations and to support those organizations. It is a call to reject the racist institutions and values of this society. . . .

. . . Black people must lead and run their own organizations. Only black people can convey the revolutionary idea—and it is a revolutionary idea—that black people are able to do things themselves. . . .

It does not mean merely putting black faces into office.[9]

One prominent theme in militant black politics is the necessity of *fostering black pride and dignity.* One of the worst effects of segregation and discrimination is that members of the minority group begin to doubt their own worth as human beings. Black leaders therefore endeavor to develop a positive image toward blackness. Carmichael and Hamilton write:

Throughout this country, vast segments of the black communities are beginning to recognize the need to assert their own definitions, to reclaim their history, their culture; to create their own sense of community and togetherness. There is a growing resentment of the word "Negro," for example, because this term is the invention of our oppressor; it is *his* image of us that he describes. Many blacks are now calling themselves African-Americans, Afro-Americans or black people because that is *our* image of ourselves.[10]

The effort to assert pride in blackness is often accompanied by African dress, African hairstyles, "soul food," "soul music," and the like.

An important political theme of black militancy is a general *condemnation of white society as "racist."* This condemnation of racism in society extends far beyond individual acts of bigotry (for example, the bombing of a black church) to encompass nearly all of the values and institutions of white society. Black militants argue that the institutions of American society are inherently racist because blacks are kept segregated in slums, because black unemployment is twice as great as white unemployment, because black incomes are only half those of whites, because the infant mortality rate among blacks is twice that among whites, because the educational level of blacks is below that of whites, and so on. In other words, the condition of blacks is itself considered sufficient proof of the racism of established institutions. Moreover, that condition also inspires black militants to condemn the value structure of American society, which either has supported the condition or at least has failed to eradicate it.

The black militant's condemnation of existing societal values and institutions as racist leads him to reject traditional democratic and organizational politics. This disparagement of democratic politics is usually accompanied by a *rejection of the ideal of coalition with white liberals.* White liberals want to reform the system whereas black radicals want to do away with it. While "limited, short-term coalitions on relatively minor issues" are possible, "such approaches seldom come to terms with the roots of institutional racism." In addition to

Angela Davis was both a college philosophy professor and an articulate spokesperson for the black militant movement. She was later jailed for her role in an escape of convicts from a Marin County, California, jail. *Wide World Photo*

black militants' concern that most white liberals are insufficiently radical in their politics, there is the fear that black people will be "absorbed or swallowed up" in white-controlled liberal organizations. There is the fear that white liberals will use black people to further white liberal objectives, claiming all the while that these objectives coincide with the aspirations of black people.

This line of reasoning inevitably leads to the conclusion that *black organizations must be led by black people* rather than by white people. The participation of whites in black organizations should be limited to "supportive roles" involving "specific skills and techniques," as for example the special knowledge of lawyers. The black militants do not welcome the participation of the

... many young, middle-class, white Americans [who], like some sort of Pepsi generation, have wanted to "come alive" through the black community and black groups. They have wanted to be where the action is—and the action has been in those places. They have sought refuge among blacks from the sterile, meaningless, irrelevant life in middle-class America. They have been unable to deal with the stifling, racist, parochial, split-level mentality of their parents, teachers, preachers and friends. . . . The black organizations do not need this kind of idealism, which borders on paternalism.[11]

The emphasis on black pride and solidarity, and the hostility toward existing social values and institutions frequently lead to a *rejection of integration*. To the militants, integration means co-optation into the white middle class society that they so vigorously condemn. It means the loss of black identity and the submergence of black culture in the prevailing culture of white society. Thus the black power movement is closely identified with "black separatism". If the prevailing values and institutions of white society were radically altered or abolished, then perhaps genuine racial integration would be possible. The black power movement generally does not envision a separate black nation but merely asserts that black pride and black solidarity are preconditions for bringing about the kinds of social conditions requisite for genuine integration. The kind of integration pictured by black power advocates is one in which the black masses will become an integral part of a radically different society, rather than one in which individual black people will be absorbed into the existing culture.

Black militancy has won widespread acceptance among black college students. At many major colleges and universities black students have organized all-black clubs whose activities frequently reflect black power philosophy. These students are critical of established values and institutions of American society; they have demanded greater emphasis on black history and culture, including the establishment of separate black studies curricula, which they usually insist must be taught only by black instructors; they have demanded that more black students be accepted for admission, often irrespective of previous academic record; they have demanded that universities hire more black faculty; and they have generally rejected integration into the white social life on campus. The black student unions have stressed black consciousness and black pride among their members.

BLACK POLITICAL POWER

In an article significantly titled "From Protest to Politics: The Future of the Civil Rights Movement," Bayard Rustin argues that the problems of blacks today—the fundamental social and economic disabilities afflicting the black masses—cannot be resolved by the same type of protest activities that eliminated legal segregation. According to Rustin, progress in overcoming the problems facing blacks today requires broad-based political power.

The future of the Negro struggle depends on whether the contradictions of this society can be resolved by a coalition of progressive forces which becomes the *effective* political majority in the United States. I speak of the coalition which staged the March on Washington, passed the Civil Rights Act, and laid the basis for the Johnson landslide—Negroes, trade unionists, liberals, and religious groups.[12]

Whether black leaders can organize a majority coalition of church, labor, and liberal groups—liberal enough to support massive public programs in education, housing, and income redistribution—is a serious political question. Attempts to build a black-poor white coalition have foundered before, as have efforts to build a black-labor alliance. However, blacks play a much more important role in national politics today than ever before. Undoubtedly, they exert a considerable liberalizing influence on American politics.

Black voters are heavily committed to the Democratic party. The pro-Democratic sentiment of blacks can be traced back to the 1930s and the presidential administration of Franklin D. Roosevelt. Harry Truman maintained the pro-Democratic bias of most blacks, through his contributions in desegregating the armed forces and advocating fair employment laws. John F. Kennedy had a strong personal following among blacks, and even though Lyndon Johnson enjoyed little personal appeal among blacks, his efforts on behalf of the Civil Rights Act of 1964 (in contrast to Barry Goldwater's opposition) won him the greatest margin of black electoral support ever received by a presidential candidate. Thus, the record of Democratic presidents in recent decades in promoting civil rights goes a long way toward explaining the loyalty of black voters to the Democratic party. Blacks also tend to look upon themselves as poor people and to regard the Democratic party as the friend of the underprivileged. They view it as the "champion of the underdog" and view themselves as "the underdog."

Blacks do not occupy public office in America in proportion to their percentage of the nation's population. However, in recent years black candidates have been more successful at the polls than at any time since Reconstruction. No blacks served in the national Congress from the Fifty-seventh Congress (1901 - 1903) to the Seventy-first Congress (1929 - 1931). But the black population migration to northern cities, the concentration of black people in ghettos, the increase in black registration, and finally the legislative reapportionment of the 1960s prompted by *Baker* v. *Carr* have combined to promote black officeholding. (*Baker* v. *Carr* [1962] required state legislatures to apportion representation on the basis of "one man, one vote." The effect of the decision was to increase urban representation in many state legislatures.) Since 1929 one or more blacks from northern cities have been members of Congress, and the number has gradually increased: The Ninety-second Congress (1971 - 1973) included 12 black representatives and one United States senator. Blacks have also been elected mayors of large cities: Carl B. Stokes in Cleveland, Ohio, Richard D. Hatcher in Gary, Indiana, Kenneth A. Gibson in Newark, New Jersey,

Maynard Jackson in Atlanta, Georgia, and Thomas Bradley in Los Angeles, California. Blacks are also winning state and local offices in the South. The best-known black southern mayor is Charles Evers of Fayette, Mississippi, brother of the slain civil rights leader Medgar Evers. Blacks have been elected to every southern state legislature. Finally, we should note that President Lyndon B. Johnson appointed Thurgood Marshall in 1967 to the United States Supreme Court, the first black ever to serve on that high tribunal.

Most successful black candidates to date have avoided racial militancy, pledging instead to represent "all of the people." Most have avoided positions that would be threatening to whites. They have been generally willing to form electoral and political alliances with white groups.

A generation ago Gunnar Myrdal wrote an essay entitled "What the Negro Gets Out of Politics" for his book *An American Dilemma*. He observed that "unquestionably the most important thing that Negroes get out of politics where they vote is legal justice—justice in the courts; police protection and protection against the persecution of the police; ability to get administrative jobs through civil service; and a fair share in such public facilities as schools, hospitals, public housing, playgrounds, libraries, sewers and street lights."[13] Contemporary research suggests that blacks can indeed help to ensure justice for

Jim Crow laws, legal racial discrimination, were largely eliminated by the struggles of the Civil Rights movement. Here the ceremonial burning of a coffin is the focal point of a celebration. *Boston Globe Photo*

themselves through the exercise of their franchise.[14] But even though legal justice is extremely important, we must ask whether this is *all* that blacks can expect to gain from politics.

Black political activity has also assisted in bringing about the legal victories of the civil rights movement. The elimination of Jim Crow—direct, lawful discrimination—was primarily a political accomplishment. American presidents and the Democratic party have been cognizant of the strategic location of large numbers of voting blacks in the big cities of northern industrial states. Presidential candidates and nominating conventions have been more "pro civil rights" than Congress, suggesting the importance of black voting power in the large urban states with big blocs of electoral votes in presidential elections. The Democratic party, which includes most big-city black voters, has been particularly interested in civil rights issues. Finally, there is some evidence that northern congressmen from districts with many blacks are, in general, more "liberal" than northern congressmen from districts with fewer blacks.[15]

However, even the victories of the civil rights movement cannot be attributed solely to black political activity. In the past, support for civil rights legislation came from a broad spectrum of the white community—from liberals, laborers, intellectuals, clergymen, and white urban middle class voters.

It is likely that black political power will continue to be most effective when joined in coalitions with whites—urban, labor, liberal, intellectual, and church groups. Black political activity will continue in support of public programs aimed at urban problems, low-income housing, welfare assistance, health care for the poor, manpower training and job placement, economic opportunity, legal services for the poor, and problems of hunger.

POWER AND RACE: A CASE STUDY

The Busing Controversy

In *Brown* v. *Board of Education*, the Supreme Court quoted approvingly the view that segregation had "a tendency to retard educational and mental development of Negro children and to deprive them of the benefits they would receive in a racially integrated school system." The U.S. Commission on Civil Rights has reported that even when segregation was *de facto*—that is, the product of segregated housing patterns and neighborhood schools—rather than the result of direct discrimination, the adverse effects on black students were still significant.[16] Black students attending predominantly black schools had lower achievement scores and lower levels of aspiration than blacks with comparable social-economic backgrounds who went to predominantly white schools. When black students attending predominantly black schools are compared with black students attending predominantly white schools, the average difference in achievement amounts to more than two grade levels. This finding is perhaps the best single argument for ending *de facto* segregation in school systems in both the North and the South.

De facto segregation is widespread. The U.S. Commission on Civil Rights has reported that 75 percent of the black elementary school pupils in large cities attend predominantly black schools (those with 95 percent or more black enrollment). This "racial isolation" is primarily a product of the ghettoization of black populations in the nation's large cities. Ending *de facto* segregation would call for drastic changes in the prevailing concept of "neighborhood schools." Schools would no longer be a part of the neighborhood or the local community but rather a part of the larger city-wide and area-wide school system. Students would have to be bused into and out of the ghettos in a massive scale. In many large cities where blacks comprise a majority of public school students, ending *de facto* segregation would mean busing city school pupils to the suburbs and suburban students to the core city. Such a program would require that separate city and suburban school districts be merged or forced to cooperate. Many suburbanites moved out of the central city in order to get their children out of city

Opposition to forced busing to achieve integrated schools is widespread, and the familiar and once innocuous school bus has become a symbol for this opposition. About 40 school buses were damaged in Pontiac, Michigan, when busing opponents struck out against these yellow symbols in 1970. *United Press International Photo*

The Busing Controversy

schools, and these persons don't favor any proposal to bus their children back into the ghettos. Finally, the ending of *de facto* segregation would oblige school districts to classify students according to race and use racial quotas as the basis for school placement. Although this would be a supposedly benign form of racial classification, it would nevertheless represent a return to both government-sponsored racial classification and the differential application of laws to the separate races (in contrast to the notion that laws should be "color blind").

The question of equality in public education is a constitutional question which is likely to be resolved by federal courts rather than public opinion or presidential or congressional action. The Fourteenth Amendment guarantees "equal protection of the laws." *If* the Supreme Court requires busing and racial balancing in all public schools in order to fulfill the mandate of the Fourteenth Amendment, *then* only another amendment to the Constitution specifically prohibiting busing and racial balancing could overturn that decision.

To date the Supreme Court has *not* held that there is any affirmative duty of school officials to correct *de facto* racial imbalances in public schools, so long as the imbalances are not a product of present or past actions of state or local governments. However, where racial imbalance and *de facto* segregation may be in part a product of past discriminatory practices by states or school districts, school officials have a duty to remove all vestiges of segregation, and this responsibility may entail busing and deliberate racial balancing to achieve integration in education. Thus, in the important case of *Swann* v. *Charlotte, Mecklenburg Board of Education,* the Supreme Court held that southern school districts have a special affirmative duty under the equal protection clause of the Fourteenth Amendment to eliminate all traces of dual school systems and to take whatever steps are necessary, including busing, to end manifestations of segregation. Moreover, the Court held that the racial composition of the school, in a southern district which had previously segregated by law, could be used as evidence of violation of constitutional rights, and busing to achieve racial balance could be imposed as a means of ending dualism in the schools. The Court was careful in saying, however, that racial imbalance in a school is not itself grounds for ordering busing, unless it is also shown that some present or past government action contributed to that imbalance. Thus, the impact of the *Swann* decision falls largely on *southern* schools.

The Supreme Court has *not* issued any sweeping order to end *de facto* segregation in the North. The constitutional question in most northern cities is somewhat different from that in southern cities; most northern cities have no history of direct discrimination by law, and it is difficult to prove that *de facto* segregation in these cities is a product of any state or local government actions. Nevertheless, several federal district courts have issued orders to northern city school officials to begin busing to achieve racial balance in their schools.

The Busing Controversy

In an important decision by the Supreme Court in 1974, involving a plan to bus students between independent suburban school districts and the city of Detroit, the Court voted five to four that the Fourteenth Amendment does *not* require busing across city-suburban school district boundaries to achieve racial balance in the schools. Where central-city schools are predominantly black and suburban schools are predominantly white, cross-district busing is not required unless it is shown that some deliberate official action brought about this segregation. The Supreme Court threw out a lower federal court order for massive busing of students between Detroit and 52 suburban school districts. Although Detroit city schools are 70 percent black, none of the Detroit metropolitan area school districts segregated students *within* their own boundaries. This decision means that largely black central cities, surrounded by largely white suburbs, will remain *de facto* segregated because there are not enough white students living within the city to achieve integration.

The argument for busing is that it is the most effective and efficient method of providing minority groups with equal opportunities in education. Currently, black ghetto schools do not supply the same educational opportunities as predominantly white outer-city and suburban schools. As a black city councilman in Detroit put it: "It's pragmatic. We don't have any desire to be close to white people just for the sake of being close to white people. We want the same thing everyone else wants so we can have the same opportunities for our kids to learn and grow."[17] Blacks have a constitutional right to equal educational opportunity. Busing is an inconvenience, but it certainly is a minor inconvenience compared with the value of equal educational opportunity. Proponents of busing maintain that busing was frequently used in the South to maintain segregation and many black children were bused past white schools closer to their home in order to attend all-black segregated schools. Now, it is argued, the same busing mechanisms should be used to achieve integration rather than segregation. Moreover, supporters of busing say that *de facto* segregation has indeed been abetted by government policies—for example, federal housing programs which build low-income public housing in central cities and promote middle class home ownership in suburbs, transportation policies which make it easier for affluent white middle class residents to leave the central city for homes in the suburbs while retaining their jobs in the cities, etc.—and therefore governments have a clear responsibility to take affirmative steps including busing to integrate public schools. Suburban residents contributed to *de facto* segregation in the central city when they moved to the suburbs, and now it is only fair that their children be bused back and forth between the suburbs and the ghettos in order to rectify the resulting racial imbalance.

Opposition to busing is widespread, and not all of it is "racist." Middle class parents feel that busing their children to ghetto schools will expose them to the social problems of ghettos—crime, drugs, and violence. White parents fear that

The Busing Controversy

Mothers of school age children have become particularly involved in both sides of the busing controversy. Here women adamantly voice their opinions. *Eugene Richards Photo*

their children will be exposed to what blacks themselves are trying to escape—the rapes, ripoffs, robberies, and dope addiction that have turned many inner-city schools into blackboard jungles. Middle class whites who have moved to a suburb for the sake of its school system resent the fact that courts will order their children to be bused back to the poorer-quality city schools. A Michigan mother argues, "I don't see any reason why they've got a right to come in here and tell me my kids can't use the school I bought and paid for."[18] The greatest opposition to busing comes when white middle class children are ordered to attend ghetto schools; opposition is much less when ghetto children are ordered to attend predominantly white middle class schools. Most whites do not believe in sending youngsters from a good school to a bad school in order to achieve racial integration. Busing also destroys the concept of the neighborhood school, where children are educated near their homes under the guidance of their parents. Neighborhood schools are said to stimulate community involvement in the educational process, bringing teachers and parents and students together more frequently. In addition, busing involves educational time wasted in riding buses, educational funds spent on buses rather than learning materials, and an unnecessary increase in the risk of accidents to many children. Proponents of busing argue that it brings children of different cultures together and teaches them to live and work and play with others who are different from themselves. But op-

The Busing Controversy

The Ku Klux Klan arose in the South in the Reconstruction era as a grass roots response to the new freedom of former slaves. In the ensuing century the Klan has reared its head in many states, both North and South. Here three Boston teenagers emulate the real Klansmen in a protest against forced busing. *Eugene Richards Photo*

ponents of busing cite the record of racial violence in mixed schools. It is difficult to justify placing the burden of racial integration of American society on school children; opponents of busing maintain that the parents should first achieve an integrated community and then there would be no need for busing. Besides, racial balancing does not always result in genuine integration; as one Pennsylvania high school student remarked concerning a city-wide busing program, "I thought the purpose of busing was to integrate the schools, but in the long run, the white kids sit in one part of the bus and the black kids in another part."[19]

———————————

NOTES

1. *Brown* v. *Board of Education of Topeka, Kansas,* 347 U.S. 483 (1954).

2. Alabama, Arkansas, Delaware, Florida, Georgia, Kentucky, Louisiana, Maryland, Mississippi, Missouri, North Carolina, Oklahoma, South Carolina, Tennessee, Texas, Virginia. and West Virginia.

3. Arizona, Kansas, New Mexico, and Wyoming.

4. A public letter by Martin Luther King, Jr., Birmingham, Alabama, 16 April 1963; the full text is reprinted in Thomas R. Dye and Brett Hawkins (eds.), *Politics in the Metropolis* (Columbus, Ohio: Merrill, 1967), pp. 100 - 109.

5. Alphonso Pinkney, *Black Americans* (Englewood Cliffs, N.J.: Prentice-Hall, 1969), pp. 124 - 125. For the two quotations, Pinkney cites, respectively, Earl R. Moses, "Differentials in Crime Rates between Negroes and Whites Based on Comparisons of Four Socio-Economically Equated Areas," *American Sociological Review,* 12 (August 1947), 420; and Thomas F. Pettigrew, *A Profile of the Negro American* (Princeton, N.J.: Van Nostrand, 1964), p. 156.

6. Kenneth Clark, *Dark Ghetto: Dilemmas of Social Power* (New York: Harper & Row, 1965), p. 11.

7. National Advisory Commission on Civil Disorders, *Report* (Washington: Government Printing Office, 1968), p. 205.

8. In June 1966, James Meredith, who in 1962 had been the first black to enroll in the University of Mississippi, was shot on a lone freedom march through Mississippi. Leaders of several civil rights organizations, including Martin Luther King, Jr., of SCLC, and Stokely Carmichael, chairman of SNCC, continued Meredith's march. During this march Carmichael and his associates employed the slogan "Black Power," although King and others disapproved of its use.

9. Stokely Carmichael and Charles V. Hamilton, *Black Power: The Politics of Liberation in America* (New York: Random House, 1967), pp. 44 and 46.

10. Ibid., p. 37.

11. Ibid., p. 83.

12. Bayard Rustin, "From Protest to Politics: The Future of the Civil Rights Movement," *Commentary,* 32 (February 1965), 28.

13. Gunnar Myrdal, *An American Dilemma: The Negro Problem and Modern Democracy,* 2 vols. (New York: Harper, 1944), Vol. I, p. 497.

14. William R. Keech, *The Impact of Negro Voting* (Chicago: Rand McNally, 1968), p. 3.

15. See Lewis A. Froman, *Congressmen and Their Constituencies* (Chicago: Rand McNally, 1963), p. 93.

16. U.S. Commission on Civil Rights, *Racial Isolation in the Public Schools,* 2 vols. (Washington: Government Printing Office, 1966).

17. *Time,* November 15, 1971, p. 64.

18. Ibid., p. 57.

19. Ibid., p. 63.

TESTING YOUR PERFORMANCE

Note to the Student. The following questions are to test how well you achieved the Performance Objectives identified for you at the beginning of this chapter. The correct answers are supplied, accompanied by corresponding pages for you to review if you have answered incorrectly. The questions are coordinated numerically with the Performance Objectives at the beginning of the chapter. This exercise will assist you in determining the type of questions you have the most difficulty in answering (discussion, identification, explanation, definition, etc.) and will prepare you for test questions likely to be asked by your instructor.

1.   (a) The initial goal in the struggle for equality in America was the _____ _____

   (b) The constitutional amendment and the clause upon which the civil rights movement is based is _____ _____

2.   (a) The U.S. Supreme Court case which ruled that the equal protection clause of the Fourteenth Amendment meant "separate but equal" was _____ _____ .

   (b) The U.S. Supreme Court case which reversed the "separate but equal" interpretation of the Fourteenth Amendment and marked the beginning of a new era in American politics was _____ _____ .

3.   A federal system of government, separation of powers between the legislative, executive, and judicial branches, and the fact that the Supreme Court must rely heavily on other branches of the federal government, the states, and private citizens to effectuate the law of the land all help to explain the _____

4.   The refusal of a school district to desegregate until it was faced with a federal court injunction, state payments of private school tuition in lieu of providing public schools, amending compulsory attendance laws to provide that no child shall be required to attend an integrated school, and the use of pupil placement laws to avoid or minimize the extent of desegregation were all examples of _____ _____ .

5.   The type of segregation that occurs when schools are predominantly white or black because of segregated housing patterns and neighborhood schools rather than direct lawful discrimination is _____

6.   Prohibition of unequal standards in voter registration procedures and of discrimination or segregation on the grounds of race, color, religion, or natural origin in any place of public accommodation and any establishment whose operations affect interstate commerce; provision for the U.S. attorney general to undertake civil action on behalf of any person denied equal access to a public accommodation and on behalf of persons attempting the orderly desegregation of public schools; establishment of the power of the U.S. Commission on Civil Rights to investigate deprivations of the right to vote and other discrimination; provision for cutting off federal funds to any federal department and agency practicing discrimination; and prohibition of firms or labor unions from dis-

criminating—all are provisions of which congressional act? _____
_____

7.   Identify the following techniques used by the civil rights movement to enable minorities to acquire power and influence in American society:

(a) A technique by which groups seek to obtain a bargaining position for themselves that can induce desired concessions from established power holders is _____ .

(b) A technique requiring mass action against laws regarded as unjust which usually results in violation of state and local laws is _____
_____ .

(c) A technique whose object is to stir the conscience of an apathetic majority and to win support for measures that will eliminate the injustices and whose users accept punishment for violation of an unjust law is _____
_____ .

8.   The individual who was the nation's leading exponent of nonviolent protest and the founder of the Southern Christian Leadership Conference (SCLC) was _____ .

9.   Contributing to the success of nonviolent direct action by disseminating the news and calling the attention of the public to the existence of unjust laws or practices, thus winning the public's sympathy when injustices are spotlighted, are some effects of the _____ .

10.   (a) The congressional act which authorized the attorney general, upon evidence of voter discrimination in southern states, to replace local registrars with federal examiners, who were authorized to abolish literacy tests, to waive poll taxes, and to register voters under simplified federal procedures was the
_____ .

(b) The congressional act which prohibited discrimination in the selling or renting of a dwelling to any person because of race, color, religion, or natural origin, discrimination against a person in the terms, conditions, or privileges of the sale or rental of a dwelling, and discrimination in advertising the sale or rental of a dwelling was the _____ .

11.   The failure to understand fully or to appreciate the distinction between nonviolent demonstrations directed against injustice, and rioting, looting, and violence directed against society itself, and the decreased effectiveness of the strategy against very subtle discrimination or *de facto* segregation are _____
_____ .

12.   Low education levels producing low income levels, preventing parents from moving out of the ghettos, depriving children of educational opportunities, producing low education levels . . . is the cycle at work in the ghettos which contributes to _____
_____ .

13.   The fact that the important institutions of the ghetto are staffed and controlled almost entirely by outsiders (whites) and the consequent feelings of powerlessness evoke analogy with an earlier era of _____ .

14.   A call for black people to unite, to recognize their heritage, to build a sense of community, to lead their own organizations, and to reject the racist institutions and values of white society was made by Stokely Carmichael and Charles Hamilton and became the basis for what movement? _____
_____

15.   Black militants reject integration because it means co-optation into the white middle class society that they condemn, loss of black identity, and the submergence of black culture in the prevailing culture of white society. For these reasons, the black power movement is closely identified with _____ .

16.   The political party to which most black voters are heavily committed is the _____ .

17.   (a) Legal justice in the courts, police protection, and protection against police persecution, as well as elimination of direct, lawful discrimination, are benefits that have been provided for blacks through _____ .

    (b) The strategy that will probably continue to be the most effective for increasing black political power is _____ .

18.   *De facto* segregation is caused by school systems that assign students to schools located close to their place of residence. These schools are known as _____ .

19.   The U.S. Supreme Court case which held that southern school districts have a special affirmative duty under the equal protection clause of the Fourteenth Amendment to eliminate all vestiges of dual school systems and to take whatever steps are necessary, including busing, to end all manifestations of segregation was _____ .

20.   (a) *De facto* segregation coupled with prior history of direct discrimination by law is characteristic of _____ cities.

    (b) *De facto* segregation where there is no history of direct discrimination by law, making it difficult to prove that *de facto* segregation is a product of any state or local governmental action, is found in _____ cities.

21.   (a) The need to provide minority groups with equal opportunities in education, prior busing in the South to maintain segregation, the "causing" of *de facto* segregation by governmental policies which have, therefore, a clear responsibility to take affirmative steps to integrate public schools, and the "fairness" of sending suburban residents' children to ghetto schools since they contributed to the existence of *de facto* segregation are all _____ .

    (b) Fear of ghetto schools' exposing children to social problems (crime, drugs, violence, etc.), suburbanites' resentment of having their children sent back to the poorer-quality city schools, destruction of the neighborhood schools and community involvement in the educational process, waste of educational time, the spending of educational funds on buses rather than on learning materials, and an unnecessary increase in the risk of accidents to many children are all _____ .

Correct Responses

1.   (a) Elimination of direct legal segregation (p. 314); (b) Fourteenth Amendment, equal protection clause (pp. 314 - 315).

2. (a) *Plessy* v. *Ferguson* (p. 315); (b) *Brown* v. *Board of Education of Topeka, Kansas* (pp. 315 - 316).

3. Limited formal power of the Supreme Court (p. 316).

4. Southern states' resistance to desegregation (pp. 316 - 317).

5. *De facto* segregation (p. 317).

6. Civil Rights Act of 1964 (pp. 318 - 319).

7. (a) Mass protest (p. 320); (b) Nonviolent direct action (p. 321); (c) Civil disobedience (p. 322).

8. Dr. Martin Luther King, Jr. (p. 322).

9. Participation of the mass media (p. 322).

10. (a) Voting Rights Act of 1965 (p. 324); (b) Civil Rights Act of 1968 (p. 325).

11. Problems posed by nonviolent direct action (p. 325).

12. Feelings of powerlessness among ghetto residents (p. 326).

13. Colonialism (pp. 328 - 329).

14. Black power movement (pp. 329 - 330).

15. Black separatism (pp. 330 - 332).

16. Democratic party (p. 333).

17. (a) Black political activity (pp. 334 - 335); (b) Coalition with urban, labor, liberal, intellectual, and church groups (p. 335).

18. Neighborhood schools (p. 336).

19. *Swann* v. *Charlotte, Mecklenburg Board of Education* (p. 337).

20. (a) Southern cities (pp. 336 - 337); (b) Northern cities (p. 337).

21. (a) Arguments for busing (p. 338); (b) Arguments against busing (pp. 338 - 340).

KEY TERMS

equal protection of the laws clause

separate but equal

Brown v. *Board of Education of Topeka, Kansas,* 1954

Plessy v. *Ferguson*

Civil Rights Act of 1964

guidelines

de facto segregation

governmental discrimination

private discrimination

mass protest

Martin Luther King, Jr.

Southern Christian Leadership Conference (SCLC)

nonviolent direct action

civil disobedience

March on Washington, 1963

Voting Rights Act of 1965

Civil Rights Act of 1968

life chances

National Advisory Commission on Civil Disorders

black power movement

black separatism

Baker v. *Carr,* 1962

"neighborhood schools" concept

Swann v. *Charlotte, Mecklenburg Board of Education*

busing

racial balancing

DISCUSSION QUESTIONS

1. Describe how the following congressional acts and Supreme Court cases helped eliminate direct legal segregation:
   (a) *Brown* v. *Board of Education of Topeka, Kansas* (1954)
   (b) Civil Rights Act of 1964
   (c) Voting Rights Act of 1965
   (d) Civil Rights Act of 1968

2. Discuss the effect of the following techniques used in the civil rights movement enabling minorities to acquire power and influence in American society:
   (a) Mass protest
   (b) Nonviolent direct action
   (c) Civil disobedience
   (d) Mass media use
   What are the problems posed by nonviolent direct action?

3. Discuss powerlessness in the ghetto:
   (a) The ghetto cycle
   (b) Poverty (income)
   (c) Family disorganization
   (d) Inequality
   (e) Social pathologies (crime, violence, mental illness)
   (f) The effect on militant mass movements

4. Discuss the themes of black militancy. Explain why black militants reject integration.

5. Discuss the development and emergence of black political power:
   (a) Formation of coalitions
   (b) Commitment to a national political party
   (c) Effect of the *Baker* v. *Carr* case
   (d) Platform of successful black candidates
   (e) What blacks get out of politics
   (f) The importance of black political activity on the civil rights movement

6. Define *de facto* segregation. Discuss:
   (a) What would have to be done to eliminate it
   (b) The ruling of the Supreme Court in *Swann* v. *Charlotte, Mecklenburg Board of Education*
   (c) Why it applies differently to southern cities and to northern cities
   (d) Arguments for busing
   (e) Arguments against busing

SUGGESTED READINGS

HARRY BAILEY, JR., (ed.), *Negro Politics in America* (Columbus, Ohio: Merrill, 1968).

STOKELY CARMICHAEL and CHARLES D. HAMILTON, *Black Power* (New York: Random House, 1967).

KENNETH CLARK, *Dark Ghetto: Dilemmas of Social Power* (New York: Harper & Row, 1965).

THOMAS R. DYE, *The Politics of Equality* (Indianapolis: Bobbs-Merrill, 1971).

MARTIN LUTHER KING, JR., *Why We Can't Wait* (New York: New American Library, 1964).

DONALD R. MATTHEWS and JAMES W. PROTHRO, *Negroes and the New Southern Politics* (New York: Harcourt, Brace & World, 1966).

ALPHONSO PINKNEY, *Black Americans* (Englewood Cliffs: Prentice-Hall, 1969).

HANES WALTON, JR., *Black Politics* (Philadelphia: Lippincott, 1972).

CHAPTER 10

Poverty and Powerlessness

PERFORMANCE OBJECTIVES

The student should be able to:

1. Discuss the different definitions of *poverty*.

2. List the groups in which poverty occurs in greater proportions than the national average.

3. Discuss poverty as relative deprivation. Contrast poverty as relative deprivation with poverty as powerlessness.

4. Cite the black sociologist who studied "the psychology of the ghetto." Discuss his findings with regard to: a sense of inferiority; crime and violence in the ghetto; personal adjustment to ghetto life; and poverty and discrimination.

5. Discuss the theory of the poverty cycle.

6. Identify the effect of slavery and segregation on blacks as seen by Daniel Moynihan. Contrast Moynihan's view of the culture of poverty with Edward C. Banfield's present-orientedness view of the culture of poverty.

7. List the criticisms of the idea of a culture of poverty.

8. Identify the goal of the War on Poverty.

9. Discuss the policy implications of the idea of a culture of poverty.

10. Outline the basic provisions of the Social Security Act of 1935.

11. Differentiate between public assistance programs and social insurance programs.

12. Identify the four categories of recipients of welfare payments partly financed by federal grants to the states.

13. Define general assistance.

14. Differentiate between Medicare and Medicaid.

15. Identify the largest, most expensive, and most controversial welfare program.

16. Discuss the problems and weaknesses of current welfare programs.

17. Outline the basic provisions of the Economic Opportunity Act of 1964. Identify the basic strategy of the War on Poverty.

18. Discuss the community action program of the Office of Economic Opportunity. Identify some of the programs and projects conducted by Community Action agencies.

19. Discuss the criticisms of the Office of Economic Opportunity.

20. Identify the purposes or strategies of income maintenance plans. Identify the basic problem of the income maintenance strategy.

21. List the provisions of President Nixon's Welfare Reform Program (the Family Assistance Plan). Identify the criticisms of the Family Assistance Plan.

POVERTY IN AMERICA

The United States is an affluent society. Indeed, this country is producing more than a trillion dollars' worth of goods and services each year. The median family income exceeds $10,000 per year. Yet many Americans live in poverty. Poverty is nothing new; it was far more widespread a generation ago than it is today. Indeed, what is new today—the reason poverty is now a focus of attention—is a national commitment to *eliminate* poverty. In the Economic Opportunity Act of 1964, Congress and the president declared that it was national policy "to eliminate the paradox of poverty in the midst of plenty in this nation." Nations throughout history have concerned themselves with the lot of the poor. But for the first time the United States has reached a point at which the elimination of poverty has become a serious national aspiration.

But the elimination of poverty—however generally this goal is shared—requires the use of power, and power is a scarce resource. Regardless of widespread agreement that poverty is undesirable, there are conflicts over what should be done about it and important struggles for power over antipoverty activity.

Conflict over poverty begins with conflict over the definition of poverty and differing estimates of its extent in America. Proponents of large-scale government programs for the poor frequently make broad definitions of poverty and high estimates of the number of poor people. They view the problem as a persistent one, even in an affluent society. They contend that millions suffer from hunger, exposure, and remediable illness, and that some people starve to death. Their definition of the problem of poverty practically mandates immediate and massive governmental programs to assist the poor.

On the other hand, opponents of large-scale governmental antipoverty programs frequently minimize the number of poor in America. They see poverty diminishing over time, without major public programs. They view the poor in America as considerably better off than the middle class 50 years ago—and even wealthy by the standards of most other societies in the world. They deny that anyone needs to suffer from hunger, exposure, remedial illness, or starvation if he will make use of the services and facilities available to him. Their definition of the problem of poverty reduces demands for massive public programs to fight poverty.

According to the U.S. Social Security Administration, there are about 25 million poor people (those below the poverty line) in the United States, or approximately 13 percent of the population. The poverty line is set by the Social Security Administration at:

Family size	Urban poverty line
One	$2,040
Two	2,633
Three	3,229
Four	4,137
Five	4,880
Six	5,489
Seven	6,751

The poverty line was derived by careful calculation of the cost of food, housing, clothing, and other items for urban families of different sizes in 1971. The dollar amounts are flexible to take into account the effect of inflation. They can be expected to rise each year with the rate of inflation.

This definition of poverty emphasizes *subsistence levels;* it seeks to describe poverty objectively as lack of enough income to acquire the minimum necessities of life. Liberals frequently view the subsistence definition of poverty as insensitive to the variety of needs—including entertainment, recreation, and the relief of monotony. Items that were "luxuries" a generation ago are now considered "necessities." John Kenneth Galbraith writes:

> People are poverty-stricken when their income, even if adequate for survival, falls markedly behind that of the community. Then they cannot have what the larger community regards as the minimum necessary for decency; and they cannot wholly escape, therefore, the judgment of the larger community that they are indecent.[1]

Moreover, the official definition of poverty does not recognize the problems of those who spend their incomes unwisely. If money goes for liquor, or dope, or expensive used cars, or is siphoned off by loan sharks, impoverished relatives

According to the U.S. Social Security Administration, approximately 13% of the American population fall below the poverty line. This kitchen, for example, is considerably less than what most Americans are accustomed to. *Eugene Richards Photo*

and friends, or high prices charged by ghetto store owners, then even a reasonably high-income family can live in poverty. Yet despite these shortcomings, the Social Security Administration definition provides the best available estimate of poverty in America.

How poor is "poor"? There is reason to believe that the 25 million Americans living in "official" poverty do not all suffer hardship and privation. About 65 percent own cars, 50 percent own their own homes, and more than half have some savings. Nearly 80 percent of the poor have television sets, and 78 percent have refrigerators or freezers. Over three-quarters have hot water, access to a telephone for receiving calls, a kitchen with cooking equipment, a flush toilet, and a bath. Yet the diets of the poor are nutritionally bad, whether from ignorance or poverty. The poor do not seek medical attention except in emergencies, the result being a great deal of illness.

But liberals charge that the problem of poverty has been seriously underestimated by government officials. By emphasizing levels of *deprivation* rather than *subsistence*, and focusing on an income required for "a healthful, self-respecting mode of life, care of children, and participation in community life," they can broaden the definition of poverty to include anywhere from 20 to 40 percent of the population.

WHO ARE THE POOR?

Poverty occurs in many different kinds of families and in all environmental settings (see Table 10-1.) However, its incidence varies sharply among groups living under different circumstances, and several groups experience poverty in greater proportions than the national average.[2] First, *blacks* are three times more likely to experience poverty than whites; the percentage of the black population of the United States falling below the poverty line is 32.1 compared to 9.9 percent for the white population. Second, *female-headed families* experience poverty far more frequently than male-headed families; 38.4 percent of all female-headed families live below the poverty line. Third, the *aged* experience more poverty than persons of working age; 25 percent of the population over 65 live below the poverty line. While we think of poverty as a characteristic of persons living in large-city ghettos, actually *rural* families experience more poverty more fre-

Being poor and black in a nation which is significantly affluent and white fosters feelings of powerlessness and despair. *Eugene Richards Photo*

TABLE 10–1. Population, by Categories, with Income Below Poverty Level
(based on total population)

	Number (in millions)	Percent of Total in Category
Total	25.5	12.6
White population	17.5	9.9
Black population	8.0	32.1
Those living in central cities	7.8	13.4
Those living in suburbs	5.1	7.3
Those living in rural areas	12.5	18.0
Under age 25	13.1	14.3
Ages 25–65	7.6	8.7
Over age 65	4.6	25.0
Families with male head	14.3	7.3
Families with female head	11.2	38.4

Source: U.S. Bureau of the Census, *Statistical Abstract of the United States, 1970*
(Washington: Government Printing Office, 1972), p. 329.

quently than do city families. On the other hand, cities have more poverty than
their surrounding suburbs.

Are the poor disappearing? Since Franklin D. Roosevelt's Depression era estimate that one-third of the nation was "ill housed, ill clad, ill nourished," the
American political and economic system has succeeded in reducing the proportion of poor from 33 percent to less than 13 percent (see Figure 10-1). If current
rates in the reduction of poverty in America continue, there will be virtually no
poverty in 25 to 30 years. However, this optimistic prediction assumes that those
remaining in poverty today can rise above the poverty line with the same speed
as those who have done so for the last two decades. But there may be a "hard
core" of poverty-stricken families and individuals who cannot achieve that
status without massive new governmental programs.

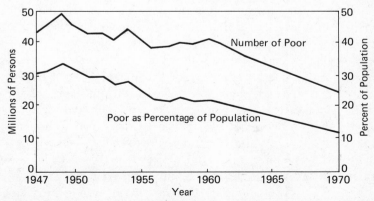

FIGURE 10-1. **Poverty in the United States** (From Thomas R. Dye, *Understanding
Public Policy, 2nd ed.* Englewood Cliffs, New Jersey: Prentice-Hall, Inc, 1975, p. 96.)

A disproportionate percentage of the elderly live below the poverty line. Most of them live on fixed incomes and many subsist on social security alone. *Eugene Richards Photo*

POVERTY AS INEQUALITY

It is possible to define poverty as *relative deprivation*, which is really to iden- tify it as *inequality*. This definition is not tied to any *absolute* level of sub- sistence or deprivation. Instead, it characterizes poverty as a sense of deprivation that some people feel because they have less income or fewer material possessions than most other Americans. Even with a fairly substantial income it is possible to feel relative deprivation in a very affluent society when commercial advertising in the mass media portray the "average American" as having a high level of consumption and material well-being.

Today the poor in America are wealthy by the standards which have prevailed over most of history, and which still prevail over large areas of the world. Nonetheless, millions of American families are considered poor, both by themselves and by others, because they have less income than most other Americans. Actually they are not any more deprived, even relative to the non- poor, than in the past. But they *feel* more deprived, they perceive a wide gap between themselves and an affluent middle class America, and they do not accept the gap as legitimate. Blacks are heavily overrepresented among the poor, and the civil rights movement made blacks acutely aware of their position in American society relative to whites. The black revolution contributed to the

TABLE 10-2. Percent Distribution of Family Personal Income
By Quintiles and Top 5 Percent of Consumer Units,
Selected Years, 1929–1962

Quintiles	1929	1935–1936	1941	1944	1947	1950
Lowest	3.5	4.1	4.1	4.9	5.0	4.8
Second	9.0	9.2	9.5	10.9	11.0	10.9
Third	13.8	14.1	15.3	16.2	16.0	16.1
Fourth	19.3	20.9	22.3	22.2	22.0	22.1
Highest	54.4	51.7	48.8	45.8	46.0	46.1
Total	100.0	100.0	100.0	100.0	100.0	100.0
Top 5 percent ratio	30.0	26.5	24.0	20.7	20.9	21.4

Source: U.S. Bureau of the Census, *Statistical Abstract of the United States, 1972,* p. 330.

1951	1954	1956	1959	1962	1968	1970
5.0	4.8	4.8	4.6	4.6	5.7	5.5
11.3	11.1	11.3	10.9	10.9	12.4	12.0
16.5	16.4	16.3	16.3	16.3	17.7	17.4
22.3	22.5	22.3	22.6	22.7	23.7	23.5
44.9	45.2	45.3	45.6	45.5	40.6	41.6
100.0	100.0	100.0	100.0	100.0	100.0	100.0
20.7	20.3	20.2	20.2	19.6	14.0	14.4

new awareness of the problem of poverty in terms of differences in income and conditions of life. Thus, eliminating poverty when it is defined as relative deprivation really means achieving equality of income and material possessions.

Let us try systematically to examine poverty as relative deprivation. Table 10-2 divides all American families into five groups—from the lowest one-fifth, in personal income, to the highest one-fifth—and shows the percentage of total family personal income received by each group over the years. (If perfect income equality existed, each fifth would receive 20 percent of all family personal income, and it would not even be possible to rank fifths from highest to lowest.) The poorest one-fifth received 3.5 percent of all family personal income in 1929; in 1970, however, this group had increased its percentage of all family personal income to 5.5. (Most of the increase occurred during World War II.) The highest one-fifth received 54.4 percent of all family personal income in 1929; in 1970, however, the percentage had declined to 41.6. This was the only income group to lose in relation to other income groups. The middle classes improved their relative income position even more than the poor. Another measure of income equalization over time is the decline in the percentage of income received by the top 5 percent. The top 5 percent received 30.0 percent of all family personal income in 1929 but only 14.4 percent in 1970. There is no doubt that income differences in America are decreasing.

Nevertheless, it is unlikely that income differentials will ever disappear completely—at least not in a society that rewards skill, talent, risk-taking, and ingenuity. If the problem of poverty is defined as relative deprivation—that is, *inequality*—then it is not really capable of solution. Regardless of how well off the poor may be in absolute terms, there will always be a lowest one-fifth of the population receiving something less than 20 percent of all income. Income differences may decline, but *some* differences will remain, and even minor differences can acquire great importance and hence pose a "problem."

POVERTY AS POWERLESSNESS

Powerlessness is the inability to control the events that shape one's life. The poor lack economic resources and are hence largely dependent upon others for the things they need. Their lack of power derives from this dependency. But powerlessness is also an attitude—a feeling that no matter what one does it will have little effect on his life. An *attitude* of powerlessness reinforces the *condition* of powerlessness among the poor. Their experiences generate feelings of meaninglessness, hopelessness, lack of motivation, distrust, and cynicism. Constant defeat causes many of the poor to retreat into a self-protective attitude characterized by indifference and a pervasive sense of futility.

The poor feel alienated because of their lack of success in obtaining important life goals. Persons who are blocked consistently in their efforts to achieve life goals are most likely to express powerlessness and alienation. These attitudes in turn become barriers to effective self-help, independence, and self-respect. Poverty can lead to apathy and aimlessness and lack of motivation.

To be *both* black and poor in a predominantly white and affluent society magnifies feelings of powerlessness and alienation. Social psychologists are not always certain about the processes by which social inequalities become perceived and influence attitudes and behaviors. But black sociologist Kenneth B. Clark has provided some interesting insights into "the psychology of the ghetto."

Professor Clark argues that human beings who live apart from the rest of society, who do not share in society's affluence, and who are not respected or granted the ordinary dignities and courtesy accorded to others will eventually begin to doubt their own worth. Every human being depends upon his experiences with others for clues to how he should view and value himself. Black children who consistently see whites in a superior position begin to question whether they or their family or blacks in general really deserve any more respect from the larger society than they receive. These doubts, Clark maintains, become the seeds of "a pernicious self- and group-hatred, the Negro's complex and debilitating prejudice against himself."

Clark observed that when Negro children as young as three years old were shown white and black dolls, or were asked to color drawings of children to look like themselves, many of them rejected the black dolls as "dirty" or "bad" and colored the picture of themselves a light color or even a bizarre shade like purple. The observations suggest that many black children suffer from serious injury to their sense of self-worth at a very young age. The results of this sense of inferiority are revealed when the child begins school—a lack of confidence in himself as a student, a lack of motivation to learn, behavioral problems, and a gradual withdrawal or growing rebellion. Lack of success in school, coupled with poor teaching and poor ghetto schools, tends to reinforce the experience of inferior achievement.

> In Negro adults the sense of inadequate self-worth shows up in a lack of motivation to rise in their jobs or fear of competition with whites; and a sense of impotence in civil affairs, demonstrated in lethargy toward voting, or community participation, or responsibility for others, in family instability and the irresponsibility rooted in hopelessness.[3]

But all human beings search for self-esteem. According to Clark, teenage blacks often pretend to knowledge about illicit activities and to sexual experiences that they have not really had. They use as their models the petty criminals of the ghetto, with their colorful swaggering style of cool bravado. The inability to succeed by the standards of the wider society leads to a peculiar fascination with individuals who successfully defy society's norms. Some young black men seek their salvation in aggressive and self-destructive behavior. Because the larger society has rejected them, they reject—or at least appear to reject—the values of that society.

Professor Clark believes that the explanation for violence and crime in the ghetto lies in the conscious or unconscious belief of many young blacks that they cannot hope to win meaningful self-esteem through the avenues available to middle class whites, so they turn to "hustling"—pimping, prostitution, gambling, or drug dealing. They are frequently scornful of what they consider the hypocrisy and dishonesty of the larger society. They point to corruption among respected middle class whites, including policemen.

But personal adjustment to ghetto life can take other forms. According to Clark, ghetto dwellers are prone to accept the "evidence" of their personal inferiority and impotence. They express a continuing sense of failure through stagnation and despair; they drop out of school; they turn to narcotics. Or they live in a world of television and motion pictures—a world which supposedly depicts the life of the American middle class. Many poor escape the harshness of poverty in dreams and fantasies of luxury and happiness.

Poverty and discrimination have also taken their toll in black family life. Professor Clark observed that under the system of slavery, the only source of family continuity was through the female; the child was dependent upon his mother and seldom knew his father. Segregation relegated the Negro male to menial and subservient jobs. He could not present himself to his wife and children as a consistent wage earner.

> His doubts concerning his personal adequacy were therefore reinforced. He was compelled to base his self-esteem instead on a kind of behavior that tended to support a stereotyped picture of the Negro male—sexual impulsiveness, irresponsibility, verbal bombast, posturing, and compensatory achievement in entertainment and athletics, particularly in sports like boxing in which athletic prowess could be exploited for the gain of others.[4]

It was the black woman who was obliged to hold the family together—to set its goals and to encourage and protect boys and girls. Many young black males had no strong father figure upon which to model their behavior. Many established temporary liaisons with a number of women. The result was a high rate of illegitimacy and family instability.

IS THERE A CULTURE OF POVERTY?

It is sometimes argued that the poor have a characteristic lifestyle or "culture of poverty" which assists them in adjusting to their life. Like other aspects of culture, it is passed on to future generations, setting in motion a self-perpetuating cycle of poverty. The theory of the poverty cycle is as follows: Deprivation in one generation leads, through cultural impoverishment, indifference, apathy, or misunderstanding of their children's educational needs, to deprivation in the next generation. Lacking the self-respect that comes from earning an adequate living, young men cannot sustain responsibilities of marriage and so they hand down to their children the same burden of family instability and female-headed households which they themselves carried. Children born into a subculture of alienation, apathy, and lack of motivation learn these attitudes themselves. Thus the poor are prevented from exploiting opportunities which are available to them.

It is probably more accurate to talk about a *sub*culture of poverty. The prefix *sub* is used because most of the poor subscribe to the "middle class American way of life" at least as a cultural ideal and even as a personal fantasy. Most poor people do not reject American culture but strive to adapt its values to the realities of economic deprivation and social disorganization in their own lives.

Daniel P. Moynihan has argued persuasively that one of the worst effects of slavery and segregation has been their impact on black family life. Segregation, with its implications of inferiority and submissiveness, damaged the male more than the female personality. The black female was not a threat to anyone. But surprisingly, in Moynihan's study [5] the female-headed black family emerged as one of the striking features of life in the ghetto. Almost 25 percent of *all* black families in the nation are headed by women. For the young black male brought up in the matriarchal setting in the ghetto, the future is often depressing, with defeat and frustration repeating themselves throughout his life. He may drop out of school in the ninth grade protesting his lack of success. Perhaps never again will he have an opportunity for further education or job training. Lacking parental supervision and with little to do, he may soon get into trouble with the police. A police record will diminish his chances of getting a job. If he gets a job, his limited job skills will seriously handicap his earning power. His pay is usually not enough to support a family, and he has little hope of advancement. His job is routine and boring. He may tie up much of his income in installment payments for a car, a television set, or the other conveniences which he sees in widespread use. Because of his low credit rating, he will be forced to pay excessive interest rates, and sooner or later his creditors will garnish his salary. If he marries, he is likely to have a large number of children, and he and his family will live in crowded, substandard housing. As pressures and frustrations mount, he may decide to leave his family, either because he has found his inability to support his wife and children humiliating or because only then will his wife and children be eligible for welfare payments. Thus the cycle is at work: Low education levels produce low income levels; low income levels prevent parents from moving out of the ghettos; forced restriction to the ghettos deprives children of educational opportunities; and so the cycle repeats. According to Moynihan.

> At the heart of the deterioration of the fabric of Negro society is the deterioration of the Negro family. . . . Three generations of injustice have brought about deep seated structural distortions in the life of the Negro American. At this point the present tangle of pathology is capable of perpetuating itself without assistance from the white world. The cycle can be broken only if these distortions are set right. In a word, the national effort toward problems of Negro Americans must be directed toward the question of family structure.[6]

Another view of the "culture of poverty" emphasizes the "present-orientedness" of the poor. Professor Edward C. Banfield argues that poverty is primarily an effect produced by extreme present-orientedness rather than a lack

of income or wealth. Individuals caught up in the culture of poverty are unable
to plan for the future, to sacrifice immediate gratifications in favor of future
ones, or to accept the disciplines that are required in order to get ahead. Banfield admits that some people experience poverty because of involuntary unemployment, prolonged illness, death of the breadwinner, or some other misfortune. But even when severe, this kind of poverty is not squalid or degrading.
Moreover, it ends once the external cause of it no longer exists. But some individuals live in a culture of poverty which continues for generations because
they are psychologically unable to provide for the future. Improvements in their
circumstances may affect their poverty only superficially. Even increased income is unlikely to change their way of life. The additional money will be spent
quickly on nonessential or frivolous items. This culture of poverty may affect no
more than 10 or 20 percent of all families who live below the poverty line, but
it generally continues regardless of what is done in the way of remedial action.[7]

Opponents of the idea of a culture of poverty argue that this notion diverts
attention from the conditions of poverty which foster family instability, present-
orientedness, and other ways of life of the poor. The question is really whether
the conditions of poverty create a culture of poverty or vice versa. Reformers are
likely to focus on the conditions of poverty as the fundamental cause of the
social pathologies which afflict the poor. Critics of the culture of poverty theme
note that even its advocates apply it only to groups who have lived in poverty for
several generations. It is not relevant to those who have become poor during
their lifetime because of sickness, accident, or old age. The cultural explanation
basically involves parental transmission of values and beliefs, which in turn
determines behavior of future generations. In contrast, the situational explanation of poverty involves social conditions—differences in financial
resources—which operate directly to determine behavior. Thus, the conditions
of poverty can be seen as affecting behavior directly as well as indirectly through
their impact upon succeeding generations. Perhaps the greatest danger in the
culture of poverty idea is that it may lead to the relaxation of efforts to
ameliorate the conditions of poverty. In other words, it may become an excuse
for inaction.[8]

Whether or not there is a "culture of poverty" is a perplexing question. The
argument resembles the classic exchange between F. Scott Fitzgerald and
Ernest Hemingway. When Fitzgerald observed, "The rich are different from
you and me," Hemingway retorted, "Yes, they have more money." Observers
who believe that they see a distinctive lower class culture will say, "The poor are
different from you and me." But opponents may reply, "Yes, they have less
money." In other words, are the poor poorly educated, underskilled, poorly
motivated, "delinquent," and "shiftless" because they are poor; or are they
poor because they are poorly educated, underskilled, unmotivated, "delinquent,"

and "shiftless"? The question is a serious one because it has important policy implications.

If one assumes that the poor are no different from other Americans, then he is led toward policies which emphasize "opportunity" for individuals rather than drastic changes in the environment. If the poor are "like" other Americans, it is necessary only to provide them with the ordinary means to achievement of the desires of other Americans—for example, job training programs, good schools, and perhaps some counseling to make them aware of opportunities that are available to them. The intervention that is required to change their lives, therefore, is one of supplying a means of achieving a level of income that most Americans enjoy. It can be argued that this kind of thinking—the denial that a subculture of poverty exists—influenced many of the programs of the Johnson administration's War on Poverty. The goal of the War on Poverty was not to directly provide resources that would end poverty but to provide opportunities so that people could achieve their own escape from poverty. But the assumption behind the programs was that the poor would respond to these opportunities in the same way most middle class Americans could be expected to respond.

On the other hand, if one believes in the notion of a culture of poverty, it is necessary to derive a strategy to interrupt the transmission of lower class cultural values from generation to generation. The strategy must try to prevent the socialization of young children into an environment of family instability, lack of motivation, crime and delinquency, and so forth. One rather drastic means to accomplish this, of course, would be simply to remove the children from lower class homes at a very early age and raise them in a controlled environment in which the conventional culture is transmitted rather than the subculture of poverty. Perhaps a less harsh version of this same idea would involve special day-care centers and preschool programs to remedy cultural deprivation and disadvantage; these programs would be oriented toward bringing about cultural change in young children through "cultural enrichment."

Another policy implication of the culture of poverty notion is that little can be done to help people escape from poverty until after there is sufficient change in their conditions of life to permit them to take advantage of opportunity programs. According to this line of reasoning, you can't change people without changing their environment; the poor cannot be changed by schooling, or man-power training, or programs to develop better attitudes while they are still poor. The emphasis on "self-help"—education, information, job training, par-ticipation—is incomplete and misleading unless it is accompanied by a program aimed at directly altering the conditions of poverty. Hence, it is argued that the *guaranteed minimum income* is required to bring the poor up to a level where they will be able to take advantage of educational and training information and other opportunity programs.

STRATEGIES IN PUBLIC WELFARE POLICY

In the Social Security Act of 1935 the federal government undertook to establish a basic framework for welfare policies at the federal, state, and local levels in America. This act embodied both an alleviative strategy (public assistance) and a new preventative strategy (social insurance). The *social insurance* concept was designed to *prevent* poverty resulting from individual misfortune—unemployment, old age, death of the family breadwinner, or physical disability. Social insurance was based on the same notion as private insurance: the sharing of risks and the setting aside of money for a rainy day. Social insurance was not to be charity or public assistance. Instead, it relied upon the individual's (compulsory) financial contribution to his own protection.

One of the key features of the Social Security Act is the Old-Age, Survivors, and Disability Insurance (OASDI) program; this is a compulsory social insurance program financed by regular deductions from earnings, which gives individuals the legal right to benefit in the event that their income is reduced by old age, death of the head of the household, or permanent disability. OASDI is not public charity but a way of compelling people to provide insurance against loss of income. Another feature of the Social Security Act was that it induced states to enact unemployment compensation programs. Unemployment compensation is also an *insurance* program, only in this case the costs are borne solely by the employer. In 1965 Congress amended social security to add comprehensive medical care for persons over 65—"Medicare." Medicare provided for prepaid hospital insurance for the aged under social security, and low-cost voluntary medical insurance for the aged under federal administration. Medicare too is based upon the insurance principle: Individuals would pay for their medical insurance during their working years and enjoy its benefits after age 65. Thus, the program resembles private medical hospital insurance, except that it is compulsory.

The distinction between the *social insurance* program and a *public assistance* program is an important one, which has on occasion become a major political issue. If the beneficiaries of a government program are required to have made contributions to it before claiming any of its benefits, and if they are entitled to the benefits regardless of their personal wealth, the program is said to be financed on the *social insurance* principle. If the program is financed out of general tax revenues, and if the recipients are required to show that they are poor before claiming its benefits, the program is said to be financed on the *public assistance* principle.

In addition to the insurance programs mentioned above, the federal government undertook in the Social Security Act to help states provide public assistance payments to certain needy persons to alleviate the conditions of poverty. The strategy of public assistance is clearly *alleviative*. There is no effort to prevent poverty or to attack its causes; the idea is simply to provide a minimum level of subsistence to certain categories of needy persons. The federal government gives grants to the states to assist them in providing welfare payments to four categories of recipients: the aged, the blind, the disabled, and dependent children. Welfare aid to persons who do not fall into any of these categories but who, for one reason or another, are poor is referred to as *general assistance* and is paid for entirely from state funds.

In 1965 in its amendments to the Social Security Act, Congress also authorized federal funds to enable states to guarantee medical services to all public assistance recipients. This program is known as "Medicaid." Unlike Medicare, Medicaid is a welfare program designed for needy persons; no prior contributions are required, but recipients of Medicaid must be eligible for welfare assistance. In other words, they must be poor.

THE WELFARE MESS

On the whole, the social insurance programs of the federal government are popular: social security, unemployment compensation, and Medicare. But public assistance has turned out to be politically one of the most unpopular programs ever adopted by the Congress. It is disliked by national, state, and local legislatures who must vote the skyrocketing appropriations for it; it is resented by the taxpayers who must bear the ever increasing burdens of it; it is denounced by officials and caseworkers who must administer it; and it is accepted with bitterness by those who were intended to benefit from it.

Dependence upon public assistance in America is increasing at a very rapid rate (see Table 10-3). Whether or not the program itself encourages dependency, one thing is certain: More Americans rely upon public assistance today than

TABLE 10-3. **Growth of Public Assistance Programs**
(millions of recipients)

	Total	AFDC	Aged	Disabled	Blind	General Assistance
1950	6.0	2.2	2.8	0.1	0.1	0.9
1955	5.8	2.2	2.5	0.2	0.1	0.7
1960	7.0	3.1	2.3	0.4	0.1	1.2
1965	7.8	4.4	2.1	0.6	0.1	0.7
1970	10.4	6.7	2.0	0.87	0.1	0.8
1971	13.5	9.5	2.0	1.0	0.1	0.9
1972	15.0	10.8	2.1	1.0	0.1	1.0

Source: *Special Analysis of the Budget of the United States, 1972* (Washington: Government Printing Office, 1971); and past issues of U.S. Bureau of the Census, *Statistical Abstract of the United States.*

ever before. Certainly our public assistance programs have not succeeded in reducing dependency. In the last decade the number of welfare recipients has more than doubled, and public assistance costs have quadrupled. Interestingly, it is not programs for the aged, blind, or disabled, or even the general assistance programs, that have incurred the greatest burdens. It is the Aid to Families with Dependent Children (AFDC) program that is the largest, most expensive, and most rapidly growing of all welfare programs—and the most controversial.

The rise in welfare rolls began during a period of high employment; it cannot be attributed to economic depression but is due to the fact that more and more people are applying for public assistance. Despite increased dependency upon welfare, and the growing burden of welfare costs, a majority of the nation's poor do *not* receive public assistance. There were 25 million poor people in America in 1970, yet only 10.4 million persons on welfare rolls. Many of the nation's poor are *working poor*, who are ineligible for welfare assistance because they hold jobs, even though the jobs pay very little. A low-income family, headed by the father, is not eligible to receive AFDC payments if the father is working, regardless of how poor the family may be.

Not only does welfare fail to assist most of the nation's poor; it does not provide enough in the way of assistance to recipients to raise them out of poverty. While welfare benefits differ from state to state, in every state the level of benefits falls well below the recognized poverty line.

State administration of welfare has resulted in wide disparities among the states in eligibility requirements and benefit levels. For example, in 1970 average AFDC monthly payments ranged from a high of $66.40 per child in New Jersey to a low of $10.20 per child in Mississippi. Monthly old age assistance payments ranged from a high of $116 in New Hampshire to a low of $39 in Mississippi.

Operating policies and administration of welfare have produced a whole series of problems, including disincentives to family life and work. Until recently, most states denied AFDC benefits if a man was living with his family, even though he had no work. This denial was based on the assumption that an employable man in the household meant that children were no longer "dependent" upon the state. Thus, if a man lived with his family, he could watch them go hungry; if he abandoned them, public assistance would enable them to eat. Moreover, an unmarried mother could get on welfare rolls easier than a married mother (who had to prove she was not receiving support from her husband). These rules have now been relaxed, but it is still more difficult for whole families to get on public assistance than for fatherless families.

In most states, if a recipient of assistance takes a full job, assistance checks are reduced or stopped. If the recipient is then laid off, it may take some time to get back on the welfare roll. In other words, employment is uncertain, while assistance is not. More importantly, the jobs available to most recipients are low-paying jobs which do not produce much more income than assistance, particularly when transportation, child care, and other costs of working are considered. All of these facts discourage work.

While such problems are serious, it is well to note that some of the charges leveled against public assistance are unfounded. For example, there are very few individuals for whom welfare has become "a permanent way of life." The median length of time on AFDC is less than three years; only one-tenth of the persons aided have been receiving assistance for more than ten years. The number of "welfare chiselers"—able-bodied employable adults who prefer public-assisted idleness to work—is probably quite small. The bulk of recipients are either aged, blind, disabled, women, or children; few employable men are on welfare rolls. The work alternative for the large numbers of AFDC mothers is fraught with problems—child care, lack of skills, no work experience, etc. It might be more costly to society to prepare these women for work than to support them.

THE WAR ON POVERTY

The War on Poverty was an attempt to apply a "curative strategy" to the problem of the poor. The most important governmental effort in the War on Poverty was the Economic Opportunity Act of 1964.[9] This act established the Office of Economic Opportunity (OEO) directly under the president with the authority to support various programs for combating poverty at the community level. The objective was to help the poor and unemployed become self-supporting and capable of earning adequate incomes. The strategy was one of "rehabilitation," not "relief." OEO was given no authority to make direct grants to the poor as relief. Instead, all of its programs were aimed, whether accurately or inaccurately, at *curing* the causes of poverty rather than *alleviating* its symptoms.

The Economic Opportunity Act established several programs oriented toward youth. The strategy appeared to be aimed at breaking the cycle of poverty at an early age. The Job Corps was designed to provide education, vocational training, and work experience in rural conservation camps for unemployable youth between the ages of 16 and 21. The Neighborhood Youth Corps was designed to provide some work, counseling, and on-the-job training for youth who were living at home. A Work Study program helped students from low-income families remain in school by giving them federally paid part-time employment with cooperating public or private agencies. Volunteers in Service to America (VISTA) was modeled after the popular Peace Corps, but volunteers were to work in poverty-impacted areas within the United States rather than in foreign countries.

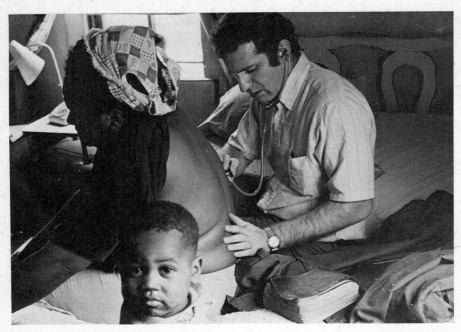

The most massive post-Depression effort to reduce poverty was President Lyndon Johnson's War on Poverty. One component was VISTA, which attracted volunteers such as this doctor to work with the poor. *Eugene Richards Photo*

But the heart of the Economic Opportunity Act was a grass-roots "community action program" to be carried on at the local level with federal financial assistance. Communities were urged to form a "Community Action Agency" composed of representatives of government, private organizations, and, most importantly, the poor themselves. The idea was that the OEO would *support the antipoverty programs* devised by local Community Action agencies to combat poverty in their own communities. Projects might include (but were not limited to) literacy training, health services, homemaker services, legal aid for the poor, neighborhood service centers, manpower training, and childhood developmental activities. The act also envisioned that a Community Action Agency would help *organize the poor* so that they could become participating members of the community and avail themselves of the many public programs designed to serve the poor. Finally, the act attempted to *coordinate federal and state programs for the poor* in each community.

Typically a Community Action Agency would begin by hiring a staff, including a full-time director, paid from an OEO administrative grant, and define a target area—generally, the low-income area of the county or the ghetto of a city. Neighborhood centers were established in the target area, embracing perhaps general counselors, employment assistance, a recreational hall, a child-care center, and some sort of health clinic. The centers assisted the poor in contacting the school system, the welfare department, the employment agencies, the public housing authority, and so on. Frequently the centers and the anti-poverty workers who manned them acted as intermediaries between the poor and public agencies. Community Action agencies also devised specific antipoverty projects for submission to Washington offices of OEO for funding. The most popular project was "Operation Headstart"—usually a cooperative program between the Community Action Agency and the school district to give preschool children from poor families special preparation before entering kindergarten or first grade. Another type of project was the "Legal Services Program," in which Community Action agencies set up free legal services to the poor to assist them in rent disputes, contracts, minor police actions, and so on. Other kinds of antipoverty projects funded by OEO included family planning programs, homemaker services, manpower training, and special educational programs. It is important to know that most of the $2 billion per year allocated to the War on Poverty went into salaries and expenses for administrators, teachers, and workers; in other words, the money was spent on efforts to "cure" poverty and not on the poor themselves.

The Office of Economic Opportunity was eventually "reorganized" by the Nixon administration, which transferred its educational and manpower training programs to other departments and then relegated OEO to the status of the "laboratory agency." Funds for the War on Poverty faced gradual reallocation. The demise of the Economic Opportunity programs cannot be attributed to political partisanship. The War on Poverty had become unpopular even before the Johnson administration left office. The reasons for the failure of this effort at a curative strategy are complex.

The Office of Economic Opportunity was always the scene of great confusion. New and untried programs were organized too quickly; there was high turnover in personnel; there was scandal and corruption, particularly at the local level. Community Action agencies with young and inexperienced personnel offended experienced governmental administrators, as well as local political figures. Frequently Community Action Agencies became involved in racial politics in local communities. Many people came to believe that the War on Poverty was a "black program." Anti-poverty workers competed with local party organizers and even with social workers for the loyalties of the poor. There was duplication of roles, inefficiency, waste, and a lack of coordination. Most damaging of all, there was little concrete evidence that the programs which were put into operation were successful in their objective—that is, in eliminating the causes of poverty.

Daniel P. Moynihan summarized the community action experiences as follows:

Over and over again the attempts by official and quasi-official agencies (such as the Ford Foundation) to organize poor communities led first to the radicalization of the middle-class persons who began the effort; next to a certain amount of stirring among the poor, but accompanied by heightened radical antagonism *on the part of the poor* if they happened to be black; next to retaliation from the larger white community; whereupon it would emerge that the community action agency, which had talked so much, been so much in the headlines, promised so much in the way of change in the fundamentals of things, was powerless. A creature of a Washington bureaucracy, subject to discontinuation without notice. Finally, much bitterness all around.[10]

POWER AND POVERTY: A CASE STUDY

Welfare Reform and the Work Ethic

Growing disillusionment over public welfare programs, combined with failures in the War on Poverty, have stimulated the search for a more effective way of dealing with poverty in America. Today most welfare reform proposals incorporate the idea of "income maintenance." Income maintenance plans come in many varieties, but essentially they propose to provide the poor with a guaranteed income to allow them to live in decency regardless of the causes of their poverty. The income maintenance strategy does not attempt to deal with the causes of poverty but simply to guarantee a minimum income. An income maintenance program can be designed to help the poor by providing minimum incomes; or it can be designed to eliminate poverty by raising their incomes high enough to remove them from poverty. That is, an income maintenance strategy can either ameliorate poverty or eliminate it altogether if the guaranteed minimum income is set high enough.

The problem, of course, is the possibility that a substantial number of recipients will view the guaranteed income as an alternative to work and will choose such an income in preference to work. The destruction of the "work ethic" would diminish total economic output, leaving society less well off than before, and it would tend to reinforce individual traits, including dependency, which affect individual dignity and self-reliance. Actually it is difficult to predict the effect of a guaranteed income on work incentive. Many people work very hard with little or no monetary incentive and prefer work to the boredom of unemployment. Initial results of experimentation on small groups of individuals who were given guaranteed annual incomes suggested that their work incentive was relatively unaffected. But there is no way of knowing what would happen to the work ethic if the guaranteed income were established for the *whole* society over a *prolonged* period of time. Whatever the results in small-scale experimental situations, how can one foresee the long-run impact of the guaranteed income in America on the qualities of personal independence, self-reliance, and responsibility that appear to be essential to the full development of the individual and to the health of society?

The income maintenance strategy is incorporated into President Nixon's Welfare Reform Program—the Family Assistance Plan. This plan was first presented to Congress in 1969 as a proposed reform of the nation's welfare policies, which the president described as "a colossal failure":

> Whether measured by the anguish of the poor themselves or by the drastically mounting burden on the taxpayer, the present welfare system has to be judged a colossal failure.

"I'm afraid this is my last visit, Mrs. Segarra. There's no money in social work."
Drawing by Weber; © 1973 The New Yorker Magazine, Inc.

Welfare Reform and the Work Ethic

Our states and cities find themselves sinking in a welfare quagmire as caseloads increase, as costs escalate and as the welfare system stagnates enterprise and perpetuates dependency. . . . The tragedy is not only that it is bringing states and cities to the brink of financial disaster, but also that it is failing to meet the elementary human, social and financial needs of the poor.

It breaks up homes. It often penalizes work. It robs recipients of dignity. And it grows.

Benefit levels are grossly unequal. . . .

The present system creates an incentive for desertion. . . .

The present system often makes it possible to receive more money on welfare than on a low-paying job. This creates an incentive not to work; it also is unfair to the working poor. . . .[11]

The president proposed a new "Family Assistance Plan" paralleling so-called guaranteed annual income proposals which had been discussed for years in liberal circles. The following features were included: (1) All low-income families with children—the *working* as well as the nonworking poor—would be eligible to receive family assistance. (2) For families with no outside income, a minimum federal payment would be provided (perhaps $3,500 for a family of four). (3) Outside earnings would be encouraged, not discouraged. A family could keep the first $750 per year of outside income without reducing federal payment; beyond that amount family assistance would be reduced by only 50 cents for each dollar earned. The break-even point—the level of income at which a family of four would cease to be eligible for family assistance benefits—would be approximately $5,000. (4) The Family Assistance program would replace the Aid to Families with Dependent Children program. (5) Adult family members would be required to register for work and accept "suitable employment" when it was offered.

The president defended the Family Assistance Plan by arguing:

Thus, for the first time, the government would recognize that it has no less of an obligation to the working poor than to the nonworking poor, and for the first time, benefits would be scaled in such a way that it would always pay to work.

With such incentive, most recipients who can work will want to work. This is part of the American character.[12]

The proposed Family Assistance program is clearly designed to remedy many of the dysfunctional consequences of previous welfare policy—disincentives to work, discouragement of family life, inequalities among the states, and discrimination against the working poor. But the long-run impact of such a policy reform is hard to predict.

The first problem with a guaranteed annual income is the increase in costs which would be involved.[13] It is likely that Congress will want to increase the minimum guarantee over the years. There is no really reliable information on

Welfare Reform and the Work Ethic

the number of working poor who would apply or what this additional load would cost. Presumably the costs of AFDC would be eliminated; but the costs of old-age, blind, and disabled assistance would continue, not to mention the spiraling cost of Medicaid for the poor.

Despite the heavy costs involved in a federally guaranteed $3,500 income for a family of four, there is no doubt that this is an inadequate income by anyone's standards. It is well below the Social Security Administration's recognized poverty line.

The work incentives of the Family Assistance Plan have been attacked as useless, and perhaps demeaning. Previous work incentive amendments to public assistance programs have not succeeded in reducing dependency. If welfare recipients could find good jobs they would have done so long ago; the real problem is that they are unskilled, uneducated, and unprepared to function effectively in the work force. Perhaps the work incentives would encourage some recipients to accept more badly paid, economically marginal jobs—maid service, gardening, window-washing, etc. But the social value of these jobs is limited, and this aspect of the reform proposal has been attacked as demeaning to the poor.

Finally, it is not certain whether such an expansion of welfare assistance to many working families would increase or reduce economic dependency in America. Possibly it would encourage dependency by making the acceptance of welfare assistance a common family practice, extending well up into the middle class. Certainly the percentage of the population receiving some form of public assistance would be greatly increased; it is conceivable that 20 percent of the population would eventually gain access to welfare rolls under a guaranteed annual income.

NOTES

1. John Kenneth Galbraith, *The Affluent Society* (New York: New American Library, 1958), p. 251.

2. U.S. Bureau of the Census, "Poverty in the United States," *Current Population Reports,* P-60, No. 86, 1972.

3. Kenneth B. Clark, *Dark Ghetto: Dilemmas of Social Power* (New York: Harper & Row, 1965), p. 67.

4. Ibid., p. 70.

5. Daniel P. Moynihan, *The Negro Family: The Case for National Action* (Washington: Government Printing Office, 1965).

6. Ibid., p. 47.

7. Edward C. Banfield, *The Unheavenly City* (Boston: Little, Brown, 1968), Chap. 6.

Welfare Reform and the Work Ethic

8.   Jack L. Roach and Orville R. Gursslin, "An Evaluation of the Concept Culture of Poverty," *Social Forces*, 45 (March 1967), 384 - 392.

9.   For a description of all of the different programs in the War on Poverty see Joseph A. Kershaw, *Government Against Poverty* (Chicago: Markham, 1970).

10.   Daniel P. Moynihan, *Maximum Feasible Misunderstanding: Community Action in the War on Poverty* (New York: Free Press, 1969), pp. 134 - 135.

11.   President Richard M. Nixon, speech on national television networks, August 12, 1969.

12.   Ibid.

13.   For an excellent example of a rational analysis of welfare reform see Theodore Marmor, "On Comparing Income Maintenance Alternatives," *American Political Science Review*, 65 (March 1971), 83 - 96.

TESTING YOUR PERFORMANCE

Note to the Student.   The following questions are to test how well you achieved the Performance Objectives identified for you at the beginning of this chapter. The correct answers are supplied, accompanied by corresponding pages for you to review if you have answered incorrectly. The questions are coodinated numerically with the Performance Objectives at the beginning of the chapter. This exercise will assist you in determining the type of questions you have the most difficulty in answering (discussion, identification, explanation, definition, etc.) and will prepare you for test questions likely to be asked by your instructor.

1.   (a) Proponents of large-scale government programs estimate that there are a large number of poor persons, view the problem as a persistent one, and emphasize levels of deprivation. Opponents of large-scale government programs estimate that there are a minimal number of poor persons, deny the necessity of being poor, and have an optimistic outlook (based on a comparison of today's poor and the middle class of 50 years ago). These represent two different approaches to defining _____ .

(b) The official definition of poverty "draws" a poverty line by carefully calculating the cost of food, housing, clothing, and other items for rural and urban families of different sizes and seeks to describe poverty objectively as lack of enough income to acquire the minimum necessities of life (subsistence level). This definition is formulated by the _____

_____ .

2.   The groups which experience poverty in the greatest proportion when compared with the national average are _____

_____ .

3.   (a) The definition of poverty as a sense of deprivation (felt by some people because they have less income or fewer material possessions than most other Americans) views poverty as _____ .

(b) The inability to control the events shaping one's life and the attitude that no matter what one does it will have little effect on his life is _____ .

4.   (a) The black sociologist who studied "the psychology of the ghetto" is

_____ .

(b) He argued that human beings who live apart from the rest of society, who do not share in society's affluence, and who are not respected or granted the ordinary dignities and courtesy accorded to others will develop a _____

_____ .

(c) The conscious or unconscious belief of many young blacks that they cannot hope to win meaningful self-esteem through the avenues available to middle class whites and their consequent turning to "hustling" is Clark's explanation for _____ .

(d) Expressing a continuing sense of personal failure through stagnation and despair, dropping out of school, living in a world of television and motion pictures, and dreaming and fantasizing of luxury and happiness are all examples of _____ .

(e) The high rate of illegitimacy and family instability, the relegation of the black male to menial and subservient jobs, the lack of a strong father figure upon which to model the behavior of young black males are the results of

_____ .

5.   The theory that deprivation in one generation leads, through cultural impoverishment, indifference, apathy, or misunderstanding of children's educational needs, to deprivation in the next generation is the _____

_____ .

6.   (a) Daniel Moynihan argues that one of the worst effects of slavery and segregation on blacks has been the _____

_____ .

(b) The view of the culture of poverty as perpetuating itself through continuation of the poverty cycle without assistance from the white world and as incapable of being broken unless the structural distortions in the lives of black Americans are abolished was expressed by _____ .

(c) The view of the culture of poverty which emphasizes the present-orientedness of the poor, rather than a lack of income or wealth, and predicts continuation of the condition, regardless of remedial action, because many persons are psychologically unable to provide for the future, was expressed by

_____ .

7.   Diverting attention from the conditions of poverty which foster family instability, present-orientedness, and other ways of life of the poor; application of it only to groups who have lived in poverty for several generations; lack of relevance to those who have become poor during their lifetime because of sickness, accident, or old age; and the relaxation of efforts to end the conditions of poverty—all are _____ .

8.   The provision of opportunities so that people could achieve their own escape from poverty, rather than direct provision of resources to end poverty, was the goal of the _____ .

9.   The derivation of a strategy to interrupt the transmission of lower class cultural values from one generation to another (such as removing the children from lower class homes at a very early age and raising them in a controlled environment in which the conventional culture is transmitted rather than the sub-culture of poverty, or culturally enriching the children through special day-care

centers and preschool programs), and the unacceptability of the idea of changing the conditions of life to permit the lower classes to take advantage of opportunity programs unless accompanied by programs aimed at directly altering the conditions of poverty (such as guaranteed minimum income), are the _____

10. The congressional act in which the federal government undertook to establish a basic framework for welfare policies at the federal, state, and local levels, which created the Old-Age, Survivors, and Disability Insurance (OASDI) program, and which induced states to enact unemployment compensation programs was the _____.

11. (a) The type of program which is financed out of general tax revenues and requires recipients to show that they are poor before claiming its benefits is a _____.

(b) The type of program which requires beneficiaries to have made contributions to it before claiming any of its benefits and entitles beneficiaries to the benefits regardless of their personal wealth is a _____

12. The categories of recipients of welfare payments (partly financed by federal grants to the states) are _____.

13. Welfare aid, paid for entirely from state funds, to persons not falling into the four categories of recipients but who, for one reason or another, are poor is referred to as _____.

14. (a) The program, passed by Congress in 1965, providing for prepaid hospital insurance for the aged under federal social security, and low-cost voluntary medical insurance for the aged under federal administration is _____

(b) The program which provides funds to enable states to guarantee medical services to all public assistance recipients is _____.

15. The largest, most expensive, and most controversial welfare program is _____

16. Ineligibility for welfare assistance as a result of holding a job, even though it pays little; failure to provide enough assistance to recipients to raise them out of poverty; disparities among the states in eligibility requirements and benefit levels; and inadequate policies and administration of welfare, and disincentives to family life and work—all are _____

17. (a) The congressional act which established the Office of Economic Opportunity (OEO) directly under the president with the authority to support various programs for combating poverty at the community level and created the Job Corps, Neighborhood Youth Corps, Work Study program, Volunteers in Service to America (VISTA), and the community action program was the _____.

(b) The basic strategy of the War on Poverty was *not* relief, direct grants to the poor, or alleviation of the symptoms of poverty but was a _____.

18. (a) A program, which was the heart of the Economic Opportunity Act, carried on at the local level with federal financial assistance by an agency com-

posed of representatives of government, private organizations, and the poor themselves and proposing to help organize the poor so that they could become participating members of the community and to coordinate federal and state programs for the poor was the _____ .

(b) Literacy training, health services, homemaker services, legal aid for the poor, neighborhood service centers, manpower training, childhood developmental activities (Operation Headstart), and family planning programs were all examples of _____ .

19. New and untried programs organized too quickly; high turnover in personnel; scandal and corruption, particularly at the local level; frequent offending of experienced governmental administrators and local political figures by young and inexperienced personnel; involvement in the racial politics of local communities; competition between antipoverty workers and local party organizers and social workers for the loyalties of the poor; confusion, duplication of roles, inefficiency, and lack of coordination; and lack of concrete evidence that the programs were eliminating the causes of poverty—all were

_____ .

20. (a) The provision of the poor with a guaranteed income to allow them to live in decency regardless of the causes of their poverty, and the designing of the program to either ameliorate poverty or eliminate it altogether (if the guaranteed income is set high enough) are the purposes and strategies of _____

_____ .

(b) The possibility that a substantial number of recipients will view the guaranteed income as an alternative to work and will choose such an income in preference to work (destruction of the "work ethic") is the basic _____

_____ .

21. (a) The eligibility of all low-income families with children to receive family assistance; provision of a minimum federal payment for families with no outside income; encouragement of outside earnings; replacement of the Aid to Families with Dependent Children program; and requirement of adult family members to register for work and to accept "suitable" employment when it is offered—these are all provisions of President Nixon's _____

_____ .

(b) Increase in welfare costs; inadequacy of the federal guaranteed income, which is below the recognized poverty line; uselessness and demeaning of work incentives for the poor; and uncertainty of the ability of expanded welfare assistance to working families to increase or reduce economic dependency—all are _____ .

Correct Responses

1. (a) Poverty (pp. 349 - 350); (b) U.S. Social Security Administration (p. 350).

2. Blacks, female-headed families, and the aged (p. 352).

3. (a) Relative deprivation (p. 354); (b) Powerlessness (p. 356).

4. (a) Kenneth B. Clark (p. 356); (b) Sense of inferiority (pp. 356 - 357); (c) Crime

and violence in the ghetto (p. 357); (d) Personal adjustment to ghetto life (pp. 357 - 358); (e) Poverty and discrimination (pp. 357 - 358).

5.　Theory of the poverty cycle (p. 358).

6.　(a) Deterioration of the Negro family (p. 359); (b) Daniel P. Moynihan (p. 359); (c) Edward C. Banfield (pp. 359 - 360).

7.　Criticisms of the idea of a culture of poverty (pp. 360 - 361).

8.　War on Poverty (p. 361).

9.　Policy implications of the idea of a culture of poverty (p. 361).

10.　Social Security Act of 1935 (p. 362).

11.　(a) Public assistance program (p. 362); (b) Social insurance program (p. 362).

12.　The aged, the blind, the disabled, and dependent children (p. 364).

13.　General assistance (p. 363).

14.　(a) Medicare (p. 000); (b) Medicaid (p. 000).

15.　Aid to Families with Dependent Children (AFDC) (p. 000).

16.　Problems and weaknesses of current welfare programs (pp. 000 - 000).

17.　(a) Economic Opportunity Act of 1964 (pp. 365 - 366); (b) Curative strategy (p. 365).

18.　(a) Community action program (pp. 366 - 367); (b) Programs and projects conducted by Community Action agencies (p. 366).

19.　Criticisms of the Office of Economic Opportunity (p. 367).

20.　(a) Income maintenance plans (p. 368); (b) Problem of the income maintenance strategy (p. 368).

21.　(a) Welfare Reform Program (pp. 369 - 370); (b) Criticisms of the Family Assistance Program (pp. 370 - 371).

KEY TERMS

Economic Opportunity Act of 1964

poverty

subsistence levels

deprivation levels

relative deprivation

powerlessness

culture of poverty

War on Poverty

opportunity programs

guaranteed minimum income

Social Security Act of 1935

social insurance concept

public assistance concept

Old-Age, Survivors, and Disability Insurance (OASDI)

employment compensation programs

Medicare

general assistance

Medicaid

Office of Economic Opportunity (OEO)

Job Corps

Neighborhood Youth Corps

Work Study program

Volunteers in Service to America (VISTA)

community action program

Community Action agencies

Operation Headstart

Legal Services program

income maintenance strategy

"work ethic"

Family Assistance Plan

DISCUSSION QUESTIONS

1. Discuss the criteria used by the U.S. Social Security Administration to define the poverty line. What is meant by this definition of poverty's emphasis on subsistence levels? What are the criticisms of this definition of poverty?

2. Identify the groups of people who are proportionately poorer than the national average.

3. Discuss the definition of poverty as relative deprivation. How would this type of poverty be eliminated?

4. Discuss the relationship between poverty and feelings of powerlessness among ghetto residents with regard to:
   (a) Self-esteem and self-confidence
   (b) Violence and crime
   (c) Sense of failure
   (d) Black family life

5. What is meant by the expression *culture of poverty?* Discuss the theory of the poverty cycle. What are the policy implications of the culture of poverty idea? What are the arguments used by proponents of the idea of a culture of poverty? What are the arguments used by opponents of the idea of a culture of poverty?

6. Discuss the differences between social insurance programs and public assistance programs:
   (a) Who pays
   (b) Who benefits
   (c) When one benefits
   (d) Strategy (alleviative or curative)
   Give examples of programs existing today for each type of program.

7. Discuss the criticisms of the public assistance (welfare) programs that currently exist. What is meant by income maintenance strategy? What are the criticisms of the strategy? Discuss the provisions of Nixon's Welfare Reform Program (Family Assistance Plan).

SUGGESTED READINGS

EDWARD C. BANFIELD, *The Unheavenly City* (Boston: Little, Brown, 1968).

JOHN C. DONOVAN, *The Politics of Poverty* (New York: Pegasus, 1967).

JOHN KENNETH GALBRAITH, *The Affluent Society* (New York: New American Library, 1958).

MICHAEL HARRINGTON, *The Other America: Poverty in the United States* (New York: Macmillan, 1962).

JOSEPH A. KERSHAW, *Government Against Poverty* (Chicago: Markham, 1970).

DANIEL P. MOYNIHAN, *Maximum Feasible Misunderstanding: Community Action in the War on Poverty* (New York: Free Press, 1969).

DANIEL P. MOYNIHAN, *The Negro Family: The Case for National Action* (Washington: Government Printing Office, 1965).

GILBERT Y. STEINER, *Social Insecurity* (Chicago: Rand McNally, 1966).

CHARLES A. VALENTINE, *Culture and Poverty* (Chicago: University of Chicago Press, 1970).

CHAPTER 11

Power, Crime, and Violence

PERFORMANCE OBJECTIVES

The student should be able to:

1. Discuss Thomas Hobbes's idea of a "social contract."

2. Identify the classic dilemma of a free government.

3. Discuss how crime rates are figured. Identify "serious crimes." Identify the factors that determine the official crime rate. Identify the types of crimes which have had the greatest increase. Identify the crime statistic which is most accurate.

4. Discuss the reasons why persons fail to report crime to the police.

5. Define the constitutional rights of defendants: guarantee of the writ of habeas corpus; prohibition of bills of attainder and ex post facto laws; prohibition of "unreasonable searches and seizures; freedom from self-incrimination; right to counsel; guarantee of a fair jury trial; protection against double jeopardy; and protection against excessive bail.

6. Define "speedy"; "public"; "impartial"; and "hung jury."

7. Describe the effect of the Warren Court of the 1950s and 1960s on the rights of accused persons in criminal cases. Outline the basic decisions in the Warren Court cases: *Mapp* v. *Ohio* (1961), *Gideon* v. *Wainwright* (1963), *Escobedo* v. *Illinois* (1964), and *Miranda* v. *Arizona* (1966).

8. Identify the major concern of Chief Justice Warren Burger's recommendations for judicial reform. List the weaknesses of the present system of criminal justice as stated by Burger in his State of the Federal Judiciary message.

9. Contrast the arguments used by opponents of capital punishment with arguments used by proponents.

10.   Discuss the 1972 Supreme Court decision regarding capital punishment. Compare the reasoning of the different Supreme Court justices.

11.   Discuss the three important functions performed by the police in urban society. Identify the typical background of police officers.

12.   Trace the use of violence in important movements throughout American history. Define vigilante violence.

13.   Compare and contrast the frustration-aggression explanation of violence with the aggressive instinct explanation of violence. Identify the type of political group which frequently espouses the frustration-aggression explanation of violence.

14.   Cite the author of *On Aggression,* who argued that aggressive behavior is rooted in man's long struggle for survival. Identify what he saw as a good way to prevent people from engaging in aggression and contrast this with the experimental psychologists' proposed remedy for aggression.

15.   Discuss the relative deprivation explanation of violence. Contrast it with the frustration-aggression explanation. Identify the political counterpart of the relative deprivation explanation of violence.

16.   Discuss James C. Davies's theory of revolutions. Identify the conditions which bring about a revolution.

17.   Discuss the use of violence as a political protest. Contrast the political protest explanation of violence with Edward Banfield's "fun" or "profit" explanation of violence.

18.   Discuss the four principal motives and the four accompanying types of riots defined by Edward Banfield.

19.   List the major ghetto riots. Outline the conclusions of the National Advisory Commission on Civil Disorders. List the three major results of white racism attitudes. List the three additional powerful ingredients of the riots. Identify the race upon which the commission laid the principal "blame" for the riots.

POWER AND INDIVIDUAL FREEDOM

For thousands of years men have wrestled with the question of balancing social power against individual freedom. How far can individual freedom be extended without undermining the stability of a society, threatening the safety of others, and risking anarchy? The early English political philosopher Thomas Hobbes (1588 - 1679) believed that society must establish a powerful "Leviathan"—the state—in order to curb the savage instincts in men. A powerful authority in society was needed to prevent men from attacking each other for personal gain—"war of every man against every man" in which "notions of right and wrong, justice and injustice, have no place." According to Hobbes, without law and order there is no real freedom. The fear of death and destruction permeates every act of life: "Every man is enemy to every man"; and "Force and fraud are the two cardinal virtues."

> In such condition, there is no place for industry; because the fruit thereof is uncertain: and consequently no culture of the earth; no navigation, nor use of the commodities that may be imported by sea; no commodious building, no instruments of moving, and removing, such things as that require much force; no knowledge of the face of the earth; no account of time; no arts; no letters; no society; and which is worst of all, continual fear, and danger of violent death; and the life of man solitary, poor, nasty, brutish, and short.

Freedom, then, is *not* the absence of law and order. On the contrary, law and order are required if there is to be any freedom in society at all.

In order to avoid the brutal life of a lawless society—where the weak are at the mercy of the strong—men form governments and endow them with powers to secure peace and self-preservation. Hobbes believed that "the social contract"—the agreement of men to establish governments and grant them the powers to maintain peace and security—is a collective act of self-preservation. Men voluntarily relinquish some of their individual freedom to establish a powerful government which is capable of protecting them from their neighbors as well as from foreign aggressors. This government must be able to maintain its existence or it cannot defend the rights of its citizens. And in order to guard its own integrity, it must be strong enough to maintain its own existence. But what happens when a government becomes too strong and infringes the liberties of its citizens? Men agree to abide by law and accept restrictions on their personal freedom for the sake of peace and self-preservation; but how much liberty must be surrendered in order to secure an orderly society? This is the classic dilemma of free government: Men must create laws and governments to protect freedom, but the laws and governments themselves restrict freedom.

THE PROBLEM OF CRIME

Crime rates are the subject of a great deal of popular discussion. Very often they are employed to express the degree of social disorganization or even the effectiveness of law enforcement agencies. Crime rates are based upon the Federal Bureau of Investigation's *Uniform Crime Reports,* but the FBI reports are based on figures supplied by state and local police agencies (see Table 11-1). The FBI has succeeded in establishing a uniform classification of the number of serious crimes per 100,000 people that are known to the police—murder and nonnegligent manslaughter, forcible rape, robbery, aggravated assault,

"Drop that gun! I'm a
plainclothesman and he's a
German shepherd!"

Drawing by Weber; © 1972
The New Yorker Magazine,
Inc.

burglary, larceny, and theft, including auto theft. But record keeping is still a problem, and one should be cautious in interpreting official crime rates. They are really a function of several factors: the diligence of police in detecting crime, the adequacy of the reporting system tabulating crime, and the amount of crime itself. Yet the evidence seems inescapable that crime in the United States is increasing at a rapid pace. The greatest increase in crime rates occurs in nonviolent crimes (burglary, larceny, theft), and lesser increases are found in crimes involving violence against the person (murder, nonnegligent manslaughter, and robbery).

Police statistics vastly understate the real amount of crime. Citizens do not

TABLE 11-1.   Crime Rate—Number of Offenses Known to Police Per 100,000 Persons

Year	Total	Murder and Nonnegligent Manslaughter	Forc-ible Rape	Rob-bery	Assault	Burg-lary	Larceny	Auto Theft
1960	1,126	5	10	60	85	502	283	182
1965	1,516	5	12	71	110	653	410	255
1970	2,747	8	19	171	163	1,071	861	454
1972	2,830	9	22	180	187	1,126	883	423
Average annual increase	9%	5%	7%	11%	7%	8%	12%	10%

Source: *Statistical Abstract of the United States, 1973,* p. 146.

report many crimes to police. The National Opinion Research Center of the University of Chicago asked a national sample of individuals whether they or any member of their household had been a victim of crime during the past year. This survey revealed that the actual amount of crime is several times greater than that reported by the FBI. There are more than twice as many crimes committed as are reported to the police. The number of forcible rapes was more than three and one-half times the number reported; burglaries were three times, aggravated assaults and larcenies were more than double, and robbery was 50 percent greater than the reported rate. Only auto theft statistics were reasonably accurate, indicating that most people call the police when their cars are stolen.

Interviewees gave a variety of reasons for their failure to report crime to the police. The most common reason was the belief that police could not be effective in dealing with the crime. This is a serious commentary on police protection in America today. Other reasons included the feeling that the crime was "a private matter" or that the victim did not want to harm the offender. Fear of reprisal was mentioned much less frequently, usually in cases of assaults and family crimes.

The current system of criminal justice is certainly no serious deterrent to crime. Most behavioral research suggests that it is not the *severity of punishment* which affects behavior but the establishment of a *sure linkage* between the criminal behavior and punishment. In other words, crime is more likely to be deterred by making punishment sure, rather than severe. However, the best available estimates of the ratio between crime and punishment suggest that the likelihood of an individual's being jailed for a serious crime is less than one in a hundred (see Figure 11-1). Most crimes are not even reported by the victim.

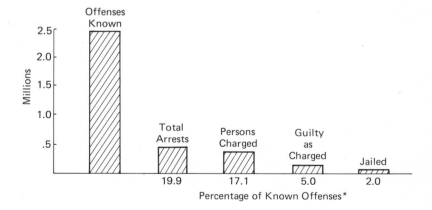

*Actual crime is estimated to be 2½ times the known offenses. If the base were actual crime, the percentages would be less than half of those appearing in the figure. Thus, persons jailed as a percentage of actual crime is less than 1 percent.

FIGURE 11-1.   Law Enforcement in Relation to Crime (From *Statistical Abstract of the United States, 1970,* p. 146.)

Police are successful in clearing only about one in five reported crimes by arresting the offender. The judicial system convicts only about one in four of the persons arrested and charged; others are not prosecuted, handled as juveniles, found not guilty, or permitted to plead guilty to a lesser charge and released. Only about half of the convicted felons are given prison sentences.

THE CONSTITUTIONAL RIGHTS OF DEFENDANTS

Guarantee of the Writ of Habeas Corpus. An ancient right in common law is the right to obtain a writ of *habeas corpus,* a court order directing a public official who is holding a person in custody to bring his prisoner into court to explain his reasons for the confinement. If a judge finds that the prisoner is being unlawfully detained, or if he finds that there is not sufficient evidence that a crime has been committed or that the prisoner could have committed it, he orders the prisoner's immediate release.

Prohibition of Bills of Attainder and Ex Post Facto Laws. Protection against bills of attainder and ex post facto laws was, like the guarantee of habeas corpus, considered so fundamental to individual liberty that it was included in the original text of the Constitution. A *bill of attainder* is a legislative act that inflicts punishment without judicial trial. An *ex post facto law* is a retroactive criminal law that works to the detriment of the accused—for example, a law that makes an act a criminal one after the act is committed, or a law that increases the punishment for a crime and applies it retroactively.

Prohibition of "Unreasonable" Searches and Seizures. The Fourth Amendment provides: "The right of the people to be secure in their persons, houses, papers, and effects, against unreasonable searches and seizures, shall not be violated, and no warrants shall issue but upon probable cause, supported by oath or affirmation, and particularly describing the place to be searched, and the persons or things to be seized." The requirement that the things to be seized must be described in the warrant is meant to prevent "fishing expeditions" into an individual's home and personal effects on the possibility that some evidence of unknown illegal activity might crop up. An exception to the requirement for a warrant is made if the search is "incident to a lawful arrest." A "lawful arrest" can be made by a police officer if he has reasonable grounds to believe a person has committed a felony or if a misdemeanor is committed in his presence; a search of the person and his property is permitted without a warrant at the time of such an arrest.

Freedom from Self-Incrimination. Although the Fifth Amendment establishes a number of procedural guarantees, perhaps the most widely quoted clause of that amendment guarantees that no person "shall be compelled in any criminal case to be a witness against himself." The sentence "I refuse to answer that question on the ground that it might tend to incriminate me" is, today, a household standard. Freedom from self-incrimination has its origins in English resistance to torture and confession. It embodies now the ideas that an individual should not be forced to contribute to his own prosecution and that the burden of proof of guilt is on the state. The constitutional protection against self-incrimination applies not only to accused persons in their own trials but also to witnesses testifying in any public proceedings, including criminal trials of other persons, civil suits, congressional hearings, or other investigations. The silence of an accused person cannot be interpreted as guilt; the burden of proving guilt rests with the prosecution.

The Right to Counsel. The right to avoid self-incrimination is closely connected with the right to counsel, as provided in the Sixth Amendment, because counsel may advise his client to remain silent and claim protection against self-incrimination. The Sixth Amendment states: "In all criminal prosecutions, the accused shall enjoy . . . the assistance of counsel for his defense." An accused individual has the right to ask for counsel before answering any police questions. If the person in custody is indigent and if he requests counsel, the police must provide him counsel.

Guarantee of a Fair Jury Trial. Trial by jury is guaranteed in both the original text of the Constitution and the Sixth Amendment: "In all criminal prosecutions the accused shall enjoy the right to a speedy and public trial, by an impartial jury . . . and to be informed of the nature and cause of the accusation; to be confronted with the witnesses against him; to have compulsory process for obtaining witnesses in his favor. . . ." The requirement of a "speedy" trial protects the accused from long pretrial waits; but the accused himself may ask for postponements if he wishes in order to prepare his defense. A "public" trial prevents secret proceedings, and "impartial" means that each juror must be able to judge the case objectively. Discrimination in the selection of the jury is forbidden. The guarantee of a fair jury trial can be violated if sensational pretrial publicity or an unruly courtroom hinders the jury from making an unbiased verdict. By old canon law a jury consisted of 12 persons, and the vote of the jurors had to be unanimous. This is still the requirement in most cases, but recently the Supreme Court indicated that unanimity might not be required in some cases.

The burden of proof rests with the prosecution. It is up to the prosecution to convince a jury "beyond reasonable doubt" that the accused is guilty. Witnesses must appear in person against the accused. He or his counsel has the right to cross-examine them. The accused may present witnesses in his own behalf and even obtain a "summons" to compel people to testify at his trial. If a guilty verdict is rendered, the defendant may appeal to a higher court any errors in his trial.

Protection Against Double Jeopardy. The Fifth Amendment states: " . . . nor shall any person be subject for the same offense to be twice put in jeopardy of life or limb. . . ." Once a person has been tried for a particular crime and the trial has ended in a decision, he cannot be tried again for the same crime. However, this right does not prevent a new trial if the jury cannot agree on a verdict (a "hung jury"), or if the verdict is reversed by an appeal to a higher court because of a procedural error. Moreover, an individual might be tried on slightly different charges stemming from the same act by different jurisdictions.

Protection Against Excessive Bail. An arrested person is considered innocent until tried and found guilty. He is entitled to go free prior to his trial unless his freedom would unreasonably endanger society, or unless there is reason to believe that he would not appear at his trial. Bail is supposed to ensure that the accused will appear for his trial. Bail can be denied for major crimes. But most accused persons are entitled to be released on bail pending their trial, and bail must not be "excessive," although there are no fixed standards in determining what is excessive.

The Warren Court—the Supreme Court of the 1950s and 1960s, under the guidance of Chief Justice Earl Warren—greatly strengthened the rights of accused persons in criminal cases. Several key decisions were made by a split vote on the Supreme Court and drew heavy criticism from law enforcement officers and others as hamstringing police in their struggle with lawlessness. These decisions included:

Mapp v. *Ohio* (1961), barring the use of illegally seized evidence in criminal cases by applying the Fourth Amendment guarantee against unreasonable searches and seizures. Even if the evidence seized proves the guilt of the accused, it cannot be presented in a trial.

Gideon v. *Wainwright* (1963), ruling that equal protection under the Fourteenth Amendment requires that free legal counsel be appointed for all indigent defendants in all criminal cases.

Escobedo v. *Illinois* (1964), ruling that a suspect is entitled to confer with counsel as soon as police investigation focuses on him, or once "the process shifts from investigatory to accusatory."

Miranda v. *Arizona* (1966), requiring that police, before questioning a suspect, must inform him of all of his constitutional rights including the right to counsel (appointed free, if necessary) and the right to remain silent. Although the suspect may knowingly waive these rights, the police cannot question anyone who at any point asks for a lawyer or indicates "in any manner" that he does not wish to be questioned.

To what extent these decisions have really hampered efforts to halt the rise in crime in America is very difficult to ascertain. The Supreme Court under Chief Justice Burger has not reversed any of these landmark decisions. Whatever progress is made in law enforcement, therefore, will have to be made within the current definition of the rights of defendants. It is important to note that Chief Justice Burger's recommendations for judicial reform center on the speedy administration of justice and not on changes in the rights of defendants.

CRIME AND THE COURTS

Chief Justice Warren E. Burger has argued persuasively that rising crime in America is partly due to inadequacies in our system of criminal justice. "The present system of criminal justice does not deter criminal conduct," he said in a special State of the Federal Judiciary message. "Whatever deterrent effect may have existed in the past has now virtually vanished."[1] He urged major reform in law enforcement, courts, prisons, probation, and parole.

A major stumbling block to effective law enforcement is the current plight of America's judicial machinery.

Major congestion on court dockets which delays the hearing of cases months or even years. Moreover, actual trials now average twice as long as they did ten years ago.

Failure of courts to adopt modern management and administrative practices to speed and improve justice.

Increased litigation in the courts. Not only are more Americans aware of their rights, but more are using every avenue of appeal. Seldom do appeals concern the suit or the innocence of the defendant; usually they focus on procedural matters.

Excessive delays in trials. "Defendants, whether guilty or innocent, are human; they love freedom and hate punishment. With a lawyer provided to secure release without the need for a conventional bail bond, most defendants, except in capital cases, are released pending trial. We should not be surprised that a defendant on bail exerts a heavy pressure on his court-appointed lawyer to postpone the trial as long as possible so as to remain free. These postponements—and sometimes there are a dozen or more—consume the time of judges and court staffs as well as of lawyers. Cases are calendared and reset time after time while witnesses and jurors spend endless hours just waiting."[2]

Excessive delays in appeals. "We should not be surprised at delay when more and more defendants demand their undoubted constitutional right to trial by jury because we have provided them with lawyers and other needs at public expense; nor should we be surprised that most convicted persons seek a new trial when the appeal costs them nothing and when failure to take the appeal will cost them freedom. Being human a defendant plays out the line which society has cast him. Lawyers are competitive creatures and the adversary system encourages contention and often rewards delay; no lawyer wants to be called upon to defend the client's charge of imcompetence for having failed to exploit all the procedural techniques which we have deliberately made available."[3]

Excessive variation in sentencing. Some judges let defendants off on probation for crimes which would draw five- or ten-year sentences by other judges. While flexibility in sentencing is essential in dealing justly with individuals, perceived inconsistencies damage the image of the courts in the public mind.

Excessive "plea bargaining" between the prosecution and the defendant's attorney, in which the defendant agrees to plead guilty to a lesser offense if the prosecutor will drop more serious charges.

CAPITAL PUNISHMENT

One of the more heated debates in correctional policy today concerns capital punishment. Opponents of the death penalty argue that it is "cruel and unusual punishment" in violation of the Eighth Amendment of the U.S. Constitution. They also contend that nations and states which have abolished the death penalty have not experienced higher homicide rates, and hence there is no concrete evidence that the death penalty discourages crime. They also argue that the death penalty is applied unequally. A large proportion of those executed have been poor, uneducated, and nonwhite. In contrast, there is a strong sense of justice among many Americans that demands retribution for heinous crimes—a life for a life. A mere jail sentence for a multiple murderer or a rapist-murderer seems unjust compared with the damage inflicted upon society and the victims. In most cases, a life sentence means less than ten years in prison, under the current parole and probation policies of many states. Convicted murderers have been set free, and some have killed again. Moreover, prison guards and other inmates are exposed to convicted murderers who have "a license to kill" because they are already serving life sentences and have nothing to lose by killing again. Public opinion polls continue to support the death penalty, although opponents have been gaining supporters over time.

Prior to 1972, the death penalty was officially approved by 30 states; only 15 states had abolished capital punishment.[4] Federal law also retained the death

The Burger court effectively eliminated the death penalty with its 1972 decision on capital punishment. Many electric chairs such as this one in Massachusetts' Walpole Prison have not been used since. *Boston Globe Photo*

penalty. However, no one had actually suffered the death penalty since 1967, because of numerous legal tangles and direct challenges to the constitutionality of capital punishment.

In 1972 the Supreme Court ruled that capital punishment *as currently imposed* violates the Eighth and Fourteenth Amendment prohibitions against cruel and unusual punishment and due process of law. The decision was made by a five to four vote of the justices, and the reasoning in the case is very complex. Only two justices—Brennan and Marshall—declared that capital punishment itself is cruel and unusual. The other three justices in the majority—Douglas, White, and Stewart—felt that death sentences had been applied unfairly; a few individuals were receiving the death penalty for crimes for which many others were receiving lighter sentences. These justices left open the possibility that capital punishment would be constitutional if it were specified for certain kinds of crime and applied uniformly. Four justices on the Court—Burger, Blackmun, Powell, and Rehnquist—dissented, mainly on the ground that the abolition of the death penalty is a decision which should be left to the people and their elected representatives, and not a decision for the Supreme Court to impose upon the nation. Some states can be expected to rewrite their laws on capital punishment to try to ensure fairness and uniformity in the application of this penalty, so even though the death penalty is currently in abeyance, the issue will continue to be debated in state capitals and federal courts.

POLICE AND LAW ENFORCEMENT

Police perform at least three important functions in urban society—law enforcement, keeping the peace, and furnishing services. Actually, law enforcement may take up only a small portion of a policeman's daily activity—perhaps as little as 10 percent.[5] The service function occupies far more of his time: attending accidents, directing traffic, escorting crowds, assisting stranded motorists, handling drunks, and so on. The function of peacekeeping is also a prominent part of his duties: breaking up fights, quieting noisy parties, handling domestic or neighborhood quarrels, and the like. It is in this function that police exercise the greatest discretion in the application of the law. In most such incidents blame is difficult to determine, participants are reluctant to file charges, and police must use personal discretion in handling each case.

Police are generally recruited from working class families; only a handful come from middle class backgrounds, and few have more than a high school education. Yet the tasks they are assigned in society would confound highly trained social scientists. Formal police training emphasizes self-control and caution in dealing with the public, but on-the-job experiences probably reinforce distrust of others. The element of danger in the policeman's job makes him naturally suspicious of others. He sees much of the "worst kind" of people and he sees even the "best kind" at their worst.

Policemen are engaged in rule enforcement as members of a semimilitary organization. They are concerned with authority themselves, and they expect others to respect authority. It is often difficult for even the most well-meaning police officer to develop respect or sympathy for ghetto residents. One policeman described the problem as follows:

> The police have to associate with lower class people, slobs, drunks, criminals, riff-raff of the worst sort. Most of these . . . are Negroes. The police officers see these

people through middle class or lower middle class eye-balls. But even if he saw them through highly sophisticated eye-balls he can't go in the street and take this night after night. When some Negro criminal says to you a few times, "you white mother-fucker, take that badge off and I'll shove it up your ass," well it's bound to affect you after a while. Pretty soon you decide they're all just niggers and they'll never be anything but niggers. It would take not just an average man to resist this feeling, it would take an extraordinary man to resist it, and there are very few ways by which the police department can attract extraordinary men to join them.[6]

VIOLENCE IN AMERICAN HISTORY

Violence is not uncommon in American society. The nation itself was founded in armed revolution, and violence has been a source of power and a stimulus to social change ever since. Violence has been associated with most of the important movements in American history: the birth of the nation (revolutionary violence), the freeing of the slaves and the preservation of the union (Civil War violence), the westward expansion of the nation (Indian wars), the establishment of law and order in frontier society (vigilante violence), the organization of the labor movement (labor-management violence), the civil rights movement (racial violence), and attempts to deal with the problems of cities (urban violence). History reveals that the patriot, the humanitarian, the pioneer, the lawman, the laborer, the black man, and the urban dweller have all used violence as a source of power. Despite pious pronouncements against it, Americans have frequently employed violence even in their most idealistic endeavors.

Perhaps the most famous act of organized mob violence occurred in 1773 when a group of "agitators" in Boston, Massachusetts, illegally destroyed 342 chests of tea. The early Revolutionary War fighting in 1774 and 1775, including the Battles of Lexington and Concord, was really a series of small guerrilla skirmishes designed more to intimidate Tories than to achieve national independence. The old American custom of tarring and feathering was a product of the early patriotic campaign to root out Tories. Aside from the regular clash of Continental and British armies, a great deal of violence and guerrilla strife occurred during the Revolution. Savage guerrilla forays along the East Coast resulted in the killing of thousands of Tory families and the destruction of their property. The success of this violence enshrined it in our traditions.

After the Revolutionary War, many armed farmers and debtors resorted to violence to assert their economic interests. If taxes owed to the British government and debts owed to the British merchants could be denied, why not also the taxes owed to state governments and the debts owed to American merchants? In several states debtors had already engaged in open rebellion against tax collectors and sheriffs. The most serious rebellion broke out in the summer of 1786 in Massachusetts, when a band of insurgents, composed of farmers and laborers,

WANTED

JOHN HERBERT DILLINGER

On June 23, 1934, HOMER S. CUMMINGS, Attorney General of the United States, under the authority vested in him by an Act of Congress approved June 6, 1934, offered a reward of

$10,000.00

for the capture of John Herbert Dillinger or a reward of

$5,000.00

for information leading to the arrest of John Herbert Dillinger.

DESCRIPTION

Age, 32 years; Height, 5 feet 7-1/8 inches; Weight, 153 pounds; Build, medium; Hair, medium chestnut; Eyes, grey; Complexion, medium; Occupation, machinist; Marks and scars, 1/2 inch scar back left hand, scar middle upper lip, brown mole between eyebrows.

All claims to any of the aforesaid rewards and all questions and disputes that may arise as among claimants to the foregoing rewards shall be passed upon by the Attorney General and his decisions shall be final and conclusive. The right is reserved to divide and allocate portions of any of said rewards as between several claimants. No part of the aforesaid rewards shall be paid to any official or employee of the Department of Justice.

If you are in possession of any information concerning the whereabouts of John Herbert Dillinger, communicate immediately by telephone or telegraph collect to the nearest office of the Division of Investigation, United States Department of Justice, the local addresses of which are set forth on the reverse side of this notice.

JOHN EDGAR HOOVER, DIRECTOR,
DIVISION OF INVESTIGATION,
UNITED STATES DEPARTMENT OF JUSTICE,
WASHINGTON, D. C.

June 25, 1934.

America has a long history of the more conventional type of criminal violence. Perhaps the best known of twentieth century criminals is John Dillinger. *The Bettmann Archive* captured courthouses in several western districts of that state and momentarily held the city of Springfield. Led by Daniel Shays, a veteran of Bunker Hill, the insurgent army posed a direct threat to the governing elite of the new nation. Shays's Rebellion, as it was called, was put down by a small mercenary army paid for by well-to-do citizens who feared that a wholesale attack on property rights was imminent. The growing domestic violence in the states contributed to the momentum leading to the Constitutional Convention of 1787, where propertied men established a new central government with the power to "ensure domestic tranquility," guarantee "the republican form of government," and protect "against domestic violence." Thus, the Constitution itself reflects a concern of the Founding Fathers about domestic violence.

The Civil War was the bloodiest war America ever fought. Total casualties of the Northern and Southern armies equaled American casualties in World War II—but the Civil War occurred at a time when the nation was only half as large as it was during the latter conflict. There were few families that did not suffer the loss of a loved one during the Civil War. In addition to military casualties, the toll in lives and property among civilians was enormous. A great deal of domestic violence also occurred both before and after the war. In 1856 the brutal events surrounding the "bleeding Kansas" issue took place. In 1859 came John Brown's raid at Harper's Ferry, meant to start the freeing of the slaves in Virginia. Brown's capture, trial for treason, and execution made him a hero to many abolitionists, though Southerners believed that he had tried to incite slave uprisings. The guerrilla war that took place in the West during the Civil War has seldom been equaled for savagery; the fearsome Kansas Jayhawkers traded brutalities with Confederate guerrillas headed by William Quantrell. Later, western bandits, including Frank and Jesse James and the Younger brothers, who had fought as Confederate guerrillas, continued their forays against banks and railroads and enjoyed considerable popular prestige and support. Moreover, after the war, racial strife and Ku Klux Klan activity became routine in the old Confederate states. The Ku Klux Klan was first employed to intimidate the Republicans of the Reconstruction era by violence and threats, and later to force blacks to accept the renewed rule of whites.

Unquestionably the longest and most brutal violence in American history was that between whites and Indians. It began in 1607 and continued with only temporary truces for nearly 300 years, until the final battle at Wounded Knee, South Dakota, in 1890. The norms of Indian warfare were generally more barbaric than those in other types of warfare, if such a thing is possible. Women and children on both sides were deliberately and purposefully killed. Torture was accepted as a customary part of warmaking. Scalping was a frequent practice among both Indians and Indian-fighters.

Vigilante violence (taking the law into one's own hands) arose as a response to

SITTING BULL. "Weep not, Great Mother; I must leave Canada, and go back to the liars and cheats. I like the excitement and tomfoolery of the double-headed Yankee system best. I crave sensation: life here is too monotonous."

One of the most brutal episodes in the history of violence in America was almost three centuries of wars against the Indians. Sitting Bull, the famous Dakota chieftan shown in this *Harper's Weekly* cartoon by Thomas Nast, was best known for his victory over General Custer at Little Bighorn. He was eventually killed by American soldiers in 1890.
Courtesy of the Boston Public Library, Print Department

a typical American problem: the absence of effective law and order in the frontier region. Practically every state and territory west of the Appalachians had at one time or another a well-organized vigilante movement. The first vigilante movement appeared in 1767 - 1769 in South Carolina, where the vigilantes were known as "regulators"—a term later used by San Francisco vigilantes in the 1850s. Vigilantes were frequently backed by prominent men; many later became senators, congressmen, governors, judges, businessmen, and even clergymen. Like Indian-fighters, vigilantes became great popular heroes. Anti-thief and anti-rustling associations flourished in the West until World War I. Vigilantes often undertook not only to establish law and order but also to regulate the morals of the citizens—punishing drunks, vagrants, ne'er-do-wells, and occasional strangers.

Violence was also a constant companion of the early labor movement in America. Both management and strikers resorted to violence in the struggles accompanying the industrial revolution. In the bitter railroad strike in Pittsburgh, Pennsylvania, in 1887 an estimated 16 soldiers and 50 strikers were killed, and locomotives, freight cars, and other property were destroyed. The famous Homestead strike of 1892 turned Homestead, Pennsylvania, into an open battlefield. The Pullman strike of 1893 in Chicago resulted in 12 deaths and the destruction of a great deal of railroad property. In 1914, Ludlow, Colorado, was the scene of the famous Ludlow Massacre, in which company guards burned a miner tent city and killed nearly a hundred persons including women and children. The Molly McGuires were a secret organization of Irish miners who fought their employers with assassination and mayhem. The last great spasm of violence in the history of American labor came in the 1930s with strikes and plant takeovers ("sit-down strikes") which accompanied the successful drive to unionize the automobile, steel, and other mass production industries.

The long history of racial violence in America continues to plague the nation. Slavery itself was accompanied by untold violence; it is estimated that one-third to one-half of the blacks captured in African slave raids never survived the ordeal of forced marches to the sea, with thirst, brutalities, and near starvation the rule; the terrible two-month voyage in filthy holes packed with squirming and suffocating humanity; and the brutal "seasoning" whereby African Negroes were turned into slaves. Nat Turner's slave insurrection in 1831 resulted in the deaths of 57 white persons and the later execution of Turner and his followers. Following the end of slavery, the white supremacy movement employed violence to reestablish the position of whites in the southern social system. Racial violence directed against blacks—whippings, torture, and lynching—was fairly common from the 1870s to the 1930s. During World War II serious racial violence erupted in Detroit. Black and white mobs battled each other in June 1943, causing 35 deaths and hundred of injuries, over a thousand arrests, and finally the dispatch of federal troops to restore order.

Racial violence has been an integral part of American history. Between the Civil War and World War II it often took the form of lynching. This 25-year-old man was lynched by a mob in North Carolina in 1935. *Wide World Photo*

Political assassinations have not been uncommon. Four presidents (Lincoln, Garfield, McKinley, and Kennedy) have fallen to assassins' bullets, and others were the intended objects of assassination. Only Lincoln was the target of a proven assassination conspiracy; the other presidential victims were the prey of presumably free-lance assassins in varying states of mental instability. In the 1930s Senator Huey P. Long of Louisiana was murdered, and a bullet narrowly missed President Franklin Delano Roosevelt and killed Mayor Anton Cermak of Chicago, who was standing near the president. The wave of political assassinations in recent years which cut down John F. Kennedy, Robert F. Kennedy, and Martin Luther King, Jr., and crippled George C. Wallace may represent a "contagion phenomenon," unstable individuals being motivated to violence by highly publicized and dramatic acts of violence. But an even more grim possibility is that political assassination may become a persistent feature of American society.

SOCIAL-PSYCHOLOGICAL
PERSPECTIVES ON VIOLENCE

Social psychologists have different explanations of violence. One explanation relies heavily upon learning theory (stimulus-response theory); we shall refer to this as the *frustration-aggression* explanation. Another relies upon Freudian notions of instinctual behavior in the "unlocking" of inhibitions; we shall call this the *aggressive instinct* explanation.

The frustration-aggression explanation is perhaps the most popular explanation of social violence—political turmoil, racial conflict, urban disorders, even crime and juvenile delinquency. Over 30 years ago psychologist John Dollard and several colleagues at Yale University set forth the proposition "Aggression is always the result of frustration."[7] They argued, "The occurrence of aggressive behavior always presupposes the existence of frustration and, contrariwise, the existence of frustration always leads to some form of aggression." Frustration occurs when there is a blocking of ongoing, goal-directed activity, and it evokes a characteristic reaction—aggression—whereby the individual seeks to reduce the emotional anxiety produced by this blocking. Aggression helps to lessen frustration brought on by the blocking of the original motive, but it fails to satisfy the original motive. The aggressive behavior merely copes with the emotional reaction to the blocking. The degree of frustration is affected by the intensity of the original need, and by the degree of expectation that the goal-

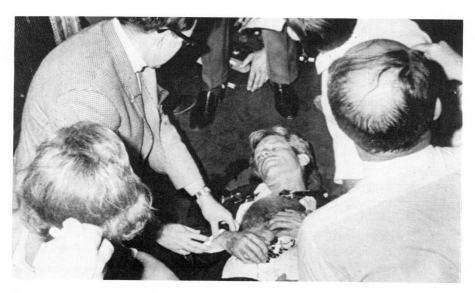

Political assassination has become an increasingly common form of violence. Senator Robert F. Kennedy was shot in the midst of his presidential primary campaign in 1968. *United Press International Photo*

directed activity would be successful. "The strength of instigation to aggression varies directly with the amount of frustration." Moreover, "The strength of instigation to aggression should vary directly with (1) the strength of instigation to the frustrated response; (2) the degree of interference with the frustrated response; and (3) the number of frustrated response sequences." In other words, aggressive behavior is a function of the degree of frustration, which in turn is determined by the strength of the original need, the degree of interference with its satisfaction, and the number of times its satisfaction has been blocked. Minor frustrations added together can produce a stronger aggressive response than would normally be expected from a frustrating situation that appears immediately before aggression. Frustration, that is, can build up over time. Of course, society attempts to inhibit aggressive behavior by threats of punishment. Dollard and his colleagues add, "The strength of inhibition of any act of aggression varies positively with the amount of punishment anticipated to be the consequence of that act."

Acts of physical violence are the most obvious forms of aggression. But other forms include fantasies of "getting even," forays against the frustrating person (stealing from him or cheating him, spreading malicious rumors about him, or verbal assaults), and generalized destructive outbursts. Dollard contends that frustration and aggression can characterize group action as well as individual action: "Remonstrative outbursts like lynchings, strikes, and certain reformist campaigns are clearly forms of aggression as well." Aggression is generally directed at the person or object which is perceived as causing the frustration, but it may also be *displaced* to some altogether innocent source, or even toward the self, as in masochism, martyrdom, and suicide. The act of aggression is presumed to reduce the emotional reaction to frustration. Dollard and his colleagues refer to the reduction as "catharsis." "The expression of any act of aggression is a catharsis that reduces the instigation to all other acts of aggression." Dollard also contends that (1) the strongest aggression is usually directed against the agent perceived to be the source of frustration, (2) the inhibition of acts of direct aggression is an additional frustration which instigates additional aggression, (3) inhibited aggression may be displaced to different objects and expressed in modified forms, (4) aggression turned against the self may occur when other forms of expression are strongly inhibited.

The frustration-aggression explanation of violence is frequently espoused by political liberals because it implies that violence is best avoided by eliminating barriers to the satisfaction of human needs and wants. In other words, liberals believe that violence can be reduced if human needs and wants are satisfied and aggression-producing frustration is reduced. In contrast, if it should turn out that aggressive behavior is innate, then no amount of need or want satisfaction would eliminate it. Only strong inhibiting forces would be able to cope effectively with innate aggressive instincts. This is frequently the view of political conservatives.

Research on the innate aggressive tendencies of organisms—humans as well as animals, fish, and birds—suggests that aggressive behavior may be deeply rooted in man's genetic history. In his interesting book *On Aggression*, an eminent zoologist, Konrad Lorenz, argues that aggressive behavior is rooted in man's long struggle for survival.[8] Man is by nature an aggressive animal. The external stimulus that seems to produce aggressive behavior only "unlocks" inhibitory processes, thereby "releasing" instinctual aggressive drives. Aggressive behavior is not just a reaction to some external condition but an inner force or instinct which is let loose only by the stimulus. "It is the spontaneity of the [aggressive] instinct that makes it so dangerous." Aggressive behavior "can explode without demonstrable external stimulation" merely because inner drives for aggression have not discharged through some earlier behavior. Lorenz believes that "present day civilized man suffers from insufficient discharge of his aggressive drive." Civilization has inhibited men from expressing themselves aggressively; for the greatest part of man's history on earth he released his aggressive drives in hunting, killing, and the struggle for survival. Now, however, they must be checked. The instincts which helped man to survive millions of years in a primitive environment today threaten his very existence. Lorenz believes that frustrations are, at best, an unimportant source of aggression. According to this formulation, an excellent way to prevent people from engaging in aggression is to provide them with "safe" ways of venting their aggressive urges. For example, competitive, body-contact sports provide such an outlet; even observing these activities, as in the case of televised professional football, affords some release of aggressive drives.

A number of experimental psychologists disagree with Lorenz's proposed remedy for aggression. Laboratory experiments have indicated that attacks upon supposedly safe targets do not lessen, and can even increase, the likelihood of later aggression. Angry people may perhaps feel better when they can attack a safe target, but their aggressive tendencies are not thereby necessarily reduced. For example, recent laboratory studies have demonstrated that giving children an opportunity to play aggressive games does not decrease the attacks they will later make upon another child but in fact actually increases the strength of subsequent attacks.[9] These studies do not rule out the notion of innate determinants of aggression; indeed, there is today among social psychologists much greater recognition of the role of inherent determinants of human behavior. However, it is clear that other factors—such as fear of punishment or learning to respond in nonaggressive ways to frustrations—can prevent man's potential for violence from being realized.

Another explanation of violence centers about the "relative deprivation" of individuals and groups. Relative deprivation is the discrepancy between people's expectations about the goods and conditions of life to which they feel justifiably entitled and what they perceive to be their chances of getting and keeping them. Relative deprivation is not merely a complicated way of saying that people are deprived and therefore angry because they have less than they want. Rather, it focuses on (1) what people think they deserve, not just what they want in an ideal sense, and (2) what they think they have a chance of getting, not just what they have. According to this theory, it is relative deprivation that creates aggression.

Contrary to the earlier frustration-aggression hypotheses, many psychologists now insist that deprivations alone are inadequate to account for most aggressive behavior. According to the newer theorizing, much greater weight must be given to the anticipations of satisfaction than to the duration or magnitude of deprivation itself. The stimulation arising from anticipation is held to be the major determinant of the vigor and persistence of the goal-seeking activity. Thus, deprivation alone does not bring about striving toward a goal; such striving is also a product of some "hope" that goals can be achieved. There is more frustration when one's hopes and expectations of success are thwarted than when one is simply deprived and without hope.

Relative deprivation is an expression of the distance between current status and levels of expectation. According to this explanation, neither the wholly downtrodden (who have no aspirations) nor the very well off (who can satisfy their aspirations) represent a threat to civil order; that threat arises from those whose expectations about what they deserve outdistance the capacity of society to satisfy them. Often rapid increases in expectations are the product of symbolic or token improvements in conditions. This situation leads to the apparent paradox of the eruption of violence and disorder precisely when conditions are getting better. Hope, not despair, generates civil violence and disorder. As Bowen and Masotti observe, "The reason why black Americans riot is because there has been just enough improvement in their condition to generate hopes, expectations, or aspirations beyond the capacity of the system to meet them." [10]

The political counterpart of this explanation of violence is frequently referred to as "the revolution of rising expectations." Poverty-stricken people who have never dreamed of owning automobiles, television sets, or new homes are not frustrated merely because they have been deprived of these things; they are frustrated only after they have begun to hope that they can obtain them. Once they have come to believe that they can get them and have anticipated having them, the inability to fulfill their anticipations is a frustrating experience. The dashing of hopes is more likely to breed violence than privation itself. Political scientist James C. Davies has employed this type of reasoning in developing a theory of revolutions. [11] Revolutions do not arise because people are subjected to long severe hardships. Revolutions occur when there is a sudden, abrupt thwarting of hopes and expectations that had begun to develop during the course of gradually improving conditions. Thus, modernization in traditionally backward societies is associated with a great increase in political instability. Hope outstrips reality, and, even though conditions are improving in society as a whole, many people become frustrated.

VIOLENCE AS POLITICAL PROTEST

Violence can also be interpreted as a form of political protest. For example, the ghetto riots of the 1960s expressed the hostility many blacks felt toward white people in general and toward established authority. To be sure, this form of political protest is a criminal one. And it may be irrational and self-defeating. The majority of casualties in ghetto riots—the dead, the injured, and the arrested—were rioters themselves. Much of the property destroyed belonged to ghetto residents. Many businesses and other conveniences will never again venture into the ghetto. Moreover, the riots may have hardened the attitudes of whites toward blacks. Certainly violence itself cannot solve the complicated social problems facing the ghetto. Nonetheless, not all riots were "senseless" or without political purpose.

The view that ghetto riots were a form of political protest is supported by evidence indicating that a large percentage of the black population in the ghettos supported the riots. For example, a survey in Watts, California, after the 1964 riot determined that roughly one-fifth of blacks in that ghetto actually participated in the riot and more than one-half of the residents supported the activities of the rioters.[12] Interviewers found that 58 percent of the Watts residents felt that the long-run effect of the riot would be favorable; 84 percent said that whites were now more aware of black problems; 62 percent regarded the riot as a black protest. In the eyes of a large proportion of blacks, riots were a legitimate protest against white society, and this protest was expected to produce improvement in the condition of the blacks. Of those blacks who claimed that riots had a political purpose, each cited one or more of the following "purposes": (1) to call attention to black problems; (2) to express black hostility to whites; and (3) to serve as an instrument for improving conditions, ending discrimination, and communicating with the "power structure."[13]

Stokely Carmichael once remarked, "Violence is as American as apple pie." And the uncomfortable fact is that the most important social movements in American history *have* been accompanied by violence. Frequently, the American political system is moved by crises when it is not moved by anything else. The civil rights protest movement sought to create *nonviolent* crises that would impel the system to end discrimination. But many black militants argue that white America will not respond to black demands for full equality until whites feel directly threatened in their own physical well-being. In commenting on the role of violence in the struggle for power, Masotti and others note:

> Perhaps the black power advocates understand better than most whites that Americans have traditionally paid lip service to their notion of consensus when critical issues arose; that in fact when critical issues arise, they can no longer be solved in the normal political channels based on common understandings; that, indeed, the only common interest a challenging minority and an unresponsive ma-

jority have is violence, with the minority offering peace only when the majority
makes the requisite concessions.[14]

Thus, in the struggle for power in America, blacks face an agonizing choice:
whether to work for the established democratic processes to effect change or to
resort to violence or threats of violence.

The vast majority of black Americans clearly reject violence. But violence in
our society, and increasing rhetoric of violence, has brought about a gradual increase in the number of blacks who believe that "the blacks will probably have
to resort to violence to win rights." Louis Harris reports that over the last ten
years the percentage of blacks who believe this is the case rose from 21 percent
in the early 1960s to 31 percent in the early 1970s. The percentage of blacks
asserting that violence is probably necessary is even higher among younger and
urban blacks.[15]

"RIOTING MAINLY FOR FUN AND PROFIT"

Another explanation of violence centers about the social and cultural
characteristics of lower class city life. Political scientist Edward C. Banfield
argues *against* the notion that urban riots are a form of black political protest, or
that they result from rage and frustration over racial discrimination. He contends that the causes of rioting are complex and deeply rooted in the culture of
lower class life. (In fact, the title of the present section is the title of Chapter 9 in
his *Unheavenly City.*) In his view there are four principal motives in riot
behavior, each of which implies a corresponding type of riot:

> *The rampage.* This is an outbreak of animal—usually young, male animal—spirits.
> Young men are naturally restless, in search of excitement, thrills, "ac-
> tion." . . . The rampage begins not because the incident made the rampagers
> angry (although they may pretend that) but because they were looking for an ex-
> cuse (signal?) to rampage. . . .
>
> *The foray for pillage.* Here the motive is theft, and here also boys and young
> adults of the lower class are the principal offenders. Stealing is ordinarily most con-
> veniently done in private, of course, but when disasters—earthquakes, fires, floods,
> power failures, blizzards, enemy invasions, police strikes—interrupt law enforce-
> ment it may be done as well or better in public. . . .
>
> *The outburst of righteous indignation.* Here the rioters are moved by indigna-
> tion at what they regard, rightly or wrongly, as injustice or violation of the mores
> that is likely to go unpunished. . . .
>
> *The demonstration.* Here the motive is to advance a political principle or
> ideology or to contribute to the maintenance of an organization. The riot is not a
> spontaneous, angry response to an incident. Rather, it is the result of the
> prearrangement by persons who are organized, have leaders, and who see it as a
> means to some end. The word "demonstration" is descriptive, for the event is a

Black Americans used violent protest to make white Americans aware of the black plight in a series of ghetto riots which struck Los Angeles, Detroit, Newark and other cities during the mid 1960's. This scene is the aftermath of the Newark riot of 1967. *United Press International Photo*

kind of show staged to influence opinion. Those who put it on are usually middle or upper class, these being the classes from which the people who run organizations and espouse political causes are mostly drawn.[16]

Professor Banfield contends that all of these motives may be operating in any particular disorder. Some individuals participate "for the fun of it," others to steal liquor and cigarettes and television sets, still others out of some momentary rage and a felt injustice, and a few (probably a tiny minority) for political purposes.

Banfield believes that television is an "accelerating cause" in riots and disorders. He contends that sensational television coverage of riots helps to recruit rampagers and pillagers. Moreover, television informs urban dwellers that they can throw a great city into turmoil by hurling rocks, smashing windows, and setting fires. Once the possibility of such action has been established, the probability of someone's taking it is very much increased. Thanks to television, the knowledge that riots are a possibility is widely disseminated. Finally, the probability of rioting is increased when spokesmen give legitimacy on television to rioting. The knowledge that "everybody is doing it" is transformed into the idea that "it can't be wrong." By explaining riots, commentators tend to justify them and hence to encourage them. Many civil rights leaders predicted that violence would occur if reforms were not accepted at a faster pace. The riots, of course, made these predictions much more credible. But as Martin Luther King, Jr., acknowledged, "A prediction of violence can sometimes be an invitation to it." Thus, explanations and predictions of disorder made rioting appear to be more natural, normal, and hence justifiable.

Professor Banfield believes that society must brace itself for a certain amount of violence.

> It is naïve to think that efforts to end racial injustice and to eliminate poverty, slums, and unemployment will have an appreciable effect upon the amount of rioting that will be done in the next decade or two. . . . Boys and young men of the lower classes will not cease to "raise hell" once they have adequate job opportunities, housing, schools, and so on. Indeed, by the standards of any former time, they have these things now. . . . As for the upwardly mobile and politically minded Negro who has a potential for outbursts of righteous indignation and for demonstrations, even serious and successful efforts at reform are likely to leave him more rather than less angry. The faster and farther the Negro rises the more impatient he is likely to be with whatever he thinks prevents his rising still faster and still farther.[17]

POWER AND VIOLENCE: A CASE STUDY

The Ghetto Riots

Even though domestic violence has played a prominent role in America's history, the ghetto riots of the 1960s shocked the nation beyond measure. More than 150 major riots were reported in American cities from 1965 to 1968, all these riots involving black attacks on established authority—on policemen, firemen, National Guardsmen, whites in general, and property owned by whites. Three riots—Watts in 1965 and Newark (New Jersey) and Detroit in 1967—amounted to major civil disorder.

The Watts riot from 11 to 17 August 1965 was set off when a white motorcycle officer arrested a black youth for drunken driving in a black district of Los Angeles known as Watts. In the words of the McCone Commission's report on the Watts violence:

> In the ugliest interval . . . perhaps as many as 10,000 Negroes took to the streets in marauding bands. They looted stores, set fires, beat up white passers-by whom they had hauled from stopped cars, many of which were turned upside-down and

burned, exchanged shots with law enforcement officers, and stoned and shot at firemen. The rioters seemed to have been caught up in an insensate rage of destruction. . . .

Of the 34 killed, one was a fireman, one was a deputy sheriff, and one a Long Beach policeman. . . . [The remainder were Negroes.][18]

The Newark riot was set off when police arrested a black cabdriver for reckless driving, driving without a license, and resisting arrest. Fellow black cabdrivers led a crowd to the police station in the overwhelmingly black central ward of Newark. Soon rocks and bottles were clattering against the station house walls. Tension mounted throughout the ghetto, some fires were set, some windows were broken, looting began, and when police and firemen arrived at the scenes of disturbances they were met with hostility and violence. Frequently police, untrained in riot control, responded in a heavy-handed and undisciplined fashion. Within 24 hours Newark was in the throes of a major civil disorder. For four consecutive days and nights, snipers fired at police and firemen, looters made off with the inventories of scores of stores, and arsonists set fire to large portions of commercial property in the black section of Newark. New Jersey's governor proclaimed Newark a city "in open rebellion," declared a state of emergency, and called out the National Guard. More than 4,000 city policemen, state troopers, and National Guardsmen were required to restore order. Before the riot was over, 23 persons had been killed, and property damage was widespread. Of the dead, only two were white—a policeman and a fireman. Of the Negro dead, two were children and six were women.

In the violent summer of 1967, Detroit became the scene of the bloodiest racial violence of the twentieth century. A week of rioting in Detroit, from 23 to 28 July, left 43 dead and more than 1,000 injured. Of the 43 persons killed during the riot, 33 were black and 10 were white. Among the dead were one National Guardsman, one fireman, one policeman, and one black private guard. Both the violence and the pathos of the ghetto riots were reflected in the following report from Detroit:

> . . . A spirit of carefree nihilism was taking hold. To riot and destroy appeared more and more to become ends in themselves. Late Sunday afternoon it appeared to one observer that the young people were "dancing amidst the flames."
>
> A Negro plainclothes officer was standing in an intersection when a man threw a Molotov cocktail into a business establishment at the corner. In the heat of the afternoon, fanned by the 20 to 25 m.p.h. winds of both Sunday and Monday, the fire reached the home next door within minutes. As its residents uselessly sprayed the flames with garden hoses, the fire jumped from roof to roof of adjacent two- and three-story buildings. Within the hour the entire block was in flames. The ninth house in the burning row belonged to the arsonist who had thrown the Molotov cocktail. . . .
>
> . . . Employed as a private guard, 55-year-old Julius L. Dorsey, a Negro, was standing in front of a market when accosted by two Negro men and a woman.

The Ghetto Riots

They demanded he permit them to loot the market. He ignored their demands. They began to berate him. He asked a neighbor to call the police. As the argument grew more heated, Dorsey fired three shots from his pistol in the air.

The police radio reported: "Looters, they have rifles." A patrol car driven by a police officer and carrying three National Guardsmen arrived. As the looters fled, the law enforcement personnel opened fire. When the firing ceased, one person lay dead.

He was Julius L. Dorsey. . . .[19]

The National Advisory Commission on Civil Disorders concluded:

1. No civil disorder was "typical" in all respects. . . .

2. While the civil disorders of 1967 were racial in character, they were not *inter*racial. The 1967 disorders, as well as earlier disorders of the recent period, involved action within Negro neighborhoods against symbols of white American society—authority and property—rather than against white persons.

3. Despite extremist rhetoric, there was no attempt to subvert the social order of the United States. Instead, most of those who attacked white authority and property seemed to be demanding fuller participation in the social order and the material benefits enjoyed by the vast majority of American citizens.

4. Disorder did not typically erupt without preexisting causes, as a result of a single "triggering" or "precipitating" incident. Instead, it developed out of an increasingly disturbed social atmosphere, in which typically a series of tension-heightening incidents over a period of weeks or months became linked in the minds of many in the Negro community with a shared network of underlying grievances.

5. There was, typically, a complex relationship between the series of incidents and the underlying grievances. For example, grievances about allegedly abusive police practices . . . were often aggravated in the minds of many Negroes by incidents involving the police, or the inaction of municipal authorities on Negro complaints about police action. . . .

6. Many grievances in the Negro community result from the discrimination, prejudice, and powerlessness which Negroes often experience. . . .

7. Characteristically, the typical rioter was not a hoodlum, habitual criminal, or riff-raff. . . . Instead, he was a teen-ager or young adult, a lifelong resident of the city in which he rioted, a high-school drop-out—but somewhat better than his Negro neighbor—and almost invariably underemployed or employed in a menial job. He was proud of his race, extremely hostile to both whites and middle-class Negroes and, though informed about politics, highly distrustful of the political system and of political leaders.

8. Numerous Negro counter-rioters walked the street urging rioters to "cool it." . . .

9. Negotiations between Negroes and white officials occurred during virtually all the disorders surveyed. . . .

10. . . . Some rioters . . . may have shared neither the conditions nor the grievances of their Negro neighbors; some may have coolly and deliberately exploited the chaos created by others; some may have been drawn into the melee merely because they identified with, or wished to emulate, others. . . .

11. The background of disorder in the riot cities was typically characterized by

The Ghetto Riots

severely disadvantaged conditions for Negroes, especially as compared with those for whites. . . .

12. In the immediate aftermath of disorder, the status quo of daily life before the disorder generally was quickly restored. Yet, despite some notable public and private efforts, little basic change took place in the conditions underlying the disorder. In some cases, the result was increased distrust between blacks and whites, diminished interracial communication, and the growth of Negro and white extremist groups.[20]

In its official report, the National Advisory Commission on Civil Disorders provided still another explanation for urban disorder: "White racism" was responsible for ghetto rioting. The commission enumerated "three of the most bitter fruits of white racial attitudes":

Pervasive discrimination and segregation. The first is surely the continuing exclusion of great numbers of Negroes from the benefits of economic progress through discrimination in employment and education, and their enforced confinement in segregated housing and schools. The corrosive and degrading effects of this condition and the attitudes that underlie it are the source of the deepest bitterness and at the center of the problem of racial disorder.

Black migration and white exodus. The second is the massive and growing concentration of impoverished Negroes in our major cities resulting from Negro migration from the rural South, rapid population growth and the continuing movement of the white middle-class to the suburbs. The consequence is a greatly increased burden on the already depleted resources of cities, creating a growing crisis of deteriorating facilities and services and unmet human needs.

Black ghettos. Third, in the teeming racial ghettos, segregation and poverty have intersected to destroy opportunity and hope and to enforce failure. The ghettos too often mean men and women without jobs, families without men, and schools where children are processed instead of educated, until they return to the street—to crime, to narcotics, to dependency on welfare—and to bitterness and resentment against society in general and white society in particular.[21]

However, the commission admitted that "these facts alone—fundamental as they are—cannot be said to have caused the disorders." The commission identified three "powerful ingredients" that had "begun to catalyze the mixture":

Frustrated hopes. The expectations aroused by the great judicial and legislative victories of the civil rights movement have led to frustration, hostility and cynicism in the face of the persistent gap between promise and fulfillment. The dramatic struggle for equal rights in the South has sensitized Northern Negroes to the economic inequalities reflected in the deprivations of ghetto life.

Legitimation of violence. A climate that tends toward the approval and encouragement of violence as a form of protest has been created by white terrorism directed against nonviolent protest, including instances of abuse and even murder of some civil rights workers in the South; by the open defiance of law and federal authority by state and local officials resisting desegregation; and by some protest groups engaging in civil disobedience who turn their backs on nonviolence, go beyond the

The Ghetto Riots

Constitutionally protected rights of petition and free assembly, and resort to violence to attempt to compel alteration of laws and policies with which they disagree. This condition has been reinforced by a general erosion of respect for authority in American society and reduced effectiveness of social standards and community restraints on violence and crime. This in turn has largely resulted from rapid urbanization and the dramatic reduction in the average age of the total population.

Powerlessness. Finally, many Negroes have come to believe that they are being exploited politically and economically by the white "power structure." Negroes, like people in poverty everywhere, in fact lack the channels of communication, influence and appeal that traditionally have been available to ethnic minorities within the city and which enabled them—unburdened by color—to scale the walls of the white ghettos in an earlier era. The frustrations of powerlessness have led some to the conviction that there is no effective alternative to violence as a means of expression and redress, as a way of "moving the system." More generally, the result is alienation and hostility toward the institutions of law and government and the white society which controls them. This is reflected in the reach toward racial consciousness and solidarity reflected in the slogan "Black Power."[22]

The commission warned that "our nation is moving toward two societies, one black, one white—separate and unequal." The principal "blame" for the riots was placed upon whites rather than blacks: "What White Americans have never fully understood—but what the Negro can never forget—is that white society is deeply implicated in the ghetto. White institutions created it, white institutions maintain it, and white society condones it."[23] The commission recommended massive federal aid programs in employment, education, welfare, and housing, but it suggested no new departures from traditional programs in these areas.

NOTES

1. Chief Justice Warren E. Burger, address on the State of the Federal Judiciary to the American Bar Association, August 10, 1970.

2. Ibid.

3. Ibid.

4. Alaska, Hawaii, Iowa, Maine, Michigan, Minnesota, New Hampshire, New Mexico, New York, North Dakota, Oregon, Rhode Island, Vermont, West Virginia, and Wisconsin (although in Michigan, New York, North Dakota, Rhode Island, and Vermont there were provisions for certain exceptions—for example, killing a prison guard).

5. James Q. Wilson, *Varieties of Police Behavior* (Cambridge, Mass.: Harvard University Press, 1968), p. 18; Arthur Niederhoffer, *Behind the Shield* (New York: Doubleday, 1967), p. 71.

6. Niederhoffer, op. cit., p. 43.

7. John Dollard et al., *Frustration and Aggression* (New Haven: Yale University Press, 1939), p. 1.

The Ghetto Riots

8. Konrad Lorenz, *On Aggression* (New York: Harcourt, Brace & World, 1966).

9. For an excellent review of the implications of laboratory studies on frustration and aggression see Leonard Buckewitz, "The Study of Urban Violence," in Louis H. Masotti and Don R. Bowen, eds., *Riots and Rebellion* (Beverly Hills, Calif.: Sage, 1968).

10. Don R. Bowen and Louis H. Masotti, "Civil Violence: A Theoretical Overview," in Louis H. Masotti and Don R. Bowen, eds., *Riots and Rebellion* (Beverly Hills, Calif.: Sage, 1968), pp. 24 - 25.

11. James C. Davies, "Toward a Theory of Revolution," in *American Sociological Review*, 27 (1962), 5 - 19.

12. President's Commission on Law Enforcement and Administration of Justice, *Crime and Its Impact—An Assessment* (Washington: Government Printing Office, 1967), p. 116.

13. William McCord and John Howard, "Negro Opinions in Three Riot Cities," in Louis H. Masotti and Don R. Bowen, eds., *Riots and Rebellion* (Beverly Hills, Calif.: Sage, 1968).

14. Louis H. Masotti, Jeffrey K. Hadden, Kenneth F. Seminatore, and Jerome R. Corsi, *A Time to Burn?* (Chicago: Rand McNally, 1969), p. 162.

15. *Time,* April 6, 1970, p. 29.

16. Edward C. Banfield, *The Unheavenly City* (Boston: Little, Brown, 1970), pp. 187, 188, 189, 190, 191.

17. Ibid., pp. 205 - 206.

18. Governor's Commission on the Los Angeles Riots, *Violence in the City—An End or a Beginning?* (Sacramento: Office of the Governor, State of California, 1965), pp. 3 - 5. The commission was headed by John A. McCone, former director of the Central Intelligence Agency.

19. National Advisory Commission on Civil Disorders, *Report* (Washington: Government Printing Office, 1968), p. 4.

20. Ibid., pp. 110 - 112.

21. Ibid., pp. 203 - 204.

22. Ibid., pp. 204 - 205.

23. Ibid., p. 2.

TESTING YOUR PERFORMANCE

Note to the Student. The following questions are to test how well you achieved the Performance Objectives identified for you at the beginning of the chapter. The correct answers are supplied, accompanied by corresponding pages for you to review if you have answered incorrectly. The questions are coordinated numerically with the Performance Objectives at the beginning of the chapter. This exercise will assist you in determining the type of questions you have the most difficulty in answering (discussion, identification, explanation, definition, etc.) and will prepare you for test questions likely to be asked by your instructor.

1. The agreement of men to establish governments and grant them the powers to maintain peace and security is a collective act of self-preservation identified by Thomas Hobbes as _____ .

2. The fact that men must create laws and governments to protect freedom and the fact that laws and governments themselves restrict freedom is the _____

_____

3. (a) Uniform classification of the number of serious crimes per 100,000 people reported to state and local police (who supply the FBI with the figures) is the _____ .

(b) Murder and nonnegligent manslaughter, forcible rape, robbery, aggravated assault, burglary, larceny, and theft are classified as _____

_____ .

(c) The diligence of the police in detecting crime, the adequacy of the reporting system tabulating crime, and the amount of crime itself are all _____

_____ .

(d) The greatest increase in crime rates occurs in what types of crimes?

_____

(e) The most accurate crime statistic is _____ .

4. The feeling that police could not be effective in dealing with crime, that the crime was a "private matter," or that the victim did not want to harm the offender are the reasons for _____ .

5. Identify the following constitutional rights of defendants:

(a) A court order directing a public official who is holding a person in custody to bring his prisoner into court to explain his reasons for the confinement _____ .

(b) Prohibition of a legislative act that inflicts punishment without judicial trial, which is known as a _____ .

(c) Prohibition of a retroactive criminal law that works to the detriment of the accused, which is known as an _____ .

(d) "The right of the people to be secure in their persons, houses, papers, and effects" provided by the Fourth Amendment, which ensures against

_____ .

(e) The Fifth Amendment guarantee that no person "shall be compelled in any criminal case to be a witness against himself." _____

_____

(f) The Sixth Amendment guarantee that "In all criminal prosecutions, the accused shall enjoy . . . the assistance of counsel for his defense." _____

_____

(g) A guarantee found in both the original text of the Constitution and the Sixth Amendment, that "In all criminal prosecutions the accused shall enjoy the right to a speedy and public trial, by an impartial jury." _____

_____

(h) The Fifth Amendment provision that once a person has been tried for a particular crime, and the trial has ended in a decision, he cannot be tried again for the same crime. _____

(i) Since an arrested person is considered innocent until tried and found guilty, most persons are entitled to be released on bail pending their trial, but there is a _____ .

6. Identify the following, which are based on the guarantee of a fair jury trial:

(a) The requirement that protects the accused from long pretrial waits.
_____

(b) The provision preventing secret proceedings. _____

(c) The requirement that each juror must be able to judge the case objectively. _____

(d) The term used when the jury cannot agree on a verdict. _____
_____

7. (a) The Supreme Court which made rulings that greatly strengthened the rights of accused persons in criminal cases was the _____
_____ .

Identify the following Supreme Court cases in which the Court ruled:

(b) That the use of illegally seized evidence was barred by the Fourth Amendment guarantee against unreasonable searches and seizures. _____
_____

(c) That equal protection under the Fourteenth Amendment requires that free legal counsel be appointed for all indigent defendants in all criminal cases. _____

(d) That a suspect was entitled to confer with counsel once "the process shifts from investigatory to accusatory." _____

(e) That police, before questioning a suspect, must inform him of all of his constitutional rights including the right to counsel, appointed free if necessary, and the right to remain silent. _____

8. (a) The Supreme Court chief justice who attacked the system of criminal justice as inadequate because it failed to deter criminal conduct was _____
_____ .

(b) Major congestion on court dockets which delays the hearing of cases; failure of the courts to adopt modern management and administrative practices to speed and improve justice; increased litigation in the courts; excessive delays in trials; excessive delays in appeals; excessive variation in sentencing; and excessive "plea bargaining" between the prosecution and the defendant's attorney—all were identified by Chief Justice Burger as _____
_____ .

9. (a) Opponents of the death penalty base their argument that it is in violation of the Eighth Amendment of the U.S. Constitution on what clause?
_____ .

(b) Failure of abolishment to increase rates as predicted, lack of concrete evidence that the death penalty discourages crime, and unequal application of the death penalty are all arguments used by _____
_____ .

(c) Retribution for heinous crimes, failure of a jail sentence to compare with the damage inflicted upon society and the victims, ease of obtaining parole and probation, and fear of murder of prison guards and other inmates are all arguments used by _____
_____ .

10. (a) In 1972 the Supreme Court ruled that capital punishment violates the Eighth and Fourteenth Amendment prohibitions against cruel and unusual punishment and due process of law but applied this ruling only to capital punishment _____ .

(b) The justices who declared that capital punishment itself is cruel and unusual punishment were _____ .

(c) The justices who felt that death sentences had been applied unfairly, and by this interpretation left open the possibility that capital punishment would be constitutional if it were specified for certain kinds of crimes and applied uniformly, were _____ .

(d) The justices who dissented, mainly on the ground that the abolition of the death penalty is a decision which should be left to the people and their elected representatives and is not a decision for the Supreme Court, were ____
_____ .

11.   (a) The important functions performed by police in urban society are
_____ .

(b) Recruitment from a working class family and having little more than a high school education are characteristic of the _____
_____ .

12.   (a) The birth of the nation, freeing the slaves and preserving the Union, the westward expansion of the nation, the establishment of law and order in frontier society, the organization of the labor movement, the success of the civil rights movement, and attempts to deal with the problems of urban society all demonstrate the _____
_____ .

(b) The violence created by taking the law into one's own hands is ____
_____ .

13.   (a) The explanation of violence relying heavily on learning theory (stimulus-response theory), perhaps the most popular explanation of social violence, is the _____ .

(b) The explanation of violence which relies upon Freudian notions of instinctual behavior in the "unlocking" of inhibitions is the _____
_____ .

(c) Those who, as a political group, frequently uses the frustration-aggression explanation of violence because of its implication that violence is best avoided by eliminating barriers to the satisfaction of human needs and wants are the _____ .

14.   (a) The author of *On Aggression*, who argued that aggressive behavior is rooted in man's long struggle for survival, is _____
_____ .

(b) Lorenz's suggestion for preventing persons from engaging in violence and aggression is to _____
_____ .

(c) Experimental psychologists' suggestion for preventing persons from engaging in violence is to have them _____
_____ .

15.   (a) The explanation of violence which (1) focuses on the distance between current status and levels of expectations and (2) identifies those who represent a threat to civil order as expecting more than society can give them is the
_____ .

(b) The giving of greater weight to the *anticipations* of satisfaction than to the duration or magnitude of deprivation itself reflects the _____
_____ .

(c) The political counterpart of the relative deprivation explanation of

violence is frequently referred to as _____ .
_____ .

16.   James C. Davies's theory that revolutions occur when there is a sudden, abrupt thwarting of hopes and expectations that had begun to develop during the course of gradually improving conditions helps explain why modernization in traditionally backward countries is associated with a great increase in _____
_____ .

17.   (a) Support of the riots among the black population in the ghettos; the citing of such purposes as calling attention to black problems, expressing black hostility to whites, and serving as an instrument for improving conditions; the ending of discrimination; and communicating with the power structure—all are evidences of the _____
_____ .

(b) The explanation of violence that centers about the social and cultural characteristics of lower class city life, and contends that the causes of rioting are complex and deeply rooted in the culture of lower class life, was expressed by _____ .
18.   Identify the type of riot exhibiting the motive(s) of:
(a) Searching for thrills, excitement and action, and the reassurance that one can "make things happen." _____
(b) Theft. _____
(c) Indignation at what the rioter regards, rightly or wrongly, as injustice or violation of the mores that is likely to go unpunished. _____
_____ .

(d) To advance a political principle or ideology or to contribute to the maintenance of an organization. _____
19.   (a) Watts, Newark, and Detroit were all _____
_____ .

(b) The nonexistence of a "typical" civil disorder; noninterraciality; nonexistence of an attempt to subvert the social order of the United States; lack of a single triggering or precipitating incident; existence of a complex relationship between the series of incidents and the underlying grievances resulting from discrimination, prejudice, and powerlessness; participation by teenagers and young adults rather than hoodlums; existence of many black counter-rioters; continuous negotiation between blacks and white officials; glaring disparities in the conditions of blacks and whites; and quick restoration of the status quo of daily life after the incident, with little basic change taking place in the conditions underlying the disorder—all were conclusions of the _____
_____ .

(c) The commission enumerated "three of the most bitter fruits of white racial attitudes," which were _____
_____ .

(d) Three additional "powerful ingredients" that helped cause the riots were _____
_____ .

(e) The race upon which the commission laid the principal "blame" for the riots was the _____ .

Correct Responses

1. The social contract (p. 381).

2. Classic dilemma of free government (p. 381).

3. (a) Crime rate (p. 381); (b) Serious crimes (pp. 381 - 382); (c) Factors determining the official crime rate (p. 382); (d) Nonviolent crimes (p. 382); (e) Auto theft (p. 383).

4. Failure to report crime to the police (p. 383).

5. (a) Writ of habeas corpus (p. 384); (b) Bill of attainder (p. 384); (c) Ex post facto law (p. 384); (d) Unreasonable searches and seizures (p. 384); (e) Freedom from self-incrimination (pp. 384 - 385); (f) Right to counsel (p. 385); (g) Right to trial by jury (p. 385); (h) Protection against double jeopardy (p. 386); (i) Protection against excessive bail (p. 386).

6. (a) "Speedy" (p. 385); (b) "Public" (p. 385); (c) "Impartial" (p. 385); (d) "Hung jury" (p. 386).

7. (a) Warren Court of the 1950s and 1960s (p. 386); (b) *Mapp* v. *Ohio*, 1961 (p. 386); (c) *Gideon* v. *Wainwright*, 1963 (p. 386); (d) *Escobedo* v. *Illinois*, 1964 (p. 386); (e) *Miranda* v. *Arizona*, 1966 (pp. 386 - 387).

8. (a) Warren E. Burger (p. 387); (b) Weaknesses in the system of criminal justice (pp. 387 - 388).

9. (a) Cruel and unusual punishment clause (p. 388); (b) Opponents of capital punishment (p. 388); (c) Proponents of capital punishment (p. 388).

10. (a) As currently imposed (p. 389); (b) Brennan and Marshall (p. 389); (c) Douglas, White, and Stewart (pp. 389 - 390); (d) Burger, Blackman, Powell, and Reinquist (p. 390).

11. (a) Law enforcement, keeping the peace, and furnishing services (p. 390); (b) Typical background of a police officer (p. 390).

12. (a) Use of violence throughout American history (p. 391); (b) Vigilante violence (p. 393).

13. (a) Frustration-aggression explanation (pp. 397 - 398); (b) Aggressive instinct explanation (p. 397); (c) Liberals (p. 398).

14. (a) Konrad Lorenz (p. 399); (b) Provide "safe" ways of venting aggressive urges (p. 399); (c) Learn to respond in nonaggressive ways to frustrations (p. 399).

15. (a) Relative deprivation explanation (pp. 399 - 400); (b) Contrast between the relative deprivation and frustration-aggression explanations of violence (p. 400); (c) The revolution of rising explanations (p. 400).

16. Political instability (p. 400).

17. (a) Use of violence as political protest (p. 401); (b) Edward C. Banfield (pp. 402 - 404).

18. (a) Rampage (p. 402); (b) Foray for pillage (p. 402); (c) Outburst of righteous indignation (p. 402); (d) Demonstration (pp. 402 - 403).

19. (a) Major ghetto riots (p. 404); (b) National Advisory Commission on Civil Disorders (pp. 406 - 408); (c) Pervasive discrimination and segregation, black migration and white exodus, and black ghettos (p. 407); (d) Frustrated hopes, legitimation of violence, and powerlessness (pp. 407 - 408); (e) White race (p. 408).

KEY TERMS

Uniform Crime Reports

crime rates

writ of habeas corpus

bill of attainder

ex post facto law

"unreasonable" searches and seizures

lawful arrest

self-incrimination

right to counsel

trial by jury

"speedy"

"public"

"impartial"

"beyond reasonable doubt"

summons

double jeopardy

"hung jury"

excessive bail

the Warren Court

Mapp v. *Ohio* (1961)

Gideon v. *Wainwright* (1963)

Escobedo v. *Illinois* (1964)

Miranda v. *Arizona* (1966)

plea bargaining

capital punishment

cruel and unusual punishment

vigilante violence

racial violence

political assassination

frustration-aggression explanation of violence

aggressive instinct explanation of violence

"catharsis"

relative deprivation explanation of violence

revolution of rising expectations

theory of revolutions

rampage

foray for pillage

outburst of righteous indignation

demonstration

National Advisory Commission on Civil Disorders

white racism

DISCUSSION QUESTIONS

1. Discuss *crime rates:*
    (a) Their use in society
    (b) Factors used in determining them; who determines them?
    (c) Uniform classification system
    (d) Reasons for their underestimation of the real amount of crime

2. Suppose you have just been arrested by the police. Discuss the relevance of each of the following constitutional rights of defendants to you:
    (a) Guarantee of the writ of habeas corpus
    (b) Prohibition of bills of attainder
    (c) Prohibition of ex post facto laws
    (d) Prohibition of "unreasonable" searches and seizures
    (e) Freedom from self-incrimination

(f) The right to counsel
(g) Guarantee of a fair jury trial
(h) Protection against double jeopardy
(i) Protection against excessive bail

3. Choose two of the following Supreme Court cases of the Warren Court era and describe how each of them strengthened the rights of accused persons in criminal cases:

(a) *Mapp* v. *Ohio* (1961)
(b) *Gideon* v. *Wainwright* (1963)
(c) *Escobedo* v. *Illinois* (1964)
(d) *Miranda* v. *Arizona* (1966)

4. Discuss the criticisms of the current system of criminal justice as elaborated by Chief Justice Warren E. Burger in his State of the Federal Judiciary message.

5. You are violently opposed to capital punishment. What arguments would you use to defend your position against someone who is for capital punishment? What did the Supreme Court rule regarding capital punishment? Was it a majority opinion? Why or why not?

6. Violence has been a source of power and a stimulus to social change in America since the time of the American Revolution. Choose four of the following important movements in American history and discuss the type of violence utilized and the results:

(a) The birth of the nation
(b) The freeing of the slaves and the preservation of the Union
(c) The westward expansion of the nation
(d) The establishment of law and order in frontier society
(e) The organization of the labor movement
(f) The success of the civil rights movement
(g) Attempts to deal with problems of urban society

7. Compare and contrast the frustration-aggression explanation of violence with the aggressive-instinct explanation of violence and the relative deprivation explanation of violence.

8. Discuss the conclusions and findings of the National Advisory Commission on Civil Disorders regarding the 150 major riots reported in American cities from 1965 to 1968. How was "white racism" responsible for ghetto rioting? What were the effects of frustrated hopes, legitimation of violence, and powerlessness of ghetto rioting?

SUGGESTED READINGS

Don R. Bowen and Louis H. Masotti (eds.), *Riots and Rebellion* (Beverly Hills, Calif.: Sage, 1968).

James C. Davies (ed.), *When Men Revolt and Why* (New York: Free Press, 1971).

John Dollard et al., *Frustration and Aggression* (New Haven, Conn.: Yale University Press, 1939).

Hugh Davis Graham and Ted Robert Gurr, *Violence in America*, A Report Submitted to the National Commission on the Causes and Prevention of Violence (New York: Bantam Books, 1969).

Konrad Lorenz, *On Aggression* (New York: Harcourt, Brace & World, 1966).

National Advisory Commission on Civil Disorders, *Report* (Washington: Government Printing Office, 1968).

Arthur H. Niederhoffer, *Behind the Shield* (New York: Doubleday, 1967).

President's Commission on Law Enforcement and Administration of Justice, *Crime and Its Impact—An Assessment* (Washington: Government Printing Office, 1967).

James Q. Wilson, *Varieties of Police Behavior* (Cambridge, Mass.: Harvard University Press, 1968).

CHAPTER 12

Power and the Quality of Life

PERFORMANCE OBJECTIVES

The student should be able to:

1. Trace the growth of the world's population. Discuss the factors that enabled the population explosion to occur. Contrast the different views of the consequences of world population growth.

2. Contrast population growth rates in developed countries with population growth rates in underdeveloped countries.

3. Cite the two constitutional amendments used by the U.S. Supreme Court to strike down state laws preventing abortion in the first three months of pregnancy.

4. Discuss the problems of the different types of environmental pollution: air pollution, water pollution, and solid waste disposal.

5. Identify the federal agency responsible for enforcing the Clean Air acts and Water Quality acts.

6. Identify the three major types of water pollutants.

7. Differentiate between primary sewage treatment, secondary sewage treatment, and tertiary sewage treatment.

8. Discuss the advantages and disadvantages of recycling. Discuss the sanitary land fill disposal method.

9. List the five causes of the energy crisis.

10. Identify the population characteristic (density or size) that primarily determines the quality of life.

11. Identify where the largest growth is occurring in metropolitan areas (suburb or city). Define a Standard Metropolitan Statistical Area.

12. Discuss the three distinguishing characteristics of urban life according to sociologist Lewis Wirth: numbers; density; and heterogeneity of urban population.

13. Define melting pot, segmentalization of human relationships, and anomie.

14. Contrast early sociological theories of primary and secondary group ties of rural and urban life with present-day sociological theories.

15. Identify the two types of urban mobility. Discuss the effects of mobility on individuals and on the community as a whole.

16. Discuss the effects of interdependence between the central city and the suburbs in a metropolitan area.

17. List the characteristics of urban life. Discuss the difficulties of trying to discuss differences between rural and urban dwellers in a highly industrialized and urbanized society.

18. Discuss the various reasons for suburbanization of America. List the positive benefits of urban life that suburbanites seek to retain.

19. Discuss the difficulties in attempting to generalize about cities and suburbs. List the factors or characteristics by which cities and suburbs *can* be differentiated. Identify the most important difference between cities and suburbs.

20. Discuss the reasons for the concentration of blacks in large central cities. Discuss the reasons for the heavy out-migration of whites to the suburbs. Identify the overall effect on American life of these two phenomena.

21. List the factors contributing to governmental fragmentation in metropolitan areas. Define "fragmented" government.

22. Discuss the advantages of metropolitan governmental consolidation (centralization). Discuss the advantages of decentralized fragmented governmental systems.

23. Identify what James Q. Wilson and others have said is a critical deficiency in federal urban policy. Identify the two federal program areas that account for the greatest expenditures of dollars for the physical improvements of cities.

24. Discuss the problems and weaknesses of the federal grant-in-aid programs for cities. Define "grantsmanship."

25. Define revenue sharing. Contrast the arguments used by proponents of revenue sharing with the arguments used by opponents of revenue sharing.

THE POPULATION EXPLOSION

Man's relationship to his environment and his ability to ensure his own survival on the planet earth is becoming a central theme of life as we approach the twenty-first century. Dr. Lee A. DuBridge, science adviser to the president, has

Food for thought.

Paul Szep, The Boston Globe

observed, "Our space craft called the Earth is reaching its capacity. Can we not invent a way to reduce our population growth to zero? . . . Every human institution . . . should set this as its prime task."[1] Ten thousand years ago, when people lived in small bands, hunting and food-gathering, the total population of the earth was an estimated 20 million—less than the current population of California. With the development of agriculture, the world's population grew to about 100 million at the time of Moses—half the current population of the United States. At the time of Christ, the world's population had reached about 250 million, a figure that rose very slowly during the famines and plagues of the Middle Ages. Following the Renaissance, advances in agriculture, commerce, and particularly public sanitation produced a world population of one billion by 1850. At this point a worldwide revolution in medical care and public health vastly reduced the death rate. Life expectancy in advanced societies leaped from 30 to nearly 70 years. In 1970 there were 3.5 billion people in the world.

The world's population is currently growing at a rate of 2 percent a year. Of all the people who *ever* lived on the earth, one in twenty is alive today. At present growth rates, the world's population will *double* in only 37 years. By the year 2000 there will be 6 billion people in the world; by 2050 there will be over 15 billion people; and by 2100 there will be over 30 billion people.[2]

What are the consequences of world population growth? It is difficult to get unbiased estimates of what the population explosion really means for mankind. Many "scare" books and articles confidently predict the doom of the human species, while other writers believe that the publicity given to population growth greatly exceeds the real dangers.

The widely quoted Dr. Barry Commoner maintains that a population of 6 billion in the year 2000 will bring the world near the "crash point"—where the earth's air, water, and soil can no longer support man. He contends that, even though sufficient food could be grown to feed such a population, the strain on the ecosystem would bring disaster. "Man will have had it." Dr. Paul R. Ehrlich makes similarly bleak predictions. He foresees the occurrence of widespread famine before the end of this century. "Hundreds of millions of people are going to starve to death unless plague, thermo-nuclear war, or some other agent kills them first. . . . Many will starve to death in spite of any crash programs we might embark upon now. And we are not embarking upon any crash programs."[3]

In contrast, the National Academy of Sciences believes that 30 million people could be fed with foreseeable increases in food supply utilizing *existing* technology. However, it warns that "a human population less than the present one would offer the best hope for comfortable living for our descendants, long duration for the species, and the preservation of environmental quality."[4] Actually less than 10 percent of the world's land is currently under cultivation. While much of the uncultivated portion is desert, mountain, or frozen tundra, it is not impossible to envision a doubling of cultivated land. Moreover, much of the cultivated area in Asia produces only 3,000 or 4,000 calories per acre per year. With modern agricultural techniques, production there could be increased to 12,000 to 15,000 calories per acre—a tripling of yield. The potential yield of food from the sea is as yet untapped. Commercial fishing is still a hunt for "wild" fish in the sea; if fish were raised on marine farms in the fashion of cattle, the sea harvest might be greatly expanded. Finally, new technologies may be

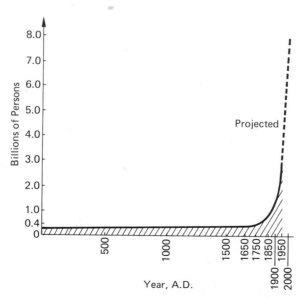

FIGURE 12-1. World Population Growth (From Congressional Quarterly, *Man's Control of the Environment,* Washington: Congressional Quarterly, 1970.)

found that could increase food production to take care of far more than the estimated 30 billion population which could be supported by existing technology.

However, the problems of population growth are compounded by the unevenness of growth rates between developed and underdeveloped countries. The rate of population increase in underdeveloped countries is twice that of advanced societies. Malnutrition, preventable disease, and starvation are frequently predicted for vast areas for Asia, Africa, and Latin America if population growth is not brought under control. Americans cannot ignore the population explosion in other parts of the world. Professor Ehrlich's comment on the interdependency of life deserves repeating: "Saying the population explosion is a problem of the underdeveloped countries is like telling a fellow passenger, 'Your end of the boat is sinking.' " Efforts in underdeveloped countries to control population growth have not yet had any significant results. Advances in productivity are often wiped out by population growth, leaving the average standard of living in many underdeveloped countries unchanged from what it was decades ago. Nevertheless, some observers believe that it is more important to control population growth in *advanced* societies, particularly the United States, than in underdeveloped countries. They argue that the United States, with only 6 percent of the world's population, uses between 30 and 50 percent of the world's annual consumption of nonreusable resources. Since the average American consumes six or seven times as many resources as the average citizen of underdeveloped nations, it is asserted that population control in the United States is essential. Finally, some representatives of underdeveloped nations view population control as a way by which wealthy nations hope to protect their own resources and limit the potential greatness of poor nations.

There is no population explosion *within* the United States. On the contrary, in recent years the birth rate in the United States has dropped to a projected zero population growth level. Family size has fallen to a point at which Americans are not even reproducing themselves—less than two children per family. (While the population will continue modest growth for a decade or more, this is because of a large number of women currently of child-bearing age.) Indeed, the problem ahead for this nation may be one of adjusting to a steady-size population, rather than continuous population growth. Moreover, compared to many other parts of the world, the United States is sparsely populated. The United States has a density of 55 persons per square mile. But the Netherlands has a density eight times greater than the United States, and England has a density ten times greater! Finally, the United States has not yet experienced the full effect of the Supreme Court's 1974 decision permitting abortions. Increased numbers of abortions may reduce the birth rate even lower than its present depressed level.

Any rate of population expansion will *eventually* saturate the planet. So a population equilibrium *must* eventually be established at some time in the future. Professor Philip M. Hauser of the University of Chicago has suggested that by bombarding people with predictions of impending disaster environmentalists may be breeding complacency. When the predictions prove false, people will be less willing to believe accurate forecasts of the real problems that lie ahead. And certainly world population growth must eventually decline. The surface of the planet is roughly 200 million square miles; about 50 million square miles is land surface. It is *not* expanding.

ABORTION AND THE LAW

Seldom has the United States embarked upon a more important social experiment than in the recent liberalization of the law and practice of abortion. Abortion can dramatically affect a nation's birth rate, its population growth, and ultimately the whole structure and quality of life.

For years, abortions in the United States for any purpose other than saving the life of the mother were criminal offenses under state laws. Then about a dozen states acted in the late 1960s to permit abortion in cases of rape or incest, or to protect the physical health of the mother, and in some cases the mental health as well. Relatively few abortions were performed under these laws, however, because of the red tape involved—review of each case by several concurring physicians, approval of a hospital board, and so forth. Then in 1970 New York enacted a law which in effect permitted abortion at the request of the woman involved and with the concurrence of her physician. Considerable controversy surrounded this law: It originally passed the New York legislature on a very close vote; later the legislature voted for repeal, but Governor Nelson Rockefeller vetoed the repeal bill and left standing the original law.

New York City quickly became a national center for abortion. The number of abortions rose above the number of live births. The number of criminal abortions in the city fell to near zero, and there was a substantial decline in the number of children placed for adoption. About half of the abortions performed on city residents involved black or Puerto Rican women; nonresident abortions largely involved white middle class women who could afford to travel to the city.

Abortion is a highly sensitive issue. It is not an issue that can be compromised. The arguments touch on fundamental moral and religious principles. Proponents of abortion argue that a woman should be permitted to control her own body and should not be forced by law to have unwanted children. They cite the heavy toll in lives lost in criminal abortions and the psychological and emotional pain of an unwanted pregnancy. Opponents of abortion generally base their belief on the sanctity of life, including the life of the unborn child which they insist deserves the protection of law—"the right to life." Many believe that the killing of an unborn child for any reason other than the preservation of the life or health of the mother is murder.

The past ten years have seen a major turnabout on the abortion question. Although the Supreme Court decision of 1973 was a milestone, the issue has been argued many times recently in many state legislatures. Here opponents and proponents discuss their viewpoints on the steps of the New Jersey State House. *Wide World Photo*

Perhaps the most significant decision about the future of the nation's population was the Supreme Court's momentous ruling in *Roe* v. *Wade* (1973) recognizing abortion as a constitutional right of women. In this historic decision the Court determined that the fetus is not a "person" within the meaning of the Constitution, and therefore the fetus's right to life is not guaranteed by law. Moreover, the Court held that the liberties guaranteed by the Fifth and Fourteenth Amendments encompass the woman's decision on whether or not to terminate her pregnancy. The Supreme Court decided that criminal abortion laws prohibiting abortions in any stage of pregnancy except to save the life of the mother were unconstitutional; that during the first three months of pregnancy the abortion decision must be left wholly to the woman and her physician; that during the second three months of pregnancy the state may not prohibit abortion but only regulate procedures in ways reasonably related to maternal health; and that only in the final three months of pregnancy may the state prohibit abortion except where necessary for the preservation of life or health of the mother. In this sweeping decision the Supreme Court established abortion not merely as permissible under law but as a constitutional right immune from the actions of popularly elected legislatures.

POLLUTION AND THE ENVIRONMENT

Mankind may suffocate in its own waste material long before the food supply runs out. The ecological problem is not solely one of balancing food supply with the number of people. Subsistence is not enough; the question is *how* we want to live—the quality of our life. The immediate environmental problems in America center about the pollution of the environment and the use of natural resources.

Air Pollution. The air we breathe is about one-fifth oxygen and a little less than four-fifths nitrogen, with traces of other gases, water vapor, and the waste products we spew into it. Most air pollution is caused by gasoline-powered internal combustion engines—cars, trucks, and buses. Motor vehicles send about 90 million tons of contaminants into the atmosphere every year—about 60 percent of the total polluting material. Industries and governments contribute another 60 million tons. The largest industrial polluters are petroleum refineries, smelters (aluminum, copper, lead, and zinc), and iron foundries. Electrical power plants are another major source of air pollution; 95 percent of the nation's electrical power is produced by burning coal or oil. The demand for electrical power has doubled every decade since 1940, and it is expected that Americans will triple their use of electricity in the next two decades. Heating is also a major source of pollution; homes, apartments, and offices use coal, gas, and oil for heat. Another source of pollution is the incineration of garbage, trash, metal, glass, and other refuse, by both governments and industries.

Air pollutants fall into two major types, particles and gases. The particles include ashes, soot, and lead, the unburnable additive in gasoline. Often the brilliant red sunsets we admire are caused by large particles in the air. Less obvious but more damaging are the gases: (1) sulfur dioxide, which in combination with moisture can form sulfuric acid; (2) hydrocarbons—any combination of hydrogen and carbon; (3) nitrogen oxide, which can combine with hydrocarbons in the sun's ultraviolet rays to form smog; and (4) carbon monoxide, which is produced when gasoline is burned.

It is difficult to assess the full impact of air pollution on health. We know that when the smog or pollution count rises in a particular city there are more deaths than would normally have been expected. Carbon monoxide is toxic and has been measured at toxic levels in the streets of certain cities at certain hours of heavy traffic. Carbon monoxide is tasteless, colorless, and odorless, but it can deprive the body of oxygen; persons exposed to relatively low levels of this gas exhibit drowsiness, headache, poor vision, impaired coordination, and reduced capacity to reason. One polluting hydrocarbon, benzo-a-pyrene, has been implicated as a possible cause of cancer; it is present in cigarette smoke, but even a nonsmoker in a highly polluted area inhales as much benzo-a-pyrene daily as he

Awareness of increasing pollution of water resources has increased markedly since the 1960's. One of the best known large bodies of polluted water is Lake Erie. This picture of Cleveland's Easterly Sewage Plant was taken with infrared film to highlight the flow of sewage into the lake. *United Press International Photo*

would from smoking. Nitrogen oxide irritates the eyes, nose, throat, and respiratory system; it damages plants, buildings, and statues. Smog is particularly dangerous to victims of emphysema. Emphysema is a pollution-related disease in which the lungs lose their capacity to function normally; it is currently the fastest growing cause of death in the United States. Finally, urban residents have been found to be twice as likely to contract lung cancer as rural residents.

What is being done? In a series of Clean Air acts passed over the last decade, the federal government has gradually raised the standards for clean air, tightened enforcement procedures, and increased penalties for violators. The Environmental Protection Agency sets standards for emission control for industries and governments. More importantly, the environmental Protection Agency enforces provisions of the Clean Air acts controlling automobile emissions. The 1975 federal standards for automobile emissions require major technological innovations that the automobile industry have to install on cars.

The laws are also forcing other industries to search for nonpolluting methods of burning fuel.

Water Pollution. Debris and sludge, organic wastes, and chemical effluents are the three major types of water pollutants. *Primary* sewage treatment—screens and settling chambers where filth falls out of the water as sludge—is fairly common. *Secondary* sewage treatment is designed to remove organic wastes, usually by trickling water through a bed of rocks three to ten feet deep, where bacteria consume the organic matter. Remaining germs are killed by chlorination. *Tertiary* sewage treatment uses mechanical and chemical filtration processes to remove almost all contaminants from water. The present federal water pollution abatement program goals call for the establishment of secondary treatment in 90 percent of American communities. In most industrial plants, tertiary treatment ultimately will be required to deal with the flow of chemical pollutants. But tertiary treatment is expensive; it costs two or three times as much to build and operate a tertiary sewage treatment plant as it does a secondary plant. Even today, however, one-third of all Americans live in communities where their sewage gets nothing but primary treatment.

The Environmental Protection Agency is responsible for enforcing a series of federal Water Quality acts. In 1972 the federal government banned production of detergents containing phosphates in the attempt to reduce the mountains of soap bubbles in the nation's waterways. Phosphates are major water pollutants which overstimulate plant life in water, which in turn kills fish. Paper manufacturing is another major industrial polluter. Municipalities are frequently unwilling to pay the high costs of secondary and tertiary sewage treatment. In 1969 the Cuyahoga River in Cleveland actually caught fire, suggesting the extent of chemical pollution in this waterway. Lake Erie has been labeled an "ecological disaster" where little marine life remains.

Waterfronts and seashores are natural resources that Americans can no longer take for granted. The growing numbers of waterfront homes, amusement centers, marinas, and pleasure boats, together with the frequent occurrence of offshore oil spills, are threatening to alter the environment of the nation's coastal areas. Marshes and estuaries at the water's edge are essential to the production of seafood and shellfish, yet they are steadily shrinking with the growth of residental-commercial-industrial development. Oil spills are unsightly and they kill fish and birds, whose bodies and gills become coated. Coastal pollution is much greater in Europe than in America, but America's coastal areas still require protection. The Water Quality acts make petroleum companies liable for the cleanup cost of oil spills, outlaw flushing of raw sewage from boat toilets, restrict thermal pollution, and set general water quality standards for all of the states. In addition, the federal government has purchased certain coastal areas to preserve the coastal wilderness.

Virginia's James River is another major waterway with industrial water pollution problems. *United Press International Photo*

Solid Waste Disposal.   Only a very wealthy country could afford to be as wasteful as the United States. Every American discards between six and eight pounds of solid waste per day! This per capita waste production is expected to double in weight in the next 20 years. The annual load of waste dumped on the environment includes 48 billion cans, 26 billion bottles and jars, 4 million tons of plastic, 8 million television sets, 7 million automobiles and trucks, and 30 million tons of paper. Already the nation spends billions of dollars annually on hauling all of this away from homes and businesses. The problem is where to put it. Burning creates air pollution. Open dumps are eyesores and create health hazards. The Environmental Protection Agency urges cities to rely on sanitary landfills—the waste is spreading in thin layers over specific land areas and covered at least once a day with a layer of earth. But many cities are running out of landfill sites.

Solving the problem of solid waste disposal requires that we either find better methods of disposal, find ways to reduce the amount discarded, or recycle wastes. Recycling could decrease the volume of solid wastes which must be disposed, and at the same time reduce the amount of virgin materials taken from the earth. Yet recycling is hampered by the difficulties of separating reusable materials from other refuse. It is frequently cheaper to use virgin materials than it is to separate refuse and recycle it.

THE ENERGY CRISIS

The energy crisis is real; it is not merely speculation about possible future disasters. Gasoline shortages and power blackouts are now facts of life. Americans guzzle a third of the world's energy production, and our appetite is growing; energy demand will more than double by the year 2000. But dwindling domestic supplies of oil and gas and unstable and costly reliance on foreign oil, combined with lagging development of new electric power plants, threatens to curtail growth in energy production in America.

The energy crisis has several causes:

1. Skyrocketing demand for energy, and styles of life (electric appliances, air conditioning, etc.) that use increasing amounts of energy (see Figure 12-2).
2. Leveling off of output of domestic fuels—particularly oil and gas—and a decline in coal production.
3. Government regulation of the price of electricity and natural gas making it more difficult for power companies to acquire the capital to construct new plants.
4. Attacks by environmentalists forcing cutbacks in the use of polluting fuels and holding up development of new power plants, particularly nuclear power plants.

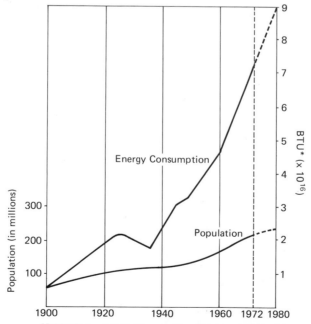

*British Thermal Unit: The quantity of heat required to raise the temperature of one pound of water one degree Farenheit.

FIGURE 12-2. U.S. Population Growth and Energy Consumption (1900–1980)
(From Congressional Quarterly, *Man's Control of the Environment,*
Washington: Congressional Quarterly, 1970.)

5. The formation of a cartel of petroleum-exporting countries (OPEC) which forced steep increases in the price of oil and threatened oil embargoes against nations that opposed the political aims of OPEC countries.

Petroleum products supply 44 percent of the nation's energy needs; natural gas, 32 percent; coal, 18 percent; and nuclear power and hydropower together, only about 5 percent (see Figure 12-3). Most of America's oil that was relatively easy to find has already been discovered and used. Oil producers must now drill deeper and costlier wells in their search for oil. Currently, the United States imports 28 percent of its oil, but dependency on foreign sources is rising. By 1980 we may be importing 50 to 65 percent. This reliance on foreign sources—particularly Middle Eastern Arab nations—raised fears of "political blackmail." Arab states are pressuring the United States to support their claims against Israel, as part of the price of supplying our nation with oil. Moreover, the cost of gasoline must certainly rise as the United States increases its dependency on imported, rather than domestic, oil. Finally, the heavy reliance on oil tankers is bound to increase the number of oil spills and contribute to coastal pollution.

In 1968 new oil reserves were discovered in Alaska. Oil from Alaska's North Slope fields can help reduce the nation's reliance on imports over the next decades. However, effective use of these reserves requires time-consuming construction of a trans-Alaska oil pipeline. Environmentalists succeeded in delaying the start of construction for five years, claiming that breaks and leaks would spill oil and the line itself would interfere with the area's ecological balance. New congressional legislation was required to authorize the pipeline, but several

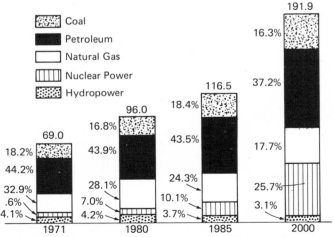

BTU: Quantity of heat required to raise temperature of one pound of water one degree Farenheit.

FIGURE 12-3. Estimated U.S. Power Consumption by Source (Quadrillion BTU's)
(From U.S. Department of Interior, "United States Energy Through the Year 2000.)

more years will pass before the flow of oil begins. Even then, the North Slope itself will not provide enough oil to solve the energy crisis.

Government regulation of the rates charged for gas and electricity have hampered investment in new drilling and new plant construction. Natural gas is clean burning and popular for heating houses and buildings; factories also consume gas. For decades gas was very cheap relative to other fuels because the Federal Power Commission held down prices. This encouraged waste, and drilling declined as investors sought more profitable ventures. *State* governments, rather than the federal government, regulate rates charged for electrical power. Power companies claim that continued delays and cutbacks in rate increases by states make it difficult to attract investment capital to expand capacity, particularly when demand is growing so rapidly.

Electrical power plants that burn coal or oil are major sources of pollution (see Table 12-1). Environmentalists actively oppose the construction of new power plants, and their legal efforts have brought new plant construction to a standstill in many parts of the country. According to a leader of the influential environmentalist lobby the Sierra Club, "Our strategy is to sue and sue and sue."

Nuclear power plants offer a new means of generating electricity without discharging pollutants into the air or water. Nuclear power does not diminish the world's supply of oil, coal, and gas, which will someday run out. A "fast breeder" reactor can create as much fissionable material as it uses to generate heat, thus solving the problem of the uranium supply. However, nuclear plants use water for cooling and send the water back into streams at a higher temperature. The result is "thermal pollution," which increases algae and chokes off fish life. Environmentalists object to the burying of radioactive waste materials in the ground from nuclear reactors. They are also concerned that overheating accidents could have dire, perhaps lethal, effects. Scare stories of nuclear reactors blowing up have been circulated, but there is little real likelihood of such an occurrence. The result of objections by environmentalists has nevertheless, been to slow the nation's conversion to this future source of energy.

TABLE 12-1. **Pollution and Its Sources: Annual Emissions of Five Major Air Pollutants; Percent of Total Emissions By Type**

Type of Emission	Automobile	Major Industries	Electrical Power	Space Heating	Refuse Disposal
Carbon monoxide	92%	3%	1%	3%	1%
Hydrocarbons	64	21	5	5	5
Nitrogen oxides	46	15	23	8	8
Sulfur oxides	4	35	46	11	4
Particulates	9	50	25	8	8
Total	60%	16%	14%	6%	4%

Source: Congressional Quarterly, *Man's Control of the Environment,* Washington: Congressional Quarterly, 1970.

Drawing by Oldden; © 1973
The New Yorker Magazine,
Inc.

Coal is the nation's most abundant fuel. But the mining of coal scars the land
and the burning of coal pollutes the air. Despite the demand for energy, coal
production has declined, owing in part to pressures from environmentalists. The
Clean Air acts have forced many electrical plants to switch from coal to oil in
order to meet air pollution standards. So far, the "gasification" of coal—its conversion to clean-burning gas before use—is too costly to be feasible.

Perhaps the overriding problem is that the United States has no coordinated
national energy policy. "Project Independence"—a presidential announcement
of an effort to make the nation independent of foreign oil import by 1980—-
quickly bogged down in bickering among various interests. Industry, labor, environmentalists, and Congress and other governmental agencies have failed to
agree on such questions as: whether to rely primarily on energy conservation or
stimulate the search for new energy sources; whether to speed up the development of nuclear energy or continue to use fossil fuels; whether or not to "trade
off" clean air standards in order to ensure adequate energy supplies; whether to
proceed slowly in developing new oil, gas, and coal reserves in the interests of
environmental protection, or to move rapidly in the interests of achieving in-

dependence from foreign powers; whether to reduce energy consumption by relying on voluntary conservation, allowing fuel prices to rise, adding new taxes to fuel, or imposing governmental allocations and rationing. These domestic issues are further complicated by delicate and dangerous Middle East politics, notably the new Arab OPEC (Organization of Petroleum Exporting Countries) cartel, which has tripled the price of foreign oil and threatened to cut off oil to the Western world if Israel does not meet Arab terms for a Middle East settlement.

In worldwide perspective, the environment is still relatively free of pollution. Most pollutants of the air and water are removed by natural processes, as long as there is time and room for dispersal and settling. But no one really knows what the limits of environmental pollution are. Actually, most of the nation's pollution problems do *not* arise from the *total* numbers of people in America or even the *total* amount of pollution produced, but rather from excessive concentration of people and pollution in the metropolitan areas of the United States. The quality of life is determined primarily by how our population has chosen to distribute itself (density) rather than by its size.

THE GROWTH OF THE METROPOLIS

Two out of three Americans live in population clusters called metropolitan areas. Most of the nation's population increase is occurring in these metropolitan areas—the increase in metropolitan area population from 1960 to 1970 was 24.4 million, in contrast to a 1.1 million *decline* in the rest of the United States (see Table 12-2). Moreover, most of this increase is taking place *outside* of the core cities—in the nation's booming suburbs. The suburban population grew by an amazing 36.0 percent in a single decade, while the core cities grew by only 8.4 percent. Today more Americans are suburbanites than either city or rural residents.

What is a metropolitan area? Briefly, it consists of a central city of 50,000 or more persons together with the surrounding suburbs, which are socially and economically tied to the central city. The Census Bureau calls a metropolitan area a "Standard Metropolitan Statistical Area" (SMSA) and defines it as a city of 50,000 or more persons together with adjacent counties which have predominantly urban industrial populations with close ties to the central city (see Figure 12-4).

In the last decade nearly 20 million Americans moved to the suburbs. No other sector of American life has grown so rapidly. Very few large *central cities* are growing in size; metropolitan areas are growing because their *suburbs* are growing. Suburbanization is due to technological advances in transpor-

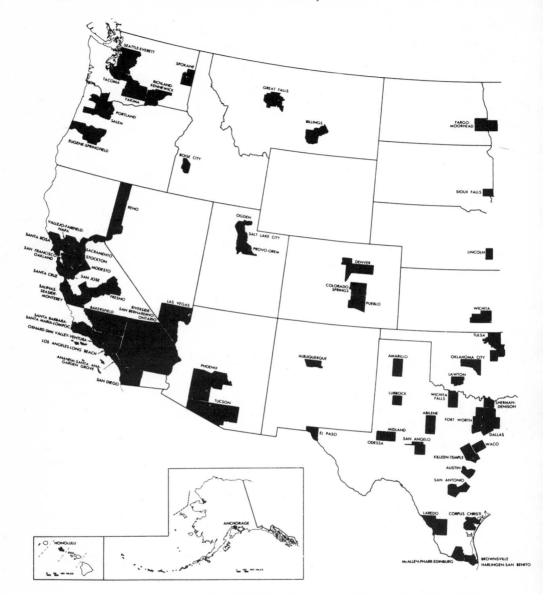

FIGURE 12-4. Standard Metropolitan Statistical Areas

tation—the automobile and the expressway. In the nineteenth century an industrial worker had to live within walking distance of his place of employment.
Hence the nineteenth-century American city crowded large masses of people
into relatively small central areas, often in tenement houses and other high-
density neighborhoods. But new modes of transportation—first the streetcar,
then the private automobile, and finally the expressway—eliminated the

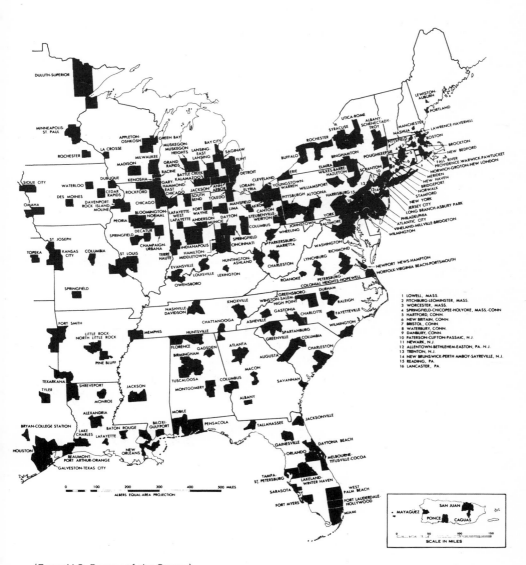

(From U.S. Bureau of the Census)

necessity for workers to live close to their jobs. Now one can spend his working hours in a central business district office or industrial plant and pass his evenings in a residential suburb miles away. The same technology that led to the suburbanization of residences has also influenced commercial and industrial location. Originally industry was tied to waterways or railroads for access to supplies and markets. This dependence has been reduced by the development of motor truck

TABLE 12-2. Population Growth in Cities and Suburbs of Metropolitan
Areas in the United States

| | Total U.S. Population | Metropolitan Areas | | | Outside Metropolitan Areas |
		Total	Central Cities	Suburbs	
1970					
Population (thousands)	203,185	136,330	62,193	74,137	66,855
Percent of U.S. total	100.0	67.1	30.6	36.5	32.9
1960					
Population (thousands)	179,993	111,886	57,360	54,526	68,107
Percent of U.S. total	100.0	62.3	31.9	30.3	37.7
Percentage increase	12.9	21.8	8.4	36.0	−1.9

Source: U.S. Bureau of the Census, *1970 Census of Population,* PC (P3)-3 (Washington: Government Printing Office, 1971).

transportation, the highway system, and the greater mobility of the labor force. Now many industries can locate in the suburbs, particularly light industries, which do not require extremely heavy bulk shipment that can be handled only by rail or water. When industry and people move to the suburbs, commerce follows. Giant suburban shopping centers have sprung up to compete with downtown stores. Thus, metropolitan areas are becoming decentralized as people, business, and industry spread over the suburban landscape.

SOCIAL PATTERNS OF URBAN LIFE

What is the impact of urbanism on the way people interact? To deal with this question, sociologists first had to formulate a sociological definition of urbanism—one that would identify those characteristics most affecting social life. Sociologist Louis Wirth provided a classic definition of urbanism more than three decades ago: "For sociological purposes a city may be defined as a relatively large, dense, and permanent settlement of socially heterogeneous individuals." Thus, according to Wirth, the distinguishing characteristics of urban life were *numbers, density,* and *heterogeneity*—large numbers of people living closely together who are different from one another.

Large numbers of people involve a great range of individual variation. The modern economic system of the metropolis is based upon highly specialized and complex division of labor. We are told that in the simple farm community a dozen occupations exhausted the job opportunities available to men. In an agricultural economy nearly everyone was a farmer or was closely connected to or dependent upon farming. But in the modern metropolis there are tens of thousands of different kinds of jobs. An industrial economy means highly specialized jobs; hence the heterogeneity of urban populations. Different jobs result in different levels of income, dress, and styles of living. An individual's job shapes the way he looks at the world and his evaluations of social and political events. In acquiring his job, he attains a certain level and type of education that also distinguishes him from those in other jobs with other educational requirements. Differences in educational level in turn produce a wide variety of differences in opinions, attitudes, and styles of living. Urban life concentrates people with all these different economic and occupational characteristics in a very few square miles.

Ethnic and racial diversities are also present. A few decades ago opportunities for human betterment in the cities attracted immigrants from Ireland, Germany, Italy, Poland, and Russia; today the city attracts blacks, Puerto Ricans, and rural families. These newcomers bring with them different needs, attitudes, and ways of life. The "melting pot" tends to reduce some of the diversity over time, but the pot does not melt people immediately, and there always seem to be new arrivals.

Urban dwellers also differ in where they live and in how they live. There is a certain uniformity to rural life; day-to-day family life on the farm is remarkably similar from one rural place to the next. But urban dwellers may live in apartments in the central city or in single-family homes in the suburbs. Some urban dwellers choose a *familistic* style of life—raising two or more children in their own single-family house, with the wife functioning as a homemaker. Others are less familistic—raising no children or a single child in a rented apartment with the wife holding down a job outside the home.

Increasing the numbers of people in a community limits the possibility that each member of the community will know everyone else personally. Multiplying the number of persons with whom an individual comes into contact makes it impossible to know everyone he meets very well. The result is a "segmentalization of human relationships," in which an individual comes to know many people but only in highly segmental, partial roles. According to Wirth, "The contacts of the city may indeed be face to face, but they are nevertheless impersonal, superficial, transitory, and segmental. The reserve, the indifference, and the blasé outlook which urbanites manifest in their relationship may thus be regarded as devices for immunizing themselves against the personal claims and expectations of others."[5]

Large numbers mean a certain degree of freedom for the individual from the control of family groups, neighbors, churches, and other community groups. But urbanism also contributes to a sense of *anomie*—a sense of social isolation and a loss of personal recognition, self-worth, and feeling of participation that comes with living in a small integrated society.

Rural life emphasized *primary group* ties—interactions within the extended family. Early sociological theory believed that urban life emphasized *secondary group* ties—interactions between members of age and interest groups rather than families and neighbors. Family life was set to center around voluntary associations and secondary group memberships—crowds, recreation groups, civic clubs, business groups, and professional and work group contacts. Sociologists believe that urban dwellers have a greater number of interpersonal contacts than rural dwellers and that the people urban dwellers are more likely to interact with are the occupants of specific social roles. In contrast, rural dwellers are more likely to interact with individuals as full personalities. Urban dwellers have greater anonymity in their social contacts; they interact with persons who have little if any knowledge of their life history. Moreover, urban dwellers frequently interact with others by utilizing them as means to an end, thus giving a utilitarian quality to interpersonal relations.

Urban society also presents problems of social control. The anonymity of urban life is believed to weaken social mores and social group controls. External controls through a series of formal institutions, such as laws, and organizations, such as the courts and the police, become more essential. Thus, social control in the cities depends in large degree upon the formal mechanisms. But laws generally express the minimum behavioral standard, and urban life involves a much wider range of behavior than rural life. Moreover, laws do not always succeed in establishing minimum standards of behavior; crime rates increase with increases in urbanism.

Another characteristic of urban life is mobility, or ease of movement. Urban mobility is both physical (from one geographic area to another) and social (from one position of social status to another). Rural communities are more stable than urban communities in both respects. Traditionally, rural dwellers were more likely to stay near the place of their birth. In contrast, urbanites frequently move from city to city, or from one section of a city to another. Social mobility is also greater in the city, because of the wider range of economic opportunities there. Moreover, the urban dweller is judged far less by his family background (which is unknown) than by his own appearance, his occupational accomplishments, and his income and lifestyle. While mobility creates opportunities for individuals, it weakens the sense of community. City dwellers do not think of their city as a community to which they belong but rather as a place they happen to live—a geographical entity commanding little personal allegiance.

Yet another fundamental characteristic is interdependence. Rural living involves little interdependence. Although the traditional farm family was not wholly self-sufficient, its members were much less dependent on the larger community for employment, goods, and services than is the modern urban dweller. Urban dwellers are highly dependent upon one another in their daily economic and social activities. Suburbanites, for example, rely upon the central city for food, clothing, newspapers, entertainment, hospitalization, and a host of other modern needs. More importantly, they rely upon the central city for employment opportunities. Conversely, the central city relies upon the suburbs to supply its labor and management forces. Downtown merchants look to the entire metropolitan area for consumers. This interdependence involves an intricate web of economic and social relationships, a high degree of communication, and a great deal of physical interchange among residents, groups, and firms in a metropolitan area. Just as specialization produces diversity among men, it also produces interdependence, and the need for coordinated activity.

Urban life presents a serious problem in conflict management. Since a metropolitan area consists of a large number of different kinds of people living closely together, the problem of regulating conflict and maintaining order assumes tremendous proportions. Persons with different occupations, income, and education levels are known to have different views on public issues. Persons well equipped to compete for jobs and income on a free market sometimes have different views about government housing and welfare programs from those of others not so well equipped. People at the bottom of the social ladder look at police—indeed, governmental authority in general—differently from the way those on higher rungs do. Persons who own their homes and those who do not regard taxation in a different light. Families with children and those without children have different ideas about school systems. And so it goes. Differences in the way people make their living, in their income and educational levels, in the color of their skin, in the way they worship, in their style of living, and so on, are at the roots of political life in the metropolis.

Thus, social theory provides us with a series of characteristics to look for in urban life:

Large numbers of people
Population density
Social and economic heterogeneity
Physical and social mobility
Economic interdependence
Physical separation of functions and groups
Numerous but superficial interpersonal interactions
Impersonality and anonymity
Segmental and utilitarian interpersonal relationships
Greater interaction in secondary groups
Reliance upon formal mechanisms of control
Greater potential for conflict

Not all of these characteristics of urban life have been documented. Indeed, in a society such as the United States which is highly industrialized and urbanized it is difficult to discern any differences between rural and urban dwellers. Moreover, urban dwellers display a great range and variation in styles of life. Some reflect the "typical" style described by social theory while others do not. Many retain their commitment to the extended family, and many city neighborhoods are stable and socially cohesive communities. Despite the plausibility of the hypothesis that urban life leads to anonymity, impersonality, and segmentalization in social relationships, it is hard to prove systematically that urban dwellers are getting more impersonal or anonymous than are rural dwellers. Finally, the sociologists cannot focus upon central-city lifestyles in describing urban living. We must now take account of suburban lifestyles, since more people live in suburbs than in central cities. And the suburban way of life is in many ways quite different from the way of life described in early sociological theory.

THE SUBURBAN TREND

One explanation of the suburbanization of America is that people strive to avoid many of the unpleasant characteristics of urban life. The move to the suburbs is in part generated by a desire to get away from the numbers, density, and heterogeneity of big-city life, the problems created by large numbers of people—the crowds, dirt, noise, smog, congestion, gas fumes, crime, and delinquency. People move to the suburbs seeking more land (less density) on which to build their own homes, enjoy backyard recreation, and give their children more room in which to play; they want sunshine, fresh air, quiet, privacy, and space.

Moreover, people often move to the suburbs to place physical distance between themselves and those whose cultures and lifestyles are different from theirs—the poor, the black, the lower class. They seek to replace the *heterogeneity* of big-city life by the *homogeneity* of the small suburban community—congenial neighbors, people like themselves, who share their interest in good schools, respectable neighborhoods, and middle class lifestyles. The suburban community, with a local government small in scale and close to home, represents a partial escape from the anonymity of mass urban life. The suburbanite identifies his community by reference to his suburban home—Scarsdale, or Mineola; he does not feel much identification with the "New York - Northeastern New Jersey Standard Metropolitan Area." A separate suburban government and school district provide him with a sense of personal effectiveness in the management of public affairs.

Suburbs offer escape from the worst problems of urban life—racial conflict, crime, violence, poverty, slums, drugs, congestion, pollution, etc. A move to the suburbs permits a family, for the time being at least, to avoid the problems of poor schools, deteriorating housing, expanding welfare rolls, muggings and robberies, violence and rioting in the central cities. Yet at the same time suburbanites wish to retain the positive benefits of urban life. The city offers economic opportunity—high-paying jobs, openings for highly skilled professionals and technicians, and upward social and economic mobility. This is the reason most people come to the city in the first place. The big city also offers theater and entertainment, professional sports, civic and cultural events, specialized shops and stores, and a host of other attractions. Suburban living allows people to enjoy the advantages of urban life while avoiding some of its hardships.

Of course, it is not really possible to argue that the major social problems of urban society—racial conflict, poverty, drugs, crime, undereducation, slum housing, and so on—are problems of central cities and not of suburbs. John C. Bollens and Henry J. Schmandt in *The Metropolis* addressed themselves to this point very effectively:

> Some myopic defenders of suburbia go so far as to say that the major socio-economic problems of urban society are problems of the central city, not those of the total metropolitan community. Where but within the boundaries of the core city, they ask, does one find an abundance of racial strife, crime, blight of housing, and welfare recipients? Superficially, their logic may seem sound, since they are in general correct about the prevalent spatial location of these maladies. Although crime and other social problems exist in suburbia, their magnitude and extent are substantially less than in the central city. But why in an interdependent metropolitan community should the responsibility for suburbanites be any less than that of the central city dwellers? Certainly no one would think of contending that residents of higher income neighborhoods within the corporate limits of the city should be exempt from responsibility for its less fortunate districts. What logic then is there in believing that neighborhoods on the other side of a legal line can wash their hands of social disorders in these sections?
>
> . . . No large community can hope to reap the benefits of industrialization and urbanization and yet escape their less desirable byproducts. The suburbanite and the central city resident share the responsibility for total community and its problems. Neither can run fast enough to escape involvement sooner or later.[6]

Generalizing about cities and suburbs is dangerous. While we will talk about some common characteristics of cities and suburbs, students are cautioned that suburbs and communities may be quite different from one another, just as there are wide differences between social and economic groups living in central cities.

Cities and suburbs can be differentiated, first of all, on the basis of occupation, income, and educational levels of their populations. The suburbs house greater proportions of white-collar employees, of college graduates, and of affluent families than any other sector in American life. And social differences between city and suburb are increasing rather than decreasing, as middle class Americans continue to flee from the central city to the suburbs, and lower income, occupational, and educational groups are concentrated in central cities.

Perhaps the most frequently mentioned reason for a move to the suburbs is the "kids." Family after family lists consideration of its young as the primary cause for the move to suburbia. The city is hardly the place for most child-centered amenities. A familistic or child-centered lifestyle can be identified in certain social statistics. There are proportionately more children in the suburbs than in the central cities; a larger proportion of suburban mothers stay at home to take care of these children; and a larger proportion of suburban families are housed in single-family homes. A nonfamilistic lifestyle is characteristic of the central city, where there are proportionately fewer children, mostly apartment living, and greater numbers of employed mothers.

But the most important difference between cities and suburbs is their contrasting *racial composition*. While blacks constitute only 11 percent of the total population of the United States, they are rapidly approaching a numerical majority in many of the nation's largest cities. Blacks are already in the majority in Washington, Atlanta, and Newark and they make up more than 40 percent of the population of Detroit, Baltimore, St. Louis, New Orleans, Oakland, Birmingham, and Gary. They are nearing a third of the population of Chicago, Philadelphia, Cleveland, Memphis, Columbus, and Cincinnati.

The concentration of blacks in large central cities is a product of the availability of low-priced rental units in older, run-down sections of central cities and of discriminatory housing practices of private owners and developers. Of course, underlying the concentration of blacks in run-down sectors of central cities is a lack of sufficient income to purchase housing in suburbs or in better city neighborhoods. The poverty and unemployment that contribute to the concentration of blacks in "ghettos" are in turn a product of inadequate training and education, low aspiration levels, and often lack of motivation. And problems in education and motivation are themselves related to a breakdown in family life, delinquency, and crime. Thus, urban blacks face a whole series of interrelated problems in addition to discrimination: poverty, slum housing, undereducation, lack of job skills, family troubles, lack of motivation, delinquency, and crime. It is difficult to talk about any one of these problems without reference to them all.

The migration of blacks into cities, particularly in the North, has been accompanied by a heavy out-migration of whites fleeing to the suburbs for a variety of reasons. The total populations of many large central cities have remained stagnant in recent years or even declined slightly; black population percentages have increased because black in-migration has compensated for white out-migration.

While these two boys seem to enjoy climbing on a sign post, this sort of play environment is looked upon with disfavor by many parents. For many families the lack of child-centered amenities is a significant cause of their move from the city to suburbia. *Eugene Richards Photo*

Many whites have fled to the suburbs to get away from concentrations of black people in central cities. One reason suburbanites may want to remain politically separate from the central cities is that they might more easily resist "invasion" by blacks. However, as blacks gain majorities in central cities, they too, may resist metropolitan governmental consolidation in order to avoid dilution of their political power through merger with white suburbs. The restriction of suburban home sales to whites only and the generally higher costs of suburban homes and property have made it difficult or impossible for blacks to follow whites to the suburbs in any significant number. The nonwhite percentage of all central cities is 21 percent.

Thus, American life is becoming more, not less, segregated. These population statistics clearly show that America is building racial ghettos in its large central cities and surrounding them with white middle class suburbs. As the exodus to the suburbs continues, cities are becoming bereft of their middle class, white, high-income, high-taxpaying populations. Increasingly, nonwhite, low-income, low-education, unskilled, nonfamilistic populations are being concentrated in the central cities. Thus the problems of these people have also been concentrated in downtown areas—racial imbalance, crime, violence, inadequate education, poverty, slum housing, and so on. By moving to the suburbs, white middle class families not only separate themselves from blacks and poor people but place physical distance between themselves and the major social problems that confront metropolitan areas.

FRAGMENTED AUTHORITY IN THE METROPOLIS

Another characteristic of metropolitan life is "fragmented" governmental authority. Suburban development, spreading out from central cities, generally ignores governmental boundaries and engulfs counties, townships, towns, and smaller cities. This suburbanization means that hundreds of separate governments may be operating in a single metropolitan area. Metropolitan government is generally "fragmented" into many smaller jurisdictions, none of which is capable of governing the entire metropolitan area in a unified fashion.

Governmental fragmentation in metropolitan areas is a function of size: the larger the metropolitan area, the more fragmented the governmental structure. Fragmentation is also related to the age of settlement and to income levels in the metropolis, although these factors are less influential than size. Apparently the older a metropolitan area, the more complex its governmental structure; and the more affluent its citizens, the more complexity in the form of separate, relatively small units of government it can afford.

Many scholars over the years have insisted that "the metropolitan problem" was essentially the problem of "fragmented" government—that is, the proliferation of governments and the lack of coordination of public programs. Advantages were claimed for metropolitan governmental consolidation. First of all, consolidation of governments was expected to *improve public service* by achieving economies of large-scale operations and providing specialized public services, which "fragmented" units of government could not provide. For example, larger water treatment plant facilities can deliver water at lower per gallon costs, and larger sewage disposal plants can handle sewage at a lower per gallon cost of disposal. Second, metropolitan consolidation would provide the necessary *coordination of public services* for the metropolis. Study after study reported that disease, crime, fire, traffic congestion, air pollution, water pollution, and so on, do not respect municipal boundary lines. Third, metropolitan consolidation would eliminate *inequalities in financial burdens* throughout the metropolitan area. Suburbanites who escaped many city taxes continue to add to the cities' traffic and parking difficulties, use city streets and parks, find employment in the cities, use city hospitals and cultural facilities, and so on. By concentrating the poor, uneducated, unskilled minorities in central cities, we also saddle central cities with costly problems of public health and welfare, crime control, fire protection, slum clearance, and the like—all the social problems that are associated with poverty and discrimination. At the same time, middle class taxpaying individuals, taxpaying commercial enterprises, and taxpaying industries are moving to the suburbs. Thus, metropolitan governmental fragmentation often succeeds in segregating financial needs from resources.

It is also argued that metropolitan government would *clearly establish responsibility for metropolitan-wide policy.* One consequence of fragmented government is the scattering of public authority and the decentralization of policy-making in the metropolis. Fragmented government divides political power into many small units with limited jurisdiction. As a result, decisions on matters of general concern, such as improving mass transit or dealing with water pollution, may be binding on only a portion of the metropolitan area. The dispersion of power among a large number of governmental units makes it possible for each of them to reach decisions without concern for the possible spillover effects, which may be harmful to other governments or residents of the metropolis.

Despite these arguments, most attempts at consolidating metropolitan governments fail. There have been a few successful mergers of city an county governments, and "metro" governments have been established in Toronto, Miami, and Nashville. But for the most part Americans have rejected metropolitan-wide governments in favor of the present fragmented system of multiple city and suburban governments. The existence of many local governments provides additional forums for the airing of public grievances. People feel better when they can publicly voice their complaints against governments, regardless of the eventual outcome. The additional points of access, pressure, and control provided by a decentralized system of local government ensure that political demands will be heard and perhaps even acted upon. Opportunities for individual participation in the making of public policy are expanded in a decentralized governmental system.

Maintaining the suburb as an independent political community provides the individual with a sense of personal effectiveness in public matters. He can feel some measure of manageability over the affairs of a small community. He is less subject to frustration and apathy, which people often feel in their relations with larger bureaucracies. He believes that his vote, his opinion, and his political activity count for more. He clings to the idea of grass-roots democracy in an organizational society.

Fragmented government clearly offers a larger number of groups the opportunity to exercise influence over governmental policy. Groups that would be minorities in the metropolitan area as a whole can avail themselves of governmental positions and enact diverse public policies. This advantage applies to blacks in the central city as well as whites in the suburbs. Fragmented government creates within the metropolitan area a wide range of governmental policies. Communities that prefer, for example, higher than average standards in their school system at higher than average costs have the opportunity to implement this preference. Communities that prefer higher levels of public service or one set of services over another or stricter enforcement of particular standards can achieve their goals under a decentralized governmental system. Communities that wish to get along with reduced public services in order to maximize funds available for private spending may do so.

Racial imbalance and the plight of central-city schools are also important forces in maintaining the political autonomy of suburban school systems in the nation's large metropolitan areas. Many suburbanites left the central city to find "a better place to raise the kids," and this means, among other things, better schools. Suburbs generally spend more on the education of each child than do central cities. Moreover, the increasing concentration of blacks in central cities has resulted in racial imbalance in central-city schools. Conditions in ghetto schools have long been recognized as a national scandal. Efforts to end *de facto* segregation within the cities frequently involve busing children into and out of ghetto schools in order to achieve racial balance. In Chapter 9 we discussed *de facto* segregation and ghetto schools in some detail. But it is important to note here that independent suburban school districts are viewed by many suburbanites as protection against the possibility that their children might be bused to ghetto schools. Autonomous suburban school districts lie outside the jurisdiction of city officials. While it is possible that federal courts may some day order suburban school districts to cooperate with cities in achieving racial balance in schools, nonetheless, the political independence of suburban schools helps assure that suburban school children will not be used to achieve racial balance in city schools.

POWER AND THE QUALITY OF LIFE: A CASE STUDY
Federal Urban Policy

In a special message to Congress the president once summarized the nation's urban problems as follows:

Federal Urban Policy

Some four million urban families living in homes of such disrepair as to violate decent housing standards.

The need to provide over 30 percent more housing annually than we are currently building.

Our chronic inability to provide sufficient low and moderate income housing, of adequate quality, at reasonable price.

The special problem of the poor and the Negro, unable to move freely from their ghettos, exploited in the quest for the necessities of life.

Increasing pressures on municipal budgets, with large city per capita expenditures.

The high human costs: crime, delinquency, welfare loads, disease, and health hazards. This is man's fate in those broken neighborhoods where he can "feel the enclosure of the flanking walls and see through the window the blackened reflection of the tenement across the street that blocks out the world beyond."

The tragic waste, and indeed, the chaos, that threatens where children are born into the stifling air of overcrowded rooms, and destined for a poor diet, inadequate schools, streets of fear and sordid temptation, joblessness, and the gray anxiety of the ill prepared.

And the flight to the suburbs of more fortunate men and women who might have provided the leadership and the means for reversing this human decline.[7]

The urban "crisis" is really a series of interrelated problems that affect the nation as a whole. Poverty, poor housing, racial conflict, crime and delinquency, social dependency, ill health, overcrowding, joblessness, ignorance, white flight to the suburbs, and fiscal imbalance are national problems. Yet their impact is increasingly concentrated in the nation's large cities.

Governments have had only limited success in dealing with the myriad problems of cities. A critical deficiency in federal urban policy is that there are no concrete goals or clear priorities in the hundreds of separate programs affecting cities. James Q. Wilson writes about urban policy:

We do not know what we are trying to accomplish. . . . Do we seek to raise standards of living, maximize housing choices, revitalize the commercial centers of our cities, end suburban sprawl, eliminate discrimination, reduce traffic congestion, improve the quality of urban design, check crime and delinquency, strengthen the effectiveness of local planning, increase citizen participation in local government? All of these objectives sound attractive—in part, because they are rather vague—but unfortunately they are in many cases incompatible.[8]

For example, the two federal program areas that account for the greatest expenditure of dollars for the physical improvement of cities are (1) the federal highway and transportation programs and (2) the federal housing and urban renewal programs. The first is operated by the Department of Transportation (DOT), the second by the Department of Housing and Urban Development (HUD). The urban portion of the interstate highway system is costing billions of

Federal Urban Policy

federal dollars; the effect of these dollars is to enable people to drive in and out of the central city speedily, safely, and conveniently, and to open up suburban areas to business and residential expansion. Of course, expressways also encourage middle class (mostly white) families to move out of the central city and enable commercial establishments to follow them. The result is further racial segregation within the metropolitan region in housing and schools, as well as reduction in the number of service jobs available to the poor living in the city. The encouragement of longer automobile trips from suburban residences to downtown offices adds to pollution and congestion.

At the same time, the Federal Housing Administration (in HUD) is helping cities tear down slum dwellings, often displacing the poor who live there and adding to their hardship, in order to make way for office buildings, hotels, civic centers, industrial parks, and middle class luxury apartments. In part, this effort is intended to lure suburbanites back to the central city. While urban renewal reduces the overall supply of housing to the poor in cities, the Housing Assistance Administration (in HUD) is assisting cities to build low-rent public housing units to add to the supply of housing for the poor.

Despite the emphasis in federal urban programs on the *physical* characteristics of cities, most observers now acknowledge that the urban "crisis" is not primarily, or even significantly, a physical problem. It is not really housing, or highways, or urban rebuilding that lies at the heart of urban discontent. Instead when we think of the challenges confronting cities, we think of racial tension, crime, poverty, poor schools, residential segregation, rising welfare rolls, fiscal crisis—in short, all of the major domestic problems facing the nation. In an urban society, *all* domestic problems become urban problems.

The federal government has never set any significant priority among its hundreds of grant programs. The result is that too few dollars chase too many goals. The maze of federal grant-in-aid programs for cities (nearly five hundred separate programs with separate purposes and guidelines) is uncoordinated and bureaucratic. Mayors and other municipal officials spend a great deal of time in "grantsmanship"—learning where to find federal funds, how to apply, and how to write applications in such a way as to appear to meet the purposes and guidelines of the program. Cities are sometimes pressured to apply for funds for projects they do not really need, simply because federal funds are available, while they may receive little or no federal assistance for more vital programs. The reason for many of these administrative and organizational problems is not merely incompetence on the part of government planners. Frequently, conflicting policies, incompatible goals, and competing government programs reflect underlying disagreements about public policy. Government institutions often accommodate conflict about public policy by enacting conflicting policies and establishing separate agencies to implement them.

As a result of widespread dissatisfaction with federal grant-in-aid programs,

Federal Urban Policy

Chicago's housing program has been called the most progressive in the nation by some experts. Vast areas of slums are being replaced by public housing such as this, in which white and black tenants are equally balanced. *Wide World Photo*

Congress was persuaded in 1972 to adopt the idea of general *revenue sharing*—the turnover of a certain amount of federal tax revenues to state and local governments with few or no strings attached. Proponents of revenue sharing, including many big-city mayors, argue that the federal government is better at collecting revenue than are state or local governments—particularly big cities. The federal individual and corporate income tax is an effective, progressive producer of large amounts of revenue, in contrast to state and local property and sales taxes. Moreover, state and local taxable resources are unequally distributed among jurisdictions; federal revenues can help equalize disparities between communities.

Further, difficulties with the haphazard and bureaucratic system of federal grants-in-aid in housing, urban renewal, antipoverty programs, manpower training, welfare, education, etc. convinced many governors and mayors that they could do a better job themselves in confronting domestic problems if federal money were made available with no strings attached. In other words, while the federal government is better at *collecting* revenue, states and communities are better at *spending* it. Hence, proponents of revenue sharing feel that it combines the best features of each level of government.

Federal Urban Policy

Opposition to revenue sharing, as one might expect, is centered in Washington. Congressmen do not like to see a system develop in which they are cast in the unpopular role of tax collector while state and local officials have all the "fun" of determining how to spend the money. Even conservative congressmen who dislike the centralized bureaucracy in Washington are fearful of separating the spending from the taxing function. They believe that the decisions to spend money must be accompanied by the burdens of collecting it, or else spending would become irresponsible. They are joined in their opposition to revenue sharing by some liberal congressmen who fear that state and local officials do not share their definition of national purposes and priorities. These congressmen wish to retain the power to control federal funds in Washington.

Power and money tend to go together in American politics. Power in the federal system has flowed toward Washington over the decades, largely because Washington has the superior taxing powers and therefore the money to deal more effectively with the nation's major domestic problems. Revenue sharing promises to revitalize state and local governments by providing new access to financial resources. If Congress refrains from adding strings over the years to shared revenues (a big *if*), states and communities will acquire both money and power to deal with the urban "crisis."

NOTES

1. Congressional Quarterly, *Man's Control of the Environment* (Washington: Congressional Quarterly, 1970), p. 9.
2. See Philip Hauser, "The Population Problem," in Sue Titus Reid and David L. Lyon (eds.), *Population Crisis: An Interdisciplinary Perspective* (Glenview, Ill.: Scott, Foresman, 1972).
3. Paul R. Ehrlich, *The Population Bomb* (New York: Ballantine, 1968), pp. 22 - 23.
4. Congressional Quarterly, *op. cit.*, p. 10.
5. Louis Wirth, "Urbanism as a Way of Life," *American Journal of Sociology*, 44 (July 1938).
6. John C. Bollens and Henry J. Schmandt, *The Metropolis* (New York: Harper & Row, 1965), pp. 249 - 250.
7. Message from the President to Congress, transmitting recommendations for City Demonstration Programs, January 26, 1966, 89th Congress, 2nd session. Reprinted in full in Thomas R. Dye and Brett W. Hawkins (eds.), *Politics in the Metropolis*, 2nd ed. (Columbus, Ohio: Merrill, 1970).
8. James Q. Wilson, "The War on Cities," *The Public Interest*, Summer, 1966.

TESTING YOUR PERFORMANCE

Note to the Student. The following questions are to test how well you achieved the Performance Objectives identified for you at the beginning of this chapter. The correct answers are supplied, accompanied by corresponding pages for you to review if you have answered incorrectly. The questions are coordinated numerically with the Performance Objectives at the beginning of the chapter. This exercise will assist you in determining the type of questions you have the most difficulty in answering (discussion, identification, explanation, definition, etc.) and will prepare you for test questions likely to be asked by your instructor.

    1.   (a) Ten thousand years ago the total population of the earth was an estimated 20 million people; by the time of Moses, it was about 100 million; at the time of Christ, 250 million. Growth was slow during the famines and plagues of the Middle Ages. By 1850 there were 1 billion people; by 1970, 3.5 billion people; and the current growth rate is 2 percent per year. These facts would all be used to _____ .

    (b) The development of agriculture, advances in agriculture, commerce, and public sanitation, and a worldwide revolution in medical care and public health are all factors contributing to the _____ .

    (c) The view of the consequences of world population growth as the doom of the human species, predicting that the earth's air, water, and soil will not be able to support man, and prognostication of the occurrence of widespread famine before the end of the century, has been expressed by _____ .

    (d) The view of the consequences of world population growth arguing that the publicity given to population growth greatly exceeds the real dangers and that 30 billion people could be fed with foreseeable increases in food supply utilizing existing technology has been expressed by the _____ .

    2.   The problems of population growth are compounded by the unevenness of growth rates between developed and underdeveloped countries. The rate of population increase in underdeveloped countries is _____

    3.   The two constitutional amendments used by the U.S. Supreme Court to strike down state laws preventing abortion in the first three months of pregnancy were the _____ .

    4.   (a) The type of environmental pollution caused by gasoline-powered internal combustion engines, electrical power plants, heating, incineration of garbage, trash, and other refuse by both governments and industries, and which falls into two types—particles and gases—is _____ .

    (b) The type of environmental pollution created by debris and sludge, organic wastes, and chemical effluents that threatens natural resources such as lakes, waterfronts, and seashores, marshes, and estuaries is _____

_____ .

    (c) The type of environmental pollution caused by discarding cans, bottles, jars, plastic, television sets, automobiles, trucks, and paper in dumps is

_____ .

    5.   The federal agency for enforcing the Clean Air acts and the Water Quality acts is the _____ .

    6.   The three major types of water pollutants are _____

_____ .

    7.   (a) The type of sewage treatment that uses screens and settling chambers where filth falls out of the water as sludge is _____

_____ .

    (b) The type of sewage treatment designed to remove organic wastes, usually by trickling water through a bed of rocks three to ten feet deep, where bacteria consume the organic matter, is _____ .

    (c) The type of sewage treatment which uses mechanical and chemical filtration processes to remove almost all contaminants from water is _____

_____ .

    8.   (a) The volume of solid wastes could be decreased by _____ .

    (b) The difficulty of separating reusable materials from other refuse and the comparatively lower cost of using virgin materials are both _____

_____ .

    (c) The disposal method which consists of spreading the waste in thin layers over specific land areas and covering it at least once a day with a layer of earth is known as a _____ .

    9.   The skyrocketing demand for energy, and styles of life that use increasing amounts of energy; the leveling off of output of domestic fuels (oil and gas) and a decline in coal production; government regulation of the price of electricity and natural gas, making it more difficult for power companies to acquire the capital to construct new plants; attacks by environmentalists forcing cutbacks in the use of polluting fuels and holding up development of new power plants; and formation of a cartel of petroleum-exporting countries (OPEC) which forced steep increases in the price of oil and threatened oil embargoes against nations that opposed the political aims of OPEC countries are identified by the author as the _____

_____ .

    10.   The population characteristic that primarily determines the quality of life is _____ .

    11.   (a) The largest growth within metropolitan areas is occurring in the ___

_____ .

    (b) The term used by the Census Bureau to refer to an area having a city of 50,000 or more persons, together with adjacent counties which have predominantly urban industrial populations with close ties to the central city, is

_____ .

    12.   Sociologist Lewis Wirth identified the distinguishing characteristics of urban life as _____

_____ .

    13.   (a) The term used to refer to ethnic and racial diversity in central cities is _____ .

(b) Multiplying the number of persons with whom an individual comes into contact makes it impossible for him to know everyone he meets very well and results in what is known as _____
_____ .

(c) The term used to define the sense of social isolation and loss of personal recognition, self-worth, and feeling of participation is _____
_____ .

14.   (a) What group ties are interactions within the extended family? _____
_____

(b) What group ties are interactions between members of age and interest groups? _____

(c) Early sociological theory believed that primary group ties were emphasized by what type of life? _____

(d) Early sociological theory believed that secondary group ties were emphasized by what type of life? _____

(e) Sociologists have found that those who are more likely to interact with individuals as full personalities are _____ .

(f) Sociologists have found that those who have greater anonymity in their social contacts are _____ .

15.   (a) Physical movement (from one geographic area to another) and social movement (from one position of social status to another) are both types of _____
_____ .

(b) The creation of opportunities for individuals and the simultaneous weakening of the sense of community are both _____
_____ .

16.   Suburbanites' reliance upon the central city for employment opportunities, food, clothing, newspapers, entertainment, hospitalization, and other modern needs, accompanied by the central city's reliance upon the suburbs to supply its labor and management forces and consumers, is evidence of an intricate web of economic and social relationships, a high degree of communication, and a great deal of physical interchange among residents, groups, and firms in a metropolitan area. This is referred to as _____ .

17.   (a) Large number of people, population density, social and economic heterogeneity, physical and social mobility, economic interdependence, physical separation of functions and groups, numerous but superficial interpersonal interactions, impersonality and anonymity, segmental and utilitarian interpersonal relationship, greater interaction in secondary groups, reliance upon formal mechanisms of control, and greater potentiality for conflict are all _____
_____ .

(b) Industrialization and urbanization, great range and variation in styles of life, difficulty of proving systematically that urban dwellers are more impersonal or anonymous, and inappropriate focus upon central-city lifestyles in describing urban living are all _____
_____ .

18.   (a) The desire to avoid the problems created by large numbers of people (crowds, crime, noise, smog) and to live near people like themselves who share their interest in good schools, respectable neighborhoods, and middle class lifestyles are some of the reasons for the process of _____ in America.

(b) Economic opportunity, upward social and economic mobility, theaters and entertainment, professional sports, civic and cultural events, and specialized shops and stores are examples of the _____
_____ .

19. (a) Because suburbs and communities may be quite different from one another, just as there are wide differences between social and economic groups living in central cities, one should be extremely careful about attempting to
_____

(b) Occupation, income, and educational levels of the population, familistic or child-centered lifestyle, and racial composition are _____ .

(c) The most important difference between cities and suburbs is their contrasting _____ .

20. (a) The availability of low-priced rental units in older, run-down sections of central cities, discriminatory housing practices of private owners and developers, and the lack of sufficient income to purchase housing in suburbs or in better city neighborhoods are all reasons for the _____
_____ .

(b) Desire to get away from heavy concentrations of blacks in central cities is one reason for the _____
_____ .

(c) The overall effect of the migration of blacks into cities and the heavy out-migration of whites to the suburbs has been to make American life _____
_____ .

21. (a) Governmental fragmentation in metropolitan areas is a function of
_____ .

(b) The term used to refer to the proliferation of governments in metropolitan areas and the lack of coordination of public programs is _____
_____ .

22. (a) The improving of public service by achieving economies of large-scale operations and providing specialized public services; better coordination of public services for the metropolis; the elimination of inequalities in financial burdens throughout the metropolitan area; and the clear establishment of responsibility for metropolitan-wide policy are all supposed advantages of _____
_____ .

(b) Greater opportunities for individual participation in the making of public policy through provision of additional points of access, pressure, and control; a greater sense of personal effectiveness in the affairs of the community; and the offering to a larger number of groups the opportunity to exercise influence over governmental policy are all considered to be _____
_____ .

23. (a) James Q. Wilson and others identified a critical deficiency in urban policy as the _____
_____ .

(b) The two federal program areas that account for the greatest expenditures of dollars for the physical improvements of cities are _____
_____ .

24. (a) The nonexistence of significant priorities, lack of coordination, bureaucratic setup, and the existence of conflicting policies, incompatible goals,

and competing government programs are all problems and weaknesses of the
_____ .

 (b) Learning where to find federal funds, how to apply, and how to write the application in such a way as to appear to meet the purposes and guidelines of the program is known as _____ .

 25. (a) The program adopted by Congress in 1972 providing for the turnover of a certain amount of federal tax revenues to state and local governments with few or no strings attached is _____ .

 (b) The superiority of the federal government in collecting revenue and the superiority of states and communities in spending it were cited by _____
_____ .

 (c) The danger of separating the spending from the taxing function and the fear that state and local officials would not share the national congressmen's definition of national purposes and priorities were cited by _____
_____ .

Correct Responses

 1. (a) Trace the growth of the world's population (p. 420); (b) Population explosion (p. 420); (c) Dr. Barry Commoner and Dr. Paul R. Ehrlich (pp. 420 - 421); (d) National Academy of Sciences (p. 421).

 2. Twice that of advanced societies (p. 422).

 3. Fifth and Fourteenth amendments (p. 424).

 4. (a) Air pollution (p. 425); (b) Water pollution (p. 427); (c) Solid waste disposal pollution (p. 428).

 5. Environmental Protection Agency (p. 426).

 6. Debris and sludge, organic wastes, and chemical effluents (p. 427).

 7. (a) Primary sewage treatment (p. 427); (b) Secondary sewage treatment (p. 427); (c) Tertiary sewage treatment (p. 427).

 8. (a) Recycling (p. 428); (b) Disadvantages of recycling (p. 428); (c) Sanitary landfill (p. 428).

 9. Causes of the energy crisis (pp. 429 - 430).

 10. Density (p. 433).

 11. (a) Suburbs (p. 433); (b) Standard Metropolitan Statistical Area (SMSA) (p. 433).

 12. Numbers, density, and heterogeneity (p. 436).

 13. (a) Melting pot (p. 437); (b) Segmentalization of human relationships (p. 437); (c) Anomie (p. 438).

 14. (a) Primary group ties (p. 438); (b) Secondary group ties (p. 438); (c) Rural life (p. 438); (d) Urban life (p. 438); (e) Rural dwellers (p. 438); (f) Urban dwellers (p. 438).

 15. (a) Urban mobility (p. 438); (b) Effects of urban mobility (p. 438).

 16. Interdependence (pp. 438 - 439).

17.   (a) Characteristics of urban life (p. 439); (b) Difficulties in distinguishing between rural and urban dwellers (p. 440).

18.   (a) Suburbanization (pp. 440 - 441); (b) Positive benefits of urban life that suburbanites seek to retain (p. 441).

19.   (a) Generalize about cities and suburbs (p. 441); (b) Characteristics by which cities and suburbs *can* be differentiated (pp. 441 - 442); (c) Racial composition (p. 442).

20.   (a) Concentration of blacks in large central cities (p. 442); (b) Heavy outmigration of whites to the suburbs (p. 443); (c) More segregated (p. 443).

21.   (a) Size, age of settlement, and income levels (p. 444); (b) Fragmented government (p. 444).

22.   (a) Metropolitan governmental consolidation (pp. 444 - 445); (b) Advantages of decentralized fragmented governmental systems (pp. 445 - 446).

23.   (a) Lack of concrete goals and clear priorities in federal urban programs (p. 447); (b) Highway and transportation, and housing and urban renewal (p. 447).

24.   (a) Federal grant-in-aid program for cities (p. 448); (b) Grantsmanship (p. 448).

25.   (a) Revenue sharing (p. 449); (b) Proponents of revenue sharing (p. 449); (c) Opponents of revenue sharing (p. 450).

KEY TERMS

ecosystem

abortion

air pollution

Clean Air acts

Environmental Protection Agency

1975 federal standards for automobile emissions

water pollution

primary sewage treatment

secondary sewage treatment

tertiary sewage treatment

water pollution abatement program

Water Quality acts

phosphates

solid waste disposal

sanitary land fills

recycling

fossil fuels

Sierra Club

"thermal pollution"

metropolis

suburb

Standard Metropolitan Statistical Area (SMSA)

central city

suburbanization

"melting pot"

familistic lifestyle

"segmentalization of human relationships"

anomie

primary group

secondary group

external social group controls

internal social group controls

mobility

interdependence

nonfamilistic lifestyle

"ghettos"

"fragmented" governmental authority

metropolitan governmental consolidation

urban "crisis"

Department of Transportation (DOT)

Department of Housing and Urban Development (HUD)

Federal Housing Administration (FHA)

Housing Assistance Administration (HAA)

federal grant-in-aid programs

"grantsmanship"

revenue sharing

DISCUSSION QUESTIONS

1. Discuss two different interpretations of the consequences of world population growth as expressed by:
   (a) Dr. Barry Commoner and Dr. Paul R. Ehrlich
   (b) The National Academy of Sciences

2. Compare and contrast the three major types of environmental pollution (air pollution, water pollution, and solid waste disposal pollution) by discussing:
   (a) Major causes and contributors
   (b) Major effects on the environment
   (c) Impacts on the health of the population
   (d) Approaches to control, reduction, and elimination

3. Discuss the energy crisis:
   (a) Causes
   (b) Relationship to environmental pollution problems

4. Discuss the rapid growth of the American metropolis:
   (a) Define Standard Metropolitan Statistical Area (SMSA)
   (b) Identify the area of greatest growth (suburb or central city)
   (c) Reasons for suburbanization

5. Discuss the effects of urbanization on:
   (a) Anomie
   (b) Problems of social control
   (c) Mobility (physical and social)
   (d) Interdependence
   (e) Conflict management

6. The most important difference between cities and suburbs is their contrasting racial composition. Discuss the reasons for:
   (a) Heavy concentration of blacks in central cities
   (b) Heavy white out-migration to the suburbs
   What has been the overall effect of these movement patterns on American society?

7. Discuss "fragmented" governmental authority in the metropolis:
   (a) Factors contributing to it
   (b) Advantages of fragmentation
   (c) Proposed remedy: metropolitan governmental consolidation. How would it improve things?

8. Define revenue sharing. Discuss the arguments in favor of it and the arguments against it.

SUGGESTED READINGS

John C. Bollens and Henry J. Schmandt, *The Metropolis* (New York: Harper & Row, 1965).

Congressional Quarterly, *Man's Control of the Environment* (Washington: Congressional Quarterly, 1970).

J. Clarence Davies, *The Politics of Pollution* (New York: Pegasus, 1970).

William M. Dobriner, *Class in Suburbia* (Englewood Cliffs, N.J.: Prentice-Hall, 1963).

Paul R. Ehrlich, *The Population Bomb* (New York: Ballantine, 1968).

Jeffery K. Hadden and Lewis H. Masotti (eds.), *Metropolis in Crisis* (Itasca, Ill.: Peacock, 1971).

Sue Titus Reid and David L. Lyon (eds.), *Population Crisis: An Interdisciplinary Perspective* (Glenview: Ill.: Scott, Foresman, 1972).

Roger Revelle and Hans H. Landsberg (eds.), *America's Changing Environment* (Boston: Houghton Mifflin, 1970).

Index